The Golden Dozen

The twelve greatest chess players
of all time.

Irving Chernev

The Golden Dozen

The twelve
greatest chess players
of all time

OXFORD UNIVERSITY PRESS
1976

Oxford University Press, Ely House, London W.1

GLASGOW NEW YORK TORONTO MELBOURNE WELLINGTON
CAPE TOWN IBADAN NAIROBI DAR ES SALAAM LUSAKA ADDIS ABABA
DELHI BOMBAY CALCUTTA MADRAS KARACHI DACCA
KUALA LUMPUR SINGAPORE HONG KONG TOKYO

ISBN 0 19 217536 X

© *Oxford University Press 1976*

This book is dedicated
to my dear wife **Selma**
with love

*Printed in Great Britain
by Fletcher & Son Ltd., Norwich*

Contents

Preface

I have always been fascinated by lists. I make note of *The Ten Greatest Novels, The Ten Greatest Pianists,* and *The Ten Worst Movies*. I read the novels, listen to the pianists, and see the movies.

Recently in an article written for *Chess*, I made a list of *The Twelve Greatest Chess Players Of All Time.* I mentioned that a book could be written in support of my opinions, and that I might be tempted to write such a book.

I have been tempted, and this is the book.

It is the culmination of a lifetime's devotion to the game. In the course of this long, but never boring, love affair with chess, I have studied the masters—from Philidor to Fischer. I have played over their wonderful games countless thousands of times, and continue to find in them new beauties. For in this expression of the art of chess play, I find poetry, architecture, music.

For the fullest enjoyment and appreciation of a masterpiece, good notes are necessary. They reveal the thoughts of the players, the subtleties that never come to light, and the ideas that need unfolding. Notes supplied by the players themselves are usually best, unless there is an annotator of the stature of Marco, Tarrasch, or Alekhine, who can tell you more about what is happening than the contestants themselves.

Take as example, the game Lasker-Capablanca (No.88 in this book). To make sure that I extracted every last morsel of pleasure from it, I played the game over with notes by the following:

Tarrasch, in *The book of the tournament,*
Lasker, in *The American Chess Bulletin* of 1914
Capablanca, in *Chess fundamentals,*
Euwe and Prins, in *Capablanca das Schachphänomen,*
Réti, in *Masters of the chessboard,*
Alexander, in *A book of chess,*
Pachmann, in *Entscheidungspartien,*
Brinckmann, in *Streifzüge und Irrtümer auf der 64 Feldern,*
Edward Lasker, in *Chess strategy,*
Fine, in *The world's great chess games,*
Znosko-Borovsky in *The middle game in chess,*
Tartakover and Du Mont, in *500 master games of chess,*
Koblenz, in *Schachtraining,*
Dufresne and Mieses, in *Lehrbuch des Schachspiels,*

Collijn, in *Lärobok I Schack*,
Purdy, in *Chess World* 1958.

This does not mean that the Lasker-Capablanca game is new to me. I saw it and revelled in its beauties ages ago.

What I am pointing out is that I am thoroughly familiar with the fine points of all the games in this book—games which support the merits of the players, and their right to be on the list of

The Golden Dozen: The 12 Greatest Chess Players Of All Time.

I give you these masters in ascending order, saving the best for the last.

Irving Chernev

Acknowledgements

The photographs were obtained from the following sources:
Nimzowitsch: *Ullstein*; Bronstein, Smyslov, and Tal: *British Chess Magazine*; Spassky, Petrosian, and Botvinnik: *Novosti*; Fischer: *The John Hillelson Agency Ltd*; Lasker: *Popperfoto*; Alekhine: *The Keystone Press Agency Ltd*; Capablanca: *Radio Times Hulton Picture Library*

We thank B.T. Batsford Ltd (London) for permission to reproduce the Bronstein-Dus Chotimirsky anecdote (p. 63) which first appeared in English in Bronstein's *200 open games* (1974).

The photograph opposite shows Irving Chernev in San Francisco, from whence he tears himself away only when the lure of visiting London or Paris becomes irresistible.

Nimzowitsch

Nimzowitsch was the most original chess player that ever lived. One has only to recall his wonderfully imaginative opening, and the subsequent combinations against Wendel (Game No. 3), or his *Immortal Zugzwang* creation against Samisch (Game No. 4), where he tied poor Samisch up hand and foot, or his blend of originality and logic in his masterpiece against Johner (Game No. 5) to realize that here was a master who did not fear putting his own ideas to the test of practical play.

Such games as the one against Behting (Game No. 2) provide convincing proof of the power of the blockade, while his wins against Hage (Game No. 7) and Mannheimer (Game No. 9) are outstanding examples of control and occupation of the weak white squares.

Nimzowitsch's games, as we shall see, are 'witch chess, heathen and beautiful.'

Nimzowitsch did more than entertain us with fascinating chess. He gave the world an extraordinary work called *My system*. This was a book that discussed such new concepts as Blockade, Over-Protection, and Prophylaxis. It elaborated familiar ideas—The Seventh Rank, The Two Bishops, The Isolated Queen Pawn, and The Pawn Chain (though even here, Nimzowitsch's advocation of an attack on the base of the pawn chain must have been an eye-opener).

There is hardly a chess player who has not been influenced (and benefitted) by *My system*. For this marvelous book has made masters out of amateurs, and grandmasters out of masters.

Nimzowitsch's tournament exploits are enviable, if only for the fact that he won the Dresden 1926 Tournament ahead of Alekhine, and the great Carlsbad 1929 Tournament ahead of Capablanca.

Nimzowitsch was strong enough to be considered one of the two leading challengers (the other being Alekhine) for Capablanca's crown. Had a match been arranged, the world would have gained a number of masterpieces, some of them demonstrating that Baroque is Beautiful.

I consider Nimzowitsch the twelfth greatest chess player of all time.

1

White **A. Nimzowitsch**   Black **O.S. Bernstein**
French Defence
Vilna, 1912

Among the unknown masterpieces of chess is this beauty by Nimzowitsch.

The ending is exquisite, and so is the preliminary maneuvering to control the black squares.

The tactical possibilities indicated in the notes (pretty ideas that the players had to consider before making their actual moves) add sparkle to the game.

1 P-K4   P-K3

2 P-Q4   P-Q4

3 P-K5

Nimzowitsch's favourite line against the French. His new philosophy of the center advocates maintaining this pawn as a spearhead in the opponent's territory. The supporting queen pawn may be sacrificed or exchanged, but the king pawn *must be over-protected* by pieces and kept alive.

3 . . .   P-QB4

4 N-KB3

Good alternatives are 4 P-QB3 and 4 Q-N4, Nimzowitsch's fascinating innovation, as in his game against Hakansson.

4 . . .   PxP

5 QxP   N-QB3

6 Q-KB4   Q-B2

7 N-B3   P-QR3

8 B-Q3   KN-K2

9 0-0   N-N3

10 BxN

White must exchange bishop for knight to save his king pawn, thereby opening a file against his king.

10 . . .   RPxB

11 N-K2

Nimzowitsch violates his own rules. The right move, in line with his theory of over-protection, was 11 R-K1.

11 . . .   B-K2

Dr. Bernstein misses a golden opportunity! After 11 . . . NxP   12 QxN (if 12 NxN, B-Q3 regains the piece with a winning game) 12 . . . B-Q3   13 QxNP (note that the queen *must* go to a black square) BxPch   14 K-R1 B-K4 dis.ch, and Black wins the queen.

12 N(K2)-Q4   NxN

13 QxN

The safer capture was 13 NxN, when 13 . . . R-R5 is met by 14 Q-Q2, and the king pawn is temporarily safe.

13 . . .   QxBP

14 B-K3   Q-B5

15 QxQ   PxQ

16 B-N6!

This isolates the bishop pawn by preventing 16 . . . P-QN4.

16 . . .   B-Q2

17 KR-B1   QR-B1

18 N-Q2!

A subtle move, whose purpose is not obvious.

18 . . .   B-KN4

Black is ready to counter 19 NxP with 19 . . . BxR 20 N-Q6ch K-K2   21 NxRch RxN, winning a piece. But White has no designs on the pawn—for the time being.

19 N-K4!

The knight leaps to the center!

19 . . .   BxR

20 N-Q6ch   K-B1

21 NxR

A diagram would seem to be in order:

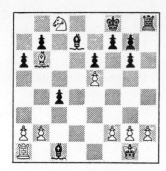

Bernstein
to move

Position after
21 NxR

Nimzowitsch

After the tempting 21 . . . BxP, Nimzowitsch had these beautiful combinations in mind:

22 R-Q1 K-K1   23 N-Q6ch K-K2 (if 23 . . . K-B1 24 NxQBP wins one of the loose bishops) 24 NxQBP B-B6   25 B-B5ch K-K1   26 N-Q6ch K-K2 (or 26 . . . K-Q1 27 NxPch winning the rook)   27 N-K4ch and the king bishop falls.

Again (after 21 . ... BxP)   22 R-Q1 BxN 23 R-Q8ch K-K2   24 RxR K-Q2 (saving the bishop by 24 . . . B-Q2 is disastrous, as 25 B-B5 (or 25 B-Q8) is instant mate)   25 R-Q8ch K-B3   26 R-Q6ch K-N4 27 B-K3!, and White threatens   28 R-Q8   winning the queen bishop, as well as   28 R-N6ch   winning the king bishop (an elegant variation).

21 . . .   B-KN4

22 P-B4!   BxN

If 22 . . . BxP   23 R-Q1 K-K1   24 N-Q6ch K-K2 25 B-B5 P-N3   26 N-B5 dbl.ch K-K1   27 N-Q6ch with a drawn result—Lasker.

23 PxB   B-Q2

24 R-Q1   K-K2

25 B-B5ch   K-K1

26 R-Q4   B-B3

27 RxP

Winning chances are usually slim in an ending where the bishops are of opposite colours. But Nimzowitsch's display of endgame wizardry in the play that follows

was enough to merit the praise of Dr. Lasker—himself a great practitioner of the art.

27 . . .   B-Q4

28 R-QN4   K-Q2

29 R-KB4   K-B3

30 B-Q6   R-Q1

31 P-QN3   R-Q2

32 P-KR4!   P-R4

33 P-KN4!

The idea is of course to create a passed rook pawn.

33 . . .   P-N4

34 P-R5   PxP

35 PxP   P-R5

36 PxP   BxP

After 36 . . . PxP, Nimzowitsch would have to choose between 37 B-B8 or 37 P-R6 as the way to win.

37 P-R5!

The first passed pawn—though it doesn't look too sturdy.

37 . . .   R-R2

38 B-B8   B-N8

In reply to 38 . . . RxP the capture by 39 RxP wins for White.

39 R-B1   B-Q6

40 R-Q1   B-B4

41 B-N4!

The precious passed pawn must be protected.

41 . . .   R-R1

42 R-Q6ch   K-B2

43 P-QR6

Not only does the pawn become more dangerous with every step it takes, but its advance institutes a threat: 44 B-R5ch K-N1   45 R-Q8ch K-R2 46 B-N6ch, and Black must part with his rook.

43 . . .   R-R1

'Well, let's attack the other rook pawn.'

44 B-B5!
Ready to penalize 44 . . . RxP with 45 B-N6ch and mate next move.

44 . . .   B-N5

45 P-R6   PxP

46 PxP
Now there are two passed pawns to worry about.

46 . . .   K-N1
The pawns are under restraint, and it's hard to see how White will make any progress.

47 K-B2
White's pieces are posted as well as they can be; so Nimzowitsch brings his king into the game. Many years later, Nimzowitsch wrote in *My system*, 'When the endgame is entered let the king set himself in motion, and strive to reach the center of the board, for from this point he can, according to need, make for the right or left, i.e., attack, the enemy king or queen's wing'.

47 . . .   B-B4
Clearly, 47 . . . RxP loses by 48 P-R7ch K-N2 49 R-Q8, and the pawn becomes a queen.

48 K-B3   P-N5

49 B-K3   K-R1

50 R-N6   R-KB1

51 RxNP   P-B3

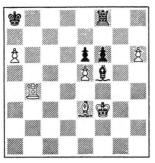

Bernstein

**Position after
51 . . . P-B3**

Nimzowitsch
to move

Black hopes to draw by simplifying the position with exchanges.

52 B-B5!   R-B1
If 52 . . . R-B2   53 R-N7! RxRch   54 PxRch KxP 55 PxP B-N3   56 P-B7 BxP (the unfortunate bishop cannot tear himself in two to stop both pawns) 57 P-R7, and White wins.

53 PxP!
Now there are three passed pawns!

53 . . .   RxB

54 P-B7   R-B1
But how can they break through when the rook guards all approaches?

55 R-N7!   B-Q6
The Bishop's Dilemma. If 55 . . . B-N3   56 R-K7 R-B1 57 R-K8ch RxR   58 PxR(Q)ch BxQ   59 P-KR7, and on to the queening square.

56 R-K7   B-N4

57 K-B4!
It would be premature to play 57 R-K8, when 57 . . . BxR (but not 57 . . . RxR   58 PxR(Q)ch BxQ 59 P-R7 follows) 58 P-B8(Q) B-B3ch, and the queen comes off the board next move.

57 . . .   R-R1

58 P-KR7   B-R5

59 K-K5   B-N4

60 K-B6   P-K4

61 K-N7   Resigns
Nimzowitsch played the ending in classic style.

2

White **A. Nimzowitsch**   Black **C. Behting**
Greco Counter-Gambit
Riga, 1919

This game shows the power of a blockader in simple, classic style. It is a brilliant piece of instruction.

Nimzowitsch's comment on his sixth move is particularly illuminating, as it reveals certain aspects of his strategy.

1 P-K4   P-K4

2 N-KB3   P-KB4

3 NxP   Q-B3

4 P-Q4   P-Q3

5 N-B4   PxP

Theory, the practice of other masters (says Nimzowitsch), recommends now 6 N-QB3 Q-KN3 7 P-KB3, but after 7 . . . PxP 8 QxP N-KB3 9 B-Q3 Q-N5 10 Q-K3ch B-K2 11 0-0 N-QB3 12 P-Q5 N-QN5 13 R-B4 Q-Q2 14 N-N6 RPxN 15 RxN, and the game is even.

6 N-K3!

Against this move (says Nimzowitsch) speak (1) tradition, which rather demands 6 N-QB3; (2) the principle of economic development; i.e., not to let one piece go a-wandering; (3) the apparently small threat effect of the blockader. And yet 6 N-K3, taken with the next move following, is in every respect a master-move. And even if all the rest of the world play here 6 N-QB3, I yet hold my move 6 N-K3 to be more correct, and this for reasons based on the 'system'.

The blockader (in this case the knight) is a piece placed directly in front of a pawn that might otherwise be mobile.

6 . . .   P-QB3

7 B-B4!!

A typical Nimzowitsch move. It seems to be time-wasting, as the bishop can be driven away at once by 7 . . . P-Q4. Nimzowitsch points out though that Black must play 7 . . . P-Q4 in order to castle, and this move will set up a target for the knight after B-N3 and P-QB4.

7 . . .   P-Q4

8 B-N3   B-K3

Black can not prevent the attack on his pawn chain by 8 . . . P-QN4, as the continuation 9 P-QR4 P-N5 10 P-QB4 strikes at the queen pawn.

9 P-QB4   Q-B2

10 Q-K2   N-KB3

11 0-0

A glance at the position shows that the knight at K3 is an ideal blockader. It hinders enemy pieces from approaching by way of White's KN4 square, it attacks the center (Q5), and it can easily spring into action, as shown in the later course of the game.

11 . . .   B-QN5

12 B-Q2   BxB

13 NxB   0-0

14 P-KB4

Threatens to advance to KB5 and win the queen pawn.

14 . . .   QPxP

On 14 . . . PxP *en passant*, there is this pretty possibility: 15 NxBP PxP 16 N-N5 Q-K1 17 NxB QxN 18 BxP N-Q4 19 NxN QxQ 20 N-K7 dbl.ch K-R1 21 RxR mate.

15 N(Q2)xBP Q-K2

Instinctive (but thoughtless) development by 15 . . . QN-Q2 would allow 16 N-Q6 Q-K2 17 N(K3)-B5 Q-Q1 18 BxBch (winning a piece . . .) K-R1 19 N-B7ch, . . . and the exchange.

16 P-B5   B-Q4

17 NxB   PxN

This capture is forced, as 17 . . . NxN 18 N-K3 Q-Q3 19 NxN PxN 20 QxP wins.

18 N-K3

Hardly has the knight at K3 disappeared (says Nimzowitsch) than a new knight at K3 stands in his place. Against such elasticity not even Death can prevail!

18 . . .   Q-Q2

19 NxP!

A sacrifice which shows that the blockader can accomplish more than merely preventing a pawn from advancing.

19 ...   NxN

20 QxP   R-Q1

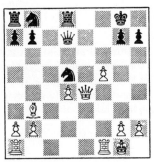

Behting

Position after
20 . . . R-Q1

Nimzowitsch
to move

21 P-B6!

The point of the sacrifice, and an illustration
of the pawn's lust to expand.

21 ...   PxP

If 21 . . . P-KN3   22 P-B7ch K-B1   23 Q-R4
K-N2   24 BxN QxB   25 Q-B6ch K-B1
26 Q-R8ch wins.

Or if 21 . . . N-QB3   22 P-B7ch K-R1
23 BxN QxB   24 QxQ RxQ   25 P-B8(Q)ch,
and mate next move.

22 R-B5   K-R1

23 RxN   R-K1

On 23 . . . Q-K1   24 B-B2 (threatening mate)
wins a whole rook. Or if 23 . . . Q-B1   24 Q-K7
RxR   25 QxBPch K-N1   26 BxRch followed
by mate.

24 RxQ   RxQ

25 R-Q8ch   K-N2

26 R-N8ch

More to the point than winning a piece by
26 R-QB1 followed by 27 R(B1)-B8.

26 ...   K-R3

27 R-KB1   Resigns

The threat of mate by 28 RxPch K-R4

29 B-B7ch (or 29 B-Q1ch) K-R5   30 R-R6 mate
is decisive.

Remarkable how quickly White's attack
became irresistible once the blockader sprang
into action!

3

White **Wendel**   Black **A. Nimzowitsch**
Nimzowitsch Defence
Stockholm, 1921

There are deep, dark, and mysterious moves in this exotic
game that could only have been produced by a strange,
original genius.

I was enchanted by this game back in the 30s, and
hastened to get it into print.

I am still enchanted by it!

1 P-K4   N-QB3

2 P-Q4   P-Q4

3 N-QB3   PxP

4 P-Q5   N-K4

5 B-KB4   N-N3

6 B-N3   P-QR3

This, and the later . . . P-QN4 is part of the Q-side expansion strategy popular today. It was rarely seen
years ago, except in the play of such free souls as
Nimzowitsch.

7 P-B3

White doesn't care for 7 NxP P-KB4 followed by
8 . . . P-B5, and the bishop is trapped.

7 ...   P-KB4!

8 PxP   P-B5!

9 B-B2   P-K4

So far we have an opening never seen on land or sea,
let alone the pages of *M.C.O.*

10 N-B3   B-Q3

Passed and semi-passed pawns must be blockaded—Nimzowitsch.

11 P-KR4   P-N4

12 P-R5   N-B1

The knight seems out of play and awkwardly placed, but it is destined for great deeds.

13 B-R4   Q-Q2

One weird move after another!

14 B-K2

A cunning move. If 4 . . . Q-N5   15 NxKP! QxNP 16 B-B3, and the queen is caught.

14 . . .   P-N5!

15 N-QN1

The knight must return home ingloriously, as does Samisch's knight in Game 4—*The Immortal Zugzwang Game* (*quod vide*).

15 . . .   N-B3!

A subtle maneuver. The attack on the king pawn and the rook pawn force White to give up one of his bishops.

16 BxN   PxB

Now the king knight file is available as a base of operations.

17 QN-Q2   Q-N2

18 K-B1   N-Q2

19 P-R6   Q-N6!

This seems silly, for White can gain time by attacking the queen, forcing her retreat to the back rank.

    But Black wants to provoke 20 R-R3!

20 R-R3   Q-N1

21 N-R4   N-B4

This knight has done a bit of wandering before getting onto a good square. It has gone from QN1 to B3, K4, N3, B1, Q2, and to B4.

    Note too, that the knight has uncovered an attack on the rook.

22 R-R1   R-N1

23 P-B3

This opens the queen knight file, but to Black's advantage.

23 . . .   PxP

24 PxP   Q-N6

25 Q-B2   R-N1

26 N-B4

If White disputes the queen knight file, he runs into trouble, as follows: 26 R-QN1 RxRch   27 NxR Q-K6   28 N-Q2 R-N6   29 P-B4 B-Q2   30 R-R2 B-R5   31 Q-B1 N-Q6 (attacks the queen and threatens mate)   32 BxN B-B4   33 Q-K1 Q-N8ch 34 K-K2 R-K6 mate.

26 . . .   B-Q2

27 NxBch   PxN

28 B-B3

Nimzowitsch to move

Position after 28 B-B3

Wendel

White seems to have consolidated his position, and has a crafty plan in the offing. After the continuation 29 N-B5 BxN   30 PxB, he threatens a curious perpetual check of the queen by 31 R-R3 Q-N4 32 R-R5 Q-N6   33 R-R3 Q-N4, and so on and on and on.

    But Nimzowitsch allows him no time for this. He has prepared a grand combination, one that bristles with beautiful points.

28 . . .   B-N4ch

29 P-B4

Interposing instead by 29 B-K2 might lead to this pretty checkmate: 29 . . . N-Q6   30 B-R5ch K-Q2   31 K-N1 Q-K6ch   32 K-R2 N-B7   33 N-B5 RxPch! 34 KxR R-N1ch   35 N-N7 Q-N6 mate.

29 . . .   BxPch

30 QxB   R-N7

31 B-K2   R-KN5

Now the other rook invades on the K-side. Nimzowitsch has this in mind: If 32 R-R3 RxN   33 RxQ R-R8ch   34 K-B2 PxRch   35 KxP RxR and wins.

32 Q-B1

What else is there? The bishop may not move, on pain of instant mate, and a move by the knight allows a quick finish by 32 . . . QxPch.

Meanwhile Black's king, though abandoned by his entire army, is perfectly safe, as the adverse queen cannot possibly approach him.

32 . . .   RxN

33 RxR   RxB

34 KxR   QxPch!

The point of the whole combination: 'the rook will not run away,' in Nimzowitsch's famous words.

35 K-Q1   Q-B8ch

36 K-Q2

But not 36 K-B2, when 36 . . . Q-Q6ch   37 K-N2 N-R5 mates neatly.

36 . . .   Q-Q6ch

37 K-K1   Q-N6ch

38 K-B1   QxR

39 K-N1   Q-N6ch

40 K-R1   Q-R6ch

41 K-N1   NxP

42 Q-B6ch   K-B2

43 Q-B7ch   K-N3

44 Q-N7ch   K-R4

45 Q-N2

Of course not 45 QxRP Q-N6ch followed by mate.

45 . . .   Q-K6ch

46 K-R2   N-B7

47 R-KB1

If 47 R-KN1 Q-K7 is decisive.

47 . . .   N-N5ch

48 K-R1   P-K5

49 R-KN1   P-B4

The passed pawns look menacing.

50 P-R4   KxP

In the midst of all the excitement the king casually snips off a pawn.

51 P-R5   K-N4

White is in a *semi-zugzwang* position. The pawn moves are exhausted, the king may not move, and the queen dare not move (if 52 Q-N2 Q-R6ch forces mate); so the rook must leave the K-side.

52 R-N1   P-B6

Now the quen must desert the king.

53 Q-N2   P-B7

This shuts off all aid to the king.

54 Resigns

If 54 Q-N7ch K-B5, and there are no more checks, while 54 K-N2 succumbs to 54 . . . Q-B6ch   55 K-B1 N-R7 mate.

'One of my best games,' says Nimzowitsch.

4

White **F. Samisch**   Black **A. Nimzowitsch**
Queen's Indian Defence
Copenhagen, 1923

Tartakover called this four-star beauty **The Immortal Zugzwang Game**.

It is a brilliancy without combinations or sacrifices. It just flows along smoothly and easily until the surprising *dénouement*.

Oh, there is a bit of a sacrifice—a knight for two pawns —but even that seems harmless enough. In fact, one is startled when an unassuming little pawn-move by Nimzowitsch compels his opponent to resign.

For Samisch realizes that he doesn't have a decent move left!

It's a game to fall in love with!

1 P-Q4   N-KB3

2 P-QB4   P-K3

3 N-KB3   P-QN3

4 P-KN3   B-N2

5 B-N2   B-K2

6 N-B3   0-0

7 0-0   P-Q4

One would expect play with the pieces, instead of blocking the path of the bishop: say 7 . . . N-K5 8 Q-B2 NxN   9 QxN (but not 9 N-N5 NxPch) 9 . . . B-K5.

8 N-K5   P-B3

9 PxP

A good alternative is 9 P-K4. Then if Black develops mechanically by 9 . . . QN-Q2, the continuation is 10 NxQBP BxN   11 KPxP PxP   12 PxP B-N2 13 P-Q6, and White wins a pawn.

9 . . .   BPxP

10 B-B4   P-QR3!

Nimzowitsch sets the Q-side pawns rolling, quite in the style popular today. He intends to follow up with . . . P-QN4, . . . N-B3, . . . N-QR4, and . . . N-B5. The knight will exert strong pressure there, or if driven off by P-N3 will have succeeded in weakening White's Q-side.

11 R-B1   P-QN4

12 Q-N3

A much superior plan was to retreat by 12 N-Q3, and follow up with 13 P-N4 and 14 N-B5, and the knight makes its presence felt.

12 . . .   N-B3

13 NxN   BxN

Has Nimzowitsch's plan miscarried? No, for the exchange has rid the board of White's annoying king knight.

14 P-KR3   Q-Q2

15 K-R2   N-R4!

16 B-Q2   P-B4

Nimzowitsch has play on both wings. He can continue either with . . . B-Q3 and . . . P-B5, or with . . . N-B3 followed by . . . P-N5 and . . . N-K5.

17 Q-Q1

White hopes to free his game with 18 P-K4, when Black could not capture the pawn, as his knight would be under attack.

17 . . .   P-N5

18 N-N1

The unfortunate knight must return home.

18 . . .   B-QN4

The bishop seizes a fine diagonal, meanwhile delaying 19 P-K4 by its attack on the rook.

19 R-N1   B-Q3!

A subtle move, the effect of which is not easily evident.

20 P-K4

Apparently a strong move, as White threatens 21 QxN as well as 21 PxQP.

20 . . .   BPxP!

21 QxN   RxP

In return for the knight, Black has two pawns, and a rook on the seventh rank. Also, White's Q-side is in a bit of a tangle.

22 Q-N5

On 22 Q-Q1 Black plays 22 . . . QR-KB1 with two big

threats: 23 . . . QR-B6, and 23 . . . BxPch   24 KxB
Q-B2ch   25 K-N4 R(B1)-B5ch, and quick mate.

22 . . .   QR-KB1

23 K-R1

This releases the bishop, as Black was threatening
23 . . . R(B1)-B6.

23 . . .   R(B1)-B4

24 Q-K3   B-Q6

Black surrounds the queen, and threatens to win her
by 25 . . . R-K7.

25 QR-K1   P-R3!!

An amazing winning move!

Nimzowitsch

**Position after
25 . . . P-R3!!**

Samisch

White resigned.

Despite having all his pieces, except one knight, on
the board, he is held fast by *zugzwang* (the compul-
sion to move) and helpless.

None of his pieces can move without immediate
loss of material. The proof:

If 26 N-B3 (or 26 N-R3) PxN

If 26 B-QB1 BxN

If 26 R-QB1 R-K7 wins the queen

If 26 KR-B1 BxR

If 26 B-KB1 BxB

If 26 K-R2 R(B4)-B6 wins the queen

(Note how 25 . . . P-R3 took away one of the queen's
flight squares).

Let's look at the pawn moves:

If 26 P-R3 P-QR4   27 PxP PxP and White has
accomplished nothing.

If 26 P-N4 R(B4)-B6   27 BxR R-R7 mate.

If 26 P-KR4 K-R1   27 P-R5 RxPch, and mate next
move.

Nimzowitsch was justifiably proud of this game.

5

White **P. Johner**   Black **A. Nimzowitsch**
Nimzo-Indian Defence
Dresden, 1926

Nimzowitsch is at his imaginative best in this fantastic
game. The strategy is unique, and the combinations
reach the heights of originality.

The game naturally won a first prize for brilliancy. It
won other accolades as well. Dr. Emanuel Lasker considered it the best game played in ten years, while Bent
Larsen recently said that this one game, more than any
other, influenced his development as a player.

Nimzowitsch himself, who saw no need for false
modesty about a notable achievement, said, 'One of the
best blockading games that I have ever played.'

1 P-Q4   N-KB3

2 P-QB4   P-K3

3 N-QB3   B-N5

4 P-K3   0-0

5 B-Q3   P-B4

6 N-B3

Routine play, but preferable might be 6 KN-K2 with
a view to strengthening the square QB3.

6 . . .   N-B3

7 0-0   BxN

Nimzowitsch liked to play against doubled pawns,
though it allowed his opponent the two bishops as
compensation.

8 PxB   P-Q3

This supports the bishop pawn, the blockader of the doubled pawns, and prepares for 9 . . . P-K4.

9 N-Q2   P-QN3

10 N-N3

White protects the queen pawn, to enable him to advance the king pawn.

Nimzowitsch suggests instead 10 P-B4 P-K4 11 BPxP QPxP 12 P-Q5 N-QR4 13 N-N3 N-N2 14 P-K4 N-K1. White could then protect the weak pawn at QB4 with his queen, and have the use of the open king bishop file.

10 . . .   P-K4

Conventional strategy to induce White to advance the queen pawn, thereby weakening the bishop pawn at his B4.

11 P-B4

If 11 P-Q5 P-K5 12 PxN (or 12 B-K2 N-K4) 12 . . . PxB 13 QxP Q-B2, and Black's position is better.

11 . . .   P-K5

12 B-K2   Q-Q2!

Only Nimzowitsch could block his bishop with the queen for the sake of preventing a pawn move (P-N4).

Nimzowitsch says, 'The text move involves a complicated system of restraint. The queen is bound for KR2!, where she will be excellently placed, for then the crippling of White's K-side by . . . P-R5 will be threatened.' He then adds, with pardonable pride, 'It must be conceded that the restraint maneuver Q-Q2, B4, R2, represents a remarkable conception.'

13 P-KR3   N-K2

14 Q-K1   P-KR4

Blockade work by a master of the art. If now 15 Q-R4 N-B4 16 Q-N5 N-R2 17 QxRP N-N6, and Black wins the exchange.

15 B-Q2   Q-B4

16 K-R2   Q-R2!

Original, profound, and powerful, as we shall see by the subsequent play.

17 P-QR4   N-B4

The threats begin: White must guard against 18 . . . N-N5ch 19 PxN PxP dis.ch 20 K-N1 P-N6, and White must sacrifice his queen to avoid mate.

18 P-N3   P-R4

This stifles any counterplay on the Q-side.

19 R-KN1   N-R3

20 B-KB1

It would be sheer suicide to play 20 Q-B2, when 20 . . . N(R3)-N5ch 21 BxN NxBch 22 PxN PxP dis.ch 23 K-N2 Q-R6 mate would follow.

20 . . .   B-Q2

21 B-B1

White's defence seems mysterious, but he clears the square Q2 for his knight, and the second rank for his queen rook to come into the game.

21 . . .   QR-B1

22 P-Q5

Otherwise Black puts on more pressure by 22 . . . B-K3, and forces the pawn to advance.

22 . . .   K-R1

23 N-Q2   KR-N1

24 B-KN2   P-KN4

25 N-B1   R-N2

26 R-R2   N-B4

27 B-R1   R(B1)-KN1

28 Q-Q1   PxP

29 KPxP   B-B1

30 Q-N3   B-R3

Nimzowitsch has built up pressure on the king knight file. If White tries to add support to the knight pawn by 31 QR-KN2, he loses on the spot by 31 . . . N-N5ch 32 PxN PxP dis.ch and mate.

Or if he defends by 31 B-Q2, there follows 31 . . . R-N3   32 B-K1 N-N5ch!   33 PxN (or 33 K-N2 BxP

Nimzowitsch

Position after
30 . . . B-R3

Johner to move

wins)PxP dis.ch   34 K-N2 BxP!   35 QxB P-K6!!
(threatens 36 . . . Q-R6 mate), and the only way to
save his king is to play 36 NxP and walk into a devastating knight fork by 36 . . . NxNch which costs
White his queen.

Truly a problem-like possibility, which shows the
scope of Nimzowitsch's imagination.

31 R-K2   N-R5

Black is ready to meet the attack on his king pawn by
32 N-Q2 with 32 . . . B-B1; then if 33 NxP Q-B4
34 N-B2 QxPch   35 NxQ N-N5 is mate. Or if
33 Q-Q1 BxP   34 KxB Q-B4ch   35 K-R2 N-N5ch
36 K-R3 N-B7 dbl.ch   37 K-R2 Q-R6 mate.

32 R-K3   B-B1

33 Q-B2   BxP

34 BxP   B-B4

This brings about a clearance which enables Black
finally to get at the king.

35 BxB   NxB

36 R-K2   P-R5

37 R(N1)-N2   PxP dis.ch

38 K-N1   Q-R6

39 N-K3   N-R5

40 K-B1   R-K1

Restraint from afar.

41 Resigns

Black threatens 41 . . . NxR   42 RxN (if 42 NxN
Q-R8 is mate) Q-R8ch   43 K-K2 QxRch (note how
Black's 40th move cleverly pins the knight)
44 K-Q1 QxQch   45 KxQ P-N7, winning easily.

If the king tries to flee by 41 K-K1, there follows
41 . . . N-B6ch   42 K-Q1 (or B1) Q-R8ch, and quick
mate.

One of my favourite Nimzowitsch games.

6

White **A. Nimzowitsch**   Black A. Rubinstein
English Opening
Dresden, 1926

Nimzowitsch rarely went in for K-side attacks. To this
one though he gives his personal touch with problem-
moves that merit exclamation marks. Take as example
his eighteenth move N-R1!, which evoked this comment
from *Le Jardin des Échecs:*

Ce coup inouï, si parfaitement 'nimzovichien,' est
bien l'un des plus mystérieux que l'on jamais vus aux
échecs. Quel autre maître aurait été capable de se rendre
compte que c'est là *le coup le plus offensif* dans cette
position? C'est du surréalisme!

1 P-QB4   P-QB4

2 N-KB3   N-KB3

3 N-QB3   P-Q4

4 PxP   NxP

5 P-K4

Nimzowitsch does not mind giving himself a backward queen pawn in exchange for other advantages.

5 . ...   N-N5

6 B-B4!

Even at this early stage one can easily fall into a trap
by the plausible 6 P-Q4, after which 6 . . . PxP
7 NxP QxN   8 QxQ N-B7ch wins a piece for Black.

6 . . .   P-K3

Three years after this game, Rubinstein tried
6 . . . N-Q6ch against Takacs and was crushed by
7 K-K2 NxBch   8 RxN P-QR3   9 P-Q4! PxP
10 QxP QxQ   11 NxQ P-K3   12 N-R4! N-Q2
13 KR-Q1 P-QN4   14 NxKP! BPxN   15 BxKP PxN
16 RxBch RxR   17 BxNch K-Q1   18 B-N4 dis.ch
B-Q3 (hoping for 19 RxBch K-B2)   19 BxR, and
White won.

7   0-0   QN-B3

8   P-Q3   N-Q5

9   NxN   PxN

10   N-K2   P-QR3

11   N-N3   B-Q3

12   P-B4   0-0

13   Q-B3   K-R1

14   B-Q2   P-B4

15   QR-K1   N-B3

16   R-K2   Q-B2

Nimzowitsch offers some good advice at this point.
He says, 'In cramped positions one should never give
away the slightest future possibility of a move. But
16 . . . Q-B2 gives away the possibility of playing . . .
Q-KB3 after 17 PxP PxP. The right move was therefore 16 . . . B-Q2, and if then 17 PxP PxP 18 KR-K1
then 18 . . . Q-B3, and Black stands much better at
any rate than he does in the game.'

17   PxP   PxP

18   N-R1!!

Wonderful! A move of sheer genius! The knight
retreats to the corner as the first step in its long
journey to N5, from whence it can take a strong
part in the attack.

18   . . .   B-Q2

19   N-B2   QR-K1

20   KR-K1   RxR

21   RxR   N-Q1

If 21 . . . R-K1   22 Q-Q5 N-K2   23 Q-B7, and Black
is a bit tied up.

22   N-R3   B-B3

'Here,' says Nimzowitsch, '22 . . . R-K1 would lead
to a combination full of pleasantries, e.g., 23 Q-R5
RxR   24 N-N5 P-KR3   25 Q-N6 PxN   26 Q-R5
mate.'

23   Q-R5   P-KN3

24   Q-R4   K-N2

25   Q-B2!

His first attempt being thwarted, Nimzowitsch attacks
the isolated pawn, and compels his opponent to re-
group his forces.

25   . . .   B-QB4

If 25 . . . Q-N3   26 P-QN4 followed by 27 B-B3 is
decisive.

26   P-QN4!   B-N3

27   Q-R4!

The problem-like switchback theme. The queen returns
with a powerful threat—28 R-K7ch winning the queen.

27   . . .   R-K1

28   R-K5!

Following the advice recommended in *My system*: An
advance post forms a base for new attacks.

28   . . .   N-B2

Of course not 28 . . . RxR   29 PxR QxP, when
30 Q-R6ch followed by mate is the penalty.
   Nor is 28 . . . P-R3 of service, as then comes
29 P-N4 PxP   30 P-B5 QxR   31 P-B6ch QxP
32 QxP mate.

29   BxN   QxB

If Black tries to simplify by more exchanges with
29 . . . RxR   30 PxR QxB, White continues 31 N-N5
Q-N1   32 P-K6 B-Q4   33 Q-B4 and wins quickly after
34 Q-K5ch.

30   N-N5   Q-N1

31 RxR   BxR

Rubinstein

Position after
31 . . . BxR

Nimzowitsch
to move

32 Q-K1!

Another switchback by the queen! Despite the few
pieces on the board, Nimzowitsch manages to
conjure up a mating attack.

His threat now is 33 Q-K5ch K-B1 (on 33 . . .
K-R3 34 N-K6 wins) 34 Q-B6ch B-B2 35 P-N5
(clearance for the bishop's check) B-B4 36 N-K6ch
K-K1 37 Q-Q8 mate.

32 . . .   B-B3

Some neat play follows 32 . . . K-B1, to wit:
33 Q-K5 B-Q1 (or 33 . . . QxP 34 Q-B6ch B-B2
35 NxB QxB 36 N-K5 dis.ch, and mate in two)
34 N-K6ch K-K2 35 Q-B5ch K-Q2 36 N-B8ch,
and Black must give up his queen.

33 Q-K7ch   K-R1

On 33 . . . K-R3 34 N-K6 wins quickly.

34 P-N5!

Sudden attack! White offers a pawn on the Q-side
to achieve mate on the K-side.

34 . . .   Q-N2

Black yields to despair and commits hara-kiri. The
alternative 34 . . . PxP leads to a forced win by
White, as follows: 35 N-K6 P-R4 (air, air!)
36 Q-B6ch K-R2 37 N-N5ch K-R3 38 B-N4
(now we see how the pawn sacrifice cleared the
way for the bishop) and the threat of 39 B-B8ch
forces Black to give up his queen.

35 QxQch   KxQ

36 PxB and wins.

One of my most elegant attacking games—Nimzowitsch.

7

White **Hage**   Black **A. Nimzowitsch**
Dutch Defence
Arnstadt, 1926

Morphy bowled over his inferiors (and who wasn't?)
with the power and energy of his attacks.

The Nimzowitsch technique is quite different. He
sets his pawns in motion all over the board, sends the
enemy pieces scurrying home, and seizes key squares
with his knight. Then, with the position so superior, the
finishing touch is mere child's play.

1 P-Q4   P-KB4

2 P-K3   P-Q3

3 B-Q3   P-K4

4 PxP PxP

5 B-N5ch   P-B3

6 QxQch   KxQ

7 B-B4   B-Q3

White has managed to relinquish the initiative after
just a few moves. True, Black has lost the privilege of
castling, but that's of little moment with queens off
the board.

8 N-KB3   N-B3

9 N-B3   K-K2

10 P-QR3   R-Q1

11 B-Q2   P-QN4

12 B-R2   P-QR4

This expanding operation on the Q-side comes up
often in Nimzowitsch games, usually with great effect.

13 0-0   P-N5

14 N-N1

A sorry-looking retreat, in order to protect the rook pawn. Surely 14 PxP PxP   15 N-K2 was preferable.

14 ...   P-B4

15 B-B4   P-K5

16 N-N5   B-R3

This will remove White's only decently developed piece.

17 BxB   RxB

18 PxP   RPxP

19 RxR   NxR

Note that in this sort of exchange, White's rook disappears from the board, while Black's is replaced by another piece.

20 P-QB3   P-R3

21 N-R3   N-N5

The knight attacks the rook pawn before settling down on K4, the center of the board.

22 P-KN3

Now that all White's pawns are on black squares, his bishop is condemned to life imprisonment.

22 ...   N-K4

23 K-N2   P-N4

24 B-B1

The useless bishop retreats, making way for the knight in the hope that he might have a more illustrious career.

24 ...   P-N6

25 N-Q2   P-QB5   (See diagram in next column.)

This paralyzes White's Q-side.

26 N-KN1

Now this knight retreats, hoping to emerge at K2 and then occupy Q4.

26 ...   N-B4

Both black knights eye the lovely square at Q6.

27 N-K2   R-KN1

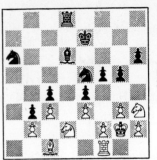

Nimzowitsch

**Position after
25 ... P-QB5**

Hage to move

28 N-Q4   P-B5

29 N-B5ch

If 29 KPxP PxP   30 R-K1 P-K6   31 PxKP PxNP   32 PxP N(K4)-Q6 wins.

29 ...   K-K3

30 NxB   P-B6ch

A *zwischenzug* (an in-between move) which puts the game on ice.

31 K-N1   KxN

32 R-Q1   K-K3

33 N-N1

Second home-coming!

33 ...   N(B4)-Q6

34 N-R3   K-Q4

35 N-N5   R-N1

36 N-R3

This poor knight has done nothing but advance a bit only to retreat again. The alternative is 36 N-B7ch K-Q3   37 N-R6 R-QR1   38 N-N4 R-R8, and Black wins the bishop.

36 ...   R-QR1

37 P-R3   K-B4

38 K-B1   NxB

39 RxN   N-Q6

40 R-N1   NxNP

41 RxN   RxN

Threatens quick mate.

42 R-N1   P-N7

White cannot prevent 43 . . . R-R8.

43 Resigns

A fine illustration of the Nimzowitsch blockading technique.

8

White **H. Mattison**   Black **A. Nimzowitsch**
Nimzo-Indian Defence
Carlsbad, 1929

Nimzowitsch's strategy to gain control of the white squares is impressive.

Raymond Keene says, 'Black's blockading knights, firmly established on white squares, create an impression of power and of pictorial beauty.'

1 P-Q4   N-KB3

2 P-QB4   P-K3

3 N-QB3   B-N5

4 N-B3   BxNch

5 PxB

White is saddled with a doubled pawn complex. In return for this weakness though, he has the two bishops and an open knight file for the convenience of his queen rook.

5 . . .   P-Q3

6 Q-B2   Q-K2

Black prepares to establish a pawn in the center by 7 . . . P-K4.

7 B-R3   P-B4

This fixes White's pawn at QB4, before making it an object of attack.

Obviously, 7 . . . P-K4 would not do, as after 8 PxP Black dare not retake.

8 P-KN3   P-QN3

9 B-KN2

The bishop no longer guards QB4, and that creates an infinitesimal weakness—but all Nimzowitsch wants is an infinitesimal weakness!

9 . . .   B-N2

10 0-0   0-0

11 N-R4

The alternative 11 N-Q2 is considerably stronger. The knight would then protect QB4 and control the central square K4.

11 . . .   BxB

12 KxB

Much better was recapturing with the knight, followed by moving to K3 with a good deal of influence on the center.

12 . . .   Q-N2ch

13 K-N1

White misses his last chance. He should play 13 N-B3, when the knight gets back into the game, and helps put up a fight.

The interposition by 13 P-B3 loses a piece after 13 . . . P-KN4 14 Q-Q2 P-KR3 and the knight is trapped.

13 . . .   Q-R3

14 Q-N3

The only move to protect his threatened bishop and bishop pawn.

14 . . .   N-B3

The knight develops with gain of time—attack on the queen pawn.

15 KR-Q1

If 15 PxP NPxP, and White is faced with loss of the bishop by 16 . . . QR-N1, and loss of the QBP by 16 . . . N-K4.

Protecting the queen pawn by 15 N-B3 is met by 15 . . . N-QR4   16 Q-N5 QxQ   17 PxQ N-B5 18 B-B1 N-Q4, and the miserable QBP falls.

Note how the doubled pawns became targets for attack after White fianchettoed his bishop.

15 . . .   N-QR4

16 Q-N5   QxQ

17 PxQ

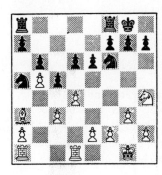

Nimzowitsch
to move

**Position after
17 PxQ**

Mattison

17 . . .   N-B5!

What a knight!

The knight attacks, by threatening the bishop and forcing it to return home.

The knight defends, by guarding the queen pawn and knight pawn against possible threats.

The knight exerts pressure by bearing down on the central squares.

Finally, the knight cannot be driven off by pawns, nor by the bishop, which is confined to black squares.

18 B-B1   P-QR3!

This pries the rook file open, enabling Black's queen rook to come into play with an attack on the isolated pawn.

19 PxRP   RxP

20 PxP   NPxP

21 N-N2

The knight returns, but it's late, too late.

21 . . .   N-Q4

22 R-Q3   R(B1)-R1

23 P-K4   N-K4!

24 Resigns

Resigning may seem premature, as pieces and pawns are even, but White must lose two or three pawns.

After 24 R-Q1 (the only safe spot for the rook) there comes 24 . . . NxP 25 R-B1 (if 25 R-K1 or 25 R-Q2, N-B6ch wins the exchange) RxP 26 RxR N-B6ch 27 K-R1 RxR, and White's king pawn is the next to fall.

This is as pretty a game as one would want for showing the power of the centralized knights.

9

White **N. Mannheimer**   Black **A. Nimzowitsch**
French Defence
Frankfurt, 1930

Why does chess fascinate us for a lifetime?

A game such as this may provide the answer.

We are impressed by Nimzowitsch's iron control of the white squares, by his mysterious 16th move of Q-R1, by the way he works up a powerful K-side attack, only to have the queen swoop down the other side of the board to snatch up a pawn, and we are amused at the nonchalance of Nimzowitsch's rook pawn as it dances gaily up the board to the queening square while his opponent seems to be too hypnotized to do anything but look on.

This sort of game should go far to dispel the notion that chess is no more than a minor art.

1 P-K4   P-K3

2 P-Q4   P-Q4

3 N-QB3   B-N5

4 PxP   PxP

5 N-B3   N-K2

Nimzowitsch preferred this development to 5 . . . N-B3, as it exerts pressure on the square KB4.

6 B-Q3   QN-B3

7 P-KR3   B-KB4

8 BxB   NxB

With the disappearance of White's king bishop the white squares lose a protector.

9 0-0   BxN

10 PxB

Again a pet idea, that of doubling the opponent's bishop pawns, further weakening his QB4 square.

10 ...   0-0

Even at this early stage, Nimzowitsch may have planned to anchor his knights firmly on the white squares K5 and QB5.

11 Q-Q3   N-Q3

12 N-N5   P-KN3

13 B-B4   Q-B3

14 B-Q2   P-KR3

15 N-B3   K-R2

16 N-R2

With a little threat of 17 BxP KxB 18 N-N4ch winning the queen. The obvious reply 16 ... Q-N2 offers no comfort after 17 N-N4 P-KR4   18 B-R6, and White wins the exchange.

16 ...   Q-R1!

An extraordinary move! But then Francis Bacon once said, 'There is no excellent beauty that hath not some strangeness in the proportion.'

This is the picture on the board:

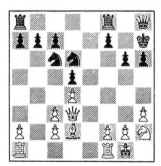

Nimzowitsch

**Position after
16 ... Q-R1!**

Mannheimer
to move

17 Q-K3   Q-N2

18 Q-B3

White could attack the pawn once more by 18 N-N4, but after 18 ... P-B4 19 QxPch (if 19 NxP N-B5 wins a piece or two) 19 ... QxQ 20 NxQ (on 20 BxQ R-R1 wins a piece) 20 ... N-K5 21 B-B1 P-KN4 leaves White's knight stranded.

18 ...   N-K5

19 B-B1   P-B4

20 Q-Q3   N-R4

This prevents any freeing attempt by 21 P-QB4, and intensifies the pressure on the white squares.

21 P-KB4!

White hopes to get some counterplay on the black squares by posting his knight at K5.

21 ...   Q-Q2

22 N-B3   Q-B3

23 N-K5   Q-K3

On principle one should not go pawn-hunting when the position calls for crushing the opponent to death. Sometimes retribution comes quickly: viz., if 23 ... QxP 24 QxQ NxQ 25 B-Q2 (skewering the knights) 25 ... N-K7ch 26 K-B2 (and now rendering them *hors de combat*).

24 R-N1   P-N3

25 K-R2   N-B5

26 B-K3

White does not relish 26 NxN PxN 27 Q-B3 Q-Q4 when he is reduced to passivity.

26 ...   P-KN4

Now that his knights are securely stationed on the vital white squares, Nimzovich starts a K-side attack.

27 P-N3   R-B3

28 QR-K1   R-KN1

29 B-B1   P-N4

An important clearance move, whose purpose we shall see later.

30 N-B3   P-KN5

31 PxP   RxP

32 N-N1

The knight is headed for K2 to help support the knight pawn.

32 ...   R(B3)-N3

Capturing the pawn instead would be premature: if 32 ... RxP 33 RxN RxQ   34 RxQ, and White wins a piece.

33 R-B3   Q-N1

34 N-K2   P-KR4

White's unfortunate pawn is attacked four times and defended four times, so Black prepares to bring another assailant into the fray.

35 K-N2

There is no rescuing the pawn by 35 R-N1, as Black plays 35 ... P-R5 followed by 36 ... PxPch 37 NxP R-R5ch 38 K-N2 NxN 39 RxN RxRch 40 QxR R-N5, and White's queen is caught in a pin.

35 ...   P-R5

36 R-R1   R-R3

37 R-R3   Q-N3!

38 B-K3   Q-R3!

Now that White's pieces are tied up on the K-side, Black's queen zooms over to the other side. The major threat is 39 ... N-N7 winning the queen.

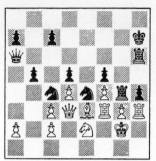

Nimzowitsch

Position after
38 ... Q-R3!

Mannheimer
to move

39 B-B2   QxP

40 B-K1   P-R4

Suddenly a new menace looms up as the passed pawn starts a promenade to the coronation.

41 K-B1   Q-N8

This clears the file for the convenience of the pawn, and initiates a threat of winning the game on the K-side by 42 ... N(B5)-Q7ch 43 K-N2 QxB, and further adversity to follow.

42 N-N1   P-R5

43 K-K2   P-R6

44 R-B1   P-R7

What nonchalance!

45 Resigns

A masterpiece in Nimzowitsch's *métier*—the strategy of white-square domination.

Rubinstein

Rubinstein was an artist of the chessboard, whose games constitute a beautiful chapter in the literature of chess, offering pleasure to all, as the moves seem simple and understandable. There is a smooth, easy flow to them, as in the games of Morphy, Pillsbury, and Capablanca. Réti describes it best, when he says, 'With Rubinstein all is refined tranquility, for with him in building up his game the position given to every piece is the necessary one. It is not a matter of a fight for him, but the working out of a victory, and so his games create an impression of a great structure from which not one stone dare be shifted.'

So much has been said of Rubinstein's astounding endgame technique—from Fine's, 'In the endgame Rubinstein is supreme,' to Tartakover's, 'Rubinstein is the rook ending of a game begun by the Gods thousands of years ago'—that we tend to overlook his accomplishments in other departments. His openings, if not so sharp and aggressive as Alekhine's, were carefully and soundly constructed. His midgames reflect profound position judgement, and the combinations he evolved were of classic beauty.

Réti (even more enthusiastic) makes this comment, 'Rubinstein has created the most perfect games of the epoch since Steinitz. The theories of Steinitz and their application in chess practice have the same history as the theories of physics and their application in technology. The games of Steinitz himself, who created the theories, were far from being the best games exemplifying them. It took an entire generation of chess masters to derive from those theories all that they contained of value for practical playing. Rubinstein was the keystone of this generation, and his games are the most perfect demonstrations of Steinitz's teachings.'

Rubinstein won brilliancy prizes galore. Who, for example, could emulate Rubinstein's feat at Teplitz-Schonau in 1922, when he won six games, of which four were awarded brilliancy prizes? As for the outstanding game of his career, *The Rubinstein Immortal* (Game No. 10), that alone should enshrine him in Caissa's Hall of Fame.

His doughty deeds in tournament play were many. Outstanding in his accomplishments were:
First prize in the great Carlsbad Tournament of 1907,
Tie with Lasker for first and second at St. Petersburg in 1909, with Rubinstein winning their individual game,
Three first prizes and a tie for first and second, out of four tournaments played in 1912,
And (this is amazing!) he defeated Alekhine, Lasker, and Capablanca, the first time he ever played them!

I consider Rubinstein the eleventh greatest chess player of all time.

10

White **G. Rotlevi**   Black **A. Rubinstein**
Queen's Gambit Declined
Lodz, 1907

The Rubinstein Immortal

The great artist of the endgame displays his virtuosity in another field.

He unleashes an attack with the fire and elegance of a Morphy, and unfolds combinations and brilliant sacrifices that would do honour to Tal or Alekhine.

The Rubinstein Immortal undoubtedly ranks with the most famous games of all time.

There is nothing like seeing this game for the first time —or the second, third, or tenth time!

1 P-Q4   P-Q4
2 N-KB3   P-K3
3 P-K3   P-QB4
4 P-B4   N-QB3
5 N-B3   N-B3
6 QPxP   BxP
7 P-QR3   P-QR3
8 P-QN4   B-Q3
9 B-N2

White heeds Nimzowitsch's injunction, 'Never play to win a pawn while your development is yet unfinished,' and avoids 9 PxP PxP 10 NxP, when the punishment would be 10 . . . NxN 11 QxN BxPch, and off comes his queen.

9 . . .   0-0
10 Q-Q2   Q-K2!
11 B-Q3

Here too the capture is risky: 11 PxP PxP 12 NxP NxN 13 QxN B-K3 14 Q-Q1 (on 14 Q-KN5, BxPch wins at once) 14 . . . NxP, with much the best of it for Black.

11 . . .   PxP
12 BxP   P-QN4
13 B-Q3   R-Q1
14 Q-K2

The queen steps aside, feeling uncomfortable on the same file as the rook.

14 . . .   B-N2
15 0-0   N-K4

With various threats, the major one being 16 . . . NxB, and if 17 QxN BxPch, and Black wins the queen.

16 NxN

Practically forced, but White parts with his king knight, the best protector of the castled position.

16 . . .   BxN

Now Black threatens to win a pawn by 17 . . . BxPch 18 KxB Q-Q3ch and 19 . . . QxB.

17 P-B4   B-B2
18 P-K4   QR-B1

Rubinstein brings up the reserves. This sort of move always reminds me of Blackburne's advice, 'Never commence your final attack until the queen's rook is in play.'

19 P-K5

This cuts down the bishop's mobility, but does not affect its career.

19 . . .   B-N3ch

The bishop merely swings over to another diagonal. giving check to the king—the first move in a magnificent combination.

20 K-R1   N-N5
21 B-K4

Rotlevi tries to exchange bishops, thereby removing one of a terrifying pair of prelates.

Against 21 N-K4 instead, the finish is neat and quick, as follows:
21 N-K4 RxB! 22 QxR BxN 23 QxB Q-R5 (threatens instant mate) 24 P-R3 Q-N6 (again threatening mate on the move) 25 PxN Q-R5 mate.

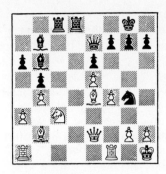

Rubinstein
to move

**Position after
21 B-K4**

Rotlevi

21 . . .   Q-R5
Rubinstein begins the display of fireworks.

22 P-N3
If White plays 22 P-R3 to prevent the mate, it
would lead to this brilliant finish: 22 . . . RxN!
23 BxR (if 23 BxB RxPch forces quick mate)
23 . . . BxB   24 QxN (on 24 QxB Q-N6   25 PxN
Q-R5 mate) 24 . . . QxQ   25 PxQ R-Q6, and the
threat of 26 . . . R-R6 mate wins the bishop.

Quite in the Alekhine style, with the sting at the
end of the combination.

22 . . .   RxN!!!
Kmoch adorns this beautiful move with three exclamation marks. I can give it no less.

23 PxQ
What choice is there? If 23 BxR BxBch   24 R-B3
BxRch   25 QxB QxRP mate. Or if 23 BxB RxNP,
and the threat of 24 . . . NxRP   25 QxN R-R6 is
decisive.

23 . . .   R-Q7!!!
A wonderful sequel to the sacrifice of the queen! This
startling rook move leaves four of Rubinstein's five
pieces *en prise*.

24 QxR
White has a bewildering choice of losing moves. Let's
look at them:
If 24 BxB RxQ   25 B-N2 R-R6!, with mate to
follow.

If 24 BxR RxQ, and White cannot parry the threats
of mate in one by the rook, and mate in two by the
bishop.
If 24 QxN BxBch   25 R-B3 RxR   26 Q-N2 R-B8ch
27 RxR BxQ mate.

24 . . .   BxBch

25 Q-N2   R-R6!
An exquisite finishing touch.

26 Resigns
Mate by the rook is inevitable.

11

White **A. Rubinstein**   Black **O. Duras**
Queen Pawn Opening
Vienna, 1908

When the powerful queen (worth two rooks or nine pawns
in today's market) is sacrificed, it's usually for the purpose
of effecting a quick mate.

Early in the game, Rubinstein sacrifices his queen brilliantly, but the only mate in sight is the one that appears
in the notes.

Rubinstein does wind up with a Q-side pawn majority
of two pawns to one. What else does an endgame specialist
need to make his opponent yield?

1 P-Q4   P-Q4

2 N-KB3   P-QB4

3 P-K3   N-KB3

4 PxP   Q-R4ch
Not a happy idea, as the queen loses time regaining
the pawn. Simpler is 4 . . . P-K3, and White cannot
keep the pawn, for if 5 P-QN4 P-QR4   6 P-B3 PxP
7 PxP P-QN3, and if then 8 B-R3 PxP   9 PxP RxB
10 NxR Q-R4ch, and Black wins two pieces for a
rook.

5 QN-Q2   QxBP

6 P-QR3   Q-B2

The queen must retreat, sooner or later.

7 P-B4

Customary procedure in queen pawn openings, to institute an attack against the queen.

7 . . .   PxP

This can only facilitate White's development. The quiet 7 . . . P-K3 should be played.

8 NxP   B-N5

Even masters should heed Lasker's injunction to develop knights before bishops.

9 P-N4   N-B3

10 B-N2   P-QN4

There was still time for development of the K-side, beginning with 10 . . . P-K3. This wild lashing-out meets with an unexpected reply.

11 N(B4)-K5!   NxN

12 NxN!

Brilliantly played, though a master of Duras's calibre should have anticipated it.

12 . . .   BxQ

13 BxPch   N-Q2

The alternative 13 . . . K-Q1 leads to this elegant finish: 14 RxBch K-B1   15 B-R6ch K-N1   16 N-B6ch QxN 17 B-K5ch Q-Q3   18 R-QB1! followed by 19 R-B8 mate.

14 BxNch   QxB

After 14 . . . K-Q1   15 RxB Q-N3, White can win in problem style by 16 N-B6ch K-B2   17 B-K5ch K-N2 18 N-R5ch K-R3   19 B-N4! Q-N3   20 B-K2ch K-N3 21 R-QB1! and mate will follow by 22 B-B7ch or 22 B-Q4ch.

15 NxQ   B-R4

16 N-K5   R-B1

17 P-N4   B-N3

Black doesn't dare seize the seventh, as after 17 . . . R-B7   18 R-QB1 forces an exchange of rooks (18 . . . RxB being met by 19 R-B8 mate).

18 NxB

White snips off the long-range bishop, even though it opens a file for Black's king rook. (Two bishops can be dangerous.)

18 . . .   RPxN

Tarrasch's *Die Moderne Schachpartie* gives the score of this game only to the 18th move, implying that the win 'is only a matter of technique.' Tarrasch deprives the reader though of seeing the Rubinstein blend of accuracy and artistry in action.

This is the situation:

Duras

Position after 18 . . . RPxN

Rubinstein to move

19 B-Q4   P-QR3

20 K-Q2

The king moves towards the centre, where it can be active in the endgame.

The king's role in the endings has been stressed by theoreticians for hundreds of years, but no one has put it more clearly and simply than Reuben Fine in *Basic chess endings*, 'The king is a strong piece: Use it!'

20 . . .   P-B3

Intending to evict the bishop, by 21 . . . P-K4, from its strong position in the center.

21 QR-QB1!

This forces Black to exchange rooks or surrender control of the open file.

21 . . .   RxR

22 RxR!

Better than capturing with the king. *The rook must*

be active in the endgame, and not be tied down to the protection of a pawn.

22 ...   P-K4
The capture 22 ... RxP succumbs to 23 R-B8ch K-B2 24 K-K2 P-K4 25 B-B5 BxB 26 RxB R-R1 27 R-B7ch K-K3 28 R-R7, and White will soon have two connected passed pawns.

23 B-B5   RxP
If 23 ... BxB 24 RxB K-Q2 25 R-R5 R-R1 26 P-QN5, and White wins the rook pawn and the game.

24 BxB   KxB

25 K-K2   P-K5

26 R-B6   R-N7

27 RxRP   RxNP
Material is even, but the two connected passed pawns constitute a powerful advantage.

28 R-R7
Almost instinctively the rook seizes control of the seventh rank.

28 ...   R-N8

29 P-N5!   R-N8

30 P-R4   P-N4

31 R-N7   R-QR8

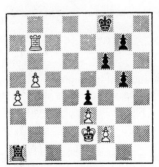

Duras

Position after
31 ... R-QR8

Rubinstein
to move

32 P-N6!
Rubinstein cheerfully gives up a pawn, as the quickest way to win.

32 ...   RxP

33 R-R7
Offers an exchange of rooks (which Black dare not accept) and clears a path for the pawn.

33 ...   R-N5

34 P-N7
Threatens 35 R-R8ch followed by 36 P-N8(Q).

34 ...   P-N5
Advancing the king by 34 ... K-K2 loses on the spot by 35 P-N8(Q) dis.ch.

35 R-R8ch   K-B2

36 P-N8(Q)   RxQ

37 RxR   K-K3

38 R-K8ch   K-B4

39 K-B1   Resigns
Duras yields just in time to avoid being polished off neatly. The finish could be 39 ... P-N6 40 PxP K-N5 41 K-N2 P-B4 42 R-K7 P-N4 43 R-KN7 P-B5 44 KPxP P-K6 45 RxP mate.

12

White **A. Rubinstein**   Black **G. Salwe**
Queen's Gambit Declined
Lodz, 1908

Rubinstein produces a strategic masterpiece in this absorbing game.

An impressive feature is the way he makes one key square uniquely his own. First he blockades the magic square QB5, to make it available for his pieces. Then he occupies it in turn with four pieces, bishop, knight, rook, and queen. Each piece taking possession of the square intensifies Rubinstein's iron grip on the position.

Eventually something must give under the strain, and Salwe finds further resistance impossible.

Rubinstein's artistry reaches the heights in this beautiful game.

1 P-Q4   P-Q4

2 P-QB4   P-K3

3 N-QB3   P-QB4

Tarrasch liked this defence for various reasons:

(a) The attack on the queen pawn disputes possession of the center.

(b) The queen knight may be developed at QB3, instead of at Q2, where it interferes with the queen bishop's career.

(c) Black can get his pieces freely and easily into play.

The disadvantage of the Tarrasch Defence is that it leaves Black with an isolated queen pawn.

4 BPxP   KPxP

5 N-B3   N-KB3

6 P-KN3

This fianchetto development, wherein the bishop bears down on the queen pawn, almost put the Tarrasch Defence out of business.

6 . . .   N-B3

7 B-N2   PxP

The books recommend simple development by 7 . . . B-K2, and 8 . . . 0-0 soon afterwards.

8 KNxP   Q-N3

There are arguments for and against an isolated pawn, some of which appear in the preamble to Game No.87.

9 NxN

Strange! Rubinstein abandons any attempt to exploit the isolated pawn. The exchange of knights lets Black unite his pawns in the centre.

9 . . .   PxN

White's plan consists in (a) preventing . . . P-B4, (b) blockading QB5, and (c) attacking the QBP with his heavy artillery.

10 0-0   B-K2

The pawns must stay put. If 10 . . . P-B4   11 NxP wins a pawn, while 10 . . . P-Q5 is met by 11 N-R4, and the reckless pawn falls.

11 N-R4!

This is not meant to frighten the queen, but to get a grip on the key square QB5. A piece stationed there could not be dislodged by enemy pawns, and would paralyse Black's entire Q-side position.

11 . . .   Q-N4

12 B-K3

Far superior to aimless development by 12 B-B4 or 12 B-N5. The bishop's role is to further the strategic plan of concentrating all forces possible on the one square—the key to the position.

12 . . .   0-0

Not having read the previous notes, Black is content to make 'good' developing moves. If there was any chance of saving the game, it lay in 12 . . . B-K3 (to protect the queen pawn) followed by 13 . . . N-Q2 and 14 . . . R-QB1—all of this to enable him to push the bishop pawn forward one square.

13 R-B1

White seizes the open file, puts more pressure to bear on QB5, and prepares to post a piece there.

13 . . .   B-KN5

14 P-B3

Hemming in his own bishop, but only temporarily, as it will soon survey a longer diagonal.

14 . . .   B-K3

15 B-B5

Invasion on the black squares! The coming exchange will accentuate the weakness of these squares, as their best defender (Black's king bishop) disappears from the board.

15 . . .   KR-K1

16 R-KB2!

A very fine move! The rook prepares to swing over

to QB2, doubling rooks on the file, and incidentally adding its protection to the tender knight pawn. The rook also vacates KB1, for the convenience of the bishop.

16 ...   N-Q2

A third attack on the bishop, with the hope of inducing it to leave.

17 BxB   RxB

18 Q-Q4!

Centralizes the queen, and restrains the freeing move 18 ... P-QB4. The queen now guards the knight pawn, making it possible for the knight to proceed to B5.

It may not be obvious to the unpractised eye, but the noose is beginning to tighten.

18 ...   R(K2)-K1

The rook of course is on its way to QB1, to help defend the pawn.

19 B-B1

A subtle means of getting the bishop into the game, and far superior to 19 P-B4, which makes K4 available to Black's pieces.

19 ...   KR-QB1

20 P-K3!

A little move, but it accomplishes a great deal. It gains time by attacking the queen, opens a diagonal for the bishop, and clears a pathway on the second rank for the rook to switch over to QB2, to add its pressure to the bishop file.

20 ...   Q-N2

'The better part of valor is discretion,' said Shakespeare, borrowing from Beaumont and Fletcher.

21 N-B5!

Blockade, in the manner prescribed by Nimzowitsch.

21 ...   NxN

22 RxN

One blockader disappear, only to be replaced by another, perhaps not as agile, but just as effective.

The rook enjoys immunity from harassment by

pawns, or by the bishop, which is confined to the white squares, and Black has no knights left.

22 ...   R-B2

23 R(B2)-B2   Q-N3

24 P-QN4!

This is the position:

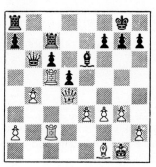

Salwe
to move

**Position after
24 P-QN4!**

Rubinstein

Now there is a threat of 25 P-N5, which forces a further weakening at Black's QR3.

24 ...   P-QR3

25 R-R5   R-N1

Other moves offer bleak prospects:
If 25 ... QxQ 26 PxQ B-B1 (protecting the rook pawn) 27 RxQP wins a pawn. Or if 25 ... Q-N2 26 Q-B5, followed by 27 P-QR4 and 28 P-N5 engineers a decisive breakthrough.

26 P-QR3

Protects the valuable knight pawn (which is destined to bring the enemy to his knees) before proceeding with the attack. Now there is no way for Black to guard all the vulnerable points. One of the three Q-side pawns must fall.

26 ...   R-R2

Saves the rook pawn at the cost of another pawn. But if instead 26 ... B-B1 27 QxQ RxQ 28 RxQP does the trick.

27 RxBP   QxR(B3)

28 QxR   R-R1

29 Q-B5

Once more does White take possession of the bishop file, and the key square, this time with the queen.

29 ...   Q-N2

The exchange of queens loses another pawn; e.g. 29 . . . QxQ   30 RxQ K-B1   31 R-R5 B-B1 32 RxQP.

30 K-B2

White consolidates his K-side position before applying the finishing touches.

30 ...   P-R4

31 B-K2   P-N3

32 Q-Q6

Further inroads into Black's territory. The queen attacks the rook pawn a third time, and also clears the square B5 for the rook to use as a springboard to the seventh rank.

32 ...   Q-B1

33 R-B5!

The rook pawn can wait! It is more important to retain control of the bishop file than to pick up stray pawns.

33 ...   Q-N2

34 P-KR4

Rubinstein, with his usual care, puts an end to any possible demonstrations on the K-side.

34 ...   P-R4

Desperation, but what else is there? If 34 . . . K-N2 35 R-B7 Q-N1   36 BxP K-N1 (or 36 . . . RxB 37 RxPch winning the queen)   37 B-N7 R-R2 38 R-B8ch BxR   39 QxQ, and White wins easily.

35 R-B7

This reduces the queen's flight squares to the minimum—one square! White is in full control of all strategic areas—the queen bishop file, the all-important square QB5, the queen file, the sixth rank, and the seventh rank.

35 ...   Q-N1

36 P-N5   P-R5

Hoping to give his rook more elbow-room.

37 P-N6

Preparing to continue with 38 P-N7 R-R2   39 R-B8ch BxR   40 QxQ, winning everything in sight.

37 ...   R-R4

38 P-N7!   Resigns

The sequel could be 38 . . . K-N2 (to avoid loss of the queen by 39 R-B8ch) 39 RxPch, and wins the queen in a different way.

Or if 38 . . . Q-K1   39 Q-N6 steals the rook in broad daylight.

Rubinstein's superb technique in exploiting QB5, the key square in the 'Pillsbury Bind,' would have delighted Pillsbury himself, who showed its power in his famous game against Tarrasch in the play-off match for first prize in the great Vienna 1898 Tournament.

13

White **A. Rubinstein**   Black **E. Lasker**
Queen's Gambit Declined
St. Petersburg, 1909

Rubinstein and Lasker finished in a tie for first place in the great St. Petersburg Tournament of 1909. They ran away with it, their 14½ points each being 3½ points ahead of the rest of the field, clearly showing their superiority to the other competitors.

It was a great feat for Lasker, who had not engaged in tournament play in five years.

For Rubinstein it was an equally notable achievement. Not only in his tie for first, but in the quality of his play, for he produced as many masterpieces over the chess-board as did Lasker, the World's Champion.

What must have added particularly to his gratification was the fact that one of the victims of his brilliant efforts was Lasker himself!

Here is the record of this, their first encounter:

1 P-Q4   P-Q4

2 N-KB3   N-KB3

3 P-B4   P-K3

4 B-N5   P-B4

A better line is 4 . . . P-KR3!, and if 5 B-R4, B-N5ch
followed by 6 . . . PxP, as the gambit pawn could be
held by . . . P-QN4.

5 PxQP   KPxP

6 N-B3

Threatens 7 BxN QxB   8 NxP, winning a pawn.

6 . . .   PxP

Practically forced, though the reply centralizes White's
king knight.

Other moves have their drawbacks;
e.g., if 6 . . . B-K2   7 PxP wins a pawn, or if 6 . . . B-K3,
7 Q-N3 can cause uncomfortable pressure.

7 KNxP   N-B3

'This gets Black into difficulties,' says Lasker, '7 . . .
B-K2 was indicated. If then 8 P-K3 0-0, exception
could scarcely be taken to Black's position.'

8 P-K3

White does not try to win a pawn by 8 BxN QxB
9 NxP, as 9 . . . QxN   10 N-B7ch K-Q1   11 NxR
B-N5ch would find him mated.

8 . . .   B-K2

9 B-N5   B-Q2

Thanks to inaccurate play in the opening (or was it
contempt for book moves?) Lasker has a bad game.

The question now before Rubinstein is, whether
to try to win the isolated queen pawn at the risk of
undergoing a powerful attack in return, or whether
to castle and defer immediate action, since the pawn
is bound to fall eventually.

10 B(KN5)xN

Rubinstein enters fearlessly into the complications,
though he will be thrown on the defensive.

10 . . .   BxB

11 NxP   BxN

12 PxB   Q-N4!

The queen comes strongly into play, with simultaneous attack on the knight and the king knight
pawn.

13 BxN   BxB

14 N-K3

Rook-hunting would be disastrous, as after 14 N-B7ch
K-Q2   15 NxR R-K1ch   16 K-B1 QxP checkmate
would be the swift penalty.

14 . . .   0-0-0

'Lasker adds to the tension,' says Réti, but Lasker
sees things differently. He comments, 'A careless
move. Black should not have given up his intention
to win the knight pawn. After 14 . . . BxP   15 R-KN1
Q-R4ch   16 Q-Q2 QxQch   17 KxQ B-K5, as well
as after   15 NxB QxN   16 Q-K2ch K-Q1   17 0-0-0
Q-N3   18 Q-Q3 (18 R-Q3? Q-B3ch) 18 . . . R-B1ch
19 K-N1 R-K1, Black would have quite a good game.'

15 0-0   KR-K1

Tarrasch, with enthusiasm he cannot quite conceal,
says, 'One sees with astonishment how brilliantly
Lasker has developed his game after sacrificing a pawn.
All his pieces are in play, and he threatens to win by
16 . . . RxN, whereas White has only one piece in
the field.'

This is the situation:

Lasker

Position after
15 . . . KR-K1

Rubinstein
to move

16   R-B1!

The start of a profound defensive plan, for which Lasker shows unrestrained admiration. 'This extraordinarily subtle move,' says he, 'shows Rubinstein to be a master of the highest order. White now retains his advantages. He threatens R-B5 and P-Q5. Black's obvious threat of 16 . . . RxN he meets as is shown by his 17th move.'

16   . . .   RxN

'I was outplayed in this combination' says Lasker, in his annotations to the game in the *Wiener Schachzeitung* of 1909. 'I should have played 16 . . . K-N1.'

A year later though, in the book of the tournament, Lasker admitted that 16 . . . K-N1 would still have given him a bad position after 17 R-B5 Q-B5 18 P-Q5 RxN 19 Q-B1 R-K5 20 PxB PxP 21 Q-B3.

17   RxBch   PxR

18   Q-B1!

'This is the miracle,' says Réti, 'Whatever move Black makes now, White turns the pawn gained to account and ultimately wins the endgame.'

18   . . .   RxP

Better chances were afforded by 18 . . . R-K4 19 QxPch (the attractive 19 P-B4 allows the equally attractive reply 19 . . . R-QB4) 19 . . . K-N1 20 PxR QxP 21 R-B1 Q-Q3, and the win offers some difficulty.

19   PxR   R-Q2

If instead 19 . . . R-Q3, to protect the queen bishop pawn, 20 RxP follows, and the rook's penetration is dangerous.

20   QxPch   K-Q1   See diagram

21   R-B4!!

An outstanding move which forces the win. Rubinstein threatens 22 Q-R8ch, followed by 23 R-K4ch or 23 R-B4ch, with a decisive attack.

21   . . .   P-B4

Counter-attack by 21 . . . R-Q8ch 22 K-B2 R-Q7ch 23 K-K1 QxP would be fatal after 24 R-Q4ch K-K2

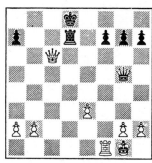

Lasker

Position after 20 . . . K-Q1

Rubinstein to move

(if 24 . . . RxR 25 QxQ) 25 Q-Q6ch K-K1   26 Q-Q8, and Black has been mated.

Meanwhile Black's rook is confined to the queen file, as 21 . . . R-K2 allows quick mate by 22 R-Q4ch, and 21 . . . R-B2 runs into 22 R-Q4ch K-K2 (or 22 . . . K-B1 23 Q-R8 mate)   23 R-K4ch, and mate at K8.

22   Q-B5!

Now mate in five moves is threatened, beginning with 23 Q-B8ch.

22   . . .   Q-K2

Lasker offers the exchange of queens. There is no hope in 22 . . . R-Q8ch   23 K-B2 R-Q7ch   24 K-K1 QxP, as 25 Q-R5ch catches the rook.

23   QxQch   KxQ

24   RxP   R-Q8ch

25   K-B2!

Rubinstein permits no drawing chances which 25 R-B1 R-Q7   26 R-B1 K-Q2 might offer.

25   . . .   R-Q7ch

26   K-B3   RxQNP   See diagram on page 31

Now we are treated to a display of Rubinstein's proverbial skill in the endgame.

27   R-QR5!

This attack on the pawn forces the enemy rook into a passive position.

27   . . .   R-N2

Lasker

Position after
26 . . . RxQNP

Rubinstein
to move

28   R-R6

While this move, confining the king to the first two
ranks, is decisive.

28 . . .   K-B1

29   P-K4

Passed pawns must be pushed!

29 . . .   R-QB2

Now before playing 30 P-K5 followed by 31 K-K4
(to escort the passed pawn up the board) White
must see to the safety of his K-side pawns, which
might be imperilled by a subsequent . . . R-B7, so he
advances them at once.

30   P-KR4   K-B2

31   P-N4   K-B1

32   K-B4   K-K2

33   P-R5

White is now ready to make further progress by
34 P-N5 followed by 35 K-B5 and 36 P-K5.

33 . . .   P-R3

This prevents the planned continuation, but at the
cost of creating a weakness at Black's KN3.

34   K-B5   K-B2

35   P-K5   R-N2

Lasker might have ventured on a swindle by 35 . . .
K-B1. Then if 36 P-K6 R-B4ch   37 K-N6 K-N1!—
and White suddenly finds himself in a mating trap!

36   R-Q6

Threatens to win by 37 R-Q7ch RxR   38 P-K6ch
K-K2   39 PxR KxP   40 K-N6, and the K-side pawns
come off the board.

36 . . .   K-K2

37   R-R6   K-B2

38   R-Q6   K-B1

39   R-QB6   K-B2

40   P-R3!

Rubinstein finds the star move! This quiet little pawn
push places Lasker suddenly in *zugzwang*—the com-
pulsion to move when there are no moves that do not
lose.

If 40 . . . K-B1   41 K-N6 (threatens 42 R-B8ch
K-K2   43 KxP) 41 . . . R-N1 (note that Black does
not now have the resource 41 . . . R-N5, as 40 P-R3!
deprived him of that pleasure) 42 R-B7 R-N3ch
43 K-R7, and White wins the knight pawn.

If 40 . . . K-K2   41 K-N6 K-Q2   42 R-Q6ch K-K1
43 P-K6 K-B1   44 R-Q8ch K-K2   45 R-Q7ch wins.

Finally, if 40 . . . R-K2   41 P-K6ch K-N1
42 K-N6 (threatens 43 R-B8ch and mate) 42 . . . R-K1
43 P-K7! R-N1   44 R-Q6 R-K1   45 R-Q8 is conclusive.

40 . . .   Resigns

A masterly game, and one of the greatest wins ever
scored against Lasker.

14

White **E. Cohn**   Black **A. Rubinstein**
Queen's Pawn Opening
St. Petersburg, 1909

One problem facing a top-ranking master is to evolve a
win from a barren position. Such a position sometimes
comes about when one of the lesser lights sweeps the
board with exchanges in order to simplify matters and
force a draw.

In this game, with pawns only to work with, Rubinstein creates an elegant win in the ending by using the particular artistry which made his name famous.

Lasker describes the finish as 'an attack finely carried through with the smallest means.'

1 P-Q4   P-Q4

2 N-KB3   P-QB4

3 P-B4   PxBP

4 PxP

This gives away the initiative. The simple 4 P-K3 is safe and sound. Another choice is the aggressive line 4 P-K4 PxP 5 QxP QxQ 6 NxQ, with an easy game.

4 ...   QxQch

5 KxQ   N-QB3

6 P-K3   B-N5

7 BxP   P-K3

8 P-QR3 BxP

9 P-N4   B-Q3

10 B-N2   N-B3

11 QN-Q2 K-K2

12 K-K2

Preferable was 12 P-R3, to compel the bishop to declare its intentions.

12 ...   B-K4!

Black seizes the opportunity (White's king knight being pinned and helpless to capture) to rid the board of White's powerful queen bishop, the chief support of his Q-side pawns.

13 BxB   NxB

14 KR-QB1 QR-QB1

15 B-N3   KR-Q1

16 N-B4

Now the pawn push is less effective: if 16 P-R3 BxNch 17 NxB NxN 18 KxN RxR 19 RxR R-Q6, and Black has the superior position.

16 ...   NxN(B5)

17 RxN   RxR

18 BxR   N-K5!

The knight leaps into the fray! The threat is now 19 . . . R-Q7ch, winning a pawn.

19 K-K1   BxN

20 PxB   N-Q3

21 B-K2

Lasker comments, 'At K2 the bishop constrains the king, and to support KB3 was not essential; therefore 21 B-Q3 was indicated, hampering the movements of White's knight.'

21 ...   R-QB1

22 K-Q2   N-B5ch!

The better move, objectively, was 22 . . . P-K4, but Rubinstein is using a bit of Lasker psychology. Convinced that his opponent will try to draw by exchanging the remaining pieces, Rubinstein offers him the chance to do so.

23 BxN   RxB

24 R-QB1

White might still have drawn with 24 P-B4 (to keep the rook from shifting over to R5, but he has an *idée fixe*.

24 ...   RxR

25 KxR   K-B3

Begins a pawn ending which would have pleased Philidor himself.

26 K-Q2   K-N4

27 K-K2

The king rushes to the aid of the precious rook pawn, the loss of which would mean clear sailing for Black's rook pawn. Going after Black's Q-side pawns instead would be too slow, as the following shows: 27 K-Q3 K-R5 28 K-Q4 K-R6 29 K-B5 KxP 30 K-Q6 K-N7 31 K-B7 P-QN4, and White is lost.

27 ...   K-R5

28 K-B1   K-R6

29 K-N1

Rubinstein's last 21 moves have been made with pieces only. Now he makes 10 pawn moves in succession and forces Cohn to resign!

20 ...   P-K4

30 K-R1   P-QN4

31 K-N1   P-B4

32 K-R1   P-N4

33 K-N1   P-KR4

34 K-R1

This is the position, before Rubinstein makes the decisive breakthrough:

Rubinstein to move

Position after 34 K-R1

Cohn

34 ...   P-N5

35 P-K4

If 35 PxP RPxP   36 K-N1 P-B5   37 PxP PxP 38 K-R1 P-N6   39 BPxP PxP   40 PxP KxP, and the king removes the remaining pawns.

35 ...   PxKP

36 PxKP

The alternative is 36 PxNP PxP   37 K-N1 P-K6 38 PxP P-K5   39 K-R1 P-N6, and Black wins.

36 ...   P-R5

37 K-N1   P-N6

38 RPxP   PxP

39 Resigns

White surrenders rather than be mated immediately after queening a pawn, thus: 39 PxB4 PxP   40 P-K5 P-N7   41 P-K6 K-N6   42 P-K7 P-B6   43 P-K8(Q) P-B7 mate!

15

White **A. Rubinstein**   Black **K. Schlechter** Queen's Gambit Declined *San Sebastian, 1912*

There are nine Muses of Caissa who are dedicated to inspiring chess masters. They are the Muses of

Imagination
Understanding . Accuracy
Confidence . Caution . Courage
Ambition . Patience
Memory

In this game, several of them inspire Rubinstein to create a masterpiece of technical skill.

1 P-Q4   P-Q4

2 N-KB3   N-KB3

3 P-B4   P-K3

4 N-B3   P-B4

This defence, which strikes immediately at the center, is intended to avoid the constricted positions which Black must endure in the Orthodox Defence.

5 BPxP   NxP

6 P-K4   NxN

7 PxN   PxP

8 PxP   B-N5ch

9 B-Q2   Q-R4

A natural move, but inferior to 9 . . . BxBch 10 QxB
0-0 11 B-B4 N-B3 12 0-0 P-QN3 13 KR-Q1 N-R4
14 B-Q3 B-N2, and the game is even.

The exchanges which result from Schlechter's
move bring White's king closer to the center, where
it can accomplish a great deal in the ending. White's
rooks too will seize the open files, making it difficult
for Black to develop his Q-side pieces.

10 R-QN1!   BxBch

There is a little trap here in 10 . . . N-B3 11 RxB
NxR 12 Q-N3 QxP 13 QxQ NxQ 14 B-B4, and
the knight cannot get out alive.

11 QxB   QxQch

12 KxQ   0-0

Schlechter assures the safety of his king by castling.
But if there is one stage of the game when the king
need not be concerned about safety, it's in the endgame, when queens are off the board, and there is
little danger of losing by checkmate.

The proper move here was 12 . . . K-K2, as the
king belongs near the center, where he can take part
in the action.

Schlechter

**Position after
12 . . . 0-0**

Rubinstein
to move

13 B-N5!!

An inspired move! It faces Black with the problem of
getting his Q-side pieces into play.

13 . . .   P-QR3

This weakens Black's QN3 square, but what else is

there? If

(a) 13 . . . B-Q2 14 BxB NxB 15 RxP, and White
wins a pawn.

(b) 13 . . . N-Q2 14 BxN BxB 15 RxP, and White
wins a pawn.

(c) 13 . . . N-B3 14 BxN PxB 15 KR-QB1 B-Q2
16 N-K5, and White wins a pawn.

(d) 13 . . . P-QN3 14 KR-QB1 B-N2 15 K-K3 R-B1
16 RxRch BxR 17 R-QB1 B-Q2 (if 17 . . . B-N2
18 R-B7 should win) 18 BxB NxB 19 R-B7 N-B3
20 N-K5, and White has a winning position.

14 B-Q3   R-Q1

If Black tries to start a pawn-roller on the Q-side by
14 . . . P-QN4, he meets with this contretemps:
15 KR-QB1 R-R2 (to prevent invasion of the seventh
rank) 16 P-QR4 R-N2 17 PxP, and White wins a pawn.

15 KR-QB1   P-QN4

If 15 . . . N-B3, the reply 16 K-K3 leaves Black embar-
rassed for a reasonable continuation.

16 R-B7!

Domination of the seventh rank! This is almost
enough by itself to win the game.

16 . . .   N-Q2

17 K-K3   N-B3

18 N-K5

With a rook in command of the seventh rank, a
knight occupying a strong outpost, and his king
centralized, White enjoys a considerable advantage.

18 . . .   B-Q2   See diagram on page 35

19 P-N4!

The idea is to make things difficult for Black, by
dislodging the knight (the best protector of the
castled position) from its present strong post.

19 . . .   P-R3

If instead 19 . . . B-K1 (to avoid losing a piece by
20 P-N5 followed by 21 RxB) there follows
20 P-N5 N-R4 21 QR-QB1, and Black faces a long,
hard winter.

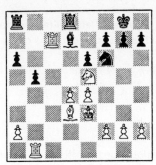

Schlechter

Position after
18 . . . B-Q2

Rubinstein
to move

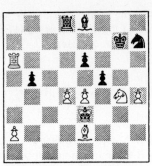

Schlechter

Position after
32 . . . P-B4

Rubinstein
to move

20 P-B4!   B-K1

21 P-N5   PxP

22 PxP   N-R2

As good as there is. If 22 . . . N-Q2   23 N-B6 wins
the exchange at once, or if 22 . . . N-R4   23 B-K2
in reply is strong enough to win.

At this point in his notes, Capablanca comments
admiringly on the precision with which Rubinstein
conducts this game.

23 P-KR4   KR-B1

24 QR-QB1   RxR

25 RxR   R-Q1

Capablanca suggests 25 . . . P-B3 as offering more
resistance.

26 R-R7   P-KB3

27 PxP   PxP

28 N-N4   B-R4

29 N-R6ch   K-R1

30 B-K2!   B-K1

But not 30 . . . BxB, which loses the exchange by
31 N-B7ch.

31 RxP   K-N2

32 N-N4   P-B4

33 R-R7ch!

This forces the king to retreat, to prevent loss of a
piece, or even mate itself. For example, if 33 . . . K-N3
34 P-R5ch K-N4   35 R-N7ch KxP   36 N-B6 dbl.ch K-R3
37 RxNch K-N3   38 P-K5, and White has gained a
piece.

Or if 33 . . . K-N3   34 P-R5ch K-N4   35 R-N7ch
K-R5   36 PxP PxP   37 N-R6! N-B1   38 NxPch K-R6
39 B-B1ch K-R7   40 R-N2ch K-R6 (on 40 . . . K-R8
41 N-N3 is mate)   41 K-B2, and there is no escape
from 42 R-N3 dbl.ch and 43 R-R3 mate.

33 . . .   K-R1

34 N-K5   PxP

35 BxP!

Same idea as before: if Black captures the bishop he
forfeits his rook by the knight check.

35 . . .   N-B3

36 BxB   RxB

With a rook dominating the seventh rank, and a
distant passed pawn waiting in the wings, all that
remains is for Rubinstein to tie things up with a
pretty coloured ribbon.

37 K-B4   K-N1

38 K-N5   R-KB1

Checking with the knight at R2 only makes matters

worse, as after 39 K-R6, the threats of mate by
40 R-N7ch followed by 41 N-N6 mate, or 40 N-N6
and then mate by the rook, are decisive.

39 K-N6!

Threatens this pretty finish:
40 R-N7ch K-R1 41 N-B7ch RxN 42 RxR N-N1
43 R-R7 mate!

39 . . .   Resigns

If 39 . . . N-K1 40 N-B7!, with the threat of
41 N-R6ch K-R1 42 R-R7 mate, should dispel any
lingering doubts.

16

White **A. Rubinstein**   Black **E. Bogolyubov**
Slav Defence
Vienna, 1922

This game was awarded First Brilliancy Prize.

Was it for its attractive combinations, or for the
superb strategy that made them possible?

Early in the game Rubinstein obtains a bit of advantage when he restricts the mobility of Bogolyubov's king
bishop. This advantage increases when his rooks gain
control of the queen bishop file, with one of the rooks
seizing the seventh rank. Then Rubinstein's heavy
pieces penetrate by way of the black squares, which
Rubinstein has skillfully managed to weaken.

Et voila! Suddenly all sorts of sparkling little combinations spring into life, apparently without any effort on
the part of Rubinstein.

1	P-Q4	P-Q4
2	P-QB4	P-QB3
3	P-K3	N-B3
4	N-QB3	P-KN3
5	N-B3	B-N2
6	B-K2	0-0

7 0-0   QN-Q2

This natural move is weak, as it lets White develop
with gain of time, and secure control of the queen
bishop file.

Better moves were 7 . . . N-K5, or 7 . . . B-N5, or
7 . . . PxP.

8 PxP   NxP

9 NxN   PxN

10 Q-N3   N-B3

Not the happiest continuation, as will be seen, but
10 . . . N-N3 is met by 11 P-QR4, with the threat of
displacing the knight by 12 P-R5.

Perhaps the knight should return home, and come
into the game by way of QB3.

11 B-Q2   N-K5

12 KR-Q1   NxB

Bogolyubov now has the two bishops, but at what a
cost! He has made four moves with the knight to
exchange it for a bishop which made only one move.
Time is too precious to be thus wasted! Moreover he
has made it possible for White to double rooks on
the open queen bishop file. Notice that when both
rooks occupy the file, there is a good chance that
one of them will get a foothold on the seventh rank,
from where there is a road leading directly to the
king.

13 RxN   Q-Q3

14 R-QB1   P-N3

The pawn needs protection before the bishop
can emerge.

15 R(Q2)-B2   B-N2

16 Q-R4!

This is to assure mastery of the open file. Black cannot dispute its possession; for example, if 16 . . .
KR-B1 17 RxRch BxR 18 Q-K8ch, and the queen
bishop falls.

16 . . .   P-QR3

This move is practically a necessity, to prevent an

inroad by 17 B-R6. It also enables the queen rook
(which was tied down to the defence of the rook
pawn) to come into play.

Withal it limits the scope of the queen bishop, so
that the two-bishop advantage obtained by Bogolyubov turns out to be a mixed blessing. Notice please
that his king bishop 'bites on granite,' in Nimzowitsch's
apt phrase.

17   R-B7

The rook zooms up to the seventh rank. The seventh
rank is seventh heaven for a rook.

Occupation of the seventh rank by a rook can strike
terror into the heart of the enemy king, however
closely guarded he may be.

17 . . .   P-QN4

This limits further the mobility of Black's queen
bishop; six of his seven pawns stand on white squares.

18   Q-R5!

And now White's heavy pieces are all stationed on the
weakened black squares, from which they cannot be
easily driven away.

18 . . .   QR-N1

19   R(B1)—B5!

The invasion continues.

19 . . .   KR-Q1

Good moves are getting scarce. On 19 . . . KR-B1 for
example, the reply 20 RxB wins a piece on the spot.
Or if 19 . . . P-K3   20 Q-B3 (threatens 21 N-K5)
20 . . . P-B3   21 N-Q2, followed by 22 N-N3 and
23 N-R5 gives White an overwhelming superiority in
position.

20   N-K5   B-KB3

This awkward-looking move is the prelude to an
ingenious defence. Should Black play 20 . . . BxN
instead, the penalty would be 21 PxB Q-K3 (or QxP)
22 RxB RxR   23 QxRch, winning the hapless bishop.

21   N-B6   P-K3

This avoids 21 . . . BxN   22 R(B5)xB, leaving the
queen with no flight square.

Bogolyubov seems to have found a way out of his
difficulties, though. If White captures by 22 NxR(Q8),
then BxN pins the rook and regains the exchange,
while if White captures by 22 NxR(N8), RxN
followed by 23 . . . B-Q1 again recovers the lost
material.

22   P-KN3!!

This is not merely a cowardly safety precaution, but
is indicative of Rubinstein's long-range planning in
preventing an unexpected mate on the last rank, or a
perpetual check in one of the variations.

Bogolyubov can do nothing meanwhile but sit tight
and await events.

22 . . .   KR-QB1

23   NxR   RxN

It would seem that Black will regain the exchange now
by 24 . . . B-Q1.

But Rubinstein has prepared a little surprise for the
occasion.

This is the situation on the board:

Bogolyubov

**Position after
23 . . . RxN**

Rubinstein
to move

24   BxP!   B-Q1

Obviously if 24 . . . PxB   25 Q-R7 in reply assures
White of an easy win.

25   B-K8!

This is where the bishop was headed for, and on the
way there he captured a pawn *en passant*, so to
speak.

25 ... Q-B1

There's no solace in 25 . . . BxR 26 QxB QxQ
27 RxQ RxB 28 RxB, and White, a pawn ahead,
and with his rook in a dominating position, has no
trouble scoring the victory.

26 RxB!

Brilliantly played, and part of the combination
foreseen by Rubinstein. There is a simple, brutal win
(given by all the annotators as a loss for White) by
26 BxPch QxB 27 RxQ BxQ 28 RxB(N7) RxR
29 RxB RxP 30 RxRP, and Black can resign.

26 ... BxQ

27 RxR

With the threat of winning the queen by 28 BxPch.

27 ... Q-Q3

28 R-N7   B-N3

29 R-B6   Q-N5

Now we can see that Rubinstein's perceptive 22nd
move, preventing mate or a possible perpetual check,
permits him time at move 30 to strike the decisive
blow.

30 BxPch   Resigns

Black faces all sorts of possibilities, none of them
pleasant. One course of play might run: 30 . . . K-B1
31 BxNP Q-K8ch 32 K-N2 (courtesy of his 22nd
move) 32 . . . B-Q1 33 R-B8 Q-R4 34 P-QN4, and
the queen must tear herself away from the unfortunate bishop.

Rubinstein gives us another fine specimen of black-
square domination.

17

White **A. Rubinstein**   Black **K. Hromadka**
King's Gambit Declined
Mahrisch-Ostrau, 1924

Rubinstein's artistry was not confined to the endgame. He
could weave combinations in the midgame to compel
admiration, and perhaps secretly envy.

He begins here with a quiet little move, ostensibly to
dislodge an annoying knight. Hardly has the knight left
when Rubinstein hurls a couple of thunderbolts at the
fortress of the enemy king. The sparkling play that
ensues makes this game a worthy runner-up to *The
Rubinstein Immortal.*

1 P-K4   P-K4

2 P-KB4   B-B4

Hromadka declines the pawn, wherein he differs from
Steinitz, who snapped up every gambit pawn that was
offered.

3 N-KB3   P-Q3

4 N-B3   N-KB3

5 B-B4   N-B3

6 P-Q3   B-KN5

An old continuation. A better move is 6 . . . B-K3, to
take the edge off White's formation. Black need not
fear an exchange of bishops, as the doubled pawns in
the center are not weak, and the open king bishop
file would be to his advantage.

7 P-KR3   BxN

8 QxB   N-Q5

9 Q-N3   Q-K2!

Superior to 9 . . . NxPch, which Pillsbury tried, to his
sorrow, in his first round game against Tchigorin in
the famous Hastings 1895 Tournament.

10 PxP

Clears a road for the bishop, and another for the rook.

10 ...   PxP

11 K-Q1   P-B3

12 P-QR4

This restrains any Q-side demonstration beginning with
. . . P-QN4.

12 ...   R-KN1

13 R-B1   P-KR3

14 N-K2   0-0-0

15 NxN   BxN

16 P-B3   B-N3

17 P-R5

This drives the bishop off the long diagonal.

17 . . .   B-B2

18 B-K3   K-N1

19 K-B2

Guards against 19 . . . NxP, and also unites the rooks.

19 . . .   K-R1

20 R-B3

Now the idea is to continue with 21 Q-B2, and the threat is to capture either rook pawn with the bishop, winning a pawn.

20 . . .   N-Q4

An ingenious means of working up an attack if White captures the knight. One possibility could be 21 PxN PxP   22 B-N3 P-K5   23 B-KB4 (if 23 R-B4, P-KN4) 23 . . . PxR   24 BxB Q-K7ch   25 K-N1 P-B7, and Black wins.

21 B-N1   N-B5

22 Q-B2   B-N1

23 P-KN3   NxRP

24 RxP   Q-Q3

After 24 . . . NxQ, White wins nicely by 25 RxQ KR-B1   26 P-R6 (threatens instant mate) 20 . . . P-QN3   27 B-K6, with the powerful 28 B-Q7 to follow.

The situation is shown in the next column.

25 Q-N6!

A staggering move!

25 . . .   R-Q2

If 25 . . . PxQ   26 PxP dis.ch B-R2   27 RxBch K-N1 28 R(B7)xPch K-B1   29 B-R6, and Black is helpless.

26 B-B5!

Another little surprise for Monsieur Hromadka. His queen hasn't a decent flight square.

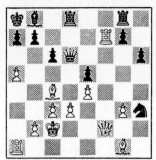

Hromadka

Position after
24 . . . Q-Q3

Rubinstein
to move

26 . . .   RxR

If 26 . . . Q-B2   27 QxQ RxQ   28 RxR BxR 29 BxR, and White has gained a rook.

27 BxQ   R-B7ch

28 QxR

Simple and effective. If instead 28 K-N3 BxB 29 Q-K3 R(N1)-KB1, and Black still needs subduing.

28 . . .   NxQ

29 B-B5

And this wins the knight, whereas 29 BxR BxB nets the exchange only.

29 . . .   Resigns

18

White **H. Mattison**   Black **A. Rubinstein**
Ruy López
Carlsbad, 1929

Rubinstein's endgame skill evoked more than mere admiration.

The editors of the Book of the Carlsbad Tournament agreed that had the ending he won from Mattison occurred 300 years earlier, it would have resulted in Rubinstein's being burned at the stage for practising witchcraft. And it still appears (say the editors) that Rubinstein did sell his soul to the Devil. Nothing else but use of black magic could have conjured up a win out of a dead-drawn position!

1 P-K4   P-K4

2 N-KB3   N-QB3

3 B-N5   P-QR3

4 BxN

The Exchange Variation of the Ruy, a pet line of Lasker's. With the black side he defeated Alekhine in the 17th round of the great St. Petersburg Tournament of 1914. Then with the white side in the next round, he disposed of his chief rival Capablanca, thus tightening his grip on first place.

4 . . .   QPxB

5 P-Q4   PxP

6 QxP   QxQ

7 NxQ   B-Q3

White's pawn structure is superior, in that he has four pawns to three on the K-side, and the prospect of creating a passed pawn in the ending—which is why he tries to simplify the play.

Black's Q-side pawns have been weakened, but he has the two bishops as compensation.

Theoretically, White should play for the ending, while Black should try to win by attack.

In line with this, a good alternative to Black's last move is 7 . . . B-Q2 followed by . . . 0-0-0.

8 B-K3   P-QB4

9 N-K2   P-B3

10 B-B4   B-K3

11 BxB   PxB

This removes any two-bishop threats, but straightens out Black's pawns.

12 N-B4   B-B2

13 N-B3   N-K2

14 0-0-0   0-0-0

15 N(B3)-Q5

White seizes a strong point in the center.

15 . . .   KR-K1

16 P-KB3   NxN

17 NxN   BxN

18 RxN   R-K4

19 R(R1)-Q1

Mattison could draw by simply playing 19 RxR QPxR 20 R-Q1, but he preferred to maintain a rook at Q5, bearing down on the backward queen pawn. He never dreamed that he could possibly lose in this position.

19 . . .   RxR

20 RxR   K-Q2

21 P-QB4   P-KN3

22 K-B2   K-K3

23 K-B3

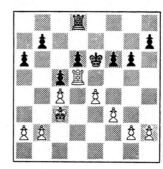

Rubinstein
to move

Position after
23 K-B3

Mattison

23 . . .   P-B4!

A glimmer of light on the horizon! The exchange of pawns will pry open a file for the rook, and this, combined with the aggressive position of his king, will assure Rubinstein of a wee bit of advantage.

24 PxPch

Or 24 K-Q3 PxP 25 KxP R-QN1, with 26 . . . P-QN4 to follow.

24 ...   PxP

25 R-Q2   P-N4

26 P-QN3   P-KR4

27 P-N3   P-B5!

28 R-K2ch   K-B4

29 R-K4   PxP

30 PxP   R-KN1

Believe it or not, but in this barren position, Rubinstein will produce two passed pawns out of thin air and these pawns will harry the enemy king to death!

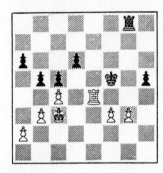

Rubinstein

Position after
30 . . . R-KN1

Mattison
to move

31 R-B4ch

White might have gambled on a win-or-lose line with 31 P-N4ch PxP   32 RxP, when Black could have gone wrong with 32 . . . RxR   33 PxRch KxP

34 PxP PxP   35 P-R4, and White wins, as the pawn cannot be headed off.

The proper continuation for Black would be 32 . . . R-KR1 (instead of 32 . . . RxR), with control of the open file and good winning chances.

31 ...   K-K3

32 R-K4ch   K-Q2

33 P-KN4   R-KB1!

Intending to meet 34 PxP with 34 . . . RxPch 35 K-B2 R-R6, netting a pawn.

34 R-K3   P-R5!

35 P-R4   PxRP

36 PxP   R-K1

37 K-Q2

Dangers begin to loom up; for example, if 37 R-Q3 P-R6   38 P-B4 P-R7   39 R-R3 R-K6ch, with knockout.

37 ...   RxR

38 KxR   P-Q4!!

The point of the whole ending. Black suddenly acquires another passed pawn, and the two separated pawns are too much for the king to cope with.

39 Resigns

The resignation deprives the spectators of seeing three pawns racing to become queens, thus: 39 PxP P-R6   40 K-B2 P-R7   41 K-N2 P-B5 42 P-N5 P-B6   43 P-N6 P-B7   44 P-N7 P-B8(Q) 45 P-N8(Q) Q-N8ch   46 K-R3 P-R8(Q) mate.

Practical jokers may be annoying, but occasionally they are amusing. One of them, in an effort to make Rubinstein switch from his favourite queen pawn opening, nailed down Rubinstein's queen pawn!

Bronstein

Bronstein is one of the most imaginative, creative players that ever lived. He delights in combinations, and seeks them out from the very opening. 'A beautiful, succulent combination containing numerous variations is my ideal,' says Bronstein.

Take as one example his game against Keres at Goteborg in 1955 (No. 25), where his genius for the fantastic fairly scintillates. He blends a combination of rare beauty from such diverse elements as a beginner-like knight move on the Q-side, a two-pawn sacrifice in the center, and a bishop sacrifice on the K-side, to conjure up an attack out of nothing. Who but Bronstein would even dream of such a wild project?

Or take his game against Khasin at Moscow in 1957, where he played what Kirby in *Chess World* calls 'the most remarkable, the most unbelievable winning move in chess.' This was the position:

Khasin

Bronstein to move

'Here Bronstein produced the extraordinary and crazy-looking 25 Q-R3!! Believe it or not, Russian analysis has shown that it is the only clearly winning move.' The game continued as follows:

25 ... BxP 26 P-B4 P-N5 27 P-K4 B-Q5ch 28 B-B2 BxBch 29 NxB BxB 30 NxB R(QB1)-Q1 31 N-N3 PxP 32 P-B5 K-R2 33 NxNP R-KN1 34 P-R3 R-N4 35 Q-K3 P-Q4 36 Q-B4 (threatens 37 NxRP KxN 38 P-R4 winning the exchange) RxN 37 PxR Q-QB2 38 Q-K3 Q-K4 39 P-N5!, and Black resigned, in view of this possible continuation: 39 ... PxP 40 QxNP R-KN1 41 Q-R5ch K-N2 42 RxQP! QxN 43 R-Q7ch K-B3 44 Q-B7ch K-K4 45 Q-Q5ch K-B5 46 R-B1ch K-K6 47 Q-Q2 mate.

Bronstein's practical successes on the field of honour include winning the Championship of Moscow in 1946, an equal first with Kotov for the Championship of the U.S.S.R. in 1948, an equal first with Smyslov for the Championship of the U.S.S.R. in 1949, a first prize without loss at Salsobaden (a 19-rounder) in 1948, an equal first with Boleslavsky at Budapest in 1950 in the Candidates' Tournament, and a victory in the play-off of 14 games, and a tied match with Botvinnik in 1951 for the Championship of the World. Despite this setback (for Bronstein was leading by a point, with only two games to go) there were later great victories, such as a first prize at Goteborg in 1955, ahead of such chess giants as Keres, Petrosian, Spassky, and Geller.

I consider Bronstein the tenth greatest chess player of all time.

19

White **D. Bronstein**   Black **M. Botvinnik**
Ruy López
Moscow, 1944

From the moment I first saw this game, I was enchanted by it.

I was fascinated by the fact that Bronstein's Q-side pieces, *still on their home squares*, proved more than a match for Botvinnik's mighty rooks dominating the center of the board.

I was intrigued by the little finesses in the ending, handled so cleverly by the young Bronstein.

I was impressed by the whole game, which is a masterpiece—and very few masterpieces are brought off against Botvinnik!

1 P-K4   P-K4
2 N-KB3   N-QB3
3 B-N5   P-QR3
4 B-R4   N-B3
5 0-0   B-K2
6 R-K1   P-QN4
7 B-N3   P-Q3
8 P-B3

This is to prevent his bishop being exchanged by 8 ... N-QR4.

8 ...   0-0
9 P-KR3   B-K3

Varies from the customary 9 ... N-QR4   10 B-B2 P-B4, known as the Tchigorin Defence.

10 P-Q4

More interesting than the line Boleslavsky tried against Botvinnik in 1947, 10 BxB PxB   11 P-Q4 Q-Q2   12 PxP PxP   13 QxQ NxQ   14 B-K3 N-B4   15 BxN BxB   16 QN-Q2 B-N3 with a drawn result.

10 ...   BxB

11 QxB

Smyslov got a strong game against Barcza in 1953 by capturing with the pawn, the next few moves being (after 11 PxB) Q-Q2   12 P-Q5 N-Q1   13 P-B4 N-N2   14 N-B3 KR-N1   15 PxP PxP   16 RxR RxR   17 P-QN4.

11 ...   PxP
12 NxP   NxN
13 PxN   P-B4
14 PxP   PxP
15 P-K5   N-Q2

Of course not the hasty 15 ... P-B5, when 16 PxN PxQ   17 PxB is painful.

16 P-QR4

In order to weaken Black's Q-side pawns.

16 ...   P-B5
17 Q-N3

With a little threat of 18 B-R6, winning the exchange —a threat often overlooked by amateurs.

17 ...   R-K1
18 R-Q1

Bronstein seems to be setting the pace, but a cold shower awaited him, as he himself says.

Botvinnik is always dangerous—until the moment he turns down his king in surrender, and that isn't often.

18 ...   B-R5
19 Q-N4

A natural move (increasing the pressure on the pinned knight) but inferior to 19 Q-B4.

19 ...   BxPch
20 KxB

Some pretty play follows 20 K-B1 P-B4   21 PxP en passant (or 21 QxKBP R-KB1   22 QxN B-Q5 dis.ch, winning the queen) 21 ... QxP   22 QxN B-N6 dis.ch   23 K-N1 Q-B7ch, and mate in two.

20 ...   NxP

21 RxQ   NxQch

22 PxN   QRxR

A strange position, and difficult to evaluate. Botvinnik has two beautifully-placed rooks gazing down from the heights like eagles, and ready to swoop down on any prey in sight.

Bronstein on the other hand has three pieces fixed on their home squares, still waiting to make their first move.

To assess the players' chances in such a position could give a computer a headache.

Botvinnik

Position after
22 . . . QRxR

Bronstein
to move

23 PxP   PxP

24 B-Q2   R-Q6

25 R-R5   R-QN6

26 B-B1

Sad, but the bishop must return, as 26 B-B3 P-N5 27 B-Q4 P-B6 is difficult to meet.

26 . . . P-B3

Assures the king against a surprise mate on the last rank.

27 R-R3   R-Q6

28 RxR   PxR

Bronstein must have sighed with relief at the disappearance of one of the dangerous rooks.

29 B-K3   R-K5

30 K-B3

Advancing the pawn would be premature, as after 30 P-N5 R-QN5   31 B-B1 PxP   32 BxP RxPch wins a pawn for Black.

30 . . . R-QN5

31 B-B1

Dispirited, the bishop returns home for the second time.

31 . . . P-N4

32 P-KN3 R-QB5

33 B-K3   P-R4

'Botvinnik underrates his young opponent,' says Eliskases, 'or he would have forced a draw by repetition of moves (33 . . . R-N5   34 B-B1 R-QB5 etc.) How was he to know that his opponent was destined to become one of the world's leading masters?'

34 PxP   P-N5ch

35 K-B2   R-B7ch

36 N-Q2   RxP

Botvinnik has ingeniously emerged with two wicked-looking passed pawns.

37 B-B4   R-R7

38 K-K3   R-R6

39 K-Q4   K-B2

40 K-K4   P-N5

41 K-Q4   R-R4

42 P-R6   R-QN4

In accordance with Tarrasch's precept, 'The rook's proper place is behind the passed pawn, whether it be his own, or an enemy one.'

43 K-B4   R-N3

44 K-B5!

The plausible 44 N-N3 is dangerous, if not fatal. The continuation could be 44 . . . R-B3ch   45 KxNP (if 45 N-B5 P-N6, or if 45 KxQP R-B6ch wins) R-B7 46 N-Q2 K-N3   47 N-B4 R-B7, and the bishop is threatened with capture.

44 ...   R-N2

45 N-N3   K-N3

46 K-B4   R-N3

47 N-B5!   K-R2

48 K-N3   P-Q7

49 BxP   R-Q3

50 B-B4   R-Q8

51 N-K4!

Careful, mustn't touch! If 51 KxP R-Q5ch 52 K-B3 RxB 53 PxR P-N6, and the pawn rushes on to become a queen.

51 ...   K-N3

52 N-B2   R-N8ch

53 K-B2   R-QR8

54 K-N2   R-R6

55 NxP   R-QB6

56 N-K3   R-Q6

57 N-B2   R-Q8

If 57 ... P-N6, White wins the pawn by 58 N-K1 R-Q8 59 N-B3 followed by 60 N-Q2.

58 NxP   K-B4

59 N-B6   R-Q2

60 K-B3   K-K3

61 K-B4   K-B4

62 N-Q4ch   K-K5

63 N-K6   K-B4

64 N-B8   Resigns

The reply to 64 ... R-Q1 would be 65 B-Q6!, and Black is powerless to prevent the rook pawn from queening.

The minor pieces did themselves proud under Bronstein's skillful guidance.

20

White **F. Zita**   Black **D. Bronstein**
King's Indian Defence
Prague-Moscow, 1946

If there were a Michelin Guide to chess masterpieces (as there is one for fine restaurants) it would award three stars to this brilliant game. (And with it, crossed knights and bishops to denote pleasant ambiance).

Who but Bronstein would sacrifice the exchange at the far end of the Q-side (with his knight under attack on the K-side) and follow it up by swinging over to the K-side to offer his knight on another square?

And that's only the beginning! From then on all sorts of diverting visual effects are conjured up by Bronstein's lively imagination, not least of which are the three zig-zag moves of the queen to finish the game.

1 P-QB4   P-K4

2 N-QB3   N-KB3

3 N-B3   P-Q3

4 P-Q4   QN-Q2

5 P-KN3   P-KN3

The English Opening has transposed into the King's Indian, the current favourite defence.

6 B-N2   B-N2

7 0-0   0-0

8 P-N3

This is inferior to 8 P-K4, for then if 8 ... P-B3 9 P-KR3 (if at once 9 B-K3 N-N5 is annoying) Q-N3 10 P-Q5 P-B4, with even chances.

8 ...   P-B3

9 B-N2   R-K1

10 P-K4   PxP!

A simple exchange, but it increases the scope of the king bishop and the king rook.

11 NxP   Q-N3!

12 Q-Q2

Superior to this was 12 N-QR4 Q-B2   13 Q-B2. Now Black seizes the initiative.

12 ...   N-B4

Threatens the king pawn.

13 KR-K1   P-QR4

Intending to break up White's Q-side pawns.

14 QR-N1   P-R5

15 B-QR1

White misses a chance to try for a swindle, as Fine points out, by 15 PxP. If then 15 . . . NxRP   16 NxN RxN, and now comes the swindly 17 NxP! QxN (or 17 . . . PxN   18 BxN, with a discovered attack on the queen) 18 P-K5, with a discovered attack on the queen.

He suggests that Black reply (to 15 PxP) Q-B2, when 16 Q-B2 gives White some counterplay.

15 ...   PxP

16 PxP   N-N5!

17 P-R3

Innocently unaware that lightning is about to strike both sides of the board.

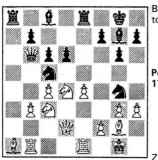

Bronstein to move

Position after 17 P-R3

Zita

17 ...   RxB!

A sacrifice which is as startling as it is profound. It is difficult to see what Black's compensation will be for the loss of the exchange.

18 RxR   NxBP!!

19 R-K3

The knight is inviolable (mustn't be touched). If 19 QxN N-Q6 attacks queen, rook, and knight; or if 19 KxN, NxNP attacks queen, the other rook, and the knight. In either case Black would have an easy win.

19 ...   NxPch

20 K-R2

After 20 BxN BxB, Black would have the two bishops, two pawns for the exchange, and threats galore.

20 ...   N-B7

The knight returns, with a threat of regaining the exchange by 21 . . . N-N5ch.

21 R-B3   N(B4)xKP

22 Q-B4

Obviously 22 NxN NxN would forfeit White's remaining knight.

22 ...   N-N5ch

23 K-R1   P-KB4

Black of course avoids the colossal blunder of 23 . . . BxN or 23 . . . QxN, when 24 QxPch and mate in two follows.

24 NxN

There is little choice, as 24 N(Q4)-K2 allows 24 . . . N(K5)-B7ch, and White must return the exchange or lose his queen.

24 ...   RxN

25 QxQP   RxN

26 Q-N8   R-Q1

27 R-R8   B-K4

28 Q-R7   Q-N5

29 Q-N1   Q-B1

Threatens 30 . . . Q-R3ch and quick mate.

30 B-R3   Q-R3

31 Resigns

If 31 Q-KB1 R-Q7   32 RxBch K-B2 and the threat

of 33 . . . R-R7ch followed by 34 . . . B-Q5ch is
decisive.

21

White **D. Bronstein**   Black **P. Dubinin**
King's Gambit
Leningrad, 1947

'It is no secret that any talented player must in his soul
be an artist, and what could be nearer to his heart and
soul than the victory of the subtle forces of reason over
crude material strength! Probably everyone has his own
reason for liking the King's Gambit, but my love for it
can be seen in precisely these terms.'

Bronstein

We, who delight in the thrills offered us by Morphy
and Anderssen, may be grateful that we have a kindred
soul, Bronstein, to give us such excitements today.

1 P-K4   P-K4

2 P-KB4   PxP

3 N-KB3   P-KN4

Black holds on to the pawn, in the old-fashioned way.
Preferable is 3 . . . N-KB3, and if 4 P-K5 N-KR4
5 P-Q4 P-Q4, and Black is safe from surprise attack.
Black can vary at his fifth move with 5 . . . P-Q3,
when 6 N-B3 B-N5   7 B-B4 N-QB3 leaves an equal
game.

4 P-KR4   P-N5

5 N-K5

The Kieseritzky Gambit, one of the strongest lines in
this opening.

5 . . .   P-KR4

Dubinin sticks to the old-fashioned way. Black should
bring his pieces out instead by 5 . . . N-KB3 or 5 . . .
B-N2.

It's rarely bad strategy to develop some pieces in
the opening.

6 B-B4   R-R2

7 P-Q4   B-R3

Some nice play follows 7 . . . B-K2. The sequel could
be 8 BxP BxPch   9 P-N3 B-N4   10 RxP RxR
11 BxPch K-B1   12 BxR BxB   13 N-N6ch K-N2
14 NxB with advantage to White.

8 N-QB3   N-QB3

9 NxBP!   RxN

10 BxRch   KxB

11 BxP!   BxB

12 0-0   QxP

13 RxBch   K-N2

14 Q-Q2

Black has a material advantage (two pieces for a
rook) but to compensate for this, White is ahead in
development, and has a strong pawn centre.

14 . . .   P-Q3

15 QR-KB1   N-Q1

Not at once 15 . . . B-Q2   18 R-B7ch, cutting short
the bishop's career. The knight move prevents the
check, and prepares to get the bishop into play.

16 N-Q5   B-Q2

17 P-K5!

Bronstein begins the decisive attack by opening
more lines leading to the king.

17 . . .   PxP

18 PxP   B-B3

The position is shown on page 50.

19 P-K6!   BxN

Clearly, the pawn was tabu. If 19 . . . NxP
20 R-B7ch K-N3 (on 20 . . . K-R1   21 Q-B3ch wins
at once) 21 Q-Q3ch, and mate follows quickly.

20 R-B7ch!

Beautiful! the doubled rooks make their presence
felt, even if one of them sacrifices itself.

20 . . .   NxR

Dubinin

**Position after
18 . . . B-B3**

Bronstein
to move

21 RxNch   K-R1

There's no relief in 21 . . . K-N3   22 Q-Q3ch K-N4
(or 22 . . . K-R3   23 Q-R7ch K-N4   24 R-B5 mate)
23 Q-B5ch K-R3   24 R-R7 mate).

22 Q-B3ch   N-B3

23 RxN   QxR

The queen sacrifice is the only way to prolong the
game, as otherwise mate follows by 24 R-B7 dis.ch,
or 24 R-N6 dis.ch.

Moving 23 . . . K-N2 instead, allows mate in two
by 24 R-B7 dbl.ch, and mate by the queen at N7.

24 QxQch   K-R2

Or 24 . . . K-N1, and 25 Q-N5ch wins the bishop.

25 Q-B5ch   Resigns

The bishop falls, and with it any flickering hope.
Quite in the style of the old gambiteers!

22

White **D. Bronstein**   Black **S. Furman**
Nimzo-Indian Defence
Moscow, 1948

Bronstein seems to be toying with his formidable
opponent. (Anyone who plays in a Soviet Championship
is formidable, and Furman scored only 1½ points less
than Bronstein and Smyslov, the two leaders).

Clever little combinations besprinkle the game, some
of them seeming to be improvised by Bronstein as he
goes along. The star of the show is the queen knight, who
leaps enthusiastically all over the board, and almost wins
the game single-handed.

1 P-Q4   N-KB3

2 P-QB4   P-K3

3 N-QB3   B-N5

4 P-K3   P-Q4

5 P-QR3   B-K2

The bishop avoids the complexities of 5 . . . BxNch,
and quietly retreats.

6 N-B3   0-0

7 B-Q3

Botvinnik played the aggressive 7 P-QN4 against
Reshevsky at The Hague in 1948, and won on the
32nd move when Reshevsky ran short of time.

7 . . .   P-QN3

8 0-0   P-B4

9 P-QN3   B-N2

Now the position has the old-fashioned look of the
Queen's Gambit Declined, when much of it was still
unexplored.

10 B-N2   N-B3

11 PxQP   KPxP

12 N-K2

The knight sees opportunities to make himself useful
at KN3 or at KB4.

12 . . .   N-K5

This knight too is ambitious, and gets a foothold in
the opponent's territory.

13 PxP   PxP

Recapturing with a piece rather than a pawn would
allow White to occupy the important square Q4 with
a piece.

The pawn capture leaves Black with 'hanging

pawns,' about which the masters have conflicting views.

They are weak because they are dangerously exposed. Or they are strong if one of them can be converted into a passed pawn, as in the game between Bernstein and Capablanca at Moscow in 1914.

Or does it depend on whose hands they are in?

14   Q-B2   Q-N3

Attacks the knight pawn, thereby parrying the threat of 15 BxN PxB   16 QxKP.

The queen's move is preferable to 14 . . . P-B4, when 15 N-B4 threatens 16 N-K6 winning the exchange, as well as 15 NxP, when 15 . . . QxN loses like a shot by the bishop's pin.

15   N-N3

The triple attack on the knight, as well as the threat of seizing the strong outpost at KB5, forces Black to weaken his pawn structure.

15   . . .   P-B4

Of course not 15 . . . NxN, when 16 BxPch K-R1 17 RPxN wins a pawn.

16   N-R5

A sudden threat to the king knight pawn.

16   . . .   R-B2

17   QR-N1

Indirectly protects his queen knight pawn, and prepares (though the possibility seems remote now) an attack on the hanging pawns by P-QN4, with a view to making Q4 accessible to his pieces.

17   . . .   R-Q1

18   KR-Q1   R-Q3

19   N-B4   K-R1

If 19 . . . Q-Q1 (returning to the defence) White plays 20 N-K5 R-B1   21 NxN BxN (or 21 . . . RxN 22 NxP)   22 P-B3, and wins a pawn.

20   B-KB1!   Q-Q1   See diagram.

21   NxP!

A little surprise for Furman!

Furman

Position after 20 . . . Q-Q1

Bronstein to move

21   . . .   B-R5

If 21 . . . RxN   22 RxR QxR   23 B-B4 impaling queen and rook.

22   NxB   QxN

23   N-B4   R(B2)-Q2

Threatens 24 . . . RxR   25 RxR RxR   26 QxR QxBPch   27 K-R1 QxKP; then if   28 Q-Q7 N-B7ch leads to mate.

24   N-R3

A good alternative, which avoids complications, is 24 RxR RxR   25 P-N3 Q-Q1   26 N-R5 R-Q2 27 P-B3.

But why should Bronstein avoid complications? He thrives on them!

24   . . .   N-Q7

Black now threatens 25 . . . NxR, as well as 25 . . . R-N3 followed either by 26 . . . QxN or by 26 . . . N-K4.

25   QxKBP

Threatens instant mate.

25   . . .   N-K2

26   Q-B7

Now there are two threats of mate on the move.

26   . . .   Q-R3

Furman

**Position after
26 . . . Q-R3**

Bronstein
to move

27 P-B4!

Prepares an outpost for the knight's entry in the attack.

27 . . . N-N1

White's rook is still immune to capture, as after
27 . . . NxR   28 RxR RxR   29 QxN B-Q4
30 BxPch QxB   31 QxR wins for White.

28 Q-B8   NxR

29 RxR   RxR

30 N-N5!

With the terrible threat of a smothered mate.

30 . . . B-Q4

As good as any. If instead 30 . . . R-Q2, then
31 N-B7ch RxN 32 QxR N-Q7 (to prevent 33 B-B4)
33 QxB, and White wins.

31 P-K4!   BxNP

If 31 . . . R-KN3 (to weaken the attack by returning
the exchange) there is a pretty win by 32 PxB RxN
33 PxR QxP   34 P-Q6 Q-N5   35 BxPch QxB
36 QxQch KxQ   37 P-Q7, and the pawn becomes a
queen.

32 P-K5!   R-Q8

This loses, as does 32 . . . R-Q7   33 P-K6 BxP
34 NxB RxB   34 N-Q8 R-N2   35 B-B4, and White
wins.

The only chance to save the game was by
32 . . . R-Q2, as was later pointed out.

33 P-K6!

Once more facing the king with mate, and forcing
Black to give up a piece.

33 . . . BxP

34 NxB

Now bearing down on the knight pawn with three
pieces.

34 . . . R-Q5

There is no defence in 34 . . . R-Q2, as 35 NxP! RxN
36 B-B4 forces mate.

35 BxR   PxB

36 N-N5!

One returns to the scene of one's first love.

36 . . . Resigns

Black must give up his queen to stop the smothered
mate.

23

White **D. Bronstein**   Black **A. Kotov**
Semi-Slav Defence
Budapest, 1950

Bronstein plays the attack in classic style.

So early in the game as the 6th move he offers a pawn
(though he has done so in the past) and on the 12th
move a rook—à la Alekhine.

The combinations that ensue are diabolically ingenious,
as Bronstein exploits the disorganized state of his
opponent's forces.

The ending is artistic and in keeping with this superb
game.

1 P-Q4   P-Q4
2 P-QB4   P-K3
3 N-QB3   P-QB3
4 P-K4   PxKP
5 NxP   B-N5ch

6 B-Q2

Quite in keeping with the Bronstein style and temperament. More timid souls would content themselves with quiet development by 6 N-B3 P-QB4 7 P-QR3 B-R4 8 B-K3 N-KB3 9 N-K2 PxP 10 BxP, with an equal (and probably dull) game in prospect.

6 . . .   QxP

Kotov accepts the challenge. Why not accept the gift of a beautiful center pawn?

He had once before tried 6 . . . BxBch 7 QxB N-B3 8 NxNch QxN 9 N-B3 0-0, but after 10 Q-K3!, he had the inferior position.

7 BxB   QxNch

8 B-K2   N-QR3

On 8 . . . QxNP, White has choice of two brilliant continuations:

(a) 9 B-KB3 Q-N4   10 N-K2 N-K2   11 R-KN1 Q-B3 12 N-N3 N-B4   13 N-K4 Q-Q1   14 RxP! NxR (if 14 . . . QxQch   15 RxQ NxR   16 N-B6 is mate) 15 N-Q6ch K moves   16 NxNP dis.ch, and White wins the queen (Tartakover).

(b) 9 Q-Q6, and if 9 . . . QxR   10 Q-B8ch K-Q2 11 R-Q1ch K-B2   12 Q-Q8 mate.

9 B-B3   N-K2

This position came up one year earlier in the Moscow-Budapest match, when Szily tried 9 . . . P-B3 against Bronstein, and was crushed after 10 Q-Q6! B-Q2   11 0-0-0 0-0-0   12 Q-N3 Q-N3   13 Q-K3 P-N3 14 N-R3 Q-R3   15 P-B4 N-K2   16 P-KN4 P-K4 17 B-Q2 N-QB4   18 Q-R3 P-K5   19 N-B2 K-N2 20 P-B5 Q-R5   21 B-K3 N-Q6ch   22 NxN PxN 23 RxP NxP 24 KR-Q1! Resigns; as 24 . . . NxB loses by 25 RxBch RxR   26 RxRch K-B1   27 QxP Q-K8ch   28 B-Q1, and Black gets mated.

10 BxP   R-KN1

If Black tries 10 . . . QxNP, disaster follows by 11 B-B6 QxR   12 Q-Q6 0-0   (on 12 . . . QxNch 13 K-Q2 wins the queen, as Black is threatened

with mate)   13 Q-N3ch N-N3   14 B-KB3, and the queen is trapped.

11 B-B3   QxNP

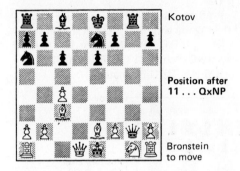

Kotov

**Position after
11 . . . QxNP**

Bronstein
to move

12 Q-Q2!!

A brilliant conception. The hasty 12 B-B3 loses after 12 . . . QxNch   13 RxQ RxRch, and Black wins a piece.

12 . . .   QxR

13 0-0-0   N-Q4

All sorts of elegant mating combinations arise after 13 . . . P-B3 (to give the king elbow room), to wit: 14 B-R5ch R-N3 (if 14 . . . N-N3   15 Q-Q8ch K-B2   16 QxPch K-K1   17 R-Q8 is mate) 15 Q-Q8ch K-B2   16 N-B3 QxRch (if 16 . . . Q-N7 17 BxP KxB   18 Q-B8 mate, and if in this 17 . . . N-KN1   18 N-K5 is mate)   17 KxQ N-KN1 18 BxP! NxB   19 N-K5ch K-N2   20 Q-K7ch K-N1 21 Q-B7ch K-R1   22 Q-B8ch and 23 N-B7 mate (Toran).

14 N-B3   QxRch

If Black tries to hold on to his queen by 14 . . . Q-N7, he runs into trouble, thus: 15 PxN KPxP (if 15 . . . QxBP   16 PxBP Q-N3   17 B-B6 wins for White)   16 Q-K3ch B-K3   17 R-N1, and White has the advantage.

15 BxQ   NxB

16 QxN   K-K2

Material is about equal, but Black's king is exposed, and his rooks are out of touch with each other.

17 N-K5   B-Q2

If 17 . . . P-B3 (to dislodge the powerfully-placed knight) then White wins by 18 Q-KR3! PxN (no better is 18 . . . R-R1   19 N-N6ch, or 18 . . . R-N2 19 Q-R6) 19 QxPch K-B1   20 B-R5 R-N2 21 Q-R8ch R-N1   22 Q-B6 mate.

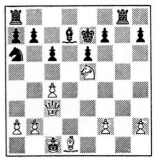

Kotov

Position after
17 . . . B-Q2

Bronstein
to move

18 Q-QR3ch!

'The brightest spot in this extraordinarily bright game,' says Kmoch. 'White forces the weakening . . . P-QB4, after which he can attack Black's QN7 and KB7 simultaneously.'

18 . . .   P-B4

The only move, as 18 . . . K-K1 succumbs to 19 Q-Q6 R-Q1   20 B-R5 R-KB1, and now, stronger than 21 NxKBP RxN   22 Q-B4 (recommended by nearly all annotators) 21 N-N4 wins *sur le champ*, as we say in Paris.

19 Q-KB3

The threats multiply: the queen now attacks two vital pawns.

19 . . .   QR-Q1

Other possibilities are:

(a) 19 . . . QR-KB1   20 QxNP N-N1   21 B-R4 R-Q1 22 BxB NxB   23 N-B6ch, and White wins the exchange.

(b) 19 . . . P-B3   20 NxB KxN   21 QxNPch N-B2 22 B-R4ch K-Q1   23 Q-B6 K-B1 (or 23 . . . R-N2 24 Q-Q6ch K-B1   25 Q-B8ch winning the rook) 24 Q-Q7ch K-N1   25 B-B6, and the queen rook falls.

20 QxBPch   K-Q3

21 Q-B4   R(Q1)-KB1

22 N-B7 dbl.ch   K-K2

The only move to avoid quick mate.

23 B-R5

Now intending 24 Q-R4ch K-K1   25 Q-Q8 mate.

23 . . .   B-B3

24 Q-Q6ch   K-B3

25 N-R6   R-N8ch

26 K-Q2   K-N2

27 N-N4

This breaks communication between the rooks, making defence that much more difficult.

27 . . .   RxN

Forced, to avoid mate. If, for example, 27 . . . R-B1 28 Q-K7ch K-R1   29 Q-B6ch K-N1   30 N-R6 mate or if 27 . . . R-KN1   28 Q-K5ch K-B1   29 Q-B6 mate does the trick.

28 Q-K7ch   K-R3

29 BxR   RxPch

30 K-K3   R-B8

31 P-KR4   K-N3

32 B-R5ch   Resigns

Mate next move is inevitable.

A nice finish to a game that is pure Bronstein from first move to last.

24

White **D. Bronstein**   Black **M. Najdorf**
Sicilian Defence
Buenos Aires, 1954

A game that floats along with ease and grace may give us as much pleasure as a ponderous masterpiece.

This game of Bronstein's charms us with its air of gay nonchalance. We derive the pleasure that comes from spontaneous wit.

Doubts and fears may have beset Bronstein though, for he took 58 minutes before deciding on his ninth move.

A bishop sacrifice at the very next turn assured him of an array of passed pawns whose relentless advance could not be curbed, though two of the pawns did fall in the ensuing struggle.

1 P-K4   P-QB4

2 N-KB3   P-Q3

3 P-Q4   PxP

4 NxP   N-KB3

5 N-QB3   P-QR3

6 B-KN5

An aggressive line, this prevents 6 . . . P-KN3 and prepares to castle Q-side, and launch an attack on the center.

6 . . .   P-K3

7 Q-B3

Or 7 P-B4 first, when 7 . . . B-K2   8 Q-B3 Q-B2 9 0-0-0 QN-Q2   10 P-KN4 gives White a strong attack.

7 . . .   QN-Q2

8 0-0-0   Q-B2

9 Q-N3!   P-N4

Najdorf may not have been happy with the more cautious 9 . . . B-K2, but the move he made gives Bronstein the opportunity to scintillate.

10 BxP!   PxB

11 N(Q4)xNP   Q-N1

12 NxPch   BxN

13 QxB   QxQ

Like it or not, Black must exchange queens, or he won't be able to breathe.

14 RxQ

Bronstein says 'As a result of the piece sacrifice White has won three pawns for the piece, leaving approxi - mate material equality. It would be wrong, however, to judge the position only from the point of material advantages. Whereas the activity of the black knight can easily be neutralized, the struggle against the white passed pawns is much more difficult. In this game Black did not fully use the possibilities open to him.'

14 . . .   P-KR3

15 B-Q2

Bronstein was not inclined to exchange his 'extremely strong black-squared bishop' for a knight (or even a rook) but the continuation 15 BxN NxB   16 KR-Q1 B-N2   17 P-B3 K-K2   18 R-N6 KR-QN1   19 P-QN3 turned out to be good enough to score a win for Fichtl against Dolezal in the same year.

15 . . .   B-N2

16 P-B3   0-0

With queens off the board, and little chance of being checkmated, the king should either castle Q-side or move to K2, in either case to help subdue the passed pawns.

17 P-QN3   KR-B1

18 K-N2   N-B4

19 B-K3   P-K4

Clears a flight square for the queen knight, but creates a weakness at his Q4 square. This little weakness won't escape Bronstein's eagle eye.

20 KR-Q1   N-K3

21 R-N6   B-B3

The position, with White to play, is shown on page 56.

22 N-Q5!

An obstreperous knight! The threat of winning the exchange by 23 N-K7ch, or a pawn by 23 NxNch, practically forces Black to remove the beast . . .

Najdorf

Position after
21 . . . B-B3

Bronstein
to move

22 ...   BxN
23 PxB
... whereupon another passed pawn springs into
being.
23 ...   N-B4
24 R-N5   N(B3)-Q2
25 P-QB4   P-K5
26 BxN   NxB
27 PxP   NxKP
28 P-Q6!
At first glance an error, as White loses a pawn, but
Bronstein has calculated carefully.
28 ...   RxPch
29 KxR   N-B6ch
30 K-R3   NxR(Q8)
31 P-B5   N-B6
32 R-R5   N-Q4
33 P-B6   N-B3
After 33 . . . RxP, the quick way to win is not by
34 RxN, but by 34 P-Q7 R-Q3 35 R-R8ch, followed
by queening the pawn, and Black must part with his
rook.
34 R-R6   K-B1
35 P-QN4   K-K1
36 P-N5   N-Q2

37 R-R7!
Bronstein is not lured into taking the knight, at the
cost of breaking up his pawns.
37 ...   R-N1
38 RxN   RxP
39 R-R7!
The threat of mate dictates Black's next move.
39 ...   R-N1
40 P-Q7ch   K-K2
41 P-Q8(Q) dbl.ch   KxQ
42 P-B7ch   Resigns

25

White **D. Bronstein**   Black **P. Keres**
Nimzo-Indian Defence
Goteborg, 1955

Bronstein won first prize at Goteborg in 1955 without
losing a single game, ahead of such mighty men of chess
as Keres, Petrosian, Geller, and Spassky—to name a few
of his chief rivals.

To sweeten the victory, he was awarded first brilliancy
prize for his game against Keres, runner-up in the tournament.

His 11th move, which looked like a stab in the dark,
could only have been made by a wildly imaginative
player—a Bronstein.

That move alone, which was instrumental in weaving
a combination out of nothing, deserved the brilliancy
prize!

1 P-Q4   N-KB3
2 P-QB4   P-K3
3 N-QB3   B-N5
4 P-K3   P-B4
5 B-Q3   P-QN3
The customary procedure is 5 . . . 0-0 followed by

6 . . . P-Q4, but if great players did not vary their defences we should have nothing but stereotyped lines, and fewer masterpieces to enjoy.

6 KN-K2

Here too the usual development of the knight is at B3, but Bronstein envisions the deployment of the knight to N3, with pressure on K4 and B5.

6 . . . B-N2

7 0-0 PxP

8 PxP 0-0

The plausible 8 . . . P-Q4 is treacherous, as after 9 Q-R4ch N-B3 10 PxP NxP 11 B-QN5 NxN 12 BxNch BxB 13 QxBch wins a piece. Or if in this 11 . . . Q-Q3, then 12 NxN PxN 13 B-KB4 Q-K3 14 BxNch BxB 15 QxB(N4), and White's knight may not be captured with impunity.

9 P-Q5!

This prevents the liberating 9 . . . P-Q4, and secures an advantage in space.

9 . . . P-KR3

If Black captures by 9 . . . PxP, there follows 10 PxP NxP (on 10 . . . BxP 11 NxB NxN 12 B-K4) 11 NxN BxN 12 BxPch KxB 13 QxB, and the isolated queen pawn looks shaky.

Black's last move is intended to prevent 10 B-N5, and it also threatens 10 . . . PxP winning a pawn.

It looks good, but appearances (as often happens) are deceiving.

10 B-B2 N-R3

Keres

**Position after
10 . . . N-R3**

Bronstein
to move

11 N-N5!!

A stroke of genius! Many a master would be content with 11 P-QR3 BxN 12 NxB R-B1 13 PxP QPxP 14 P-QN3, retaining the advantage of the two bishops.

White's obvious threat is 12 P-QR3 B-B4 13 P-QN4 B-K2 14 P-Q6 winning a bishop but there's more to this than meets the eye.

To begin with, White sacrifices a pawn or two, and Black, to make any progress, must accept the offer. What does White hope to gain by this?

The knight's leap, at first glance purposeless, is actually the beginning of a profound series of moves. The knight's move is linked, strange as it may seem, with a bishop sacrifice at the other end of the board, which sets off the fireworks.

11 . . . PxP

12 P-QR3 B-K2

13 N-N3!

Offers another pawn. The astute observer will note that the knight now has access to B5, a lovely square.

13 . . . PxP

This is not mere pawn-grabbing, as it opens a long diagonal for the bishop.

14 BxP!!

Beautiful! White gives up a piece, though he is two pawns down—and this against Keres, one of the greatest masters of tactical play that ever lived!

14 . . . PxB

Otherwise 15 BxP follows, with a dangerous attack, one possibility being 15 . . . KxB 16 N-B5ch K-R1 17 Q-Q4 K-N1 18 Q-R4 N-Q4 19 NxBch and mate in two.

15 Q-Q2 N-R2

The pawn cannot be saved by 15 . . . K-N2, as 16 N-B5ch in reply is too strong to withstand.

Later analysis, mostly by Bronstein, showed this possibility after 15 . . . N-B4 (bringing another piece to the defence): 16 QR-K1! N-Q6 17 BxN PxB 18 N-B5 B-K5 19 N(N5)-Q4 R-K1 20 NxPch K-B1

21 Q-N5 B-N3   22 RxB! (Very tempting is 22 R-K6, and if 22 . . . QPxR   23 QxB! PxQ   24 NxP, mating beautifully with the two knights) 22 . . . RxR (if 22 . . . QxR   23 N(R6)-B5 BxN   24 NxB wins the queen) 23 QxN R-K5   24 Q-R8ch K-K2   25 N(R6)-B5ch BxN   26 NxBch K-K3   27 Q-R3!, and White's attack should prevail.

That is reminiscent (says Purdy) of some of Alekhine's combinations in which no win is clear until the final move. Just a word now for those who wonder if Bronstein saw all this when he offered the bishop. It is possible, but it was not necessary. The necessity is not to see every variation to the end, but rather to be able to recognize intuitively a winning position at an earlier stage than is possible for ordinary players.

16 QxRP   P-B4
Black is ready to return some of his booty to stem the attack.

17 NxBP   RxN
If 17 . . . B-KB3 to prevent being mated, 18 QR-K1 threatening 19 N-K7ch is very strong.

18 BxR   N-B1
Material is approximately even, but the black king is denuded of pawn protection, and White's attack is still flourishing.

This is how things look:

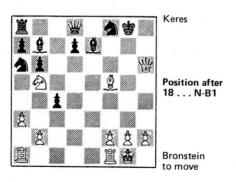

Keres

Position after
18 . . . N-B1

Bronstein
to move

19 QR-Q1
Obviously to continue with 20 R-Q4 and 21 R-N4ch, but also with the beautiful tactical threat of 20 RxP!, and if 20 . . . NxR B-K6 mate!

19 . . .   B-N4

20 Q-R5   Q-B3
Keres puts up a hard fight, and the win is not easy.

21 N-Q6
The knight, idle for so long, comes into the game with strong effect.

21 . . .   B-B3

22 Q-N4
Menaces the bishop by the threat of 23 P-KR4.

22 . . .   K-R1

23 B-K4!
White avoids the simplifying 23 QxB QxQ   24 N-B7ch K-N2   25 NxQ K-B3, and Black has chances.
The move he makes eliminates Black's active queen bishop, the threat being 24 BxB PxB   25 N-K4 winning the other bishop.

23 . . .   B-R3

24 BxB   PxB

25 QxP
White picks up a stray pawn or two, to equalize the material.

25 . . .   N-B4

26 P-QN4   N(B4)-K3

27 QxP   R-N1
The alternative is 27 . . . R-Q1, when White clears away some pieces by 28 N-B7ch QxN   29 RxR NxR 30 QxBch with advantage.

28 N-K4   Q-N3

29 R-Q6   B-N2

30 P-B4   Q-N5

31 P-R3   Q-K7

32 N-N3

But not the hasty 32 RxN NxR   33 QxN, when
33 . . . B-Q5ch is the painful response.

32 . . .   Q-K6ch

The first check of the game!

33 K-R2   N-Q5

If 33 . . . NxP, White wins neatly by 34 Q-B7 R-K1
35 QxBch KxQ 36 N-B5ch K-B2   37 NxQ RxN
38 RxNch (Pachmann).

34 Q-Q5   R-B1

35 N-R5

Now the idea is to dispose of the bishop who guards
the approaches to the king.

35 . . .   N-K7

36 NxB   Q-N6ch

But not 36 . . . KxN   37 Q-N5ch K-R2 (or K-B2)
38 Q-B5ch, catching the rook.

37 K-R1   NxP

Here if 37 . . . KxN 38 Q-K5ch regains the piece,
while if 37 . . . QxN 38 Q-R5ch does likewise.

38 Q-B3   N-K7

39 R-R6ch

White's first check of the game, and it is decisive.

39 . . .   Resigns

A modern immortal game!

26

White **D. Bronstein**   Black **E. Rojahn**
Two Knights' Defence
Moscow, 1956

Chess may be a science or an art, but in the hands of a
master who has wit and imagination it can be an entertainment.

Bronstein discovers a gambit in an opening that goes
back to the days of Polerio, who described its features
in 1590. In return for two pawns and nebulous chances,

Bronstein sacrifices a bishop at his eighth move.

Nebulous, that is, except to Bronstein, who starts an
army of pawns marching up the board.

So relentless is their advance as to overwhelm Rojahn,
who cannot find the time, or the moves, to prevent them
from engulfing him.

1 P-K4   P-K4

2 N-KB3   N-QB3

3 B-B4   N-B3

4 N-N5   P-Q4

5 PxP   N-QR4

Countless amateurs have played 5 . . . NxP, and
succumbed to the Fegatello or Fried Liver attack
when 6 NxBP KxN 7 Q-B3ch starts the black
king wandering.

6 P-Q3   P-KR3

7 N-KB3   P-K5

8 PxP!

The usual move is 8 Q-K2. In this case Bronstein's
sacrifice deceived his opponent completely. He
thought Bronstein had blundered and simply left a
piece *en prise.*

8 . . .   NxB

9 Q-Q4   N-N3

10 P-B4   P-B4

Black wants to stop 11 P-B5, but a better course
was 10 . . . P-B3 to dispute the center. He might
have to return a piece for two pawns, but at least
he would have a tenable game.

11 Q-Q3   B-N5

12 QN-Q2   B-K2

13 0-0   0-0

14 N-K5

Probably intending 15 NxB NxN   16 P-B4, and the
pawns begin to look menacing.

14 . . .   B-R4

15 P-QN3   N(N3)-Q2

16 B-N2   NxN

17 BxN   N-Q2

18 B-B3   B-B3

Black tries to exchange as many pieces as he can, and be left with a superiority in material.

19 QR-K1

Bronstein musters all his forces in preparation for 20 P-B4 and 21 P-K5.

19 . . .   BxB

20 QxB   Q-B3

Preferable was 20 . . . P-B3, to restrain White from advancing the king pawn. If then 21 P-B4 Q-K2 continues to dispute the critical square.

Rojahn

**Position after
20 . . . Q-B3**

Bronstein
to move

21 P-K5

This is superior to the plausible 21 Q-R3 (attacking two two loose pieces) which might allow Black sufficient counterplay to change the aspect of things: 21 . . . . Q-N7 22 N-N1 B-K7 23 QxN BxR 24 RxB QxRP, and Black can put up a fight.

21 . . .   Q-B4

22 P-B4   B-N3

23 N-K4

This prevents any intrusion by 23 . . . Q-Q6. There is no danger in a counter-sacrifice of the queen, as

after 23 . . . QxN 24 RxQ BxR 25 P-B5, Black's bishop is unhappily placed, while his king faces untold dangers.

23 . . .   QR-N1

24 Q-B3

With two fearsome threats: 25 P-KN4 (embarrassing the queen) and 25 N-N3 Q-B7 26 R-K2 Q-Q6 27 P-B5 (regaining material).

24 . . .   B-R2

Clears a flight-square for the queen.

Had he tried 24 . . . B-R4 instead, the play might have gone as follows:
25 N-N3 BxQ 26 NxQ B-N5 27 N-K7ch K-R1 28 P-B5, and Black is left with the worry of saving his bishop (threatened with 29 P-KR3 and 30 P-KN4) and the prospect of White's obtaining two connected passed pawns on the sixth rank.

25 P-KN4   Q-N3

26 P-B5   Q-N3

27 Q-N3

Protects the king pawn and prepares for 28 P-KR4 and 29 P-N5, to break through on the K-side.

27 . . .   P-B3

28 P-K6

Seven white pawns on seven white squares—what a pretty picture!

Bronstein says that he had little to think about for the next few moves, as the pawns could win the game by themselves!

28 . . .   N-K4

29 P-KR4   K-R1

30 P-N5   R(N1)-B1

Obviously there is little joy in 30 . . . RPxP 31 PxP, when the threat of 32 P-N6 is fatal.

31 K-R1

Clears the square N1 for the rook, with this possibility: 32 R-KN1 (threatens 33 PxBP followed by 34 QxP mate, or 34 QxN) 32 . . . Q-B2 (guards both delicate points)   33 P-Q6 Q-N3   34 PxBP, and Black is help-less.

31 ...   Q-Q1

32 P-N6

Bronstein says that he could have played 32 NxKBP! PxN   33 RxN! PxR   34 QxPch with fatal effect, but the idea of pushing the pawns up as far as possible must have intrigued him.

32 ...   BxP

No better is 32 . . . B-N1   33 P-Q6.

33 PxB   P-N4

34 P-Q6   Q-N3

35 P-Q7   NxQP

'For every pawn—a piece!' says Bronstein.

36 PxN   R(QB1)-Q1

37 NxKBP   Q-B3ch

Or 37 . . . RxN   38 R-K8ch and quick mate.

38 Q-N2

And Black lost by overstepping the time limit.

Too bad that Bronstein was deprived of this pretty finish: 38 . . . QxQch   39 KxQ PxN   40 R-K7 and the threat of 41 P-N7ch winning a rook could lead to 40 . . . R-KN1   41 R-R7 mate!

Bronstein has the consolation of achieving this problem-like mate in the notes at least, if not in the actual game.

27

White **D. Bronstein**   Black **A. Palmiotto**
Pirc Defence
Munich, 1958

In describing his feelings before sitting down to play, Bronstein once said, 'I cannot stop thinking that today, right now, I have the very fortunate possibility of playing the most beautiful, the most fighting, and the most pro-found game since the time of my birth, and since long before it.'

Here then is a little-known specimen of Bronstein's skill, in which the demolition of a heavily-guarded king's position is brought about with art and ingenuity. There are some surprise moves, of which I commend the seventh, tenth, and sixteenth to your attention.

1 P-K4   P-Q3

2 P-Q4   N-KB3

3 N-QB3   P-KN3

4 P-B4   B-N2

5 N-B3

Marshall played the bold 5 P-K5 against Pillsbury at Cambridge Springs in 1904, and scored a quick victory after 5 . . . PxP   6 BPxP N-Q4   7 N-B3 N-QB3 8 B-QB4 P-K3   9 B-KN5! NxN   10 PxN N-K2 11 0-0 P-KR3   12 B-B6! BxB   13 PxB N-B4 14 Q-K2 QxP   15 P-N4 N-Q3   16 N-K5 Q-K2 17 B-Q3 0-0   18 R-B2 K-N2   19 QR-KB1 B-Q2 20 R-B6 R-KN1   21 NxNP QxR   22 RxQ KxR 23 Q-K5 mate!

5 ...   0-0

6 P-K5

This may be stronger (it is certainly more vigorous) than the customary 6 B-Q3 or 6 B-K2.

6 ...   KN-Q2

7 P-KR4!

This sort of bayonet attack was rarely, if ever, seen in Morphy's day, as it inhibited K-side castling. Later on, strategists like Steinitz and Tarrasch would con-demn this sort of 'wild advance,' before development was complete.

It has its points though!

7 ...   P-QB4

8 P-R5   BPxP

Black has at least broken up the pawn center.

9 QxP   QPxP

10 Q-B2!

But not 10 PxP NxP with advantage to Black.

10 . . .   KPxP

11 PxP   RPxP

Black misses the opportunity to be on the wrong end of a miniature 'brilliancy' by capturing 11 . . . BPxP, when 12 B-B4ch K-R1   13 RxPch KxR   14 N-N5ch followed by 15 Q-R4ch forces checkmate.

12 BxP   N(Q2)-B3

13 Q-R4

Planning to continue with 14 B-KR6, to force an exchange of Black's stalwart king bishop.

13 . . .   Q-R4

The queen is prepared to swing over to KR4, to drive off the attackers.

14 N-KN5   B-N5

15 B-Q3   QN-Q2

16 0-0!

Nothing more can be accomplished on the rook file, so White brings his king into safety.

16 . . .   B-R4

Black's king seems as secure as though he were in a fortress.

How does White get rid of all those pieces protecting the king?

17 QR-K1   P-K4

18 B-Q2   Q-B4ch

19 B-K3   Q-B3

20 B-N5   Q-B2

21 B-K2!

This move forces the exchange of one of Black's guardian bishops.

21 . . .   BxB

There is no choice, since otherwise the advance 22 P-KN4 wins a piece.

22 RxB   KR-B1

The plausible 22 . . . QR-B1 succumbs to 23 N(B3)-K4 Q-B3   24 NxNch NxN   25 RxN!, and Black will be mated.

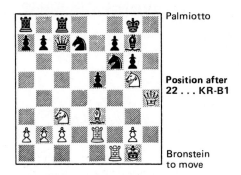

Palmiotto

Position after 22 . . . KR-B1

Bronstein to move

23 N(B3)-K4

Obviously with the idea of killing off one or two of the king's musketeers.

23 . . .   K-B1

The king flees before 24 R(K2)-B2 makes his stay unbearable.

24 NxN   NxN

25 RxN!   BxR

26 N-R7ch   K-K2

Or 26 . . . K-N2   27 Q-R6ch and mate next move.

27 QxBch   K-K1

28 R-Q2   P-R4

29 Q-N7

The most accurate, as mate is forced in two more moves; e.g., 29 . . . K-K2   30 B-N5ch K-K3   31 Q-B6 mate.

29 . . .   Resigns

In his delightful book *200 Open Games*, Bronstein describes his meeting with Dus-Chotimirsky in the Moscow match 'Locomotive' against 'Dynamo,' as follows:

'It is commonly thought that chess is a game for silent people.

As soon as my opponent had played 2 P-KB4 (after 1 P-K4 P-K4) I suddenly heard an angry, "And I'm having no refusal! Accept the sacrifice! If you don't take the pawn I won't continue the game."

There was nothing I could do. I accepted the old maestro's gambit.

Several moves later Dus-Chotimirsky played a hurried move, and whilst I was considering my reply, decided . . . to change his move!

The spectators gasped, the judges wanted to stop the clocks, but Fedor Ivanovich suddenly shouted at everyone, "What on earth is this? Look, I made a bad move, and now I'm changing it for a good one. Rules, you say? To hell with your rules, this is chess! Besides, you don't object?" said my opponent, turning to me.

"Please, it's my pleasure!"
And the game went on as if nothing had happened.'

(P.S. Bronstein won his game against Dus-Chotimirsky, the Giant-killer who had defeated the two men who tied for first at the great St. Petersburg 1909 Tournament, World Champion Lasker and Russian Champion Rubinstein).

Time is precious, and a grandmaster needs every golden moment allotted to him. There are occasions though, when he wants time to collect his thoughts, or perhaps to get into the right mood.

Such occasions as at Moscow in 1967, when Bronstein faced Stein, and took twenty-five minutes to meditate before playing his first move. By no means did he startle the spectators, as he opened with the conventional 1 P-Q4. This must have amused them, though, as they gave him a good-natured round of applause.

Spassky

Spassky was on Fischer's list of the ten greatest players that ever lived, long before he (Spassky) became World's Champion.

Spassky is a master for all seasons. Aggressive when there is an opportunity to attack, he is perfectly at home on the defence. He is alert to error, and punishes any inaccuracy quickly and inexorably. Spassky plays all openings (even those considered inferior) fearlessly, and delights in beating other masters with their own favourite weapons.

As a case in point, take his 23-move victory over Bronstein (No.31) in a King's Gambit. A King's Gambit! Why, it's Bronstein's speciality and particular delight! And look again at his 15th move, where he lets Bronstein capture a rook with a pawn, the pawn promoting to a queen with check! Simply incredible!

Or consider his 17-move brilliancy (No. 36) against Larsen, whom he defeated in sparkling style, though Larsen played Larsen's Opening.

As for other flights of imagination, what move can equal his 13th in the game against Pilnik at Goteborg (No. 30), where he puts a bishop *en prise*, the bishop attacking the ghost of a knight! The fact that Spassky is poker-faced can also be disturbing to his opponent, who has no clue as to whether a sacrifice is sound, or merely a desperate venture.

Spassky was a *wunderkind*, learning the moves at the age of five. At nine, he began to study the game seriously, and progressed to such effect as to become a first-category player at eleven, a candidate-master at twelve, an International Master at sixteen, and a Grandmaster at eighteen.

Spassky has a long list of triumphs to his credit. Most impressive to me is the manner of his climb to a match for a title in 1966:

In the Soviet Qualification Tournament at Kharkov in 1963, Spassky won 6 games, drew 8, lost none.

In the 31st Soviet Championship at Leningrad in 1963-4, Spassky won 5 games, drew 14, lost none.

In the Soviet Zonal, at Moscow in 1964, Spassky won 4 games, drew 6, lost 2.

In the Interzonal at Amsterdam in 1964, Spassky won 13 games, drew 8, lost 2.

In his match against Keres at Riga in 1965, Spassky won 4 games, drew 4, lost 2.

In his match against Geller, Spassky won 3 games, drew 5, lost none.

In the final match against Tal at Tiflis in 1965, Spassky won 4 games, drew 6, lost one.

All this (39 wins, 51 draws, and 7 losses) was in order to get a crack at the title held by Petrosian.

Petrosian held on to the crown, but in 1969 Spassky outplayed him and took it away, after defeating such mighty men as Geller, Larsen, and Korchnoi in preliminary matches.

Spassky was World Chess Champion until 1972, when Fischer defeated him—but it is no disgrace to lose to Fischer.

I consider Spassky the ninth greatest chess player of all time.

28

White **B. Spassky**   Black **V. Smyslov**
Nimzo-Indian Defence
Bucharest, 1953

This game created a great deal of excitement when it was played, and brought Spassky's name into the limelight.

For Spassky was only sixteen at the time, while Smyslov was a seasoned grandmaster, close to the top of his form. Smyslov in fact took first prize in the powerful Zurich Tournament which took place later in the same year, and went on the following year to play a drawn match with Botvinnik for the title of world champion.

Spassky's play in this game is simple, clear, and straightforward. The theme of the strategy that brings him victory can be summed up in one word—centralization. In the face of this strategy, Smyslov's attempts to work up a K-side attack are doomed to failure.

1 P-Q4   N-KB3

2 P-QB4   P-K3

3 N-QB3   B-N5

One reason for the popularity of this defence is that it is a fighting line. It begins by preventing P-K4 (a desideratum for White in queen pawn openings) and allows chances for counter-attack.

White has a wealth of choice for his next move:
4 Q-B2 is the Classical Variation,
4 Q-N3 is the Spielmann Variation,
4 P-K3 is the Rubinstein Variation,
4 P-QR3 is the Samisch Variation,
and that's only the beginning!

Lesser-known, but perfectly sound lines are 4 P-B3, or 4 P-KN3, or 4 B-Q2, or 4 N-B3.

So—chess openings are far from being exhausted!

4 B-N5

Spassky varies from the lines listed above, and plays a little-known but effective variation called the Leningrad System.

4 ...   P-KR3

5 B-R4   P-B4

6 P-Q5   P-Q3

7 P-K3   PxP

8 PxP   QN-Q2

9 B-QN5

Various motives could be ascribed to this move. It might be in order to meet 9 . . . Q-R4 with 10 BxNch BxB 11 N-K2, with the better position for White.

More likely is the possibility that the bishop has no better square for its development, as Soltis points out. The square K2 should be reserved for the king knight, at Q3 it leaves the queen pawn hanging, and at B4 it is exposed to attack, at some time or other, by . . . N-K4 or . . . P-QN4.

9 ...   0-0

Porath tried 9 . . . P-KN4 against Spassky in 1964, but was slaughtered after 10 B-N3 Q-R4 11 BxNch BxB 12 N-K2 B-N4 13 P-QR3 BxNch 14 NxB B-B5 (the losing move; preferable was 14 . . . N-K5) 15 Q-B3! K-K2 (if 15 . . . Q-Q1 16 N-K4 wins at once) 16 BxPch KxB 17 QxNch K-B2 18 QxPch K-N1 19 Q-B6 R-Q1 20 Q-K5ch Q-B2 21 QxQch KxQ 22 P-K4, and Porath resigned ten moves later.

10 N-K2   N-K4

11 0-0   N-N3

12 B-N3   N-R4

13 B-Q3

This is not an admission that the bishop's development at N5 was inappropriate. Circumstances have changed and in view of that fact the bishop can now be more usefully employed at Q3.

For example, if Black plays 13 . . . P-B4, the reply 14 P-B4 confers a three-fold advantage on White:

(1) His bishop, posted at Q3, exerts pressure on sensitive points along the diagonal.

(2) The square K6, weakened by Black's pawn advance, might be accessible to one of White's pieces.

(3) The range of Black's queen bishop has been sharply cut down.

13 ...   NxB

Black has gone to a great deal of trouble to obtain the two bishops, only to find a couple of moves later that his own king bishop has so little future that it can be dispensed with.

14 NxN   N-K4

15 B-K2   BxN

Black is prompted to this exchange by the fact that his bishop has little scope with so many of his pawns standing on black squares.

16 PxB   Q-R5

17 P-KB4!

An astute move, as will be seen.

17 ...   N-N5

18 BxN   BxB

19 Q-R4!

Like the magician's trick of misdirection, the queen's move to the Q-side masks a threat on the other wing. White intends to continue with 20 P-B5 (pinning the bishop) followed by 21 R-B4 or 21 Q-KB4.

19 ...   B-B1

The bishop runs home, not relishing the prospect of being shut in by 20 P-B5.

20 P-K4

The pawns begin to look ominous.

20 ...   Q-N5

21 Q-B2   P-KR4

22 R-B2   P-QN4

Smyslov seems to show indecision. He wavers between continuing operations on the K-side, and starting his pawn majority rolling on the Q-side.

23 P-K5

Whereas Spassky has no doubts about his objectives. He simply strengthens his center, in line with the injunctions of the masters, from Capablanca, who said,

'Control of the centre is essential to a successful attack against the king,' to Nimzowitsch who said, 'Your eye on the wings, your mind on the center, that is the deepest meaning of position play.'

23 ...   P-R5

24 N-B1

The knight is out of play for the moment, but it is destined for great deeds.

24 ...   B-B4

25 Q-Q2   PxP

Smyslov tries desperately to obtain more room for his pieces. Much better was the patient 25 ... QR-Q1, followed by 26 ... KR-K1, to await events.

26 PxP

The recapture results in Spassky's having a passed pawn, the square KB4 for the convenience of his pieces, and the threat of winning a piece by 27 N-K3.

26 ...   B-N3

27 R-K1   P-R6

28 P-Q6   B-K5

29 N-K3

The knight leaps into action! It attacks the queen, protects the knight pawn, and is poised to take an active part in the K-side attack.

29 ...   Q-K3

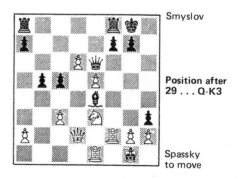

Smyslov

Position after
29 ... Q-K3

Spassky
to move

30 R-B4!

The rook follows the knight's lead, actuated by the same noble motives.

30 ... BxP

But not 30 . . . QxKP, when 31 N-N4 attacks the queen, and uncovers defence for the rook, and an attack on the bishop as well.

31 N-B5!

The attack gains in momentum, the primary threat being 32 N-K7ch K-R2   33 R-R4ch, and Black must give up his queen.

31 ... KR-K1

32 R-K3   QR-Q1

Too late, too late! There is no way to avert the catastrophe.

33 NxP!

A blow from which there can be no recovery.

33 ... RxP

Capturing the knight is immediately fatal, thus: 33 . . . KxN   34 R-N3ch K-B1   35 RxPch KxR (or 35 . . . QxR   36 Q-R6ch)   36 Q-B4ch and mate next move.

  Black's last move is predicated on the chance (say one in a million) that Spassky will reply 34 QxR or 34 PxR.

34 NxQ   Resigns

As 34 . . . RxQ allows 35 R-N3ch and mate next move.

29

White **B. Spassky**   Black **M. Taimanov**
Ruy López
U.S.S.R. Championship, 1955

There are all sorts of pleasantries in this little game.

  There is Spassky's nonchalant offer of a knight on the Q-side, while his other knight is under attack on the K-side.

Then there is a sort of casual air about the queen, as she snips off one pawn after another, and presents Taimanov with the problem of halting five ambitious passed pawns.

1 P-K4   P-K4

2 N-KB3   N-QB3

3 B-N5   P-QR3

4 B-R4   P-QN4

5 B-N3   N-R4

6 0-0

White can go in for a gambit, recommended by Svenonius, by 6 BxPch KxB   7 NxPch K-K2 8 P-Q4 N-KB3   9 B-N5 Q-K1   10 P-KB4 K-Q1 11 0-0 , with good attacking chances.

6 ...   P-Q3

7 P-Q4   NxB

The tempting 7 . . . PxP   8 QxP P-QB4 does not win a piece, as after 9 BxPch KxB   10 Q-Q5ch wins at least the exchange, since the interposition by 10 . . . B-K3 succumbs to 11 N-N5ch K-K1 (if 11 . . . K-N3 12 NxB attacks the queen and also threatens mate) 12 NxB Q-B1   13 QxR!, and White wins neatly.

8 RPxN   P-KB3

Black decides to fortify his K4 square.

  An interesting possibility after 8 . . . N-B3 is this (which I hope is sound): 9 PxP NxP   10 Q-Q5 B-B4 11 Q-B6ch K-K2   12 N-B3! NxN   13 B-N5ch P-B3 14 PxBPch PxP   15 BxPch! KxB   16 QxNch, and White wins.

9 N-B3   B-N2

10 N-KR4   N-K2

11 PxP   QPxP

This is a safer recapture than 11 . . . BPxP, when 12 B-N5 gives strong pressure to White.

12 Q-B3

Protects the king pawn from loss by 12 . . . P-N5.

12 ...   Q-Q2

13 R-Q1   Q-K3

14 B-K3   P-N4

Black tries to free his game by violent means.

The alternative 14 . . . P-N3 has little appeal for Taimanov, as after 15 N-Q5! NxN   16 PxN Q-Q3 17 P-B4, White is in sight of a win.

Nevertheless, White's reply to the move he made must have come as a shock.

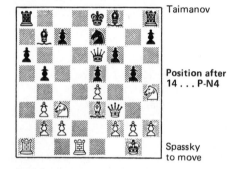

Taimanov

Position after 14 . . . P-N4

Spassky to move

15 NxP!!

A powerful blow! Suddenly White seems to be attacking from all sides.

15 . . .   RPxN

What else is there? If 15 . . . R-B1 (to prevent loss of his queen) 16 Q-R5ch Q-B2 17 NxPch RxN 18 R-Q8ch KxR 19 QxQ PxN 20 R-Q1ch R-Q2 21 B-N6ch forces mate.

16 Q-R5ch   Q-B2

Still worse is 16 . . . N-N3 17 RxRch BxR 18 NxN Q-B2 19 Q-N4 PxN (if 19 . . . P-KB4 20 NxR wins, or if 19 . . . QxN 20 Q-Q7 is mate) 20 Q-B8ch K-K2 21 Q-Q7 mate.

17 RxRch   BxR

18 R-Q8ch   KxR

19 QxQ   PxN

Black has rook, knight, and bishop for the queen— enough material—but his pieces are disorganized, and his pawns are weak, and easy prey for a ferocious queen.

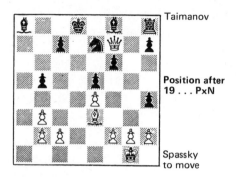

Taimanov

Position after 19 . . . PxN

Spassky to move

Here is the rest of the story:

20 QxBP   R-N1

21 P-KB3   P-R6

22 P-N3   K-K1

23 QxP   R-N3

24 QxPch   B-B3

25 Q-N8ch   K-B2

26 QxP

White has five passed pawns, each of them a potential queen.

26 . . .   R-B3

27 B-N5   R-K3

Black can try a last-minute swindle with 27 . . . RxP 28 BxN BxB 29 QxB B-N4, but after 30 Q-Q7ch K-B3 31 QxP(R3) B-K6ch 32 K-R1, there is nothing left to live for.

28 P-QN4   K-N1

29 Q-N8   N-N3

30 K-B2   N-K4

31 P-N5   B-K1

32 B-K3   B-Q3

33 Q-B8   K-B2

34 P-N6   R-B3

35 B-B4   B-Q2

36 P-N7   B-K3

37 BxN   BxB
38 P-N8(Q) B(K3)xQ
39 QxB(K5) Resigns

30

White **B. Spassky**   Black **H. Pilnik**
Sicilian Defence
Goteborg, 1955

When Keres, who is modest about his accomplishments, says of a game he played, 'This exceptionally exciting game, full of sacrifices, is of a type rarely seen in a game between grandmasters,' you may be sure that the game he is praising is an extraordinary one.

And it is a wonderful game! Keres was mistaken though about the rarity of its occurrence. For on the same day that Keres was playing Najdorf, and in that very room, two other Soviet players were facing two other Argentinians, and all three Soviet grandmasters won their games in the same way. Keres won from Najdorf, Spassky won from Pilnik, and Geller won from Panno by the same series of remarkable moves!

The Argentine team had prepared a certain line of play which they thought to be effective, and the three Soviet players refuted it move for move in the same way. Whether they had been following a previously worked-out plan, or whether the three games duplicated each other by almost incredible coincidence, no one will ever know, but out of it emerged a masterpiece—in triplicate!

There is one idea in the game which I doubt has ever before been seen on a chessboard, and that alone is worth the price of admission:

White makes a move with his bishop which attacks a piece that is not there; it attacks the ghost of a knight!

This amazing move had not been taken into account by the Argentinian analysts!

1 P-K4   P-QB4

2 N-KB3   P-Q3

3 P-Q4   PxP

4 NxP   N-KB3

5 N-QB3   P-QR3

6 B-KN5   P-K3

7 P-B4   B-K2

Two rounds earlier, Panno had tried 7 . . . Q-N3 against Keres—to his sorrow.
Keres was in fine form, and won it in glorious style. This is how he did it: 8 Q-Q2 N-B3   9 0-0-0 QxN 10 QxQ NxQ   11 RxN N-Q2   12 B-K2 P-R3 13 B-R4 P-KN4   14 PxP N-K4   15 N-R4 B-K2 16 N-N6 R-QN1   17 B-N3 PxP   18 KR-Q1 P-B3 19 P-B4 0-0   20 R(Q4)-Q2 P-B4   21 P-B5 P-B5 22 PxP BxP   23 RxB PxB   24 PxP R-B2   25 K-N1! R-B2   26 R-Q8ch K-N2   27 R-QB1! N-B3   28 P-K5 K-N3   29 B-Q3ch K-B2   30 R-R8 K-K2   31 B-N6! Resigns

Black can move none of his pieces without loss, and is threatened in addition with 32 R-K8 mate. 'This game,' says Keres, 'would have given Grandmaster Nimzowitsch much pleasure.'

The scene now shifts to Goteborg:

8 Q-B3   P-R3

9 B-R4   P-KN4

This was the innovation of the Argentine players. Black offers a pawn to enable him to occupy K4 with his pieces.

10 PxP   KN-Q2

11 NxP!

A fairly obvious sacrifice, as White gets two pawns for his knight, and attacking chances on the exposed king.

11 . . .   PxN

12 Q-R5ch K-B1

At this point one might expect the plausible development by 13 B-B4, but it would occasion the opponent no difficulty, as after 13 . . . N-K4   14 0-0 ch K-N2

15 B-KN3 QN-B3, and Black maintains a knight at his K4 outpost.

Obviously, White must try to prevent 15 . . . QN-B3, the key move to the defence. I give this explanation for the better appreciation of White's next move.

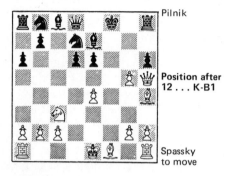

Pilnik

Position after
12 . . . K-B1

Spassky
to move

13 B-N5!!

The beauty of this move lies not in the simple fact that 13 . . . PxB allows a White win by 14 0-0 ch, but because the bishop attacks a piece that is not there! *The bishop attacks the ghost of a knight (the queen knight which has not yet moved), and is poised to capture it the moment it moves to B3 or Q2.*

This is as subtle a move as I have ever seen on a chessboard.

White is now prepared for this continuation: 13 . . . N-K4 14 B-N3 N(N1)-B3 (in order to replace the knight at K4 with another knight, in the event of its capture) 15 B(N5)xN PxB 16 BxN PxB 17 0-0 ch B-B3 (otherwise mate on the spot) 18 RxBch, and White wins.

13 . . .   K-N2

There is no relief in 13 . . . Q-K1 14 0-0 ch K-N2 15 PxPch K-R2 16 R-B7ch, and White wins.

At this point Panno varied with 13 . . . N-K4, and lost quickly to Geller. The other two games continued on the same course until the 23rd move, when Spassky pushed his rook pawn forward one square, while Keres moved it two squares.

14 0-0

Threatens mate in one.

14 . . .   N-K4

If 14 . . . Q-N1 15 P-N6! BxB 16 QxB (stronger than 16 R-B7ch) 16 . . . Q-Q1 17 R-B7ch KxP 18 R-K7!, and Black has no defence (Keres).

15 B-N3   N-N3

Developing the queen knight in support of the knight at K4 fails, as after 15 . . . QN-B3 16 B(N5)xN PxB 17 BxNch PxB 18 Q-B7 is mate.

Or if 15 . . . Q-N1 16 BxNch PxB 17 B-K8! QxB 18 PxPch K-R2 19 R-B7ch and Black must give up his queen.

This is the state of affairs:

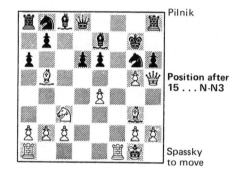

Pilnik

Position after
15 . . . N-N3

Spassky
to move

16 PxPch   RxP

17 R-B7ch

This freshens up the attack: Black must not be allowed a breathing spell.

17 . . .   KxR

18 QxR   PxB

Finally Black removes the Bishop, which has been waiting patiently to be captured.

Keres shows this pretty win after 18 . . . Q-R1: 19 R-B1ch B-B3 20 B-K8ch KxB (if 20 . . . QxB 21 Q-R7ch) 21 QxNch K-K2 22 RxB!, and the recapture by 22 . . . QxR forfeits the queen after 23 BxPch.

White is still two pieces down. He can regain one piece, but at the cost of letting the king go into hiding.

19 R-B1ch   K-K1

Or 19 . . . B-B3   20 Q-R7ch K-B1   21 QxN, and White wins the Bishop and with it the game.

20 QxNch   K-Q2

21 R-B7   N-B3

The king seems sheltered from his pursuers, but they find the means to get at him.

A diagram seems to be in order:

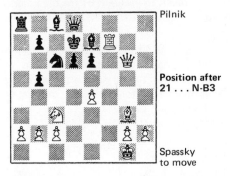

Pilnik

Position after 21 . . . N-B3

Spassky to move

22 N-Q5!

Beautiful! White's immediate threat is 23 NxB NxN 24 B-R4, winning the pinned knight and the game.

22 . . .   RxP

Capturing the knight loses, as follows: 22 . . . PxN 23 QxPch K-K1   24 Q-N6 PxP (or 24 . . . K-Q2 25 PxP, and Black must lose a piece)   25 R-N7 dis.ch K-Q2   26 Q-Q6ch K-K1   27 R-N8ch, and mate follows next move.

23 P-R3

Keres varied here with 23 P-R4.

23 . . .   Q-R1

24 NxB   NxN

25 Q-N5

Najdorf (Keres's opponent) resigned here in view of 25 . . . Q-Q1   26 QxPch K-B2   27 Q-B5ch K-N1

28 BxPch K-R1   29 BxN, and there's nothing left.

Pilnik (Spassky's opponent) fought on for a few more moves, thus:

25 . . .   R-R8ch

26 K-R2   Q-Q1

27 QxPch   K-B2

28 Q-QB5ch   K-N1

29 BxPch   K-R1

30 BxN   R-R4

31 Q-N4   Resigns

After 31 . . . Q-B2ch   32 B-Q6 Q-Q1   33 R-B8 the game is over.

31

White **B. Spassky**   Black **D. Bronstein**
King's Gambit
Leningrad, 1959

Spassky is one of the few grandmasters who dares play the King's Gambit in tournaments.

In this game he defeats Bronstein in 23 moves in typically Morphy style, though Bronstein is a tougher opponent than were the victims of Morphy's brilliancies.

One move by Spassky—a fantastic move—lights up the whole position. 'Fantastic' is a strong word, and should be used sparingly, but how else can one describe Spassky's inspired 15th move? Instead of removing an impudent pawn that attacks his rook, Spassky blithely permits this pawn to capture his rook with check!

Truly, it is a move in a million!

1 P-K4   P-K4

2 P-KB4   PxP

3 N-KB3   P-Q4

After accepting the gambit, either 3 . . . P-Q4 or 3 . . . N-KB3 (each of which is a developing move) offers the best practical defence.

The old-fashioned 3 . . . P-KN4, holding on to the pawn, is dangerous, as Black breaks up his own K-side position.

4 PxP   B-Q3

A safer alternative is 4 . . . N-KB3, following Lasker's principle of developing knights before bishops.

Bronstein may have planned to continue with 5 . . . N-K2 and 6 . . . N-N3 to protect the bishop pawn, or he may have intended 5 . . . N-K2 followed by 6 . . . N-Q2 and 7 . . . N-KB3—a sort of hedgehog defence.

5 N-B3   N-K2

At this early stage the players are probably out of the books, and left to their own resources.

6 P-Q4   0-0

7 B-Q3   N-Q2

8 0-0   P-KR3

Bronstein may have wanted to prevent 9 N-KN5 followed by 10 N-K4, but the move he makes is slow, timid, and weakening.

The natural move is 8 . . . N-KB3, which frees his queen bishop, threatens to win a pawn, and helps guard his king.

This would comply also with the old precept (which has not yet been abandoned) 'A knight at KB3 is the best defence of a castled K-side position.'

Bronstein had nothing to fear (after 8 . . . N-KB3) from 9 N-K5 N(K2)xP 10 NxN NxN 11 Q-R5 P-KN3 12 Q-R6 Q-B3, as Spassky later pointed out.

9 N-K4!   NxP

If 9 . . . P-KN4, to guard against losing a pawn by 10 NxB PxN 11 BxP, the reply 10 P-B4 is strong for White.

10 P-B4   N-K6

Black plunges into the complications, as that seems more attractive than 10 . . . N-N5 11 B-N1, followed by 12 P-QR3, and White's position looks imposing.

11 BxN   PxB

12 P-B5   B-K2

The bishop must retreat, as 12 . . . B-B5 13 P-KN3

B-N4   14 N(B3)xB PxN   15 Q-R5 gives White a winning attack.

13 B-B2!

Spassky prepares to arrange queen and bishop in battery formation along the highway leading to the king.

13 . . .   R-K1

Perhaps there were chances of holding the position by 13 . . . N-B3   14 Q-Q3 NxN   15 QxN P-KN3 16 QxKP K-N2.

Bronstein's idea is to vacate KB1 for the knight to guard the square R2 against the threat of mate.

14 Q-Q3   P-K7

Bronstein hopes to gain time by luring the queen into capturing the king pawn, but the queen (unlike Atalanta, who stopped to pick up the golden apples in the race against her suitor) resists the temptation to pick up the insolent pawn.

This is the position:

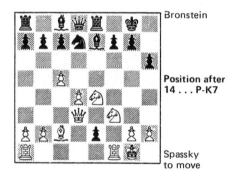

Bronstein

Position after
14 . . . P-K7

Spassky
to move

15 N-Q6!!

A magnificent move! Spassky lets his rook be captured with check!

'One of the deepest sacrifices this side of The Evergreen Game,' says Soltis.

15 . . .   N-B1

Bronstein refrains for the moment from capturing the rook, on the chance that Spassky might have last-minute misgivings about the soundness of his rook sacrifice. He might then take the king pawn and thereby lose a tempo for the attack.

The fact that Bronstein had only 20 minutes left for his next 26 moves, was not helpful to his frame of mind.

16 NxBP!

I am sure that Spassky did not consider such a move as 16 NxR for more than two seconds.

16 ...   PxR(Q)ch

17 RxQ   B-B4

Capturing the knight instead lets White win quickly and neatly, thus: 17 ... KxN 18 N-K5 dbl.ch K-N1 19 Q-R7ch NxQ 21 B-N3ch K-R1 22 N-N6 mate.

Black could have put up more resistance with 17 ... Q-Q4, but even then the continuation 18 B-N3 QxN(B2) 19 BxQch KxB 20 Q-B4ch K-N3 21 Q-N8 (cuts the king off from his army) 21 ... B-B3 22 N-R4ch BxN 23 Q-B7ch K-R2 24 QxR gives White a position in sight of a win, especially with Bronstein in extreme time-pressure.

18 QxB   Q-Q2

19 Q-B4   B-B3

20 N(B3)-K5   Q-K2

21 B-N3   BxN

22 NxB dis.ch   K-R2

23 Q-K4ch   Resigns

Bronstein sees the mate that follows after 23 ... K-R1, by 24 RxNch RxR 25 N-N6ch K-R2 26 NxR dbl.ch K-R1 27 Q-R7 mate.

The final position appeared in the James Bond picture *From Russia with Love*, indicating that chess books may some day be sold to the movies.

32

White **B. Spassky**   Black **L. Evans**
King's Indian Defence
Varna Olympiad, 1962

Spassky turns out a beautiful little specimen of K-side attack.

In so tightly-knit a formation as the King's Indian Defence, he manages to pry open the rook file as early as the 13th move, for the delectation of his pieces.

Once in control of the valuable file, Spassky's attack proves irresistible.

It is an elegant game, one of the best in the Olympics, and destined to find a place in the anthologies.

1 P-Q4   N-KB3

2 P-QB4   P-KN3

3 N-QB3   B-N2

4 P-K4   P-Q3

White has built a strong pawn centre in order to cramp his opponent's game.

Black's objective in allowing this luxury to his opponent is the hypermodern idea of undermining the centre.

He has two courses of action, both based on inducing White to advance his queen pawn, and then striking at the supporting king pawn or queen bishop pawn. One method is to play ... P-B4, following that up (after White plays P-Q5) with ... P-K3 and ... P-QN4. Another way is to play ... P-K4 and (again after P-Q5) to follow with ... N-R4 or ... N-K1, and start a pawn roller on the K-side by ... P-KB4, ... P-KB5 and ... P-KN4, which can lead to a powerful Black attack.

Indeed the popularity of the King's Indian Defence stems from the fact that it's a fighting line, which offers winning chances to Black as well as White.

5 P-B3

This quiet little move, a favourite of Spassky's, contains a good deal of poison.

5 ...   P-B3

One would expect the conventional 5 ... 0-0, or 5 ... N-B3 followed by 6 ... P-K4.

6 B-K3   P-QR3

7 Q-Q2   P-QN4

8 0-0-0   PxP

9 BxB   0-0

This sets up a target for Spassky, who has excellent aim.

There was still time to get the Q-side pieces in motion by 9 . . . QN-Q2   10 KN-K2 N-N3   11 B-N3, B-K3, with a fairly decent game.

10 P-KR4!

Spassky doesn't waste a moment! He intends to pry open the file in double-quick time. (An open file leading to the king is the road to happiness.)

10 . . .   P-Q4

Black should either make the breakthrough more difficult by playing 10 . . . P-KR4, or oppose bishops by 10 . . . B-K3, to weaken the pressure exerted on his king bishop pawn.

11 B-N3   PxP

Practically forced, to prevent 12 P-K5 driving off his knight from its ideal post.

12 P-R5!

Evans may have expected 12 PxP, when 12 . . . B-N5 13 N-B3 QN-Q2 lets him bring two pieces into the game.

12 . . .   KPxP

13 RPxP   RPxP

14 B-R6   PxP

The queen pawn has wandered down to KN7, somewhat in the way Winter's bishop pawn wandered down to QN7 in his game against Keres at Warsaw in 1935.

Eleven out of the fourteen moves made by Evans have been pawn moves. Such trifling with the principles of development can hardly go unpunished.

Meanwhile Spassky, whose role it is to mete out the punishment, has given up all his K-side pawns.

This is how things look:

Evans

Position after
14 . . . PxP

Spassky
to move

15 R-R4!   N-N5

Blocking the file by 15 . . . N-R4 loses like a shot: 16 RxN PxR   17 Q-N5, and it's all over.

16 BxB   KxB

17 QxP!

Offers Black a tempting knight fork. If Black yields to temptation by 17 . . . N-K6, the sequel would be 18 Q-R2 NxR (if 18 . . . R-R1   19 RxR QxR, and 20 Q-K5ch removes the presumptuous knight) 19 R-R7ch K-N1   20 R-R8ch K-N2   21 Q-R6ch K-B3   22 N-K4ch K-B4   23 Q-N5ch KxN 24 R-R4ch K-Q6   25 Q-Q2 mate.

17 . . .   N-R3

18 N-B3   N-B4

19 R-R2   Q-Q3

If 19 . . . R-R1   20 BxP KxB (20 . . . RxR   21 QxPch K-R1   22 NxR is hopeless for Black)   21 N-K5ch K-N2   22 QxNPch and mate next move.

The knight fork by 19 . . . N-K6 is still of no avail, as after 20 Q-N5 NxR   21 Q-R6ch K-B3   22 Q-B4ch K-N2 (if 22 . . . B-B4   23 Q-K5 is mate)   23 N-K4!, and mate follows.

20 N-K5   N-Q2

The first and last move of Black's Q-side pieces.

21 N-K4   Q-B2

22 QR-R1

In contrast, all White's pieces are actively engaged in the attack.

22 ...   R-KN1

23 R-R7ch   K-B1

24 RxPch   K-K1

25 QxP!

This flashy queen sacrifice is not intended to give the spectators a thrill, but it is the quickest way to break down any resistance.

25 ...   NxN

Naturally, 25 ... RxQ runs into mate by 26 R-R8ch.

26 R-B8 dbl.ch   Resigns

If 26 ... KxR   27 QxR is mate, or if 26 ... K-Q2 mate follows by 27 N-B5, or by 27 B-K6, or by 27 Q-K6, or by 27 Q-K8.

33

White **Klovan**   Black **B. Spassky**
Ruy López
U.S.S.R. Championship, 1963-4

An amusing game—except to Klovan, of course!

Spassky sacrifices a pawn early in the game, for the sake of rendering a bishop impotent. The unfortunate bishop is reduced to zigzagging about, in a vain effort to reach a diagonal where it can make itself useful.

Particularly annoying to Klovan must have been the circumstance that this white-squared bishop is unable to exploit the fact that Spassky's position is full of white-square weaknesses.

In compensation for this, Spassky's iron grip on the black squares makes it almost impossible for his opponent to break through in order to free his pieces.

· The ending, with Spassky's king wandering down towards the end of the board, is an attractive piece of play, and in keeping with this fine game.

1 P-K4   P-K4

2 N-KB3   N-QB3

3 B-N5   P-QR3

4 B-R4   N-B3

5 0-0   B-K2

6 R-K1   P-QN4

7 B-N3   0-0

8 P-QR4

Klovan does not venture on 8 P-B3 P-Q4, which could lead to the sharp complications of the Marshall attack, a gambit line with which Spassky is thoroughly familiar.

8 ...   B-N2

9 P-Q3   P-Q3

10 N-B3

The usual move is 10 P-B3, which provides a good square for the bishop, in the event that Black plays 10 ... N-QR4.

10 ...   N-QR4

11 B-R2   P-N5

12 N-K2   P-B4

13 N-N3

Klovan, blissfully unaware of potential danger on his Q-side, continues with the customary procedure of establishing an outpost by N-B5.

13 ...   P-N6!

This must have caught Klovan by surprise!

Spassky's offer of a pawn is strongly reminiscent of the famous Dus Chotimirsky-Capablanca game, played at Moscow in 1925, where Capablanca gave up two pawns (one at B5 and one at N6) apparently to no tangible purpose.

Spassky's sacrifice has a similar deep, dark design. The position is shown on page 78.

14 PxP

A better reply, thanks to the gift of hindsight, is 14 BxP.

Spassky

Position after
13 . . . P-N6!

Klovan
to move

14 . . .   N-B3

15 N-B5   N-QN5

A fine spot, from which the knight exerts a great
deal of influence.

16 B-N1   P-QR4

17 B-N5   B-B1

This bishop too seeks greener pastures.

18 NxBch   QxN

19 N-Q2

Obviously, the knight is headed for B1 and N3, in
order to attack the white squares.

19 . . .   P-R3

20 B-K3   P-N4

Spassky's three musketeers, the pawns at N4, K4, and
B4, maintain a tight grip on the black squares.

21 N-B1   N-K1

22 N-N3   N-N2

Just in time to stop White from playing 23 N-B5.

23 Q-Q2   P-B3

Spassky's position is full of holes, and an enemy
white-squared bishop would have a field day wandering through those wide-open spaces. But Klovan's
bishop is still imprisoned behind the lines.

24 B-B2   Q-KB2

25 B-Q1   Q-N3

26 B-K2   P-R4!

Spassky prepares to cut down the limited scope of
the bishop still more by 27 . . . P-N5, or to banish
the knight by 27 . . . P-R5—or both!

27 Q-Q1   P-N5!

28 P-B4

A desperate bid for freedom.

28 . . .   PxP *en passant*

29 BxP

Of course not 29 PxP, when 29 . . . P-R5 wins a
piece.

29 . . .   P-R5

30 N-R5   R-R2

The rook is ready to enter the game, by way of the
second rank, which is conveniently vacant.

31 R-KB1   P-B4

32 NxN

White loses patience in the face of such threats as
32 . . . B-R3 or 33 . . . PxP, and exchanges knights,
though at the cost of letting the rook into the game.

32 . . .   RxN

33 PxP   BxP

34 Q-Q2

Threatens to win the exchange by 35 B-R6, his
queen pawn being beyond help.

34 . . .   BxP

35 B-R6   BxR

36 RxB   P-K5

37 BxR   KxB

38 B-K2   RxRch

39 BxR

White has managed to escape material loss, but not
positional disadvantage. Black's two connected
passed pawns should assure the win, provided his
king does not run into a perpetual check.

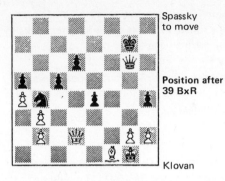

Spassky
to move

**Position after
39 BxR**

Klovan

39 ...   Q-B3
Threatens to exchange queens at Q5, and win in a
flash.

40 Q-K2   Q-B5
Protects the king pawn, and plans a decisive penetration by 41 ... N-Q6.

41 Q-N5   K-R3

42 Q-K8   Q-K6ch

43 K-R1   Q-B7

44 Q-R8ch   K-N4

45 Q-N7ch   K-B5
Despite the open position, Spassky's king cannot be
annoyed much longer. If 46 Q-R6ch K-K4 47 Q-N7ch
Q-B3, and White must exchange queens or be mated.
Or if 46 Q-B6ch K-K6 47 Q-B3ch (on 47 Q-N5ch
Q-B5 forces the queen exchange) N-Q6 48 BxN
PxB 49 Q-B1ch P-Q7, and White can give it up.

46 P-N3ch   PxP

47 PxPch   QxP

48 Q-R6ch   K-B6

49 Q-Q2
Would you believe that White, with the aid of his
hitherto miserable king bishop, actually threatens
mate in three moves? The play would be:
50 B-K2ch K-B7 51 B-Q1 dis.ch K-B8 52 Q-K2
mate.

49 ...   K-N5

50 B-N5
The Ruy López bishop starts life all over again.
   It's strange that Klovan did not try 50 B-K2ch as
a last resort, when 50 ... K-R5 allows 51 Q-R6,
mate on the move, and 50 ... K-R6 is met by
51 Q-R6ch Q-R5 52 Q-K3ch Q-N6 53 Q-R6ch, and
White draws by perpetual check.

50 ...   N-Q6!
The knight has been waiting patiently for 35 moves
on the sidelines, but now it comes in with irresistible
effect, its threat being 51 N-B7ch, winning the queen.

51 BxN   PxB

52 QxRP
And White resigned without waiting for Black's next
move. The continuation would be 52 ... Q-R6ch
53 K-N1 Q-K6ch followed by 54 ... P-Q7.

34

White **L. Portisch**   Black **B. Spassky**
Queen's Gambit Accepted
Amsterdam, 1964

Spassky wins a fascinating ending, though he is a pawn
down, and his opponent has the two bishops.
   Though he has little material to work with, Spassky
makes use of his meager forces to excellent effect, his
king especially making a valuable contribution by its
energetic advance into enemy territory.
   This is in accord with what Philidor prescribed almost
200 years ago, 'The king may be of service, either in
protecting some pawns of your own which may be more
advanced than the rest, and on their passage to queen; or
in taking or harassing any adverse pawns, traversing the
board with the same design.'
   The language may be old-fashioned, but the advice is
still good today.

1 P-Q4   P-Q4

2 P-QB4   PxP

This line is considered, by most theorists under the influence of Tarrasch, as slightly inferior, for Black exchanges a centre pawn for a side pawn.

From time to time, however, there is a revival of interest in accepting the pawn, dangerous though it may seem. Black gets an open game and good tactical chances, instead of the cramped positions that are usually his lot in the Queen's Gambit Declined.

3 N-KB3   N-KB3

4 Q-R4ch   P-B3

Black can play to exchange queens with 4 . . . Q-Q2, when 5 QxBP Q-B3   6 N-R3 QxQ   7 NxQ P-K3   8 P-QR3   P-QR4   9 B-B4 P-QN4 leaves an even game.

5 QxBP   B-B4

6 N-B3   P-K3

7 P-KN3   QN-Q2

8 B-N2

So far the players have followed the 23rd game of the 1934 world championship match between Bogolyubov and Alekhine.

8 . . .   B-Q3

At this point, Alekhine played 8 . . . B-B7, surrounding the queen, and threatening to capture her by 9 . . . N-N3. His intention was to force 9 P-K3 (the queen needing a flight square) and shut in White's queen bishop.

Bogolyubov suffered no inconvenience, built up a good position by 9 P-K3 B-K2   10 0-0 0-0   11 P-QR3 P-QR4   12 Q-K2 B-N3   13 P-K4 Q-N3   14 P-R3 Q-R3   15 Q-K3, and went on to win the game.

9 0-0   0-0

10 N-KR4   B-KN5

11 P-KR3   B-R4

12 P-K4

The threat is of course 13 P-K5, winning a piece.

Portisch is ready to reply to 12 . . . P-K4 with 13 N-B5, a square available to his knight thanks to the bishop having been driven off.

12 . . .   N-K1

White's center looks strong, but 'appearances are deceptive,' as Aesop said long ago in *The wolf in sheep's clothing.*

13 B-K3   B-K2

14 N-KB3   N-Q3

15 Q-N3

Centralizing the queen by 15 Q-Q3 would be hazardous in view of the annoying pin 15 . . . B-N3 in reply.

15 . . .   BxN

To allow the opponent the two bishops seems strange, but after 16 N-Q2, Spassky's queen bishop has little future.

16 BxB   Q-N3

17 P-Q5   QxQ

18 PxQ   BPxP

19 PxP   P-K4

Spassky sacrifices a pawn, rather than play 19 . . . P-QR3, when 20 PxP PxP saddles him with an isolated king pawn.

20 RxP   RxR

21 BxR

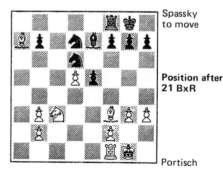

Spassky to move

Position after 21 BxR

Portisch

Spassky has lost a pawn, and his queen knight pawn is isolated. To offset this, his opponent has weaknesses in a doubled pawn on the knight file, and an isolated queen pawn.

White has tactical advantage in the long-range action open to his two bishops. Black has strategic advantage in his four-to-three majority of pawns on the K-side, which offer the prospect of creating a passed pawn.

21 ...   P-B4!

There was little hope of imprisoning the bishop, as after 21 ... P-QN3 the sequel would be 22 N-R4 N-B1   23 R-B1 NxB   24 R-B7, and White regains the piece.

22 B-K2   R-B1

23 B-K3   K-B2

Spassky wastes no time in getting his king into play for the endgame.

24 N-N5   N-B3

25 NxNch   BxN

26 R-R1   K-N3

Black does not snap at the pawn, as the penalty would be (after 26 ... NxP)   27 B-QB4 K-K3 28 R-Q1, and White wins the greedy knight.

27 B-QB4   P-R4

28 R-R7   R-QN1

Spassky's rook seems terribly out of play, tied down as it is to defending a pawn—but keep an eye on it!

29 R-R5   P-R5!

39 R-N5

Clearly 30 PxP P-B5, followed by 31 ... P-K5 and 32 ... K-B4 has little appeal for Portisch.

30 ...   PxP

31 PxP   N-Q2

32 R-R5

Dispirited, the rook returns to the open file.

At first glance, 32 B-R7 driving the rook off from the pawn's defence looks attractive, but

Spassky's reply would be 32 ... R-QR1, and 33 RxP is followed by 33 ... RxB   34 RxR B-B4ch, netting a piece for Black.

32 ...   K-B3

The king makes room for 33 ... P-KN4.

33 P-R4

Which of course White's move prevents—for the moment.

33 ...   P-B5!

34 PxP   PxP

Lo and behold! The pawn majority has yielded a passed pawn, and with it definite winning chances.

35 B-B2   P-KN4!

36 PxPch   KxP

37 K-N2   N-K4

38 B-B5

Object: to destroy the blockader of his passed pawn.

38 ...   P-B6ch

39 K-B2   BxBch

40 RxB   K-B5

41 R-B7

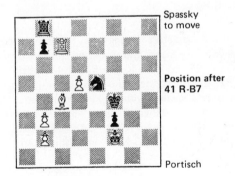

Spassky
to move

Position after
41 R-B7

Portisch

41 ...   R-QR1!

Now Spassky gladly gives up a pawn to get his rook into action.

42 RxP

Portisch accepts the gift, but he thought for 30 minutes before deciding to do so.

He could have saved the game by a pretty line of play which Spassky and his second Bondarevsky later pointed out: 42 B-K2! N-N5ch (or 42 ... . PxB 43 RxP, and the king pawn falls next) 43 K-K1 PxB 44 KxP R-QN1   45 P-Q6 N-K4   46 P-Q7 P-N4 47 R-N7, and after the loss of the pawn, the ending of rook and knight against rook is a theoretical draw.

42 ...   R-R7

43 K-K1

No chance is offered by 43 R-K7, when 43 ... RxPch 44 K-K1 (or 44 K-B1 R-N8ch   45 K-B2 N-N5 mate) P-B7ch   45 K-B1, and 45 ... K-B6 forces mate.

43 ...   K-K6

44 K-Q1   NxB

The bishop must be destroyed, as it stands guard over the pawn's queening square.

45 PxN   R-R8ch

46 K-B2   P-B7

47 R-KB7   P-B8(Q)

48 RxQ   RxR

49 K-B3   K-K5

50 K-N4

Most of the spectators thought that Portisch missed a draw with this move, and suggested this line of play: 50 P-Q6 K-K4   51 P-B5 K-Q4   52 P-N4 R-B6ch 53 K-B2, and the connected pawns assure the draw.

The indefatigable Bondarevsky demonstrated the Black win thus: 50 P-Q6 R-B8ch!   51 K-N4 K-K4 52 P-B5 K-K3   53 K-N5 K-Q2   54 P-N4 R-QN8 55 K-B4 K-B3   56 K-B3 K-N4, and White is in *zugzwang* and must lose.

50 ...   K-K4

51 K-B5   R-B1

52 Resigns

35

White **P. Keres**   Black **B. Spassky**
Ruy López
Candidates' Matches, Riga, 1965

Spassky plunges from the opening directly into the ending, skipping the midgame complications completely. In no time at all he has obtained a passed pawn.

'A passed pawn,' says Nimzowitsch, 'is a criminal who must be kept under lock and key.

Only one little pawn—but it radiates enormous power!

1 P-K4   P-K4

2 N-KB3   N-QB3

3 B-N5   P-QR3

This is the *Morphy Defence*, though played by Morphy only twice in serious games, both times against Anderssen, the result being a draw and a win for Morphy.

4 B-R4   N-B3

5 0-0   B-K2

The Closed or Strong Point Defence is based on the maintenance of a pawn at K4 as a strong point.

6 R-K1   P-QN4

Black plays this before 6 ... P-Q3, as after 7 P-B3 P-QN4 White plays 8 B-B2, and the bishop is tucked away and secure against being exchanged.

7 B-N3   P-Q3

8 P-B3   0-0

9 P-KR3

A prophylactic move, to prevent the knight's being pinned after 9 P-Q4.

9 ...   P-R3

The standard, time-honoured procedure is 9 ... N-QR4   10 B-B2 P-B4   11 P-Q4 Q-B2, which has occurred countless times in master play.

Spassky's move, known as the *Smyslov Variation*, is based on a regrouping of pieces with ... R-K1 and

... B-B1, to strengthen the K4 strong point before starting operations on the Q-side.

Moving 9 ... R-K1 at once would be premature, as 10 N-N5 in reply would send the rook scurrying back to B1.

10 P-Q4   R-K1

11 QN-Q2   B-B1

12 N-B1

The knight's destination, as in many forms of the López, is B5, by way of N3 or K3.

12 ...   B-Q2

The bishop stays on the diagonal leading to the critical square.

13 PxP

Complications could continue with 13 N-N3 N-QR4 14 B-B2 P-B4   15 P-Q5 (or 15 P-N3 first) P-B5, but Keres decides to simplify matters a bit.

13 ...   QNxP

14 NxN   PxN

15 Q-B3   P-B4

Spassky is unconcerned about his K-side, which is tightly guarded, and starts the pawns rolling on the Q-side.

16 R-Q1   P-B5

17 B-B2   Q-K2

18 P-QN3

One would expect the more vigorous 18 P-QR4 or 18 N-N3 (with a view to a K-side attack) from Keres.

18 ...   PxP

19 PxP   See diagram

19 ...   KR-B1

The rook adds pressure on the Q-side, the theatre of battle.

20 B-N2   P-QR4!

This little pawn and its successor will create trouble with every step they take.

21 N-K3   P-R5

Spassky to move

Position after 19 PxP

Keres

22 PxP   PxP

A distant passed pawn at last, but it has some giants in its path that it must slay, before it reaches the eighth square and glory.

23 P-B4

'If White did not want to allow the advance of the passed pawn,' say Tal and Koblentz, 'he could play 23 B-R3, but in that case he has to reckon with the queen sacrifice 23 ... QxB   24 RxQ BxR   25 N-Q5 NxN   26 PxN B-N7   27 Q-K4 P-N3, and Black has a nice game. Black could also reply 23 ... Q-K1 if he did not want to go in for such committal lines of play.'

23 ...   P-R6!

24 B-B3   B-R5!

Cleverly killing off White's king bishop, as otherwise 25 N-Q5 NxN   26 KPxN brings it into active play.

25 BxB   RxB

26 KR-N1   Q-K3

Begins a regrouping which Keres should have prevented with 26 Q-B5.

27 Q-Q1   See diagram on page 84

This and the previous move are strangely quiescent for an energetic Keres! Did he perhaps overlook Spassky's knight fork on the 29th move?

27 ...   NxP!

28 BxP

On 28 QxR NxB regains the exchange. The desperado bishop (so named by Lasker) wins back a

Spassky
to move

Position after
27 Q-Q1

Keres

pawn by the capture, but the difficulties (for White), increase with each reduction of pieces.

28 ...   QxB

29 QxR   N-B6

30 Q-B2   NxR

31 RxN

This is preferable to 31 QxN, when 31 . . . R-N1 lets the rook penetrate to the seventh rank.

31 ...   R-R1

Threatens 32 . . . P-R7, winning a rook.

32 Q-R2

Unhappy queen, reduced to blockading a pawn!

32 ...   B-B4

33 R-N5

Pins the bishop which was ready to eliminate the knight, White's only active piece.

33 ...   R-N1!

34 RxR   QxR

Object: 35 . . . Q-N7 and *finis*.

35 N-Q5   See diagram

White is prepared to meet 35 . . . Q-N7 with 36 QxQ PxQ 37 N-B3 B-Q5 38 N-N1.

35 ...   Q-KN6!

Plans a quick finish by 36 . . . QxBPch 37 QxQ BxQch 38 KxB P-R7, and the pawn promotes next move.

36 K-B1

Now the plan would fail, as after 36 . . . QxBPch 37 QxQ BxQ 38 N-B3 (the king does not have to capture!) and the pawn is held back.

36 ...   Q-Q6ch

37 K-K1   Q-Q5

Renews the theme of capturing twice with check.

38 Q-N3

The king may not return to B1 as 38 . . . Q-Q8 mate would follow.

38 ...   QxPch

39 K-Q1   P-R7

This last step is decisive.

40 Resigns

A last attempt to prevent queening by 40 Q-R4 fails after 40 . . . P-R8(Q)ch 41 QxQ Q-B8ch, and Black wins the queen.

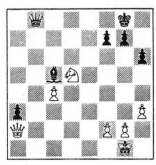

Spassky
to move

Position after
35 N-Q5

Keres

36

White **B. Larsen**   Black **B. Spassky**
Larsen's Opening
World v. U.S.S.R., Belgrade, 1970

Spassky crushes Larsen in a game that is not only a brilliancy in miniature—it is an astonishing *tour de force!*

At the time, Larsen was one of the two leading non-Soviet players (Fischer being the other) regarded as outstanding contenders for the crown of World Champion Spassky.

In this game, Larsen was facing Spassky on Board No.1 in a match between the Soviet players on one side, and a team picked from the leading masters of *The Rest of the World* on the other. (Fischer incidentally was holding down Board No.2 against Petrosian).

The first game of the four-round series between Spassky and Larsen had ended in a draw, and the watching audience anticipated a featureless draw in the second game.

Contrary to expectations though, Spassky managed to bring most of his pieces into play quickly and to penetrate his opponent's territory. A startling breakthrough followed that took Larsen (and several thousand spectators) completely by surprise, and ended the affair in short order.

The whole game took only 17 moves, with Spassky winning it by a knockout.

1 P-QN3

Larsen's play has been greatly influenced by Nimzowitsch, and like *The Great Original*, he is willing to venture on unexplored paths.

1 ...   P-K4

2 B-N2   N-QB3

3 P-QB4   N-B3

4 N-KB3

Larsen, who is fearless, welcomes the complications that attend this move. He could avoid them by playing 4 N-QB3, and then fianchettoing his king bishop.

4 ...   P-K5

5 N-Q4   B-B4

6 NxN   QPxN

Black has a doubled pawn, but in compensation he exerts pressure on the backward queen pawn.

7 P-K3   B-B4

Three units (Black's queen, king pawn, and queen

bishop) now bear down on the enemy's weakened Q3 square.

8 Q-B2   Q-K2

9 B-K2   0-0-0

Practically all of Black's pieces are in play, and poised for a K-side attack.

10 P-KB4

This leads to trouble, but good moves are hard to find. A better line (though it does not look too appetizing) is 10 BxN QxB   11 N-B3.

10 ...   N-N5!

With a multitude of threats, *par exemple:*

(a) If 11 N-B3 RxP!   12 QxR BxP   13 Q-B2 B-B7ch, and White must choose between losing his queen by a knight fork or by a discovered attack.

(b) If 11 0-0 RxP!   12 NxR NxKP   13 Q-B1 NxR dis.ch   14 KxN Q-R5   15 Q-K1 QxPch   16 N-B3 PxN   17 B(K2)xP (if 17 PxP B-R6 is mate)   17 ... B-Q6ch, and Black wins the queen.

(c) If 11 BxP KR-N1   12 B-N2 Q-R5ch   13 P-N3 NxKP!   14 PxN RxP!   15 PxR QxPch!   16 K-B1 BxP   17 B-R5 B-R6ch   18 RxB Q-N8ch   19 K-K2 Q-E7 mate (Byrne).

All three variations are pretty ways to lose.

11 P-N3

Further weakening his white squares, but Larsen keeps the queen out—or so he thinks!

11 ...   P-KR4!

12 P-KR3

And this is intended to frighten off the knight.

It's too late for quiet development, as 12 N-B3 allows 12 ... RxP!, and Black wins as in the previous note—with a variation or two added.

The scene on the board is shown on page 86.

12 ...   P-R5!

The beginning of a remarkable breakthrough that thrilled the more than 2000 spectators filling the hall to watch the match.

Spassky
to move

Position after
12 P-KR3

Larsen

None of them, I dare say, anticipated the extra-ordinary finish planned by Spassky.

13 PxN

Larsen took almost an hour before deciding to capture the knight.

He saw no hope in 13 BxN BxB   14 PxB PxP
15 R-N1 R-R8! (as happened later in the actual game)
16 RxR P-N7   17 R-N1 Q-R5ch   18 K-K2 QxPch
19 K-K1 Q-N6ch   20 K-K2 (if 20 K-Q1 Q-B7 wins)
20 . . . Q-B6ch   21 K-K1 B-K2, and threats of mate are in sight.

13 . . .   PxP

14 R-N1

Larsen played this move almost instantaneously, realizing instinctively that exchanging rooks was fatal, as after 14 RxR RxR   15 PxB R-R8ch   16 B-B1 P-N7, it's all over.

14 . . .   R-R8!!

An exciting move to bring about in grandmaster chess!

Spassky took 17 minutes on the move, to assure himself of the win, before swooping down with the rook to the eighth rank. (Morphy took 12 minutes before sacrificing his queen against Paulsen in their famous game at the First American Congress at New York in 1857.)

15 RxR

Or 15 K-B1 RxRch   16 KxR Q-R5, and mate is inevitable.

15 . . .   P-N7

16 R-B1

If 16 R-N1 Q-R5ch   17 K-Q1 Q-R8, and Black wins quickly.

16 . . .   Q-R5ch

17 K-Q1   PxR(Q)ch

18 Resigns

After 18 BxQ BxPch   19 B-K2 Q-R8 mate is the *coup de grâce*.

Smyslov

Smyslov has a love of chess, and of the beauty to be found in chess ideas. One would expect him to create works of art in his games. And so he does, but he does not let his pursuit of the aesthetic lure him from the prime object of the game—to win quickly, efficiently, and painlessly.

Smyslov has a gift for making something out of nothing, and then turning the advantage to account with the cool, dispassionate skill of a scientist. His technique is enormous, and his strategy in the middle-game shows imagination, logic, and depth of thought. Once Smyslov gets a grip on the game, it is relentless and crushing in its power. His operations are on so large a scale that many of his greatest productions are simply referred to as 'massive.'

Smyslov's openings show a wealth of originality, and he has contributed many new ideas to the Ruy López, and to the French, Grünfeld, Caro-Kann, and Nimzo-Indian Defenses.

Combination play? He is a brilliant tactician, and has produced many fine specimens of sparkling midgame combinations and slashing K-side attacks. As Bronstein once said, 'The title of positional player does not mean that a grandmaster is not gifted with amazing combinative vision.'

There is one department of the game in which Smyslov surpasses his rivals, and that is in the end-game. There he is entitled to the privilege of being considered the greatest endgame artist of the day—one whose play may be mentioned in the same breath with that of Capablanca or Rubinstein.

Smyslov's games—a blend of art and science—are a continual source of pleasure.

Smyslov's greatest triumphs in tournament play, before he became World Champion in 1957, were at Zurich 1953 in the Candidates' Tournament, and at Amsterdam 1956, also in the Candidates' Tournament. In the first-named, Smyslov came in first ahead of Bronstein, Keres, Reshevsky, Petrosian, and Geller, losing only one game out of 28 played; in the second, he came in first ahead of such élite as Keres, Spassky, Petrosian, Geller, and Bronstein, again losing only one game out of 18.

Smyslov prepared himself carefully for the Championship match with Botvinnik, by writing out about 800 of Botvinnik's games, studying them and commenting on his analytical discoveries. This bore good enough fruit to enable him to draw the first match between them, and win the second. He kept the title for a year, but then Botvinnik wrested it away from him. This was a defeat, but an honourable one, and the result of their three encounters showed that the two great masters were about evenly matched. Out of their 69 match games for the World's Championship, Smyslov won 18 games and lost 17, while 34 games were drawn.

I consider Smyslov the eighth greatest chess player of all time.

37

White **V. Smyslov**   Black **V. Makogonov**
Caro-Kann Defence
Moscow, 1944

One of Smyslov's most delightful efforts is this little-known beauty, played early in his career.

The chief performer is the queen, who dances gaily all over the board, pausing only to pick up a pawn here and there.

It isn't all honey and roses though, as there are menaces to be faced in the form of fierce-looking passed pawns.

But, as in all enchanting stories, there is a happy ending to reward the reader.

1 P-K4   P-QB3

2 P-Q4   P-Q4

3 P-KB3

The *Fantasy Variation*, a favourite line with Tartakover, who played it with success.

Two miniatures to show some pretty possibilities:

Tartakover-Przepiorka at Budapest 1929 continued: 3 . . . PxP 4 PxP P-K4 5 N-KB3 PxP 6 B-QB4 B-K3 7 BxB PxB 8 0-0! B-K2 9 NxP Q-Q2 10 Q-R5ch K-Q1 (if 10 . . . P-N3 11 Q-K5 wins) 11 B-K3 P-B4 12 R-Q1 PxN 13 RxP B-Q3 14 P-K5 N-KB3 15 PxN PxP 16 N-B3 Resigns, as after 16 . . . N-B3 17 RxB QxR 18 R-Q1 wins the queen.

Kiriloff-Grigoriev at Moscow 1931 went this way: 3 . . . PxP 4 PxP P-K4 5 N-KB3 PxP 6 B-QB4 B-K3 (if 6 . . . B-N5ch 7 P-B3 PxP 8 BxPch KxB 9 QxQ PxP dis.ch 10 K-K2 PxR(Q) 11 N-N5ch and White mates quickly) 7 BxB PxB 8 0-0! Q-K2 9 B-N5 Q-B4 10 P-QN4! Q-N3 (on 10 . . . QxNP instead, there is a nice finish by 11 N-K5 N-KR3 12 BxN PxB 13 Q-R5ch K-K2 14 R-B7ch K-Q3 15 N-Q3 Q-N4 16 N-R3! QxQ 17 N-B4 mate) 11 N-K5 P-Q6 dis.ch 12 K-R1 Q-Q5 13 RxBch! KxR 14 Q-B3ch N-B3 15 BxN K-K1 16 P-B3

Q-Q3 17 BxP R-B1 18 QxRch Resigns. Back to Moscow, 1944.

3 . . .   P-K3

Black shuns the unknown perils, and hopes to turn the game into a variation of the French Defence by something like this: 4 N-B3 N-B3 5 P-K5 KN-Q2 6 P-B4 P-QB4 7 N-B3 N-QB3, with a fair game.

4 B-K3   Q-N3

Attacks the knight pawn, and prepares to dispute control of the centre by 5 . . . P-QB4, the customary strategy to cope with White's body of pawns.

5 N-Q2   N-Q2

If at once 5 . . . P-QB4, then 6 KPxP KPxP 7 PxP BxP 8 BxB QxB 9 N-N3 leaves Black with an isolated queen pawn to worry about.

6 B-Q3   P-QB4

7 P-B3   P-B5

8 B-QB2   QxNP

Makogonov disregards the Hungarian proverb: It is never safe to capture the queen knight pawn—even when it is safe!

9 N-K2   Q-R6

10 0-0   N-N3

11 PxP   PxP

12 R-K1

In return for the pawn he sacrificed, White has most of his pieces poised for action.

12 . . .   B-Q2

13 N-KB1   0-0-0   See diagram on page 91

14 B-B1

The queen must be dislodged from her strong position, so that the queen rook pawn may be free to advance.

14 . . .   Q-R4

15 P-QR4   B-Q3

16 N-K3   N-K2

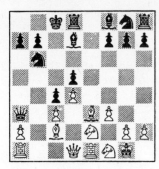

Makogonov

Position after
13 . . . 0-0-0

Smyslov
to move

Makogonov

Position after
23 . . . P-B4

Smyslov
to move

17 B-Q2   QR-K1

This provides a flight square for the queen, who
now has little mobility.

18 N-N3

By this threat of 19 N-R5, Smyslov hopes to induce
Black to weaken his pawn position with 18 . . . P-N3.

18 . . .   P-R4

This is superior to 18 . . . P-N3, after which there
follows 19 N-N4, and the prospect of further intrusion by 20 N-B6 or 20 N-K5 would compel an
exchange of pieces to White's advantage.

19 N(K3)-B5   NxN

20 NxN   BxN

21 BxBch   K-N1

22 P-B4

Obviously this is to enable the queen to get into the
game by way of KB3.

  The move is singular nevertheless: It limits the
range of both black-squared bishops at one stroke!

22 . . .   P-N3

23 B-B2   P-B4

And this reduces the range of Smyslov's white-
squared bishop. Makogonov seems to be building a
bomb-proof shelter, and it is difficult to picture how
Smyslov will break through.

24 Q-B3

The queen starts out on a journey, 'to traverse
climes beyond the western main.'

24 . . .   R-K5

'A fine positional idea,' says Smyslov, 'which is the
logical complement of Black's previous strategy:
White's activity after 25 Q-N3 is curtailed. If now
25 BxR, then 25 . . . QPxB   26 Q-N3 R-N1 followed
by 27 . . . N-Q4, and Black's position is impregnable.'

25 Q-N3!   R-N1

26 Q-N5   B-K2

27 Q-R6   B-B3

28 Q-R7   R-N2

29 Q-R8ch   N-B1

30 BxR

White accepts the offer of a rook for his bishop, now
that the knight is unable (for the time being) to
occupy the good defensive square Q4.

30 . . .   QPxB

31 Q-B8   Q-Q1

32 Q-N4

Smyslov refrains from the exchange of queens, preferring to keep his opponent on the run, with little time
to reorganize his forces.

32 . . .   R-QB2

33 P-R5   P-R3
34 QR-N1

Black has nothing to fear yet, but Smyslov threatens to threaten.

34 ...   B-K2
35 Q-R4   Q-Q2
36 Q-R2   Q-Q4
37 R-N2   N-R2

Smyslov's queen has been beaten back, and it would appear that Black might assume the initiative.

38 R-N6

Smyslov must have made this move instantly, as otherwise 38 . . . N-N4 would make Black's position air-tight.

38 ...   N-B3

Black plays to win the queen rook pawn, thereby creating a passed pawn for himself. A safer course was 38 . . . R-B3, offering an exchange of rooks.

39 R(K1)-N1   K-B1
40 Q-N2

Triple attack! After this powerful move Black must part with his queen knight pawn, or his king knight pawn!

40 ...   NxRP
41 RxKNP

Destroys the base of Black's pawn chain, making the other K-side pawns vulnerable to attack.

41 ...   N-N6
42 B-K3   P-R4
43 Q-K2   P-QR5
44 R-N2   Q-R4
45 R-N8ch   B-Q1
46 R-R2   P-N4
47 QxRP   QxP

Black has created promising counterchances. His three connected passed pawns look menacing, and he threatens mate in one.

Has the hunted become the hunter?

48 QxPch   R-Q2
49 K-B2   Q-R4

The tempting 49 . . . NxP loses to 50 Q-B5ch K-N2 51 R-Q2, and White wins a piece.

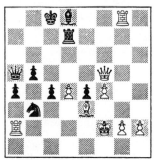

Makogonov

Position after
49 . . . Q-R4

Smyslov
to move

50 Q-K6!   Q-B2
51 P-B5   K-N2

A desperate try to free his pieces from the pins.

52 R-N6

This will hurt a bit! White aims at winning the queen by 53 Q-R6ch K-N1   54 R-QB6 Q-N2 55 B-B4ch B-B2   56 R-QN6, and Black again succumbs to the power of a pin.

52 ...   K-B1
53 QxKP

Once again threatening the life of the queen.

53 ...   Q-N2
54 R-B6ch   K-N1
55 P-Q5

Clears another diagonal for the bishop, supports the rook, cuts down the scope of the adverse rook, and advances a passed pawn—four achievements at one blow! What more can one little move by a pawn accomplish?

55 ...   N-R4
56 Q-K5ch   K-R1

57 Q-K6

New threats loom up, such as 58 R-R6ch K-N1
59 B-B4ch K-B1 (if 59 . . . R-B2   60 R-N6 wins the
queen)   60 R-B6ch B-B2   61 RxBch, and again
White wins the queen.

57 . . .   K-N1

58 R-N2

Smyslov is ready to meet 58 . . . P-R6 with 59 RxNP!
QxR(N4)   60 QxR NxR   61 PxN, and there is no
way to ward off his threats.

58 . . .   N-N6

59 B-B4ch   K-R2

60 R-R6ch   Resigns

After 60 . . . QxR   61 QxRch, and White wins the
bishop and the game.

38

White **V. Smyslov**   Black **I. Rudakovsky**
Sicilian Defence
Moscow, 1945

For many years chess masters, writers, and teachers of
the game, have stressed control of the centre as a necessary preliminary to an attack on the wings.

In the 1930s (to go no further back than that)
Capablanca said clearly and simply, 'Control of the centre
is essential to a successful attack against the king.'

In the 40s, Fine elaborated on the theme by saying,
'The centre retains its importance throughout the game
because it is the region of maximum mobility. Combinations are most effective when the pieces are in or near
the centre; attacks should not be begun unless control
or neutralization of the centre is assured.'

In the 70s, modern theoreticians confirm these
admonitions. Sokolsky, for example, says, 'One of the
prerequisites for an attack is control of the centre. It is
easier to bring the forces from the centre to the K-side

and often an opponent who has lost control of the
centre finds his forces in scattered disarray.'

Smyslov, who is well aware of the importance of
the center, is always on the *qui vive* for the right
opportunity to come along.

A golden opportunity does present itself in the
form of a square in the centre—a square which could
be a magnificent outpost for a knight. Unfortunately
though, there are two pieces standing guard over the
critical square.

How Smyslov disposes of the two guardians, secures
the outpost for his knight, and then launches a K-side
attack is the substance of the following story:

1 P-K4   P-QB4

2 N-KB3   P-K3

3 P-Q4   PxP

4 NxP   N-KB3

5 N-QB3   P-Q3

This prevents 6 P-K5, and is preferable to the
aggressive 5 . . . B-N5. Play after that might run as
follows: 6 P-K5 N-K5   7 Q-N4! Q-R4   8 QxN
BxNch 9 PxB QxPch   10 K-Q1 QxR   11 N-N5
P-Q4 12 PxP *en passant* N-R3   13 B-Q3!, with
advantage to White.

6 B-K2   B-K2

7 0-0   0-0

8 B-K3   N-B3

9 P-B4   Q-B2

10 Q-K1

The queen is headed for N3, where she will be
strongly placed for attack.

Meanwhile, the square Q1 has been cleared for the
convenience of the queen rook.

10 . . .   NxN

11 BxN   P-K4

This thrust at the bishop seems a bit risky. Modest
development by 11 . . . B-Q2 and 12 . . . B-B3 has
its good points.

12 B-K3

Smyslov prefers this to 12 PxP PxP   13 Q-N3
B-QB4, when the consequent exchange of bishops
reduces White's attacking chances.

12 . . .   B-K3

Plausible, as the bishop guards the square Q4, but
this purpose could have better been served by
12 . . . B-Q2 and 13 . . . B-B3.

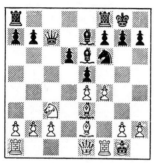

Rudakovsky

Position after
12 . . . B-K3

Smyslov
to move

13 P-B5!

This is the move White wanted to make, but now he
does so with gain of time.

13 . . .   B-B5

There was still time for 13 . . . B-Q2, though White
could complicate matters with 14 P-KN4 B-B3
15 B-B3 P-Q4   16 PxP P-K5   17 NxP NxQP, when
White enjoys a slight advantage.

　　Black's actual move is a strategic error, as Smyslov
promptly demonstrates.

14 BxB   QxB

The disappearance of Black's queen bishop rids the
board of one of the defenders of his Q4 square.

15 B-N5!

Now Smyslov sets about disposing of the other!

　　As he himself says, 'An instructive example of how
to take advantage of the weakness at Q5 in such positions. The exchange at KB6 is unavoidable, whereupon the white knight becomes firmly entrenched

at Q5. This gives White good prospects of a direct
attack on the king.'

15 . . .   KR-K1

16 BxN   BxB

17 N-Q5   B-Q1

The bishop pawn is safe from harm, as after 17 . . .
QxBP   18 R-B2 Q-B4   19 R-QB1, followed by
20 N-B7, costs Black the exchange.

18 P-B3   P-QN4

19 P-QN3   Q-B4ch

20 K-R1   R-QB1

21 R-B3   K-R1

Passive defence by 21 . . . P-B3 has its drawbacks.
The scope of Black's bishop is cut down, and the
king's position is still not safe from assault by the
heavy pieces, beginning with 22 Q-R4 and 23 R-R3.

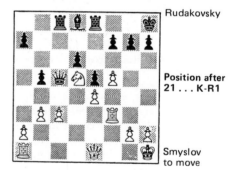

Rudakovsky

Position after
21 . . . K-R1

Smyslov
to move

22 P-B6!

This forces a breach in the pawn barrier shielding
the king.

22 . . .   PxP

Immediate loss follows 22 . . . P-N3   23 Q-Q2 R-KN1
24 Q-R6, for the threat of mate by 25 QxPch is
decisive.

　　Or if 22 . . . BxP   23 NxB PxN   24 Q-R4
(threatens mate in four, beginning with 25 QxBPch)
24 . . . R-K3   25 R-R3 K-N2   26 Q-R6ch K-N1
27 R-N3ch, and mate next move.

23 Q-R4   R-KN1

24 NxP

Threatens 25 QxP mate—a queen-and-knight mate.

24 . . .   R-N2

25 R-N3

Now the threat is 26 QxPch RxQ   27 R-N8 mate—
a rook-and-knight mate.

25 . . .   BxN

A pretty possibility is 25 . . . B-K2   26 RxR KxR
27 QxPch KxN   28 Q-R6 mate.

26 QxB

Threatens an immediate queen-and-rook mate.

26 . . .   R-KN1

27 R-Q1   P-Q4

28 RxR!

More efficient than 28 RxP Q-KB1, and Black's
queen is safe for the time being.

28 . . .   Resigns

The recapture by 28 . . . RxR allows 29 RxP, and
White wins the queen, whether or not she returns to
KB1.

39

White **V. Smyslov**   Black **S. Reshevsky**
Ruy López
U.S.A.-U.S.S.R. Radio Match, 1945

Smyslov's game against Reshevsky, played in the radio
match between teams representing the United States and
the Soviet Union, took an exciting turn when Smyslov
sacrificed his queen for a rook and bishop. True, he was
left with two powerful bishops, but in compensation for
this, Reshevsky had a flock of dangerous pawns under
his command.

Despite the fact that Smyslov enjoyed the advantage
of being more familiar with the analysis of this line of the
López than his redoubtable opponent, the game between

them is a masterpiece, of historical importance, and
worthy of the players and the occasion.

1 P-K4   P-K4

2 N-KB3   N-QB3

3 B-N5   P-QR3

4 B-R4   N-B3

5 0-0   NxP

Unusual for Reshevsky, who generally plays 5 . . .
B-K2, the Closed Defence.

Did Reshevsky have something especially prepared
for the occasion?

6 P-Q4   P-QN4

7 B-N3   P-Q4

8 PxP   B-K3

9 P-B3

Keres's continuation 9 Q-K2, followed by 10 R-Q1,
exerting pressure on the queen file, is an excellent
alternative.

9 . . .   B-QB4

This leads to sharper play than the customary 9 . . .
B-K2. One drawback to Reshevsky's move, though, is
that it lets White gain a tempo by an attack on the
bishop when the queen knight moves to Q2 and
then to N3.

10 QN-Q2   0-0

11 B-B2   P-B4

Black avoids 11 . . . NxN   12 QxN, after which White
can continue with 13 Q-Q3, forcing black to weaken
his K-side pawns.

12 N-N3   B-N3

13 KN-Q4   NxN

14 NxN   BxN

Reshevsky could have avoided complications with
14 . . . Q-K2, or 14 . . . Q-Q2 and 15 . . . P-B3, but
he plunged cheerfully into a sacrificial line of play
that he was familiar with.

As it happened, the Soviet players had analyzed this line thoroughly—and published their findings in *Schachmaty* several months before this game was played—and knew more about its intricacies than did Reshevsky.

15 PxB   P-B5

16 P-B3   N-N6

This offer of the knight goes back as far as the game between Fleissig and Mackenzie, played at Vienna in 1882.

Reshevsky's comment after the game is revealing, 'Had I known at that time that Smyslov made his first fifteen moves in one minute, indicating a thorough familiarity with the variation, I would have been more discreet.'

Being discreet had its troubles too at this stage, as after 16 . . . N-N4   17 P-KR4 N-B2   18 BxP QxP 19 Q-Q2, White has the better prospects.

Reshevsky

Position after 16 . . . N-N6

Smyslov to move

17 PxN   PxP

18 Q-Q3

White intends to parry 18 . . . Q-R5 with 19 QxPch QxQ   20 BxQch KxB   21 B-Q2, followed by 22 B-K1 and 23 BxP, and the extra pawn should carry the day.

Or if 18 . . . P-N3 instead, then 19 Q-K3 Q-R5 20 Q-R6 puts an end to threats against the king.

Smyslov's 18 Q-Q3 move is an improvement on Duras's 18 R-K1, which he played against Maroczy at Ostend in 1906. Duras won the game, though not convincingly, for the position reached when Maroczy resigned appears to be no more than a draw.

18 . . .   B-B4

19 QxB!   RxQ

20 BxR

This queen sacrifice, prepared for by White's 18th move, is the contribution of Boleslavsky.

20 . . .   Q-R5

21 B-R3

The only defence, but it does the trick.

21 . . .   QxPch

22 K-R1   QxKP

'With only a queen for rook and two bishops,' says Reshevsky, 'Black must try to pick up as many pawns as possible. His one chance to get his resulting passed pawns in motion is before White's bishop gets to work.'

23 B-Q2

Fine writes in *The world's a chessboard*, 'Hereabouts we radioed for time consumed by the other team. Reshevsky, who had taken about an hour and a half for the first 23 moves, discovered to his dismay that Smyslov had taken exactly one minute! The whole variation, we later discovered, had been published in the June 1945 issue of *Schachmaty* (official Soviet chess magazine). Foreign material has always taken a long time to reach the United States, and during the war the delay was of course much worse than before.'

'Actually,' says Chernev, 'hardly anyone on the team ever looked at material published in foreign chess magazines. Had they done so, they would have found that the play up to this point was not new, but had occurred in several games played in 1942 and 1943, notably Boleslavsky against Ragozin, Moscow 1943, Cortlever against Euwe, Amsterdam 1942, and Boleslavsky against Botvinnik, Sverdlovsk 1943—to name some of the games.'

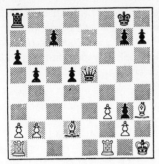

Reshevsky
to move

Position after
23 B-Q2

Smyslov

23 ...   QxP

This may be a bit greedy. Better chances were offered
by 23 . . . P-B4 24 QR-K1 QxP 25 B-B4 P-Q5
26 BxP P-Q6 27 B-K5 QxRP 28 B-Q6, with possibilities for both sides, as in Boleslavsky-Botvinnik,
Sverdlovsk 1943 (Yes, Virginia, we're still in the
books.)

24 B-B4   P-B4

Reshevsky could have put up stouter resistance with
24 . . . P-Q5, but he was terribly short of time at this
stage.

25 B-K6ch   K-R1

26 BxQP   R-Q1

The seemingly powerful 26 . . . Q-Q5, with an attack
on both bishops and an incipient threat of mate, is
easily refuted by 27 B-K4 followed by 28 BxNP.

27 QR-Q1   P-B5

28 BxNP

Interesting play follows 28 BxBP RxR 29 RxR
Q-B3 30 B-K6 P-R3 (but not 30 . . . P-N3, when
31 R-Q8ch lets White win neatly) and Black wins.

28 ...   P-B6

Reshevsky does not snap at 28 . . . QxRP, when
29 BxP RxR 30 RxR leaves him helpless.

29 B-K5!

Look at those beautiful bishops!

29 ...   P-N5

Smyslov was prepared to meet 29 . . . Q-K7 with
30 BxP (not 30 KR-K1 P-B7!) 30 . . . RxB 31 QR-K1
R-R4ch   32 K-N1, and White's threat of mate is conclusive.

30 B-QN3   R-Q7

31 P-B4!

Now the threat is 32 RxR QxR 33 R-Q1, and
death on the last rank.

31 ...   P-KR4

32 R-QN1   R-KB7

Reshevsky, pressed for time, puts up a hard fight.

33 KR-K1

Naturally, Smyslov does not go in for 33 RxQ,
when 33 . . . RxRch 34 K-R2 PxR 35 BxP RxP
leaves Black with a rook and two pawns against the
two bishops, with fair drawing chances.

33 ...   Q-Q7

Further opposition on the seventh rank fails; e.g.
33 . . . R-K7 34 R(K1)-Q1 R-Q7 35 RxQ and wins,
as the rook on Q1 is defended.

34 QR-Q1   Q-N7

Smyslov refutes 34 . . . R-K7 with 35 R-KN1 Q-K6
36 R-Q8ch K-R2   37 B-N8ch K-N3   38 R-Q6ch
K-B4   39 B-R7ch, and White has a winning attack.

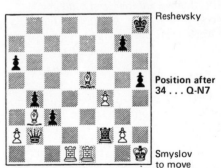

Reshevsky

Position after
34 . . . Q-N7

Smyslov
to move

Now half-a-dozen checks bring about the dénouement.

35 R-Q8ch   K-R2

36 B-N8ch   K-N3

Reshevsky says, 'I had enough seconds left to appreciate the beauty of 36 . . . K-R3   37 R-Q6ch P-N3   38 R-Q7 P-N4   38 R-Q6 mate! What bishops!'

37 R-Q6ch   K-B4

38 B-K6ch   K-N3

39 B-Q5 dis.ch   K-R2

40 B-K4ch   K-N1

If 40 . . . P-N3   41 R-Q8 forces mate.

41 B-N6   Resigns

On 41 . . . K-B1, White can choose between 42 R-K6 followed by 43 R-K8 mate, or 42 R-Q8ch K-K2 43 B-B6 dbl.ch KxB   44 R-Q6 mate.

40

White **V. Smyslov**   Black **C. Kottnauer**
Sicilian Defence
Groningen, 1946

Smyslov scintillates in this masterpiece in miniature.

A slight inaccuracy by his opponent in the opening offers an alert Smyslov the opportunity to whip up an attack.

One sacrifice follows another, and suddenly all Smyslov's pieces spring to life. A couple of lightning strokes, and Kottnauer's position is thoroughly demolished.

1 P-K4   P-QB4

2 N-KB3   P-Q3

3 P-Q4   PxP

4 NxP   N-KB3

5 N-QB3   P-QR3

6 B-K2   P-K3

7 0-0   P-QN4

A risky demonstration in view of Black's undeveloped position. Much better is the Paulsen procedure of 7 . . . Q-B2, followed by 8 . . . B-K2 and castling. Black's game then may look cramped, but it is solid, and offers chances for counter-attack.

8 B-B3!

Smyslov pounces like a tiger on the long diagonal—a diagonal which his opponent dare not dispute.

If 8 . . . B-N2   9 P-K5! PxP   10 BxB R-R2 11 N-B6 NxN (definitely not 11 . . . QxQ   12 RxQ RxB   13 R-Q8 mate)   12 BxNch N-Q2   13 B-K3 R-B2   14 B-N6, and White wins.

8 . . .   R-R2

9 Q-K2!

A subtle move, and far superior to the obvious 9 B-K3, with overt designs on the rook. The move 9 B-K3 would be met adequately by 9 . . . R-Q2 followed by 10 . . . B-N2 and the advance of the queen pawn.

After Smyslov's move, the reply 9 . . . R-Q2 is unsatisfactory, as after 10 P-K5! PxP   11 N-B6 Q-B2 12 NxN QxN   13 B-B6, White wins the exchange.

9 . . .   R-B2

Black must therefore deploy his rook to B2 instead, where it is unhappily placed, interfering as it does with the movements of the queen.

It's worthy of note that Kottnauer had not expected 9 Q-K2, as he admitted after the game.

10 R-Q1   QN-Q2

11 P-QR4

Trouble! Trouble!

This powerful move initiates an attack on the weakened Q-side.

11 . . .   PxP

If 11 . . . P-N5   12 N-R2 P-QR4   13 N-N5 and the rook has no safe refuge. On 13 . . . R-B3   14 P-K5 N-Q4   15 BxN PxB and 16 PxP dis.ch is fatal. Or if 13 . . . R-B4   14 B-K3 traps the hapless rook.

12 NxRP   B-N2

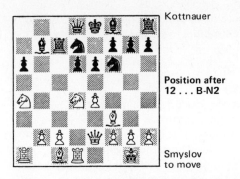

Kottnauer

Position after
12 . . . B-N2

Smyslov
to move

13 P-K5!
Smyslov strikes while the iron is hot. Black is given no time to complete his development.

13 . . .   NxP
The other possibilities are:

(a) 13 . . . PxP   14 BxB PxN   15 BxP, and the queen pawn will fall—or worse.

(b) 13 . . . BxB   14 NxB PxP, and the rook pawn is not long for this world.

14 BxB   RxB

15 QxP   Q-N1

16 N-B6   NxN

17 QxNch   N-Q2

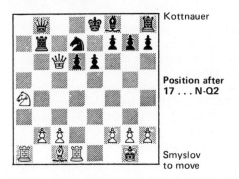

Kottnauer

Position after
17 . . . N-Q2

Smyslov
to move

It would seem that little harm can come to Black, but Smyslov uncorks a beautiful and original combination, whereby all his pieces are enabled to take part in the attack.

18 N-B5!!
Smyslov gives this move two exclamation marks. I can award it no less.

Should Black now refuse the knight, and move 18 . . . R-B2, White finishes him off with 19 NxN RxN 20 R-R8 pinning the queen.

18 . . .   PxN
If Kottnauer now expected 19 RxN RxR   20 R-R8 QxR   21 QxRch, leaving him with two rooks for the queen, he was sadly disappointed.

19 B-B4!
The point of the first sacrifice! Smyslov gave away a knight to clear the path for the offer of a bishop!

19 . . .   B-Q3
Accepting the bishop instead would not help: 19 . . . QxB   20 Q-B8ch K-K2   21 QxR K-B3 22 RxN K-N3   23 P-KN3 Q-B4   24 R-R7, and the heavy pieces penetrate with irresistible effect.

20 BxB   R-N3

21 QxNch!   Resigns
After 21 . . . KxQ   22 BxQ dis.ch, the ending would be a breeze for Smyslov.

41

White **V. Smyslov**   Black **A. Denker**
Sicilian Defence
Match U.S.A.-U.S.S.R., Moscow, 1946

Smyslov's victory over Denker won the prize for the best-played game in the 1946 match between United States and Soviet Union's chess masters.

It is a fine specimen of the strategy of blockade, a theme greatly to the taste of Nimzowitsch.

It is an equally admirable illustration of *zugzwang*, another of Nimzowitsch's favourite concepts.

Smyslov achieves a picturesque finale in his *zug-zwang* effect, when he brings about an arrangement consisting of seven pawns and pieces in one straight line along a diagonal!

1 P-K4   P-QB4

2 N-QB3   N-QB3

3 P-KN3   P-KN3

4 B-N2   B-N2

5 P-Q3   P-K3

6 B-K3   N-Q5

7 QN-K2

A refinement introduced by Smyslov, and superior to the routine 7 KN-K2.

Smyslov's move clears the way for building up a strong pawn center by 8 P-QB3 and 9 P-Q4.

7 . . .   P-Q3

If Black goes pawn-hunting by 7 . . . NxN   8 NxN BxP   9 R-QN1 Q-R4ch   10 B-Q2 QxP, the boomerang combination   11 RxB QxR   12 B-QB3 followed by 13 BxR regains material with advantage to White.

8 P-QB3   N-QB3

9 P-Q4   PxP

10 NxP

The attempt to establish a strong pawn center by 10 PxP is neutralized by 10 . . . P-Q4   11 PxP PxP, followed by 12 . . . KN-K2.

10 . . .   NxN

11 BxN   P-K4

Denker does not exchange bishops, as that would deprive his K-side of a valuable defender, so he tries to dislodge the enemy bishop from its centralized position.

The move is natural enough, but it saddles him with a backward pawn on an open file, and cuts down the scope of his king bishop as well.

Routine development by 11 . . . N-B3 was the

proper specific to avoid a dangerous weakening of the pawn structure

12 B-K3   N-K2

13 N-K2   0-0

14 0-0   B-K3

Denker is now ready to rid himself of the backward pawn, and free his game as well, by playing 15 . . . P-Q4 next move.

But Smyslov, who is thoroughly familiar with the Nimzowitsch formula 'Restrain! Blockade! Destroy!,' is prepared to use these mighty weapons.

Denker

Position after 14 . . . B-K3

Smyslov to move

15 Q-Q2!

Now the strategic thrust 15 . . . P-Q4 will be refuted by the tactical reply 16 B-B5!, winning a pawn for White.

15 . . .   Q-B2

This guards against the bishop's *coup* (mentioned in the previous note) and plans 16 . . . KR-Q1 followed by 17 . . . P-Q4.

White would like to restrain the queen pawn once for all by P-QB4, but if he tries to prepare the move by 16 P-N3, the reply 16 . . . P-QN4 puts an end to that little scheme.

How then can Smyslov enforce P-QB4?

16 KR-B1!

Here's how! This rook move, as subtle as it is strong, will be the means of enforcing 17 P-QB4, the strategical device to cramp Black's game severely.

Smyslov shows that 16 . . . P-QN4 would be bad, if not fatal, for Black: 16 . . . P-QN4   17 P-QR4 P-QR3   18 R-Q1. Then if:

(a) 18 . . . QR-Q1   19 PxP PxP   20 R-R7!

(b) 18 . . . KR-Q1   19 PxP PxP   20 RxR RxR 21 QxP.

(c) 18 . . . B-N6   19 QxP QxQ   20 RxQ BxP 21 N-B1, and the threat of 22 P-N3 is decisive.

16 . . .   P-B4

So—Denker tries to initiate complications on the K-side, to distract Smyslov from the pursuit of his strategical objectives.

17 P-QB4   PxP

Denker

Position after 17 . . . PxP

Smyslov to move

18 N-B3!

A fine move. Smyslov indicates this beautiful refutation of 18 . . . BxP: 19 NxP P-Q4   20 N-N5 P-Q5 21 N-K6 PxB   22 QxP Q-Q3   23 NxR B-B2 (if 23 . . . B-Q4   24 BxBch NxB   25 Q-B5 BxN   26 QxQ BxQ   27 R-Q1!)   24 R-Q1 N-Q4   25 Q-N3 R-Q1 26 NxNP! PxN   27 BxN BxB   28 RxB QxR 29 R-Q1!, and wins. (A superb illustration of the power of a pin).

18 . . .   N-B4

19 NxP

White's knight is centralized, his king bishop has the use of a long diagonal and pressure has been maintained against his opponent's position.

What more could mortal man desire?

19 . . .   NxB

20 QxN   P-KR3

21 R-Q1

Smyslov regroups his rooks, this one bearing down on the QP, while the other will support his QBP.

21 . . .   KR-Q1

If 21 . . . BxP   22 QR-B1 (better than 22 NxP) 22 . . . P-Q4   23 RxP (threatens 24 R-B5 and 24 P-N3)   23 . . . Q-B2   24 N-Q6, and the bishop is doomed.

22 QR-B1   QR-B1

23 P-N3   P-N3

24 N-B3

Smyslov now aims at an exchange of white-squared bishops. His knight or a rook could then dominate the board at Q5, a square from whence it could not be dislodged. Black would be left with the 'bad' bishop, one hampered in its movements by pawns occupying squares of the same colour.

24 . . .   Q-K2

25 B-Q5   K-R2

26 BxB   QxB

27 R-Q3   R-B2

28 R(B1)-Q1   R-B2

Denker tries for a counter-attack on the king bishop file, as the queen pawn can not be adequately defended.

29 N-K4   B-B1

30 R-Q5   Q-N5

31 R(Q1)-Q3

Smyslov carefully sidesteps the little trap 31 NxP BxN   32 RxB QxRch!   33 RxQ RxRch, and Black has excellent drawing chances.

31 . . .   B-K2

Denker in turn avoids stubborn defence of the pawn, as it could lead to this: 31 . . . Q-K3   32 Q-Q2 R(B2)-Q2   33 P-B5 NPxP   34 NxBP, and White wins the exchange.

32　NxP

Last step in the process: Destroy!

32 . . .　BxN

33　RxB　R(Q1)-KB1

34　QxKP　RxP

It looks as though something might be developing for Black, but Smyslov has calculated everything with cold-blooded precision.

35　R-Q7ch　R(B7)-B2

36　RxRch　RxR

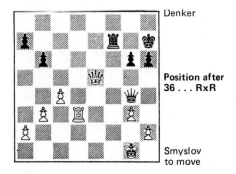

Denker

Position after 36 . . . RxR

Smyslov to move

37　R-Q8!

With a threat of mate that relegates Black's rook to a passive role.

Despite the wide-open position, Black strangely enough does not have a single check that might postpone his inevitable doom.

37 . . .　R-KN2

38　Q-K8　P-KN4

39　Q-R8ch　K-N3

40　R-Q6ch　K-B2

41　QxP　Q-B4

42　R-Q1　Q-B4ch

43　K-N2　Q-K2

44　R-B1ch　K-N1

45　Q-KB6　Q-K1

46　Q-B5

Once more Smyslov regroups his pieces—this time for the final assault.

46 . . .　P-N5

47　R-B2　Q-K2

48　Q-Q3　R-N4

Denker's queen check at N2 would be countered by Smyslov's queen check at Q5, and the ensuing exchange of queens would leave White with an easily won rook ending.

49　R-K2　Q-B1

50　Q-K4　R-N2

51　Q-Q5ch　Q-B2

On 51 . . . R-B2　52 R-KB2 forces a wholesale exchange of pieces, while 51 . . . K-R2 yields to 52 Q-R5ch K-N1　53 R-K8, and White wins the queen.

52　R-K6!

This is the pretty picture:

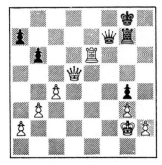

Denker to move

Position after 52 R-K6!

Smyslov

Smyslov fills up the diagonal and creates a beautiful semi-*zugzwang*, to finish this great game.

If the rook moves, say to R2, then 53 Q-Q8ch K-N2 (or 53 . . . Q-B1　54 R-K8)　54 R-K7 wins the queen.

If the queen moves to QB2, there follows 53 R-K8 dbl.ch K-R2　54 Q-R5 mate. Or if the queen moves to B1, 53 R-K8 dis.ch wins the queen.

If the king moves to R1, 53 R-R6ch K-N1 (on 53 . . . R-R2 54 QxQ leaves the rook unable to recapture) 54 Q-K8ch Q-B1 55 R-R8ch wins the queen.

If 52 . . . K-R2 53 Q-K4ch K-R1 54 R-K8ch R-N1 55 R-K7! Q-R4 (to guard his R2 square) 56 Q-Q4ch, and White forces mate.

Black's only move is 52 . . . Q-N2, pinning the White queen, and even that succumbs to the brutal 53 QxQ RxQ 54 R-N6ch R-N2 55 RxRch, with an elementary pawn ending.

52 . . . Resigns

42

White **V. Smyslov**   Black **S. Reshevsky**
Ruy López
Moscow, 1948

Smyslov gets a positional advantage early in the game. He has a knight beautifully placed in the center, a rook bearing down on the queen file, and a couple of energetic bishops. This gives him an iron grip on the game which increases move by move in the style reminiscent of Tarrasch.

To avoid being crushed to the wall, Reshevsky is forced to weaken his pawn position. This is all that Smyslov needs to bring it down to an ending, which he conducts as skillfully as Rubinstein ever did.

Altogether it is a fine performance by Smyslov against an opponent notably difficult to subdue.

1 P-K4   P-K4

2 N-KB3   N-QB3

3 B-N5   P-QR3

4 B-R4   P-Q3

5 P-B3   KN-K2

Steinitz favoured this development of the knight, as it can swing over to N3 and secure the strong point K4.

6 P-Q4   B-Q2

7 B-N3

Obviously with the intention of continuing with 8 N-N5, and a double attack on the delicate bishop pawn.

7 . . .   P-KR3

8 QN-Q2

Customary strategy in many forms of the López, the idea is to maneuver the knight to Q5, a fine outpost in the center, by way of QB4 and K3.

8 . . .   N-N3

9 N-B4

To delay this move, and castle instead, would permit Black to play 9 . . . N-B5, and then secure the knight in its advanced position by 10 . . . P-KN4.

9 . . .   B-K2

10 0-0   0-0

11 N-K3   B-B3

12 N-Q5   R-K1

Reshevsky tries to improve on the game Euwe-Keres, played in the first round of the same tournament, where Keres moved 12 . . . PxP, and the continuation was 13 NxQP R-K1 14 NxBch QxN 15 P-B3 N-B5 (threatens to win a pawn by 16 . . . NxN 17 PxN QxP 18 QxQ N-K7ch) 16 NxN BxN 17 B-K3, with the better game for White.

Reshevsky's move gives Smyslov the opportunity to obtain a slight positional edge.

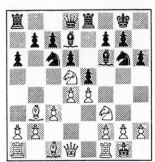

Reshevsky

Position after 12 . . . R-K1

Smyslov to move

13 PxP!

An exclamation point for this move! White gets the advantage with this capture, no matter how the opponent recaptures—and he has five different ways of doing so!

If 13 . . . PxP 14 NxBch PxN (but not 14 . . . QxN, as 15 QxB wins a piece for White) 15 BxRP, and White wins a pawn.

If 13 . . . KNxP 14 NxN NxN   15 P-KB4 N-B3 (on 15 . . . N-N5 16 P-KR3 wins a pawn) 16 Q-B3, with a fine position for White.

13 . . .   BxP

14 NxB   PxN

15 Q-B3

The queen is strongly placed here, while her departure from Q1 leaves room for the rook to make its presence felt.

15 . . .   B-K3

Reshevsky is anxious to be rid of the annoying knight which paralyzes most of his pieces. If he tries to do so by 15 . . . N-R4 16 B-B2 P-QB3, then after 17 N-K3 the knight will come in at B5 with equally disturbing effect.

16 R-Q1

Not only does the rook exert pressure on the file, but it institutes two threats of winning material by discovered attack. One is by 17 N-N6, netting the exchange, the other by 17 BxP PxB 18 N-B6ch, winning the queen for rook and bishop.

16 . . .   BxN

17 RxB

Very good, as White obtains control of the queen file, but 17 PxB had its points: if then 17 . . . P-K5 18 Q-N4, and the threats of 19 PxN as well as 19 QxN!, would set some problems for Black.

17 . . .   Q-K2

18 Q-B5!

Simple and strong! The threat is 19 R-Q7 winning instantly, as the queen is attacked, and also the

tender bishop pawn behind the queen.

There is also a hidden attack on the king knight. If for example, 18 . . . QR-Q1 (the most natural move on the board, as it disputes the file) 19 BxP PxB 20 RxR RxR 21 QxNch, followed by 22 QxRPch, brings in a couple of pawns for White.

18 . . .   N-B1

It speaks well for Reshevsky's tactical skill that he avoids the instinctive 18 . . . QR-Q1, but keeps the enemy rook out by his knight move.

19 B-K3   N-K3

And now he keeps the bishop from reaching B5 and disturbing his queen.

20 QR-Q1   KR-Q1

21 P-N3!

Euwe points out the merits of this quiet little move:

(a) It provides the king with a flight square against threats of mate on the back rank.

(b) It prevents an unwelcome intrusion by the knight at B4.

(c) It protects the square R4, the importance of which will be evident later on.

21 . . .   R-Q3

To avoid being crushed to death, Reshevsky offers an exchange of rooks, though it will leave him with a weak pawn on an open file.

The plausible 21 . . . P-KN3 would lead to 22 22 RxRch RxR 23 RxRch QxR 24 Q-R3, and Black must lose a pawn.

22 RxR   PxR

The pawn seems secure enough, but Smyslov finds an ingenious way to get at it.

23 Q-N4

A subtle move. The direct threat is 24 BxP winning a pawn; the indirect threat is 24 R-Q2 followed by 25 Q-Q1, bearing down on the unfortunate queen pawn.

23 . . .   K-R1

Black would have no picnic after 23 . . . K-B1, suggested by some commentators. Smyslov refutes it with 24 B-N6, which threatens to win by 25 BxN PxB   26 Q-B3ch K-K1   27 Q-Q3 K-Q2   28 B-B5 and the queen pawn cannot be saved.

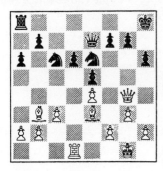

Reshevsky

Position after
23 . . . K-R1

Smyslov
to move

24 B-N6!

Very strong! It prevents 24 . . . R-Q1, protecting the pawn, and also deprives Black of counterplay, beginning with 24 . . . N-R4. White intends (if undisturbed) to win the queen pawn by doubling his pieces on that file.

24 . . .   N-N1

A rather ponderous attempt to bring the knight to the protection of the queen pawn. Reshevsky wants to move the knight to K1, by way of Q2 and KB3.

The move is awkward though, as it shuts off the rook, a circumstance which Smyslov immediately exploits.

What other defences were there? If for instance:

(a) 24 . . . N-B4   25 BxN PxB   27 R-Q7, winning a pawn.

(b) 24 . . . N(B3)-Q1   25 R-Q2 P-B3 (in order to protect the pawn by 26 . . . N-KB2)   26 BxN! NxB   27 Q-Q1, and the pawn falls.

(c) 24 . . . R-QB1   25 R-Q2 N-N1   26 Q-Q1 R-B3   27 B-R7 N-Q2   28 B-Q5 R-B2   29 BxN QxB   30 RxP, and White has won a pawn.

25 BxN   PxB

Capturing with the queen instead costs Black an extra pawn, thus: 25 . . . QxB   26 QxQ PxQ   27 RxP, and a king pawn comes off next move.

26 Q-R4!

Smyslov cleverly forces an exchange of queens, removing the defender of the queen pawn.

26 . . .   Q-Q2

The doubled pawns that ensue as a result of 26 . . . QxQ   27 PxQ, would be feeble compensation for the unavoidable loss of the queen pawn.

27 Q-Q8ch!

'The harmonious co-operation of pieces behind the enemy lines,' says Smyslov,' resulting logically from systematic strategy, is rare in practice.'

27 . . .   QxQ

28 BxQ   N-Q2

There is no saving the pawn by 28 . . . N-B3, as 29 B-N6 keeps the rook at bay.

29 B-B7   N-B4

If Black tries 29 . . . N-B3, then White proceeds with 30 RxP N-K1   31 R-Q7 N-B3   32 R-K7, and removes both king pawns.

30 RxP

The hasty capture by 30 BxP suffers this consequence: 30 . . . R-Q1   31 P-B3 P-QN3, and Black's next move 32 . . . N-N2 will trap the pinned bishop.

30 . . .   R-QB1

After 30 . . . NxP there comes 31 RxP, and the second king pawn cannot be saved.

Reshevsky's rook move is intended to break up White's Q-side.

31 B-N6   N-R5

32 RxP   NxNP

33 RxKP   N-B5

If 33 . . . RxP   34 B-Q4! R-B8ch   35 K-N2 N-Q6   36 R-K7, with an easy win for White.

34 R-K6   NxB

35 RxN   RxP

36 RxNP   R-B7

37 P-KR4

White cannot rescue his queen rook pawn, but he has a healthy pawn majority on the K-side.

37 . . . RxRP

This is the situation:

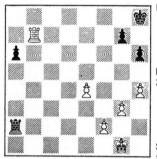

Reshevsky

Position after
37 . . . RxRP

Smyslov
to move

Capablanca said of similar endings, 'Endings of one rook and pawns are about the most common sort of endings arising on the chess board. Yet though they do occur so often, few have mastered them thoroughly. They are often of a difficult nature, and sometimes while apparently very simple they are in reality extremely intricate.'

We can appreciate this particular ending if we have an outline of Smyslov's general plan.

White's rook will assume its best position—at QR7, where it dominates the all-important seventh rank, and at the same time keeps the adverse passed rook pawn under constant attack, *no matter how far it advances on the file.*

White's king will advance under a pawn shelter to KN6, where it is in position, assisted by the rook, to remove Black's K-side pawns. The pawn shelter is necessary to prevent Black from checking and then queening his pawn, this pawn having reached QR7, with the rook defending it at QR8.

38 K-N2   P-QR4

39 P-R5   P-R5

40 R-R7

The rook occupies the best spot on the board: behind the passed pawn, in accordance with the Tarrasch recipe, and on the seventh rank (to imprison the king), in accordance with the Nimzowitsch recipe.

40 . . . K-N1

41 P-N4   P-R6

Black cannot restrain White's king (in retaliation) by 41 . . . R-R6, as there follows 42 P-B3, and then K-N3 K-B4 and P-K5.

42 K-N3   R-K7

43 K-B3   R-R7

44 K-K3   K-B1

45 P-B3   R-R8

46 K-B4

White plans 47 K-B5 and 48 P-B4.

46 . . . P-R7

47 P-K5

White must exercise care to avoid drawing swindles. The hasty 47 K-K5 permits 47 . . . R-KB8 48 RxRP (the pawn must be removed) 48 . . . RxP, and the win is none too easy.

47 . . . K-N1

Black has little choice, as his rook is tied down to the defence of the valuable QRP. King moves are all that he has left.

If he plays 47 . . . K-K1, then 48 K-B5 R-KB8 49 RxP RxPch 50 K-K6 (with a threat of mate) 50 . . . K-Q1 51 R-R8ch K-B2 52 R-R7ch, and White wins.

48 K-B5!   R-KB8

If 48 . . . K-R2 49 P-B4 K-N1 50 K-N6, and it's all over.

49 RxP   RxPch

50 K-N6   K-B1

On 50 . . . R-B2 instead (to protect the knight pawn) White forces the play by 51 R-R8ch (carefully avoid-

ing 51 P-K6 R-B3 mate!) R-B1   52 RxRch, (simpler
than 52 R-R7 K-R1, when 53 RxP falls into 53 . . .
R-B3ch and stalemate after the compulsory recapture)
52 . . . KxR   53 P-K6 K-K2 (or 53 . . . K-N1   54 P-K7
and mate next)   54 KxP, and White wins.

51 R-R8ch   K-K2

52 R-R7ch   Resigns

After 52 . . . K-B1   53 RxP R-B5   54 KxP, and
White's pawns can not be stopped.

43

White **I. Lipnitzky**   Black **V. Smyslov**
Nimzo-Indian Defence
Moscow, 1951

In 1914 when Capablanca was in Vienna, prior to playing in the St. Petersburg Tournament, he was invited
to be Réti's partner in a consultation game against
Fahndrich and Kaufmann. They played the black pieces,
and reached this position after the 14th move of White:

Réti & Capablanca
to move

Fahndrich &
Kaufmann

Réti says, 'The opportunity presented itself to develop
a hitherto undeveloped piece, and indeed with an attack
(on the queen). The move 14 . . . R-K1 would have had
that effect, and was in accordance with the principles
prevailing when I grew up, and which corresponded
almost entirely with Morphy's principles (for he would
without considering have chosen that move).

To my great astonishment Capablanca would not even
consider the move at all. Finally he discovered the following maneuver by means of which he forced a deterior-
ation of White's pawn position and thereby later on his
defeat:

14 . . .   B-Q5

15 Q-Q3   B(Q5)xN

16 QxB   N-K5!

17 Q-Q4   P-KN4

18 N-K5   B-B4

19 P-KB3   PxB

20 PxN   BxP

21 R-B2   P-R6!

22 R-K1   P-B4

23 PxP   Q-B3

With this game began a revolution in my conviction as
to the wisdom of the old principle, according to which in
the opening every move should develop another piece. I
studied Capablanca's games and recognized that contrary
to all the masters of that period he had for some time
ceased to adhere to that principle.'

In the following game, Smyslov too seems to be dis-
regarding normal development. He moves pieces twice
in the opening, and then develops them to the side of the
board.

His opponent, adhering to the principles governing
the proper disposition of the pieces, plays the opening in
straightforward fashion.

The result of the game must have shattered Lipnitzky's
faith in the weight of authority. For in the short space of
23 moves, his position was invaded and his king faced
with inevitable checkmate.

1 P-Q4   N-KB3

2 P-QB4   P-K3

3 N-QB3   B-N5

4 Q-B2   N-B3

5 N-B3   P-Q4

The usual build-up in this variation is 5 . . . P-Q3, followed, when feasible, by 6 . . . P-K4.

6 P-QR3

A simple line for White is 6 PxP PxP   7 B-N5 0-0   8 P-K3 R-K1   9 N-Q2 BxN   10 QxB, with a good game.

6 . . .   BxNch

7 PxB

White, with the two bishops, and an open file for his queen rook, must have been pleased with his position.

7 . . .   N-QR4

This seems to violate two principles at one blow: one, of moving the same piece twice in the opening; the other, of developing pieces to the side of the board. Nevertheless, the knight's move is a subtle one, and is an indication of Smyslov's keen positional sense, in espying a slight weakness and then pouncing down on it.

He intends to exert pressure on QB5, a fine spot for a black piece, as it could not easily be dislodged from there.

8 N-K5   N-Q2

Another tempo lost, as the second knight makes two moves in the opening! As we shall see, it is more important to exploit the weaknesses of critical squares than to develop pieces mechanically.

9 NxN   BxN

Smyslov has killed off White's knight which was strongly stationed at K5, and which guarded the QBP, and (just as important) the square QB4 itself.

10 PxP   PxP

11 B-B4

A routine move which brings the bishop into play, but one that is not suitable to the requirements of the position. The tender point is White's QB4, which needs all the care it can get.

Better chances were offered by 11 P-K3 0-0 12 B-Q3, followed by 13 0-0.

11 . . .   B-N4!

Beautiful positional play—even though the bishop moves a second time, and to the side of the board!

Three units (knight, bishop, and queen pawn) now bear down on White's QB4, the key square.

12 P-KR4

On 12 P-K3 instead, Black exchanges bishops, and then anchors his knight at QB5, a fine post and a springboard as well to other important squares.

White could still have managed to castle by 12 P-N3 0-0   13 B-N2 R-K1   14 B-B3, followed by 15 0-0.

Instead of this line of play, he tries to whip up an attack, where he might put up some sort of fight, rather than be crushed to death.

12 . . .   0-0

13 R-QN1   Q-Q2

14 R-R3

This rook is headed for KN3. The tempting 14 BxP would not gain a pawn, but lose a piece after 14 . . . B-R5.

14 . . .   KR-K1

15 R-KN3

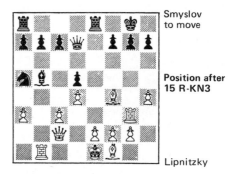

Smyslov to move

Position after 15 R-KN3

Lipnitzky

15 ...   N-B5!

The key to Smyslov's strategy! The knight radiates power in every direction.

16 B-R6   P-KN3

17 Q-B1

The queen guards against loss of the exchange by 17 . . . NxP, and prepares to swing over to the K-side.

17 ...   N-Q3!

The knight is now ready to leap in at KB4, to subdue any incipient attack.

18 Q-B4   B-R3

But not the hasty 18 . . . N-B4, when the sequel could be 19 RxB! NxR (if 19 . . . QxR 20 QxN) 20 PxN QxR 21 Q-B6, and it's Black who gets mated.

19 P-K3   N-B4

'The knight has trod an interesting path,' says Smyslov, 'from QN1→B3→R4→B5→Q3→KB4. Black now goes over to the counter-attack.'

20 BxB   PxB

21 R-N7

White seems to have created attacking chances, with all four of his pieces bearing down on Smyslov's king.

All the more surprising is it to discover that it is not Smyslov's king that is in danger, but Lipnitzky's!

Within three moves the whole scene changes, and the play comes to a sudden end.

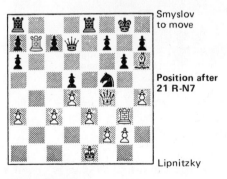

Smyslov to move

Position after 21 R-N7

Lipnitzky

21 ...   QR-N1!

22 RxBP   R-N8ch

23 K-K2   Q-R5!

Mate follows next move by 24 . . . Q-Q8 (or if 24 P-B3, by 24 . . . Q-B7).

24 Resigns

44

White **V. Smyslov**   Black **P. Trifunović**
Réti Opening
Zagreb, 1955

There is an easy grace about this game which is reminiscent of the elegant style of Morphy, Pillsbury, and Capablanca, all of whom made chess look easy.

Right from the start, Smyslov places his pieces where they will do the most good. So great is their influence that combinations seem to spring up almost by themselves.

Smyslov gains a positional advantage sufficient for him to win a pawn. He spurns the pawn, and in a manner befitting a great master, gives up the exchange instead.

There is still play left in the game, but Smyslov handles it with effortless ease.

1 P-QB4   N-KB3

2 N-QB3   P-K3

3 N-B3   P-Q4

4 P-K3   B-K2

5 P-QN3   O-O

6 B-N2   P-B4

7 PxP   NxP

If Black recaptures with 7 . . . PxP, then 8 P-Q4 P-QN3 9 PxP PxP leaves him with hanging pawns in the center that will require constant attention.

8 NxN   QxN

9 B-B4   Q-Q1

10 N-K5   N-Q2

11 0-0

Pillsbury would surely have played 11 P-B4, when
11 . . . NxN 12 BxN offers prospects of a K-side
attack.

11 . . .   NxN

12 BxN   B-B3

13 P-Q4

Only thus can White hope to gain a slight advantage.
If Black exchanges bishops, the square Q6 will provide a fine outpost for White's pieces.

13 . . .   PxP

14 PxP   B-Q2

15 Q-R5   B-B3

16 QR-Q1 B-K5

An attractive idea: Black wants to transfer the bishop
to KN3, where it will drive off the queen, and also
secure his king's position.

It loses time, though that was difficult to foresee.
A safer continuation (if he were playing to draw) was
16 . . . BxB 17 PxB Q-R4, followed by exchanging
rooks on the queen file.

17 KR-K1 B-B7

18 R-Q2   B-N3

19 Q-K2   B-K2

With the transparent threat of 20 . . . B-N5, winning
the exchange.
Trifunović does not care for 19 . . . BxB 20 QxB,
followed by 21 P-KR4, and White has the initiative.

20 R(Q2)-Q1 Q-N3

Smyslov says that preference should have been given
to 20 . . . B-N5 21 R-KB1 Q-K2, parrying the threat
of the breakthrough 22 P-Q5 by 22 . . . PxP 23 RxP
K-R1 and then . . . P-B3.
Note that 21 . . . Q-N3 (in this variation) is met by
22 P-Q5 PxP 23 RxP and White threatens 24 R-N5
winning a piece, as well as 24 Q-N2 winning the valuable king knight pawn.

21 P-Q5!   PxP

22 RxP

Suddenly there are threats! One is 23 BxP, winning
the KNP; another is 23 R-N5 Q-R3 24 B-Q5, winning the QNP. A third (if a third is necessary) is
24 B-Q4, winning the bishop.

22 . . .   B-B3

Where else can the unhappy bishop flee?
If 22 . . . B-N5 23 R-N5 wins, or if 22 . . . B-R6
23 R-N5 Q-R3 and 24 B-Q5 is embarrassing.
Finally, if 22 . . . KR-K1 (to protect the bishop)
the sequel would be 23 B-Q4! Q-B2 24 R-K5 K-B1
25 RxB! RxR 26 BxPch K-K1 27 B-N5ch K-Q1
28 B-KB6, and the rook is caught.

23 R-Q6!

Played in the grand manner! Smyslov could win a
pawn, and eventually the game, by 23 R-N5 Q-Q1
24 BxB followed by 25 RxP, but he prefers to attain
the victory like an artist of the chessboard.

23 . . .   Q-B4

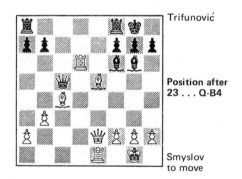

Trifunović

**Position after
23 . . . Q-B4**

Smyslov
to move

24 RxB!

Instead of chasing after a pawn, Smyslov sacrifices
the exchange.

24 . . .   PxR

25 BxP

No mating attack is in sight, but Smyslov's control

of the center, and his long-range bishops, will keep
his opponent busy warding off the various threats.

Trifunović must now provide against death on the
black squares by way of KR6 or by means of 26 B-R1
followed by 27 Q-N2.

Smyslov shows that 25 . . . Q-B3 fails after
26 Q-N2 KR-K1   27 R-QB1 P-N4   28 B-R8 K-B1
29 B-N7ch K-N1   30 B-R6, and White wins.

25 . . .   Q-KR4

26 Q-K3   P-KR3

27 P-KR3

Threatens 28 P-KN4 and 29 QxKRP, winning
instantly.

Meanwhile Black may not oppose the enemy
queen with 27 . . . QR-K1, as 28 QxR RxQ
29 RxRch K-R2   30 R-R8 mate is the painful
result.

27 . . .   Q-KB4

28 B-B3

Clearance for 29 Q-Q4 (or QxKRP), and mate on
the long diagonal.

28 . . .   K-R2

29 P-KN4!

Cuts down Black's choice of reply, 29 . . . Q-B7
(for example) losing immediately to 30 B-Q2.

29 . . .   Q-KN4

30 P-B4   Q-R5   See diagram

Trifunović is prepared to meet the tempting 31 P-B5
with 31 . . . QR-K1   32 PxBch PxP   33 B-K5 RxB
34 QxR Q-B7ch   35 K-R1 Q-B6ch, and Black draws
by perpetual check.

31 K-N2!   R-KN1

There is no comfort in 31 . . . QR-K1, when 32 QxR
RxQ   33 RxR P-B3 (to stop mate)   34 B-K1 corners
the queen.

32 Q-K7!

The simplest way to bring about capitulation. Black

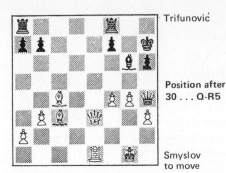

Trifunović

Position after
30 . . . Q-R5

Smyslov
to move

is forced to exchange, his queen having no flight
square.

32 . . .   QxQ

33 RxQ   QR-K1

On 33 . . . QR-KB1   34 K-B3 (threatens 35 P-B5)
B-N8   35 BxP, and White wins whatever is not nailed
down.

34 RxR   RxR

35 P-B5

'Steals a piece in broad daylight,' as Tartakover used
to say.

35 . . .   P-R3

36 K-B3   R-QB1

37 B-Q4   P-N4

38 B-Q3   R-B8

39 PxBch   PxP

40 P-KR4

With an eye to winning the pinned pawn by P-R5.

40 . . .   R-Q8

41 K-K2   R-KR8

42 P-R5   R-R7ch

43 B-B2   K-N2

44 PxP

At last a passed pawn!

44 . . .   P-KR4
45 PxP   RxP
46 B-Q4ch   K-N1
47 B-K4   P-R4
48 K-B3   Resigns

> After 48 . . . P-N5 49 K-N4 R-QN4 50 B-Q3, the rook is forced away from the fourth rank, and 51 B-B4ch followed by 52 P-N7ch ends the affair.
> A masterpiece of strategy by Smyslov.

45

White **E. Geller**   Black **V. Smyslov**
Nimzo-Indian Defence
Candidates' Tournament, Amsterdam, 1956

The artistic touches in this game make it one of Smylov's most fascinating efforts.

There is the switching of the attack from one side of the board to the other—from threats on the doubled-pawn complex to threats on the king himself.

There is the subtle retreat of the knight to K1 (quiet aggression!) in order to reappear effectively at Q3.

There is the sudden offer of the queen (which Geller dare not take) to the probable surprise of his opponent.

Finally, there is a neat finish, to round out the game. Smyslov is at his best in this strategic masterpiece.

1 P-Q4   N-KB3
2 P-QB4   P-K3
3 N-QB3   B-N5
4 P-QR3

> The Samisch Variation, which allows White the two bishops, in return for which he has a doubled pawn to watch over.

4 . . .   BxNch
5 PxB   P-B4
6 P-K3   P-QN3

7 N-K2

> Geller's idea is to tempt Black to win a pawn by 7 . . . B-N2 8 N-N3 0-0 9 B-Q3 BxP, when 10 R-KN1 B-N2 11 N-R5 (or 11 P-K4) gives White a strong attack.

7 . . .   N-B3

> Above all in positions of this sort, Black must not play . . . P-Q4, and dissolve the doubled pawn.

8 N-N3   0-0
9 B-Q3   B-R3

> It is more important to exert pressure on the doubled pawns than to develop the bishop at N2.

10 P-K4   N-K1!!

> A brilliant blockading maneuver, originated by Capablanca in his game against Johner at Carlsbad in 1929.
>
> The knight will emerge later at Q3, to increase the pressure on White's queen bishop pawn. Meanwhile it clears the way for K-side action, beginning with . . . P-KB4.
>
> A superb strategical concept!

11 B-K3   N-R4
12 Q-K2   R-B1

> Strikes a third time at the pawn. After 13 . . . PxP 14 PxP, Black's queen rook, knight, and bishop attack the pawn.

13 P-Q5   See diagram on page 113

> White could add a guard to the pawn by 13 R-QB1, but the reply 13 . . . N-Q3 would threaten it with a fourth piece.
>
> White decides to advance his queen pawn, thereby preventing the opening of the queen bishop file by . . . PxP.

13 . . .   Q-R5!

> Her Majesty makes a powerful entrance! On R5 she prevents attack by 14 P-K5, when 14 . . . BxP wins a pawn, or by 14 Q-R5, when 14 . . . QxQ 15 NxQ BxP again wins the luckless pawn.

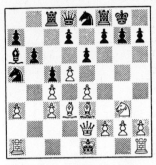

Smyslov
to move

Position after
13 P-Q5

Geller

Smyslov postpones the expected 13 . . . N-Q3—reinforcement of the attack on the bishop pawn—for the continuation 14 P-K5 N(Q3)xP 15 Q-R5 P-N3 16 Q-R6 NxB (or 16 . . . P-B4 17 B-N5) 17 N-R5!, is deadly.

The great master, as we see, must blend caution with daring.

14 0-0   N-Q3

15 QR-Q1   P-B4

Much stronger than capturing the pawn. Smyslov maintains the threat (to worry Geller) while instituting a new threat of 16 . . . P-B5, winning a piece.

A third threat is 16 . . . PxP 17 B-B2 BxP, and Black wins the exchange.

16 QPxP   QPxP

Smyslov sees no need to complicate things by 16 . . . P-B5 17 PxQP QR-Q1 18 P-K5.

17 PxP   PxP

18 Q-B3   B-N2

After 18 . . . P-B5 19 Q-Q5ch N-B2 20 N-B5, Black loses his KBP, or even his queen (20 . . . Q-N4 21 P-KR4 Q-N5 22 P-B3 Q-R4 23 N-K7ch)—Kmoch.

19 Q-B4

White has managed to retain material equality, though sooner or later the weakling (the pawn at his QB4) is bound to fall.

19 . . .   Q-B3

Here too, Smyslov refrains from winning the pawn, as after 19 . . . QxQ 20 BxQ N(Q3)xP 21 BxN NxB 22 R-Q7 R-B2 23 RxR KxR 24 NxP regains it.

20 B-N1   N-K5

The position is trappy. Smyslov could easily burn his fingers with 20 . . . N(R4)xP 21 B-R2 P-QN4 22 RxN, and White wins a piece.

21 R-Q7

Geller hopes to complicate matters, even at the cost of the exchange.

The alternative offers no hope. For example, if 21 NxN PxN 22 QxQ RxQ 23 R-Q7 R-B2 24 KR-Q1 B-B3, and the rook must leave the seventh rank. The resulting ending would be an easy Black win, as the doubled pawns are sitting ducks.

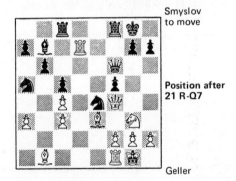

Smyslov
to move

Position after
21 R-Q7

Geller

21 . . .   Q-B3

Attacks the rook, and also threatens 22 . . . N-Q7 winning the exchange, as the king must guard against mate.

22 RxB

If 22 KR-Q1 instead, 22 . . . N-B3 wins the exchange by the threat of mate.

22 . . .   QxR

23 NxP

White has a pawn for the exchange, and two bishops

that could cause trouble. It will take all of Smyslov's
skill to subdue his opponent.

23 ...   QR-K1

Very good, as the rook adds its support to the
strongly-placed knight. This is better than 23 . . .
N(K5)xQBP, when 24 Q-R4, threatening 25 N-K7ch,
could be annoying.

24 Q-N4   K-R1

25 N-N3   NxN

26 RPxN   Q-KB2

Smyslov regroups his forces, meanwhile threatening
to win a piece by 27 . . . RxB.

27 Q-R4   P-KR3

28 B-Q3   Q-B3

29 Q-R5   R-Q1

Care is needed every step of the way. If, for example
29 . . . QxP 30 Q-N6 sets Black on the defence.
   Smyslov's move compels the bishop to abandon
the long diagonal, or the pawn.

30 B-K2   Q-B4

31 Q-R4   Q-B3

Both players, being in time-pressure, repeat moves to
gain time on the clock.

32 Q-R5   N-B3

33 P-N4

With the hope of breaking up the K-side position by
34 P-N5.

33 ...   Q-B2

34 Q-R4   N-K2

35 Q-R3

Now 35 P-N5 would be harmless after 35 . . . N-B4
followed by 36 . . . NxB.

35 ...   N-N3

36 Q-R2   N-B5!

Finally Black goes over to the attack.

37 B-B3   QxP

And finally the pawn falls.

38 P-N5   R-Q3

39 R-B1

Capturing the pawn instead leads to this pretty
finish: 39 PxP RxP 40 Q-N3 QxRch! 41 KxQ R-R8
mate!

39 ...   R-N3

40 PxP   RxP

41 Q-N3

Smyslov
to move

Position after
41 Q-N3

Geller

41 ...   Q-K5!

A spectacular move!
   If White should accept the offer of the queen,
practically everything comes off the board, thus:
42 BxQ N-K7ch 43 K-B1 NxQch 44 K-K1 R-R8ch
45 K-Q2 NxBch 46 K-B2 RxRch 47 KxR NxP
(either one) and wins.

42 QxN

White is forced to simplify, in view of Black's
threat of 42 . . . Q-R2, after which mate for White
is inevitable.

42 ...   QxQ

Smyslov has one more chance to go wrong with
42 . . . RxQ, when 43 BxQ RxB 44 BxR lets
White escape with a draw.

43 BxQ   RxB

44 R-K1   R-QR5

45 R-K8ch   K-R2

46 B-K4ch   P-N3

47 P-N4   RxP

48 R-K6   RxP

There is no need to fear 49 P-N5 R-R5   50 BxPch K-N2   51 B-B5 R-KB5   52 R-KB6 R(B6)-KB6.

49 K-N2   P-QN4

50 P-B3   P-N5

51 P-N5   R-R5

52 BxPch   K-N2

53 K-N3   R-Q5

54 B-K8

White can play 54 B-R5, with the threat of drawing by 55 R-K7ch, and inescapable perpetual check, but the reply 54 . . . R-Q2 would put an end to that little idea.

54 . . .   P-N6

55 P-N6   R-Q1

56 R-K7ch

Just as Geller made this move, he overstepped the time-limit.

The finish would have been 56 . . . K-B3 57 P-N7 RxB!, and Black wins.

Tal

Tal is the greatest living combination player. He is a genius of attack, a wizard who makes the pieces come alive and dance to his bidding. No-one else holds the spectator so enthralled as Tal, for at his board there are bound to be fireworks, no matter how placid the position, no matter how strong the opponent.

Tal has been called the Paganini of Chess, the Magician of Riga, and the Chevalier *sans peur et sans reproche.* He has brought off brilliancies against all the mighty men of chess, and has subdued players from Aronson to Zaitsev—no letter of the alphabet being safe from Tal.

His imagination is on tap at all times, and his inspiration bubbles, since he pours out dazzling com-`binations in a steady stream. There are sacrifices galore in Tal's games, but they are not there to thrill the gallery. The sacrifices are made because they offer the most winning chances, and are the result of lightning-quick analysis and assessment of the position. Tal has an amazingly swift sight of the board, and can see through a half-dozen variations in a twinkling.

Tal is not overawed by the importance of the occasion, nor the reputation of his opponent. He may have a hard game to play in the afternoon, but that does not prevent his playing thirty or forty skittle games in the forenoon, just for fun.

For Tal loves chess passionately, and communicates his feeling in the beautiful games he creates. He has entertained millions, and will entertain millions more in the future, who (like you and me) are mad about the game, and are attracted by brilliant, exciting, imaginative play.

Early in his career, Tal thrilled the chess world with his devil-may-care style of play. Onlookers were delighted with his willingness to plunge into unfathomable complications, and his readiness to sacrifice pawns or pieces in order to stir up activity. There were skeptics who predicted that he would come to grief with this seemingly reckless play.

But the critics were confounded when Tal came in first in the 1957 U.S.S.R. Championship, ahead of such stalwarts as Bronstein, Keres, Spassky, and Petrosian, to become at the age of 20 the youngest winner of the title of Soviet Champion. Simagin commented, 'Tal is a born chess player. He almost inevitably finds the strongest line, and in double-edged complications his splendid combinative powers present themselves.'

Then, to prove it was not luck, Tal won the Championship of the U.S.S.R. the following year, and the Interzonal Tournament at Portoroz as well. In the latter event, Tal out-distanced a strong field, among whom were Petrosian, Gligorić, Fischer (the new young terror), and Bronstein. This feat he accomplished in heroic style, by capturing first prize without loss of a game.

At Zurich the next year, Tal again took first prize, beating out such opposition as Gligorić, Fischer, Keres, and Larsen, and a few months later won the Candidates' Tournament held at Bled, Zagreb, and Belgrad, ahead of Keres, Petrosian, Smyslov, Fischer, and Gligorić. He was particularly tough on Fischer, beating him four straight(!), and on Ólafsson, Gligorić, and Benko, beating each of them three games and drawing the fourth. (His *bête noire* though was Keres, who defeated him three times, against one loss).

One man stood in the way of Tal's winning the World's Championship—Mr. Soviet Chess, the mighty Botvinnik. Nothing daunted, and no respecter of reputations, Tal proceeded to win the first game in an hour and a half! He followed up his victory by drawing four games and then winning the next two. Botvinnik came back with two straight wins, but those were the only games he won, and the match ended with a victory for Tal by 12½ points to 8½. Tal thus became at the age of 23 the youngest world champion in the history of the game.

Tal's triumph was short-lived, for Botvinnik took back his crown the following year, inflicting a 13 to 8 defeat on Tal. So Tal became the youngest champion ever to lose his title, a distinction one could do without.

However, Tal had not lost his magic touch! At Bled in the same year, Tal finished first in a powerful tournament of 20 contestants, ahead of such tough men as Fischer, Gligorić, Keres, Petrosian, and Geller. Tal finished a point ahead of Fischer, but the latter had the pleasure of winning a stunning game from Tal (No. 76) which helped repay any blow to his pride.

Tal today still turns out beautiful, beautiful games, and will probably do so for many years to come.

I consider Tal the seventh greatest chess player of all time.

46

White **M. Tal**   Black **G. Lissitzin**
Sicilian Defence
Leningrad, 1956

Like D'Artagnan, hero of *The three musketeers*, Tal is a gallant fighter, whose bravery borders occasionally on the reckless.

Who but Tal would dream of letting his king wander out into enemy territory, terrorize the pawns, and win the game almost all by himself?

Little wonder that this beautiful game has always been one of my favourites.

1 P-K4   P-QB4

2 N-KB3   P-Q3

3 P-Q4   PxP

4 NxP   N-KB3

5 N-QB3   P-KN3

6 P-B4   N-B3

Lissitzin is on the *qui vive.* The natural move 6 . . . B-N2 could land him in a trap, thus: 7 P-K5 PxP (7 . . . N-R4 is the saving move) 8 PxP N-N5 9 B-N5ch K-B1 (on 9 . . . B-Q2 or 9 . . . N-Q2 10 QxN wins a piece) 10 N-K6ch, and White wins the queen.

7 NxN   PxN

8 P-K5   N-Q2

9 PxP   PxP

10 B-K3

Black gets a good game after 10 Q-B3 P-Q4   11 B-K2 B-KN2   12 Q-K3ch Q-K2   13 QxQch KxQ   14 0-0 R-QN1.

10 . . .   B-K2

11 Q-B3   P-Q4

12 0-0-0   B-B3

13 B-Q4

Rather than continue developing his pieces mechanically, Tal immediately disputes control of the long diagonal.

13 . . .   0-0

14 P-KR4

Intending to open the rook file by 15 P-R5.

14 . . .   R-N1

Black plays for counter-attack along the open knight file, which leads right to the king's address.

It would not do to capture the rook pawn, as after 14 . . . BxP   15 Q-R3 P-N4   16 P-KN3 N-B3 17 P-B5 the bishop is lost.

15 Q-B2

Black was threatening 15 . . . BxB   16 RxB Q-N3, with an attack on the rook as well as the queen knight pawn.

15 . . .   R-N5

16 BxB

It would be dangerous to pick up a stray pawn, as this could be the result: 16 BxP Q-R4   17 B-K3 RxNP!   18 KxR BxNch   19 K-B1 Q-R6ch   20 K-N1 Q-N7 mate.

16 . . .   NxB

17 P-R3

Here too taking the pawn leads to trouble. If 17 QxP Q-Q3   18 P-KN3 RxNP!   19 KxR Q-N5ch   20 K-B1 QxN, and Black has a strong attack, one threat being 21 . . . Q-R8ch   22 K-Q2 N-K5ch   23 K-K1 Q-B6ch   24 K-K2 B-N5 mate.

17 . . .   Q-N3

18 QxQ   RxQ

Time for a diagram. See page 120.

19 N-R4!

An excellent move, though the knight moves to the side of the board. The idea is to fix Black's center pawns so that they may not advance, and to dominate the opponent's weakened black squares.

19 . . .   R-N2

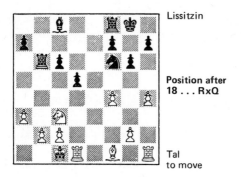

Lissitzin

Position after
18 . . . RxQ

Tal
to move

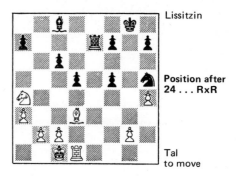

Lissitzin

Position after
24 . . . RxR

Tal
to move

20 B-Q3   N-R4

21 KR-B1   R-K2

22 P-B5!

A fine positional sacrifice. At the cost of a pawn (and when does Tal hesitate to give up a pawn?) Tal disrupts his opponent's pawn structure on the K-side. In addition to this, the acceptance of the sacrifice leaves Black's bishop hemmed in by pawns occupying white squares.

22 . . .   PxP

This leads to Black's ruin, though Tal's continuation is far from obvious.

23 R(B1)-K1

Tal does not hesitate to exchange pieces, though he is a pawn down. He must dispute control of the open file before Black doubles rooks, and gains complete possession of it.

23 . . .   R(B1)-K1

24 RxR   RxR   See diagram at top of next column.

25 K-Q2!

The king starts out on a remarkable journey. He intends to stroll up the Q-side, and spread havoc among the pawns.

Certainly it is a striking conception at this stage of the game.

25 . . .   N-N6

26 K-B3   P-B5

This enables the bishop to take active part in the game.

27 K-Q4

The king continues his journey along the black squares.

27 . . .   B-B4

Black wants to exchange bishops (being a pawn ahead), but he also threatens 28 . . . BxB 29 KxB R-K6ch 30 K-Q4 R-K7, with possession of the seventh rank, and the prospect of picking up a pawn or two as booty.

28 R-Q2   R-K3

Foiled in one attempt, the rook tries his luck elsewhere.

29 N-B5   R-R3

30 K-K5!   BxB

31 PxB   RxP

32 K-Q6   R-R3ch

33 K-B7

Despite being two pawns down, White has better chances in the ending. His king is so wonderfully active, and Black's so woefully passive, that he is in effect a king ahead!

33 . . .   N-B4

34 K-N7   N-Q5

Black defends well. His knight protects the bishop

pawn, enabling the rook to become aggressive. In fact, Black poses a threat of winning another pawn by 35 . . . R-R7, followed by 36 . . . P-B6.

35 R-KB2   P-R4

36 RxP   N-K3

37 R-N4ch   K-B1

If Black tried to exchange rooks (being a pawn ahead) the consequences would be painful, the play going like this: 37 . . . R-N3   38 RxRch RPxR   39 NxN PxN   40 KxP K-B2   41 P-QN4, and White will have a passed pawn, which will turn into a queen in a few moves.

38 KxP!

A heroic king! He fears naught, not even discovered check!

38 . . .   NxN dis.ch

39 KxN   R-K3

40 KxP

One by one the soldiers fall.

40 . . .   R-QN3

41 P-N4   PxP

42 PxP

Tal now has a passed pawn as reward for his efforts. All that remains is to escort the pawn to the queening square.

42 . . .   K-K2

43 K-B5   R-KB3

44 R-Q4

This cuts off Black's king from the Q-side.

44 . . .   R-B4ch

45 K-N6

This is preferable to interposing the rook, when 45 . . . R-B5 (threatening 46 . . . R-N5) might be annoying.

45 . . .   R-B3ch

46 K-B7   R-B4

Black fights hard to restrain the dangerous pawn.

47 R-K4ch

And this check forces the king further away from the Q-side, the theater of action.

47 . . .   K-B3

48 K-B6   R-B7

49 P-N4   P-R4

Black is willing to give up one pawn for the sake of creating a passed pawn of his own.

50 PxP   K-N4

51 P-N5   P-B4

52 R-QN4

The ideal position for the rook—behind the passed pawn.

52 . . .   P-B5

53 P-N6   P-B6

54 P-N7   Resigns

Lissitzin is convinced that there is no hope. Had he played on, the finish would have been 54 . . . R-B7ch 55 K-Q5 P-B7   56 P-N8(Q) P-B8(Q)   57 Q-N3ch K-B3 (or 57 . . . K-B4   58 Q-N6 mate)   58 Q-N6ch K-K2   59 R-N7ch, and quick mate.

47

White **M. Tal**   Black **V. Simagin**
Irregular Defence
Leningrad, 1956

Those who are lucky enough to watch Tal in action are bound to see chess that is exciting.

No matter how strange the opening, Tal is sure to whip up a ferocious attack, which he conducts with ceaseless energy. In the course of the play, he usually manages to come up with a fantastic move or two, much to the surprise of his opponent (and the rest of the chess world, as well).

Here, from one of his early tournaments, is a game where Tal held the spectators spellbound throughout the forty-five moves.

1 P-K4   P-QB3

2 P-Q4   P-Q3

We are out of the books—and it's only the second move!

3 N-QB3   N-B3

4 P-B4

Naturally enough, White seizes control of the center.

4 . . .   Q-N3

5 N-B3

Tarrasch would probably play 5 B-K2 instead, to prevent Black from pinning the knight, and then, by an exchange of pieces, freeing his game somewhat.

5 . . .   B-N5

6 B-K2   QN-Q2

7 P-K5

This interrupts Black's plans to develop his bishop by 7 . . . P-K3 or 7 . . . P-N3.

7 . . .   N-Q4

Clearly, 7 . . . PxP   8 QPxP, sending the king knight home, is out of the question.

8 0-0   NxN

9 PxN

The doubled pawns do not disturb Tal at all, as he has acquired an open file for his rook.

9 . . .   P-K3

10 N-N5!

Did Tal even at this early stage envision sacrificing his knight for the precious king bishop pawn?

10 . . .   BxB

11 QxB   P-KR3

Black tries to force the knight to a decision before such moves as 12 P-B5, or 12 Q-R5 add to his difficulties.

There was no relief in 11 . . . B-K2, when White has choice of two powerful continuations:

(a) 12 P-B5 0-0 (or 12 . . . BxN 13 BxB 0-0 14 P-B6) 13 P-B6 PxBP 14 NxRP, and the king is

exposed to the fury of a Tal attack.

(b) 12 PxP BxP 13 NxKP PxN 14 QxPch B-K2 15 R-K1 Q-Q1 16 B-R3 P-B4 17 PxP N-B1 18 Q-K4, and White has an irresistible attack.

12 NxBP

Sacrificing a piece to get the king out into the open (and to give the spectators a thrill) is a familiar enough device, but Tal invests the theme with his own touches of genius.

12 . . .   KxN

13 P-B5

Sets Black some difficult problems. If 13 . . . PxBP 14 P-K6ch K-K2 15 PxNch KxP 16 R-K1, and the threat of 17 Q-K6ch cannot be met satisfactorily.

Or if 13 . . . K-N1 (running away from it all) 14 PxKP NxP 15 Q-B2! N-B5 16 Q-B7ch K-R2 17 R-B6!, and mate follows by 18 RxP.

Finally, if 13 . . . NxP 14 Q-K3 (or even more simply 14 K-R1) and the knight dare not move for fear of 15 QxP checkmate. Hence . . .

13 . . .   QPxP

14 BPxP dbl.ch   KxP

At this point, ordinary mortals would spend time analyzing the effects of such moves as 15 Q-N4ch or 15 Q-B4ch, or 15 B-B4, or even 15 B-K3 (threatening 16 P-Q5ch), but Tal finds a truly fantastic move for the pursuance of his attack.

This is the situation:

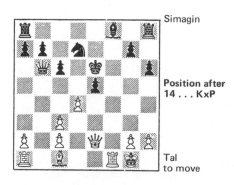

Simagin

Position after 14 . . . KxP

Tal to move

15 R-N1!   QxR

On principle, Black might just as well take the rook, as otherwise it comes into the game with gain of time.

The alternative 15 . . . Q-R3 is not attractive, as after 16 Q-N4ch K-Q3 17 PxPch K-B2 (or 17 . . . NxP 18 R-Q1ch K-B2 19 B-B4 Q-R4 20 Q-K6 and White wins a piece) 18 R-B7 R-Q1 19 P-K6, and White wins.

16 Q-B4ch   K-Q3

The king must go to a black square, permitting White a bishop check, and the capture of the queen.

On 16 . . . K-K2, there follows 17 B-R3ch K-Q1 18 RxQ BxB 19 RxP R-QN1 20 RxP R-N8ch 21 K-B2 R-B1ch 22 K-K2 B-K2 (or to Q3) 23 Q-K6, and White wins.

17 B-R3ch   K-B2

18 RxQ   BxB

Black has rook, knight, and bishop for the queen, but Tal has something more valuable than material goods. He possesses what Bronstein calls 'the most powerful weapon in chess—the next move!'

19 Q-N3!

This double attack (which Tal must have long ago foreseen) either wins the bishop, or dislodges the king from his hiding place, and subjects him to harassment from all quarters of the board.

19 . . .   B-K2

The only move, as 19 . . . B-Q3 or 19 . . . B-B1 costs a rook after 20 QxPch.

20 QxPch   K-Q3

21 PxPch   NxP

Forced, as 21 . . . K-K3 22 QxPch wins the knight.

22 R-Q1ch   K-K3

23 Q-N3ch   K-B4

The least of the evils. If 23 . . . K-B3 24 R-B1ch K-N3 (or 24 . . . K-N4 25 Q-K6 B-B3 26 Q-B5ch K-R5 27 P-N3 mate) 25 Q-K6ch B-B3 26 Q-B5ch K-B2   27 QxN and White wins.

24 R-B1ch   K-K5

The king must continue his peregrinations.

25 R-K1ch   K-B4

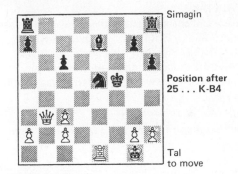

Simagin

Position after
25 . . . K-B4

Tal
to move

26 P-N4ch   K-B3

The king is compelled to retreat, as advancing to B5 lets Tal mate in a hurry, thus: 26 . . . K-B5 27 Q-R4ch! (the key move) K-N4 (or 27 . . . K-B6 28 Q-K4 mate) 28 RxNch K-N3 (on 28 . . . K-R5 29 R-R5 is mate) 29 Q-K4ch K-B2 30 RxBch K-N1 31 Q-N6 R-R2 32 R-K8ch RxR   33 QxR mate.

27 R-B1ch   K-N3

28 Q-K6ch   K-R2

Here too, 28 . . . B-B3 loses a piece by 29 Q-B5ch followed by 30 QxN.

29 QxN

At long last, Tal wins back a piece.

29 . . .   KR-K1

30 R-B7

Threatens mate, and forces . . .

30 . . .   B-B1

31 Q-B5ch   K-N1

32 K-B2   B-B4ch

33 K-N3   R-K6ch

34 K-R4   QR-K1

Suddenly Black has a counter-attack going, and Tal will have to find a magic winning move!

35 RxPch!

So he sacrifices a second rook!

35 ...   KxR

36 QxB   R(K1)-K3

There were still chances to save the game, as Ragozin points out: 36 . . . R(K1)-K2 37 QxBP R-KB2, and 38 . . . R(B2)-B6 might have drawn for Black.

By this time though, Simagin must have been exhausted, and played what seemed to be reasonably good moves.

37 QxRPch

Tal now has an extra trump in his passed rook pawn.

37 ...   K-N3

38 Q-R8

This prepares to meet 38 . . . RxP with 39 Q-N8ch K-B3 (protects one rook, but loses the other) 40 Q-R8ch, and White wins a rook.

38 ...   K-B3

39 P-R4   K-K4

40 P-R5   K-Q4

41 Q-Q8ch   K-K5

Against 41 . . . K-B4, White mates in three by 42 Q-Q4ch K-N4 43 Q-N4ch K-R3 44 Q-N6 mate.

42 P-R6   K-B6

43 P-R7   R-K7

Black actually threatens mate on the move!

44 Q-Q3ch   R(K3)-K6

45 QxR(K3)ch   Resigns

48

White **M. Tal**   Black **A. Tolush**
Sicilian Defence
Leningrad, 1956

Tal scintillates in positions that offer complications. He might be a piece down, with one or two others under attack. But will he try to rescue them from capture? Not if he can add to the excitement by sacrificing yet another piece!

So great is Tal's wealth of tactical ideas, that combinations seem to spring to life when his talented fingers pick up the chess pieces.

Here as evidence, is a sparkling game against Tolush:

1 P-K4   P-QB4

2 N-KB3   P-Q3

3 P-Q4   PxP

4 NxP   N-KB3

5 N-QB3   P-QR3

6 B-N5

A vigorous move, popular with modern masters. It prevents 6 . . . P-KN3, and prepares for Q-side castling, with attacking prospects beginning with P-KB4.

6 ...   P-K3

The customary response. Care is needed after 6 . . . QN-Q2, when 7 B-QB4 P-K3 8 0-0 Q-B2 leads into 9 BxKP! PxB 10 NxP, as in the famous game Keres-Sajtar, played at Amsterdam in 1954, which Keres won quickly and brilliantly. The remaining moves of that game were: 10 . . . Q-B5 11 N-Q5 K-B2 12 BxN KxN 13 B-B3! N-B3 14 BxN PxB 15 N-N6 Q-B3 16 NxR B-K2 17 P-QR4 P-N3 18 Q-Q5ch K-Q2 19 R-R3 B-Q1 20 NxPch! Resigns, as 20 . . . BxN 21 Q-B7ch K-Q1 22 QxPch wins the rook, or if 20 . . . QxN 21 Q-B5ch K-B2 22 R-B3ch wins the bishop.

7 P-B4

This may be stronger than 7 Q-B3, when 7 . . . P-KR3! 8 B-R4 B-K2 9 0-0-0 Q-B2 10 B-Q3 N-B3 11 NxN PxN 12 B-QB4 R-QN1 13 B-KN3 0-0 maintains equality.

7 ...   Q-N3

Safer (comparatively) is 7 . . . B-K2 8 Q-B3 Q-B2 9 0-0-0, but Tolush, who revels in complications, is not interested in safety.

8 Q-Q2   QxP

Tolush goes into the *Poisoned Pawn Variation.*
Fischer, as Black against Spassky in their world
championship match in 1972, took the pawn in their
seventh game. The game ended in a draw, after Fischer
missed good winning chances. In the eleventh game,
Fischer again accepted the poisoned pawn, but
Spassky, well-prepared this time, won Fischer's
queen on the 25th move, and the game on the 31st.

9 R-QN1

Spassky played 9 N-N3 in both games of the match,
the next few moves of the 11th running as follows:
9 . . . Q-R6   10 BxN! PxB   11 B-K2! P-KR4   12 0-0
N-B3   13 K-R1 B-Q2   14 N-N1!, a move which
offered Fischer much food for thought.

9 . . .   Q-R6

10 P-K5!

Energetic, and superior to 10 BxN PxB   11 P-B5,
when 11 . . . B-R3 changes the complexion of the
game.

10 . . .   PxP

11 PxP   KN-Q2

On 11 . . . N-Q4, White probably would have played
12 NxN PxN   13 P-B4 with good prospects.

12 N-K4

Attractive, as the knights are centralized à la Nimzowitsch, but an equally good alternative was
12 B-QB4, when the natural developing move 12 . . .
B-K2 allows the nice response 13 BxKP!.

12 . . .   QxP   See diagram

Tolush plunges *faute de mieux* into the complications.
Apparently he did not relish 12 . . . B-B4   13 R-N3
QxP   14 Q-B3! N-N3   15 N-Q6ch.

13 R-N3

This cuts off the queen from returning to Q4.

13 . . .   Q-R8ch

Other continuations of the attack meet brusque
refutations:
    If 13 . . . N-B4   14 N-N5!, and White threatens

Tolush

Position after
12 . . . QxP

Tal
to move

two mates in one, while the reply to 13 . . . B-B4
is 14 Q-B3, with the threat (besides 15 NxB) of
15 N-Q6ch winning the other bishop.

14 K-B2   Q-R5

Having made castling for White impossible, the queen
pursues the attack from another angle.
    Against 14 . . . B-B4, Tal's procedure would have
been 15 NxB NxN   16 B-N5ch PxB (if 16 . . . K-B1
17 Q-N4!)   17 RxQ N-K5ch   18 K-K2 NxQ
19 RxR NxR   20 NxN, and White nets another
piece next move.

15 B-N5!

A brilliant move, but Tal has lots of brilliant moves
at his disposal.

15 . . .   PxB

Practically forced, as 15 . . . Q-R7 loses instantly by
16 Q-B3, when the king's life is threatened by 17 QxB
mate, and the queen's life by 18 R-R1.

16 NxNP

This too threatens instant mate.

16 . . .   P-B3

There is no relief in 16 . . . N-R3, when 17 N(K4)-
Q6ch BxN   18 QxB wins, while 16 . . . B-K2 proves
disastrous after 17 BxB KxB   18 Q-N5ch, and Black
has no defence.

17 PxP   PxP

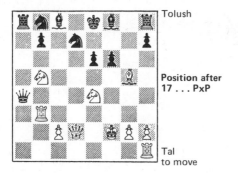

Tolush

**Position after
17 . . . PxP**

Tal
to move

Tal is a piece down, and two more of his pieces are under attack, but he continues with unflagging vigour, in line with Pillsbury's advice, 'So set up your attack, that when the fire is out, it isn't out!'

18 R-K1!
Beautiful centralization, and the best way to maintain the pressure.

18 . . .   R-R3
It is fatal to accept the bishop, as after 18 . . . PxB 19 N-B7ch K-K2 (if 19 . . . K-B2 20 R-B3ch wins) 20 Q-Q6ch K-B2 21 QxPch K-N2 22 N-K8 is mate.

19 BxP   NxB

20 NxNch   K-B2

21 R-KB3
Tal protects one knight, but abandons the other.

21 . . .   Q-R5ch
If 21 . . . QxN, White either wins the queen or forces mate, thus: 22 N-Q5 dis.ch K-N1 (on 22 . . . K-K1 23 N-B7ch attacks king and queen, while 22 . . . K-N3 allows quick mate by 23 R-B6ch) 23 Q-N5ch B-N2 24 N-K7 mate (and wins the queen too!).

22 K-B1   P-K4
'Always check, it might be mate!,' does not avail Black, as after 22 . . . Q-B5ch 23 K-N1 B-B4ch 24 K-R1 QxN 25 N-Q5 dis.ch K-N3 26 R-B6ch, it's White who does the mating.

23 Q-Q5ch   B-K3

24 N-Q7 dis.ch   K-N3

25 NxPch   K-N2

26 R-N3ch   QxR
Desperation, but 26 . . . K-B3 loses after 27 Q-Q8ch, while 26 . . . K-R3 runs into loss by 27 N-B7ch BxN 28 Q-Q2ch K-R4 29 R-K5ch and mate next move.

27 QxPch   N-Q2

28 PxQ   R-N3

29 Q-B7   B-QB4

30 NxN   B-B5ch

31 R-K2
Black overstepped the time-limit. He was lost though, after 31 . . . BxRch 32 KxB R-K1ch 33 N-K5 dis.ch, followed by 34 QxB, as well as after 31 . . . BxRch 32 KxB R-K3ch 33 N-K5 dis.ch B-K2 34 N-Q4, when White wins the exchange.

49

White **M. Tal**   Black **G. Fuster**
Caro-Kann Defence
Portoroz, 1958

Tal sacrifices pieces cheerfully, if doing so gives him a glimmer of opportunity to display his tactical skills. Given the slightest chance Tal can make a great master seem like a rank amateur by the speed and power of his attack.

In this game, a slashing stroke by Tal rips the game wide open, and the combinations come tumbling down.

1 P-K4   P-QB3

2 P-Q4   P-Q4

3 N-QB3   PxP

4 NxP   N-Q2

The order of moves is important; if at once 4 . . .
N-KB3, then 5 NxNch disrupts Black's pawn position.

5 N-KB3

A trappy alternative is 5 B-QB4, after which there
could follow 5 . . . KN-B3   6 N-N5 P-K3   7 Q-K2
N-N3 (definitely not 7 . . . P-KR3   8 NxBP KxN
9 QxPch K-N3   10 B-Q3ch K-R4   11 Q-R3 mate)
8 B-N3 QxP   9 KN-B3 B-N5ch (preferable is a move
by the queen, when 10 N-K5 gives White positional
compensation for his pawn)   10 P-B3 BxPch   11 K-B1
and White wins.

5 . . .   KN-B3

6 NxNch   NxN

7 B-QB4   B-B4

Carefully avoiding 7 . . . B-N5, which loses a pawn by
8 BxPch KxB   9 N-K5ch, followed by 10 NxB.

8 Q-K2   P-K3

9 B-KN5   B-K2

10 0-0-0   P-KR3

An instinctive attempt to brush the bishop away, but
it weakens the pawn position. It seems dangerous to
castle, since White can initiate an attack by 11 N-K5
followed by a pawn storm starting with P-KN4 and
P-KR4.

More to the point was freeing himself without disturbing the pawn position, say by 10 . . . N-Q4; then
after 11 BxB QxB, he is prepared to castle Q-side or
K-side, whither he listeth.

11 B-R4   N-K5   See diagram

With the expectation that Black would reply 12 B-N3,
when he could eliminate one of the bishops, and enjoy the simple life, but Tal throws a monkey wrench
into the machinery.

12 P-KN4!

A little surprise for Monsieur Fuster!

Various possibilities suddenly open up:
if (a) 12 . . . BxP   13 BxB BxN (or QxB   14 QxN,
winning a piece)   14 QxB QxB   15 QxN, and White

Fuster

**Position after
11 . . . N-K5**

Tal
to move

has won a piece. Or if (b) 12 . . . BxB   13 PxB NxP
14 PxP NxQR   15 PxP dbl.ch K-Q2 (or 15 . . . K-B1
16 N-K5)   16 B-K6ch K-B2   17 NxB QxN
18 Q-K5ch K-N3   19 RxN Q-N4ch   20 K-N1, and
White should win.

12 . . .   B-R2

A prudent retreat.

13 B-KN3   NxB

14 BPxN

The books say, 'Capture towards the center!,'
but this and other principles are for general guidance,
and not to be applied indiscriminately.

In this case, the open bishop file offers more
attacking opportunities than would the rook file.

14 . . .   Q-B2

Develops the queen, with a view to castling Q-side—
if Tal permits.

15 N-K5   B-Q3

16 P-KR4   P-B3

Black wants to evict the knight by force, since he
dare not castle K-side on account of the reply
17 P-N5, breaking into his position, and if 16 . . .
0-0-0   17 NxKBP QxN   18 BxPch, and White wins
the queen.

The move Black does make gives Tal the chance
he wants—a sacrifice which tears away the king's
pawn protection.

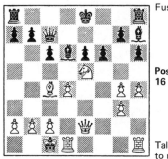

Fuster

**Position after
16 . . . P-B3**

Tal
to move

17 BxP!
A second surprise!

17 . . .   PxN
The knight sacrifice must be accepted, after which
Black's king remains in the center, exposed to
attack on the two open files.

18 PxP   B-K2
Black loses quickly after 18 . . . BxP 19 KR-K1.
The combinations are easy, but pretty.

(a) 19 . . . BxKNP 20 B-Q7 dbl.ch K-B2 21 Q-K7ch
K-N3 22 P-R5 mate.

(b) 19 . . . B-B3 20 B-B8 dis.ch K-B2 (if . . . B-K2
21 B-Q7ch, and Black must give up his Q—as a start)
21 Q-K6ch K-N3 22 P-R5ch K-N4 23 Q-K3ch, and
mate next.

(c) 19 . . . B-B3 20 B-B8 dis.ch Q-K2 21 Q-Q2
RxB 22 Q-Q7ch K-B2 23 RxQch BxR 24 R-B1ch
K-N3 25 Q-B5 mate.

19 KR-B1
With mating intentions : 20 B-B7ch K-B1
21 B-N6 dis.ch K-N1 22 Q-B4 mate.

19 . . .   KR-B1
A pretty reply to 19 . . . B-N1 is 20 Q-K4!

20 RxRch   BxR

21 Q-B3
To this, the natural reply 21 . . . R-Q1 is fatal:

22 RxRch KxR (or 22 . . . QxR 23 Q-B7 mate)
23 QxB mate.

21 . . .   Q-K2

22 Q-N3
Institutes a new threat: 23 B-Q7ch QxB 24 RxQ
KxR 25 QxPch, winning an innocent rook that wasn't
even in the fight.

22 . . .   R-N1
On 22 . . . R-Q1, White wins by 23 B-B7ch QxB
24 RxRch K-K2 25 R-Q7ch, and Black's queen
comes off next move.

23 B-Q7ch   QxB
On 23 . . . K-Q1 24 B-B5 dis.ch wins the bishop.

24 RxQ   KxR

25 Q-B7ch   B-K2

26 P-K6ch   K-Q1

27 QxP   Resigns
The bishop is lost. After 27 . . . B-K5 28 Q-K5
attacks two unprotected pieces.

    The game is a good illustration of the power of
the queen (or is it the power of Tal?)

50

White **M. Tal**   Black **S. Gligorić**
Queen's Indian Defence
Candidates' Tournament, Zagreb, 1959

Another fascinating game by Tal (but aren't all Tal's
games fascinating?).

    The excitement begins with the 15th move, when Tal
offers a pawn in return for control of a key square. The
excitement is sustained throughout the length of the ensuing 49 moves by the liveliness of the action.

    A delightful feature of the game is the zigzag journey
undertaken by Tal's king bishop, which turns out to be
as effective as it is amusing.

1 P-Q4   N-KB3

2 P-QB4   P-K3

3 N-KB3   P-QN3

The Queen's Indian Defence, to which Gligorić resorts, after his favourite King's Indian has suffered a defeat at the hands of Tal in an earlier round.

4 N-B3   B-N2

5 B-N5   B-N5

6 P-K3   P-KR3

7 B-R4   P-KN4

Timid souls, who hesitate to break up the K-side pawn structure, are advised to play the safer line 7 . . . BxNch   8 PxB P-Q3   9 B-Q3 QN-Q2   10 0-0 Q-K2, followed by castling Q-side.

8 B-N3   N-K5

9 Q-B2   BxNch

10 PxB   P-Q3

11 B-Q3   NxB

In an earlier Candidates' Tournament game, Taimanov had played 11 . . . P-KB4 against Gligorić, and the continuation 12 0-0 N-Q2   13 N-Q2 N(Q2)-B3 14 NxN BxN   15 BxB NxB   16 P-B3 NxB   17 PxN Q-Q2 led to an even game.

Tal improved White's play though in his game against Duckstein at Zurich in 1959, with the vigorous 12 P-Q5, and after 12 . . . PxP   13 PxP BxP   14 N-Q4 Q-B3   15 P-B3 NxB   16 PxN N-Q2   17 BxP N-B4 18 N-N5, eventually scored a win.

12 RPxN   N-Q2

13 P-R4

This is to discourage Q-side castling, while the threat of opening the rook file by 14 P-R5 compels Black to weaken his pawn position.

13 . . .   P-QR4

14 R-QN1   P-N5

Forces the knight to the side of the board, where strangely enough it turns out to be happily placed.

15 N-R4   N-B3

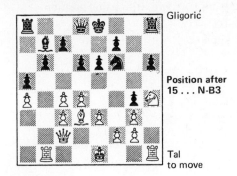

Gligorić

Position after
15 . . . N-B3

Tal
to move

16 P-Q5!

This offer of a pawn, typical of Tal, must have been made in a split-second!

16 . . .   Q-K2

Relying on instinct alone, Black should be wary of accepting the sacrifice, since it cedes White's knight (and bishop) the beautiful square KB5.

17 0-0

It would not do to go in for 17 PxP QxP   18 N-B5 0-0-0   19 NxRP when 19 . . . N-K5! turns the tables.

17 . . .   N-Q2

After 17 . . . 0-0-0, Tal intended to play 18 P-K4. He indicated that 18 PxP PxP   19 N-N6 Q-N2 20 NxR RxN allowed Black possibilities of counter-attack by . . . P-R4 and . . . P-R5.

18 PxP   QxP

Black recaptures with the queen, as after 18 . . . PxP 19 N-N6 Q-N2   20 NxR QxN   21 B-N6ch puts an end to his hope of castling, and keeps the king in the center.

19 B-B5!   QxBP

This looks good, as the queen captures a pawn and protects the king knight pawn at the same time—but Tal has a few good moves in store to meet the situation.

20 KR-Q1

The threat is now 21 R-Q4 Q-B4   22 R-N5 Q-R6

(if Q-B3   23 B-K4 catches the bishop) 23 BxP, and
White regains the pawn, with a fine position.

20 . . .   N-B3

21 R-Q4   Q-B3

Gligorić

Position after
21 . . . Q-B3

Tal
to move

22 B-K6!

Beautiful, and perhaps unexpected. Black's queen
is surrounded, and threatened with loss by 23 R-QB4.

22 . . .   R-KN1

Clearly 22 . . . PxB succumbs to 23 Q-N6ch K-K2
24 Q-N7ch, followed by removal of the rook from the
board.

Gligorić's move is meant to counter 23 R-QB4 with
23 . . . PxB   24 RxQ BxR, leaving him with rook,
bishop, and pawn for the queen.

23 B-B4!

Another zigzag move by the bishop, this time with
even more vicious intent—winning the queen by
24 B-N5.

23 . . .   K-B1

Better chances were offered by 23 . . . 0-0-0
24 Q-B5ch N-Q2

24 B-N5   Q-B4

25 R-QB4   Q-K4

26 RxBP

Equalizing the material assets, but the position is
manifestly in favour of White.

26 . . .   B-K5

27 B-Q3   P-Q4

28 R-B6   R-N1

29 P-QB4! R-N4

On 29 . . . PxP, White can choose between 30 BxB
QxB   31 RxBP, and 30 RxBP BxB   31 QxB, followed
by 32 R-B4, in either case with advantage.

30 P-B5   P-Q5

Obviously not 30 . . . PxP, when 31 RxRch QxR
32 RxN wins a piece by 'the overworked queen'
theme.

31 KPxP   QxQP

32 BxB   QxB

33 PxP   QxQ

34 RxQ   N-Q2

35 P-N7   N-B4

This is the situation:

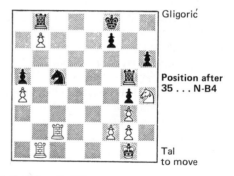

Gligorić

Position after
35 . . . N-B4

Tal
to move

36 R-N5!   NxNP

37 R(B2)-N2!

Several annotators have said that Homer nods, and
suggested 37 N-B5 to win, the threat being
38 RxN RxR   39 R-B8 mate. Then if 37 . . . P-B3
38 R-B7 wins a piece, or if 37 . . . K-N1   38 NxPch
followed by 39 RxR wins.

Homer may nod, but Tal does not, as P.H. Clarke
shows: if 37 N-B5, Black escapes the pin on his

knight by simply abandoning it! He plays 37 . . .
R-K1, and White cannot touch the beast, as his own
knight needs protection.

37 . . .   RxR

38 RxR   K-K2

Of course not 38 . . . K-N2, to protect the rook pawn,
as 39 N-B5ch K-N3   40 N-Q6 costs him the exchange.

Black's actual move is intended to relieve the rook
in its defence of the knight, enabling it to go after
White's rook pawn.

39 N-B5ch

After sitting patiently on the side-lines for 24 moves,
the knight decides to take a hand in the activities.

39 . . .   K-Q2

40 NxP   K-B2

41 NxBP   R-KB1

But not 41 . . . R-K1   42 RxNch KxR   43 N-Q6ch
and White wins.

42 N-R6   R-Q1

43 R-N5   R-Q8ch

44 K-R2   R-R8

45 RxP   N-B4

46 R-QB4   K-B3

47 N-B5   RxP

48 N-Q4ch   K-N3

The king stays close to the pawn, in order to protect
it. If instead 48 . . . K-Q4   49 RxR NxR   50 N-N3,
and the pawn is lost.

49 RxR   NxR

50 P-N4   N-B6

51 K-N3   P-R5

52 K-B4

More precise was 52 N-B2, holding back the pawn.

52 . . .   P-R6

53 N-B2!

Careful! Instead of this, if White is hasty and plays
53 P-N5 N-K7ch ruins everything.

53 . . .   P-R7

54 P-N5   K-B4

55 P-N6   K-B5

56 P-N7   N-Q4ch

57 K-N5   N-K2

Black fights hard. His knight stops the pawn, while
his king will capture the knight, and queen the
rook pawn.

58 P-B4!   K-B6

59 N-R1   K-N7

60 P-B5   KxN

61 P-B6   K-N8

62 PxN   P-R8(Q)

63 P-K8(Q)   Q-R4ch

If 63 . . . QxPch   64 Q-N3ch forces an exchange of
queens and wins.

64 K-R6   Resigns

If 64 . . . Q-N3ch   65 Q-N6ch wins, or if 64 . . .
Q-Q7ch   65 K-R7 Q-Q6ch   66 Q-N6 brings about
the exchange, and wins.

In the course of the game, this was the tour taken
by Tal's king bishop:

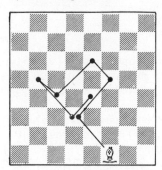

51

White **M. Tal**   Black **R. Fischer**
King's Indian Defence
Zagreb, 1959

Tal was at the top of his form in winning the Candidates' Tournament in 1959, and with it the right to play Botvinnik for the title.

Though he found Keres his *bête noire*, losing three out of four games to him, Tal qualified easily by scoring 20 points, outdistancing such tough competitors as Keres, Petrosian, Smyslov, Gligorić, and Fischer.

Evidence of his prowess may be gathered from the fact that he won four games in a row from Bobby Fischer—a feat no one has ever accomplished before or since!

In the course of the tournament, Tal produced some beautiful games, the following being one of his masterpieces.

1 P-Q4   N-KB3

2 P-QB4   P-KN3

3 N-QB3   B-N2

Fischer's loss to Tal in an earlier round did not deter him from trying the King's Indian Defence again.

4 P-K4   P-Q3

5 B-K2   0-0

6 N-B3   P-K4

7 P-Q5   QN-Q2

8 B-N5

Petrosian's pet variation, one purpose of which is to clamp a pin on the knight, making it difficult for Black to get in the . . . P-KB4 break, practically essential in the defence.

If Black tries to release himself from the pin by . . . P-KR3 and . . . P-KN4, it's at the expense of weakening his white squares.

The continuation 8 0-0 N-B4   9 Q-B2 P-QR4 10 N-K1 KN-Q2   11 B-K3 P-B4   12 PxP PxP

13 P-B4 PxP   14 BxP N-K5   15 NxN PxN   16 P-KN3 Q-B3   17 R-QN1 Q-Q5ch   18 K-R1 N-B4, offers no problems to Black.

8 . . .   P-KR3

Quick, before 9 Q-Q2 makes this move impossible!

9 B-R4   P-R3

P.H Clarke best explains this move, 'Black wants to prevent N-QN5 so that he can move his queen, so that he can move his knight, so that he can move his king bishop pawn. The whole conception is too tortuous.'

Benko had tried 9 . . . P-KN4 in a previous round against Smyslov, but after 10 B-N3 N-R4   11 0-0 N-B5   12 N-Q2 P-KB4 (to stop 13 B-N4)   13 PxP NxBch   14 QxN N-B3   15 P-B5 BxP   16 QR-B1 PxP   17 Q-B4 N-Q2   18 P-N4!, he had the inferior position, and he eventually lost the game.

10 0-0   Q-K1

11 N-Q2

White prepares for P-KB4, the thematic move in attacking the King's Indian.

11 . . .   N-R2

Black prepares for . . . P-KB4, the thematic move in defending the King's Indian.

12 P-QN4   B-B3

This varies from their 6th round game, when Fischer played 12 . . . N-N4, and succumbed to a Tal attack. Fischer was not the only victim, as Gligorić tried the move several rounds later against Petrosian—to his sorrow.

The break by 12 . . . P-KB4 would be premature, as after 13 PxP PxP (13 . . . RxP is better) 14 B-R5, White wins the exchange.

13 BxB   N(R2)xB

14 N-N3

The knight takes the first step in supporting the contemplated advance of the pawn to B5.

14 . . .   Q-K2

15 Q-Q2   K-R2

16 Q-K3

And the queen takes the second step.

16 ...   N-KN1

Fischer of course intends to continue with 17 . . .
P-KB4, the only possible chance there is for counterplay.

17 P-B5!   P-B4

18 PxBP

Tal must prevent any demonstration by 18 . . . P-B5.

18 ...   PxP

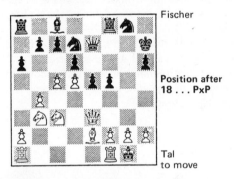

Fischer

Position after
18 . . . PxP

Tal
to move

19 P-B4!

Tal offers a pawn, the first of his gifts. The open files
resulting from its acceptance will favour the player
whose development is superior.

19 ...   PxP

There is little choice, as 19 . . . P-K5 not only cedes
White the square Q4 for the use of his pieces, but also
allows him attacking chances by P-KN4.

20 QxP   PxP

This turns out to be fatal, but there was little consolation in 20 . . . Q-K4, which still left him the
weakling king bishop pawn to worry about, or in
20 . . . N-K4, after which White plays 21 QR-K1
followed by 22 N-Q4 with advantage.

21 B-Q3!

Aims directly at the king, and meanwhile clears the
center file for the queen rook.

21 ...   PxP

22 QR-K1   Q-B3

Fischer could have put up more resistance with
22 . . . Q-Q3, though 23 BxPch K-R1   24 Q-Q4ch
Q-B3   25 QxP Q-N3ch   26 Q-Q4ch QxQch   27 NxQ
would still have left White with the better game.

This is the position, with Tal to play:

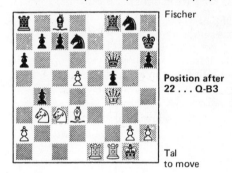

Fischer

Position after
22 . . . Q-B3

Tal
to move

23 R-K6!

Tal cheerfully sacrifices a piece to lure the queen
away from the theater of action.

23 ...   QxN

24 BxPch   RxB

Quick loss follows 24 . . . K-N2 by 25 R-N6ch
K-B2 (or 25 . . . K-R1   26 RxPch NxR   27 QxNch
and mate next)   26 BxNch dis.ch KxR   27 QxR,
and White wins.

25 QxRch   K-R1

26 R-B3   Q-N7

If 26 . . . Q-N2 there follows 27 R-N3 Q-B1 (or
27 . . . Q-R2   28 R-K8! QxQ   29 R(K8)xNch, and
mate next move)   28 QxQ NxQ   29 R-K8, and
White wins a knight or two.

27 R-K8!

Every move a hammer-blow! This one threatens
28 RxNch, with mate or loss of the queen to follow.

27 ...   N(Q2)-B3

This returns the piece, and is the only move for the time being.

Strangely enough, Black's queen has no checks with which to delay the inevitable.

28 QxNch   QxQ

29 RxQ   K-N2

30 R(B6)-B8

Attacks knight and bishop.

30 ...   N-K2

This saves both pieces.

Fischer

Position after
30 . . . N-K2

Tal
to move

31 N-R5!

Effectuates an almost complete *zugzwang*. Of all Black's pieces, only the rook may move without immediate loss of a piece, and that only to N1.

If 31 . . . K-N3   32 RxN wins a piece.
If 31 . . . B-N5   32 RxR wins a piece.
If 31 . . . NxP   32 RxB wins a piece.
If 31 . . . R-R2, 32 R-B1 wins a piece.

31 ...   P-R4

32 P-KR4   R-N1

33 N-B4

Threatens 34 P-Q6 PxP   35 NxP with a triple attack on the unfortunate bishop.

33 ...   P-N4

34 N-K5   Resigns

The threat of 35 R-B7ch K-R3   36 R-R8 mate is too much to withstand.

52

White **M. Tal**   Black **Y. Averbach**
Ruy López
U.S.S.R. Team Championship 1961

Tal manages somehow to introduce excitement in staid positions that have occurred thousands of times before in master games.

A few waves of his magic wand, and pleasing combinations spring up out of soil that seemed barren.

Tal cleverly maneuvers matters so that he scores the win in the early midgame—the way to do it if you are playing an endgame specialist!

1 P-K4   P-K4

2 N-KB3   N-QB3

3 B-N5

One reason for the popularity of the Ruy López is that White gets a good game simply by making natural moves.

3 ...   P-QR3

4 B-R4   N-B3

5 0-0   B-K2

The *Strong Point* variation, which aims to maintain a pawn at K4, to prevent White from getting too powerful a center.

6 R-K1   P-QN4

7 B-N3   P-Q3

8 P-B3   0-0

9 P-KR3

This prevents the pin of the knight, and is important if White wants to play P-Q4. Should he play 9 P-Q4 first, then 9 . . . B-N5 threatens 10 . . . BxN, breaking up the K-side.

Should White then continue with 10 P-Q5, the continuation 10 . . . N-QR4 11 B-B2 P-B3 strikes at White's center. Or if 10 B-K3, the sequel 10 . . . PxP 11 PxP N-QR4 12 B-B2 N-B5 13 B-B1 P-B4 allows Black good counterchances.

9 . . .   N-QR4

10 B-B2   P-B4

11 P-Q4   Q-B2

The Tchigorin system, whose intricacies no one has yet mastered. It offers such a wealth of fascinating possibilities that many of its devotees are happy to play either side of the variation.

12 QN-Q2

The knight is headed for an outpost at Q5 or KB5, from either of which squares it can take active part in an attack on the king.

12 . . .   N-B3

The knight returns towards the center—the theater of war.

The alternative 12 . . . B-N2 leads to an equal game—unless White is the better player.

13 PxBP

Stein obtained a good game against Ivkov in the Interzonal Tournament of 1964 by 13 P-Q5 N-Q1 14 P-QR4 R-N1 15 P-B4 B-Q2 16 RPxP PxP 17 PxP BxP 18 B-R4! R-R1 19 R-K3 N-N2 20 R(K3)-R3.

Tal, however, wants the square Q5 open and available to his knight.

13 . . .   PxP

14 N-B1   R-Q1

15 Q-K2   P-N3

Bisguier tried 15 . . . N-KR4 against Fischer in the U.S. Championship of 1963-4. Fischer replied 16 P-KN3!, a move which, he said, 'bankrupts Black's strategy. The slight weakening of the K-side is inconsequential. but Black's loss of time with his king

knight is.' After 16 . . . P-N3, White's response 17 P-KR4!, was characterized by Fischer as 'a tremendous improvement over Bronstein's game against Reshevsky.'

Fischer won the game on the 35th move, one of his 11 straight wins in that tournament.

16 N-K3   R-N1

This is the position, with White to play:

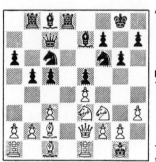

Averbach

Position after 16 . . . R-N1

Tal
to move

17 N-N5!

En avant! Tal wastes no time! In a position that is apparently even, Tal launches an attack which forces capitulation in less than a dozen moves.

17 . . .   B-B1

18 Q-B3   B-KN2

19 N-Q5   Q-Q3

20 B-K3   P-R3

Black attacks the knight, which has no flight-square. Has Tal miscalculated, or does he have a combination up his sleeve?

21 NxNch   BxN

After 21 . . . QxN instead, there follows 22 QxQ BxQ 23 N-B3, and the bishop picks up one of the two loose pawns.

22 QR-Q1   Q-K2

The knight is still *en prise* and doomed, but its fate was foreseen, and is part of the master plan.

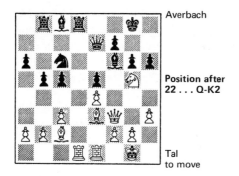

Averbach

Position after
22 . . . Q-K2

Tal
to move

23 BxP!

Begins a beautiful combination, with a problem-like finish.

23 . . .   RxR

If 23 . . . QxB   24 QxB threatens mate in two, as well as 25 RxRch, winning easily. If then 24 . . . R-B1 25 B-N3 PxN (otherwise 26 BxPch wins) 26 QxNPch K-R1   27 Q-R6ch K-N1   28 R-Q6 B-K3 (on 28 . . . N-K2   29 QxPch forces mate) 29 RxB PxR 30 BxPch R-B2   31 Q-N6ch wins.

24 RxR

Far better than 24 BxQ RxRch   25 K-R2 NxB 26 QxB PxN   27 QxN B-K3, when Black still needs subduing.

24 . . .   QxB

25 QxB   PxN

So the knight did not escape after all! But Tal has not been unprepared, and he now unfolds the rest of the combination.

26 B-N3!

This quiet little move initiates two threats: 27 QxBPch, and 27 QxNPch.

26 . . .   R-N2

27 QxNPch   K-B1

28 Q-R6ch   Resigns

The rest, which is certainly not obvious, would go like this:

28 . . .   K-K2

If 28 . . . K-N1   29 R-Q6, with the threat of 29 R-N6ch, is decisive.

29 R-Q5

Attacks the queen, which must stay near the knight.

29 . . .   Q-N3

30 R-Q6

Doubles the attack on the knight (which may not move) and forces Black to defend it.

30 . . .   R-B2

Protecting the knight by 30 . . . B-Q2 loses by 31 Q-B6ch K-K1   32 BxPch K-B1   33 B-N6 dis.ch K-N1   34 Q-B7ch, and mate next move.

Black's rook move though unguards the queen, and that is the whole point of Tal's combination.

31 Q-B6ch   K-K1

32 R-Q8ch!

and Black must play 32 . . . NxR, exposing his queen to capture.

53

White **M. Tal**   Black **R. Letelier**
Ruy López
Havana, 1963

Even in the sober Ruy López opening, one may stray into strange territory where, as O. Henry says, 'The hand of man has never set foot.'

Tal acclimatizes himself quickly, and in no time at all, little combinations follow each other in rapid succession. There is such an air of spontaneity about them that one is tempted to call this little opus of Tal's—
Impromptu Havanaise.

1 P-K4   P-K4

2 N-KB3   N-QB3

3 B-N5   P-QR3

4 B-R4   P-Q3

5 P-B3   B-Q2

6 P-Q4   KN-K2

Unusual at this point. Black generally develops in simple, straightforward style by 6 . . . N-B3   7 O-O B-K2   8 R-K1 O-O   9 QN-Q2 B-K1 (the Kecskemet Variation) or by 6 . . . P-KN3   7 O-O B-N2   8 PxP PxP   9 B-K3 N-R3 (the Alekhine system).

7 B-N3   P-R3

To prevent 8 N-N5.

8 N-R4   P-KN4

If Black expected to drive the knight off, he is under a grave delusion, as Tal's pieces rarely retreat.

9 Q-R5

Mate takes precedence over everything else!

9 . . .   R-R2

10 BxNP   PxP

11 P-KB4

He must stop 11 . . . N-K4, with dishonourable intentions (12 . . . B-N5) towards the queen.

11 . . .   Q-B1

Still pursuing the queen by 12 . . . B-N5.

12 P-B5   PxP

13 NxP   N-K4

14 B-B6

Castling instead would allow 14 . . . PxB   15 QxR PxN, and Black wins two pieces for a rook.

14 . . .   N-N1

This will eliminate the troublesome bishop, but not in the way pictured by Black.

15 BxN   PxB   See diagram at top of next column.

16 N-N6!   B-Q3

Obviously 16 . . . PxN   17 QxPch loses the exchange, so Black protects his valuable king pawn.

17 BxPch!

Tal strikes at once, forcing the king out into the open.

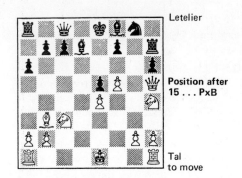

Letelier

Position after 15 . . . PxB

Tal to move

17 . . .   KxB

Capturing with the rook loses by 18 N-R8 B-K3 19 PxB QxP   20 QxRch, and White wins the exchange and the game.

18 N-Q5!

There being no worthwhile discovered check, this move introduces one—19 N(N6)-K7 dis.ch, winning the queen.

18 . . .   K-N2

19 O-O

Now the threat is 20 P-B6ch, and Black must give up his knight.

19 . . .   N-B3

20 NxN   KxN

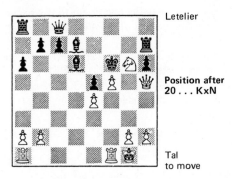

Letelier

Position after 20 . . . KxN

Tal to move

21 NxP!

Tal always finds fresh resources, generally beginning with a sacrifice.

21 ...   Q-K1

If 21 . . . BxN 22 Q-N6ch gets the rook in return, while 21 . . . KxN is met by 22 P-B6 dis.ch K-K3 (on 22 . . . KxKP 23 QR-Q1 is enough to frighten the poor king to death) 23 Q-Q5 checkmate.

22 NxBch   RxN

Quick loss follows 22 . . . QxN 23 P-K5ch KxKP (23 . . . BxP 24 Q-N6ch wins the rook) 24 P-B6 dis.ch K-K3 24 Q-B5ch.

If 22 . . . K-N2, there is a pretty win by 23 Q-N4ch K–R1 24 N-B6 R-N2 25 QxRch KxQ 26 NxQch, and the rest is easy.

23 P-K5ch!

Tal never seems to run out of ideas.

23 ...   BxP

Other captures lose the queen, viz: 23 . . . KxP 24 QR-K1ch, or 23 . . . QxP 24 Q-N6ch K-K2 25 QR-K1, and the pin does it.

24 QxPch   K-B2

25 QR-K1

The right order of moves. Premature would be 25 P-B6, when 25 . . . B-Q5ch 26 K-R1 Q-R1 holds the fort.

25 ...   R-Q4

Frees the queen from being tied down to the bishop, let alone from the menace of the enemy rook on the file.

The tempting 25 . . . B-Q5ch 26 K-R1 R-K2 goes down to glorious defeat after 27 P-B6 RxR 28 Q-N7ch K-K3 29 RxRch B-K4 30 RxBch KxR 31 P-B7 dis.ch, and the queen falls.

26 Q-R7ch   K-B3

There are some nice touches after 26 . . . K-B1, when 27 P-B6 Q-B2 28 Q-R6ch K-K1 (if 28 . . . K-N1 29 R-K4! wins) 29 Q-R8ch Q-B1 30 RxBch! RxR 31 P-B7ch K-Q2 32 QxR wins for White.

Again, if 26 . . . K-B1 27 P-B6 B-Q5ch 28 K-R1 Q-B2 29 Q-R8ch Q-N1 30 Q-R6ch K-B2 31 R-K7 is mate.

Letelier's move leads to an equally neat finish.

27 R-K4   B-Q5ch

28 K-R1!   Resigns

After 28 . . . QxR 29 Q-N6ch, Black must decide between losing his queen by 29 . . . K-K2 30 P-B6 dis.ch, or his king by 29 . . . K-K4 30 Q-K6 mate, the latter finish making this pretty picture:

54

White **M. Tal**   Black **R. Bogdanovich**
Sicilian Defence
Match U.S.S.R.-Yugoslavia, Budva, 1967

Tal's opponent is perfectly familiar with Nimzowitsch's precept, 'Never play to win a pawn while your development is unfinished,' but he is lured nevertheless into going pawn-hunting early in the game. Perhaps he was influenced by Steinitz's own policy after he had captured a hot pawn, 'A pawn is worth a little trouble.'

It's true that Tal gives away pawns with a generous hand (sometimes throwing in a piece or two) but for this he exacts punishment from the recipient.

This time he works up a slashing attack, studded with

enough sparkling moves to require a goodly supply of
exclamation marks.

The spirit of Morphy lives on!

1 P-K4   P-QB4

2 N-KB3   P-Q3

3 P-Q4   PxP

4 NxP   N-KB3

5 N-QB3   P-QR3

6 B-KN5

An energetic line, designed to draw the fangs of the
Najdorf Variation.

6 . . .   P-K3

7 P-B4   Q-N3

8 Q-Q2   QxP

Yielding to temptation, Black captures the poisoned
pawn. His position is solid, and (he hopes) able to
withstand assault.

9 R-QN1

The older line of play, but Spassky's defeat of Fischer
in the 11th game of their Championship Match,
beginning with 9 N-N3, will undoubtedly become
fashionable for a while.

9 . . .   Q-R6

10 P-B5

This varies from Keres-Fuderer, Gothenberg 1955,
which took this short but brilliant course: 10 P-K5
KN-Q2 11 P-B5! NxP 12 PxP PxP 13 B-K2
QN-B3 14 NxN PxN 15 N-K4! P-Q4 16 0-0 Q-R5
17 B-R5ch K-Q2 (if 17 . . . P-N3 18 N-B6ch wins,
or if 17 . . . N-N3 18 BxNch PxB 19 Q-B2, and
mate to follow) 18 RxB Resigns.

10 . . .   N-B3

Though Geller played this move against Fischer and
won, he suggested 10 . . . P-N4, securing more Q-side
space, as a better defence.

11 PxP   PxP

12 NxN   PxN

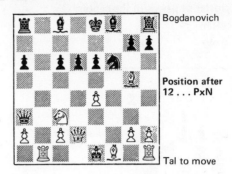

Bogdanovich

Position after
12 . . . PxN

Tal to move

13 P-K5!

Tal wants to open some files, so he sacrifices another
pawn.

13 . . .   N-Q4

14 NxN

Since an exchange of knights can hardly be avoided,
Tal proceeds with it at once, in order to go about
the business of bringing new pieces into the field.

The alternative 14 N-K4 allows 14 . . . PxP, and
the threat of 15 . . . B-N5 will delay the attack.

14 . . .   BPxN

15 B-K2   PxP

This pawn had to be eliminated, as it interfered with
Black's freedom of movement.

16 0-0   B-B4ch

Gligorić put it picturesquely, 'The tension is at its
peak. Black's king has no safe place, the winds are
blowing all around along open files and diagonals, but
still Black's central pawn mass allows hope for the
protection of the sable sovereign.'

17 K-R1   R-B1

Black is keenly interested in reducing the number of
pieces, as their diminution would lessen the force of
the attack.

18 P-B4

White, on the other hand, is concerned about splitting up the cluster of pawns in the center.

18 ...   RxRch

19 RxR   B-N2

Bogdanovich

Position after
19 . . . B-N2

Tal
to move

20 Q-B2!

Fischer, who reached this position in his game against Geller at Monte Carlo earlier in the same year, played 20 B-N4, but suffered a debacle after 20 . . . PxP 21 BxP Q-Q6 22 Q-K1 B-K5! 23 B-N4 R-N1 24 B-Q1 K-Q2 (to avoid the threat of 25 B-R4ch) 25 R-B7ch K-K3, and White resigned, as 26 RxP loses by 26 . . . BxPch 27 KxB R-N7ch 28 K-R1 Q-Q4ch, and Black forces mate.

Tal's move is excellent, but equally potent is 20 B-Q1 (Lilienthal's suggestion) with the threat of winning by 21 R-B3 Q-N5 22 QxQ BxQ 23 B-R4ch and mate next move.

After this subtle 20 B-Q1 move, there are all sorts of interesting possibilities. If Black for example plays 20 . . . PxP, the reply 21 Q-QB2, with threats of 22 Q-R4ch, and 22 QxRP, is crushing.

22 ...   P-K5

21 B-N4!   B-K2

Unfortunately, Black cannot play the powerful-looking 21 . . . Q-Q6, as the reply 22 Q-R4ch is fatal.

22 Q-KB2!   0-0-0

Perhaps this may offer a modicum of safety. The alternative 22 . . . BxB loses quickly by 23 Q-B7ch K-Q1 24 QxB R-B1 25 BxP R-B2 26 Q-N8ch K-K2 27 Q-KB8ch, and White wins the queen.

23 B-B4!

This fine move precludes any attempt by the king to flee to the corner.

23 ...   B-Q3

24 BxPch   K-N1

On 24 . . . K-B2, White can choose between pursuing the attack by 25 PxP, or by 25 R-QN1 (threatening 26 Q-N6ch) Q-R4 26 Q-R7.

25 Q-N6!   BxB

Black must give up the exchange, as a rook move, say to K1, is more expensive, the reply 26 BxBch winning the queen.

26 QxRch   K-R2

27 R-QN1   Q-Q3

Black had to prevent 28 Q-N6ch.

28 BxP!

Played with the customary Tal elegance.

28 ...   BxB

Black refuses the queen, as it's only a temporary loan. After 28 . . . QxQ 29 RxBch K-R1 30 R-Q7 dis.ch, Tal gets the queen back, with a bishop as interest.

29 QxQ   BxQ

30 PxB   Resigns

Petrosian

Petrosian plays like no other master, past or present.

   Petrosian does not play for the attack; you get the impression that he regards a K-side attack as a primitive attempt to force a win. Nor does he try to improve his position at every turn, nor play to weaken that of his opponent. Very often he seems to be devoting his time to maneuvering his pieces to the first rank, or even into a corner of the board.

   N'importe! Petrosian can be dangerous from the first rank!

   Petrosian has mastered the art of prophylaxis far beyond the teachings of Nimzowitsch, and can nip in the bud any aggressive attempts by his opponent. He can smell danger a mile off, and knows how best to avert it. Petrosian has enormous patience, and can maneuver tirelessly, waiting for the right moment to spring. When he does, the pent-up energy in his pieces can be devastating.

   Wedded to fascinating technique is enormous tactical ability. Sharpened by thousands of blitz games (in blitz play he is second only to Fischer) he sees combinations in a flash, most of which he dismisses. For Petrosian embarks on a combination only if it is correct, and conclusive in every detail. In this (Euwe says) Petrosian resembles Capablanca. Both feel at home in all the nooks and crannies of the chessboard. Both prefer simple positions, and are accurate and deep in calculation. And both of them have a dislike of wild play in chess. A sacrifice is either correct or incorrect. A semi-correct sacrifice does not exist in Petrosian's vocabulary. In this Petrosian differs from Botvinnik in the same way that Capablanca differed from Lasker. This is not to say that Lasker and Botvinnik play wildly, but they are more willing to allow a role to the accidental in their games.

   Petrosian's style is unique unto himself. A study of his games show such ideas as these:

1. Opening moves which seem to contradict established principles.
2. Late development of several pieces.
3. Castling which is long-delayed.
4. Castling to a wing where the king seems exposed to danger.
5. Retreat of seemingly well-placed pieces to the back rank, or into a corner.
6. Early advance of the king rook pawn, a step which seems premature and makes castling on the K-side dangerous.
7. A series of strange, apparently purposeless moves.
8. Unexpected *zwischenzuge*—in-between moves.
9. Little stabbing pawn pushes, alternating from one side of the board to the other, which nibble away at the enemy position.

10. Subtle defensive touches, when his position seems in no danger of attack.

Small wonder then, that Petrosian's opponents are often bewildered by his mysterious maneuvers, and seem at times to put up insufficient resistance.

Petrosian's games are fascinating, and I recommend them for your delectation.

Petrosian enjoyed his first big triumph in the year 1951, when he became Champion of Moscow, and also finished first in the semi-finals of the U.S.S.R. Championship.

This was followed by a second prize in the 1952 Interzonal Tournament, and a second prize in the 1953 Candidates' Tournament.

In 1956 he repeated his 1951 stunt by again becoming Champion of Moscow, and again finishing first in the semi-finals of the U.S.S.R. Championship.

Two years later, Petrosian finally came in first in the Tournament for the Championship of the U.S.S.R.

Other victories in the next few years sweetened his career, culminating in his winning of first prize without loss in the Candidates' Tournament held at Curaçao in 1962, ahead of Keres, Geller, Fischer, and Korchnoi—to name his toughest rivals.

Petrosian was now ready for the supreme test, facing Botvinnik for the title of Champion of the World.

The match was contested in 1963, and Petrosian passed the test with flying colors, by defeating the title-holder 12½ to 9½

Now that he had possession of the crown, Petrosian had to beat back the assaults of the next challenger, in the person of Spassky. In preparation, Petrosian studied more than 500 of Spassky's games, to see if he could spot weaknesses that were not obvious to most annotators. Apparently he found some that he could exploit, for he defeated Spassky by 12½ points to 11½

That was in 1966, but Spassky turned the tables in 1969, and took the crown away to the tune of 12½ to 10½ points in a hard-fought match.

I consider Petrosian the sixth greatest chess player of all time.

55

White **Jopen**   Black **T. Petrosian**
French Defence
Belgrade, 1954

Petrosian plays the opening like a beginner—or a genius!

He develops bishops before knights, blocks his own pieces, brings his queen out too early, exchanges a long-range bishop for a harmless knight, and indulges in a few other eccentricities.

In short, Petrosian smashes all the maxims, precepts, principles, and advice that have been handed down in the past 200 years—and goes on to win the game beautifully!

1 P-K4   P-K3

2 P-Q4   P-Q4

3 N-QB3   B-N5

'Knights before bishops', say the authorities.

4 P-K5   P-QN3

Prepares for 5 . . . B-N2, fianchettoing the bishop on a closed diagonal.

5 Q-N4   B-B1

Two violations at one blow: moving the same piece twice in the opening, and undeveloping his bishop.

6 N-B3   Q-Q2

Two more violations: brings his queen out early in the game, and blocks the path of the bishop.

7 N-QN5   N-QB3

This move obstructs the bishop pawn. Dr. Lasker says, 'You will sometimes, especially in Q-side openings, find it a better plan to advance the queen bishop pawn two squares before obstructing it with your knight.'

True, this is not a Q-side opening, but the strategy recommended for Black in the French Defence is to attack the center by . . . P-QB4.

8 P-B3   P-QR3

9 N-R3   P-B4

10 Q-N3   BxN

Not only does Petrosian exchange his long-range bishop for a knight posted at the side of the board, but he allows his opponent the advantage of the two bishops. .

11 PxB   B-N2

Black's remaining bishop bites on granite—in commanding a diagonal that is blocked by his own queen pawn.

12 N-N5   0-0-0

'Castle as early as possible, preferably on the K-side,' says everybody, beginning with Howard Staunton.

13 P-KR4   N-R3

This knight develops at the side of the board, there being no other choice.

14 B-Q3   K-N1

15 Q-B3   N-B2

16 N-R3   P-N3

17 Q-K2   K-R2

18 B-KN5   NxB

19 NxN   P-R3

20 N-R3   See diagram on page 146.

The knight could have returned to B3, but what was its future? From B3 the knight could move to Q2 and to N3, and then what? The knight could find no secure foothold anywhere.

From R3 though, the knight envisions a possibility of getting into the game by way of B4.

20 . . .   Q-K2!

Suddenly the queen strikes in two directions at once, and menaces both of White's rook pawns!

21 N-B4   P-KN4

22 N-R3

The alternatives are not inviting: If 22 N-N6 QxP 23 NxR QxBPch   24 Q-Q2 QxRch, and Black wins a piece. Or if 22 PxP PxP   23 RxR RxR   24 N-R3 P-N5 25 N-N1 R-R8   26 K-B1 (if 26 Q-B1, QxP wins) 26 . . . Q-R5, and White is lost.

Petrosian
to move

Position after
20 N-R3

Jopen

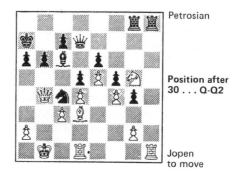

Petrosian

Position after
30 . . . Q-Q2

Jopen
to move

22 . . .   QxP

23 Q-Q2   Q-K2

White cannot now regain his pawn, as after 24 PxP PxP, he dare not recapture with either queen or knight.

24 0-0-0   QR-KN1

25 K-N1   N-R4

26 PxP   PxP

27 P-B4

Of course not 27 NxP, as 27 . . . RxR 28 RxR QxN wins a piece for Black.

27 . . .   P-N5

28 N-N5

The knight's third visit to this square.

28 . . .   B-B3

29 Q-N2   N-B5

30 Q-N4   Q-Q2

This seems to lose a pawn, but Petrosian is never caught napping.

See diagram at top of next column, with White to play.

31 BxN   P-R4

A *zwischenzug* (an in-between move) to drive the queen away from the protection of the bishop.

32 Q-N2

But not 32 Q-N3 (guarding the bishop), as 32 . . . B-R5 in reply would be painful.

32 . . .   PxB!

Suddenly new vistas are opened to Petrosian's bishop!

33 Q-Q2   B-Q4

34 R(Q1)-N1   Q-B3

35 RxR   RxR

36 P-N3

Otherwise 36 . . . R-R7 wins another pawn for Black.

36 . . .   Q-K1

37 K-N2   Q-R4

38 K-B2   Q-R7

39 QxQ

Forced, as a rook move loses the knight pawn.

39 . . .   RxQch

40 K-N1   K-R3

41 Resigns

White is helpless:

A move by his rook allows the reply 41 . . . R-N7, winning the knight pawn, and leaving Black with a passed pawn.

His knight can move only to B7 and Q8, and back again—to no avail.

Meanwhile, Black's king is free to wander down to R6, help capture the rook pawn, and win as he pleases.

A characteristic Petrosian game, unconventional and thoroughly captivating.

56

White **T. Petrosian**   Black **H. Pilnik**
Benoni Defence
Candidates' Tournament, Amsterdam, 1956

This game is one of the most impressive examples of profound modern-day strategy.

Petrosian blends positional subtleties with clever
tactical touches, in action that takes place over the entire
board.

This is sophisticated chess on a grand scale!

1 P-Q4   N-KB3

2 P-QB4   P-B4

3 P-Q5   P-K4

4 N-QB3   P-Q3

5 P-K4   P-KN3

6 N-B3

A good line is 6 B-K2, reserving the possibility of
playing 7 P-B4.

If 6 P-B4 at once, then 6 . . . N-R4   7 B-K3 N-Q2,
and Black controls his important K4 square.

6 . . .   B-N2

7 B-N5

Petrosian just loves this move! The pressure on his
K-side tempts Black to shake off the pin by 7 . . .
P-KR3 and 8 . . . P-KN4, with a consequent weakening
of his pawn position.

7 . . .   N-R3

8 B-K2   N-B2

The usual procedure. The knight supports . . . P-N4,
in order to obtain counterplay on the Q-side.

9 N-Q2!

A thoughtful, farsighted move, with more in it than
meets the eye. *Par exemple:*

After the almost inevitable exchanges at QN5 (as
a result of Black playing . . . P-N4) the square QB4
is available to White's knight.

Clearance of the king bishop's diagonal also
circumvents any counterplay by 9 . . . P-KR3, 10 . . .
P-KN4, and 11 . . . N-R4.

9 . . .   B-Q2

A better plan to enforce the pawn push . . . P-N4
was to play 9 . . . P-QR3. If then 10 P-QR4, Black
replies 10 . . . P-N3, and follows with 11 . . . R-QN1
and 12 . . . B-Q2.

10 P-QR4   P-N3

Whereas now 10 . . . P-QR3   is met by 11 P-R5!,
and 11 . . . P-N4 is rendered futile by 12 PxP *en
passant*.

11 N-N5!

This puts a halt to the proceedings, whether Black
captures the knight or not.

11 . . .   BxN

The knight had to be removed, as it threatened to
take the queen pawn, and 11 . . . B-QB1 allowed
12 P-R5 in reply.

The capture should have been made by the knight
though, as the bishop was needed to guard his QB3
square.

12 BPxB   0-0

White's shrewd 11th move has deprived Black of
effective counterplay on the Q-side.

Meanwhile, Petrosian's knight eyes the dream
square at QB4.

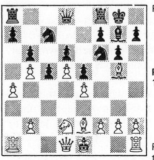

Pilnik

**Position after
12 . . . 0-0**

Petrosian
to move

13 P-QN4!

Beautiful! White now maintains a constant threat of PxP (naturally, when the time is ripe).

Black meanwhile, is restrained from playing . . . PxP, as that hands over the queen bishop file, and the square QB6, to White's rook.

13 . . .   P-KR3

14 BxN!

An important move, though by no means an obvious one. If 14 B-K3 instead, Black plays 14 . . . PxP followed by 15 . . . N-Q2 and 16 . . . N-B4, making his position impregnable.

As John Hammond puts it, 'The exchange of a good bishop for a harmless knight is altogether in Petrosian's style. Having acquired a quarter of the board, he wants quiet enjoyment of it, and no interference from . . . N-Q2 and . . . N-B4.'

14 . . .   QxB

15 0-0

White avoids 15 PxP, as after 15 . . . QPxP, Black is enabled to play . . . N-K1 and . . . N-Q3, blockading the passed pawn (and the rest of the position).

15 . . .   KR-Q1

16 N-B4

The knight is ideally posted at this square, poised to take part in any action that may develop.

16 . . .   B-B1

17 P-N3!

Very deceptive, as this quiet little move on the K-side will help support a break-through on the Q-side!

The plan is to play 18 PxP QPxP   19 P-B4, therewith setting in motion a formidable pawn-roller, which would render a blockade of the queen pawn impossible.

A fine point involved, which shows the importance of proper timing, is that the pawn capture undertaken without the preparatory 17 P-N3 move, leads to this continuation: 17 PxP QPxP   18 P-B4 PxP   19 P-K5

Q-N4   20 B-B3 N-K3!, and the knight anchors itself firmly at Q5!

17 . . .   PxP

Restraining the K-side pawns by 17 . . . P-N4 does not appeal to Black. For one thing, it weakens his K-side. For another, it permits the intrusion 18 B-N4 and 19 B-B5, and eventually P-B4 with an attack.

18 Q-N3   K-N2!

A little trap. If 19 QxP N-K3!   20 PxN, (otherwise 20 . . . N-B4 sets up a barricade) P-Q4!, and Black frees himself. (The king's move incidentally, is to prevent (in this line) the bishop pawn being taken with check).

19 KR-B1

Petrosian is in no hurry.

19 . . .   P-KR4

20 N-K3

White clears the file for his rook.

20 . . .   N-K1

21 QxP   KR-B1

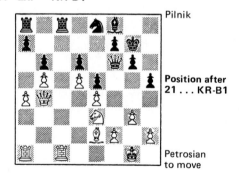

Pilnik

Position after 21 . . . KR-B1

Petrosian to move

22 R-B6!

The strategic crowning of Petrosian's previous efforts.

22 . . .   Q-Q1

Exchanging rooks was unavailing, as White recaptures 23 NPxR with 24 B-R6 and 25 B-N7 to follow, or 23 QPxR with 24 N-Q5 to follow.

23 QR-QB1   N-B3

Black is still hoping that he can get in 24 . . . N-Q2 and 25 . . . N-B4, thus battening down the hatches.

24 B-B1

White is ready to circumvent the idea. If Black plays 24 . . . N-Q2, then 25 B-R3 pins the knight, and after 25 . . . RxR 26 QPxR N-B4 he continues with 27 N-Q5, and the advance of the passed pawn will cost Black the exchange.

24 . . .   KR-N1

25 B-R3!

The bishop's entrance on the scene, combined with the power of the doubled rooks, assures White of complete domination of the queen bishop file.

25 . . .   P-R3

Black must get some air, or chance being smothered.

26 R-K1

This protects the king pawn, in preparation for 27 N-B4.

26 . . .   PxP

27 PxP   N-R2

28 N-B4   R-R7

29 B-N2

Petrosian plays safe, being in time-pressure. The Tournament Book indicates as more precise 29 Q-N3 (to drive off the annoying rook). Should the rook be supported by 29 . . . R(N1)-R1 (instead of leaving) then the continuation 30 RxNP N-N4 31 B-N2 Q-B3 32 Q-K3 gives White a winning advantage.

29 . . .   Q-B3

30 R-KB1

He must stop the mate in two.

30 . . .   N-N4

31 Q-N3   R(N1)-R1

32 P-R4

White repels one of the invaders before picking up the first bit of booty.

32 . . .   N-R2

33 RxNP   R-R8

34 R-B6   R(R1)-R7

Black is getting obstreperous, actually threatening 35 . . . QxPch and mate next move!

35 Q-K3   Q-Q1

36 RxR

The advance 36 P-N6 was simpler, but Petrosian was still in time-trouble.

36 . . .   RxRch

37 K-R2   N-B3

38 P-B3

The queen was in danger, so this or 38 B-R3 had to be played.

38 . . .   Q-N1

39 Q-N3   N-Q2

40 P-N6   N-B4

41 Q-N2   R-R5

42 Q-N5   R-R7

43 R-B7   P-N4

Desperately attempting to divert White from carrying out such threats on the Q-side as 44 Q-B6 and 45 P-N7, or 44 N-R5 and 45 N-B6, either with decisive effect.

44 N-K3   PxP

45 N-B5ch   K-N1

46 PxP   R-R3

Sets a last trap: If 47 RxN (to remove the rook's protector) 47 . . . RxP followed by 48 . . . PxR is an unpleasant surprise.

47 P-N7   R-R2

But not 47 . . . QxR of course, the response being 48 P-N8(Q).

48 R-B8   QxP

The pawn does not promote, after all!

49 Q-K8

And the win does not come on the Q-side, after all!

49 . . . N-Q2

50 NxP   Resigns

After 50 . . . Q-N3 51 QxPch K-R1 52 N-B5 wins
at once.

57

White **R. Fischer**   Black **T. Petrosian**
Caro-Kann Defence

Candidates' Tournament, Bled, 1959

An entertainment in 68 moves is this battle-royal
between Fischer, a man who usually wins, and Petrosian,
a man who rarely loses.

Despite the length of the game, it holds the reader
fascinated every step of the way. A highlight of the
performance is the ardous journey undertaken by a fearless king, who has decided to make his role an active one.

1 P-K4   P-QB3

2 N-QB3   P-Q4

3 N-B3   B-N5

4 P-KR3   BxN

Concedes White the two bishops.

The Soviet masters prefer the two bishops—if they
have them. And they prefer the two knights—if they
have *them*. (This could be a tribute to Tchigorin,
though, whose predilection for the knights, and his
prowess with them, is legendary).

5 QxB

Tal surprised Botvinnik in their 1960 match by recapturing with the pawn, but it was an experiment
he did not care to repeat.

5 . . .   N-B3

6 P-Q3   P-K3

7 P-KN3   B-N5

8 B-Q2   P-Q5

9 N-N1   BxBch

Keres varied with 9 . . . Q-N3 in two later rounds of
the tournament, both times against Fischer.
Keres won both games.

10 NxB   P-K4

11 B-N2   P-B4

Petrosian giveth, and Petrosian taketh away. Fischer
is left with one bishop only, its efficacy sadly limited
by pawns standing on white squares.

12 0-0   N-B3

13 Q-K2

Obviously to make way for the advance 14 P-KB4.

13 . . .   P-KN4!

'Not through the Iron Duke!' as bridge players say.

14 N-B3

Riskier (for both sides) was 14 P-KB4 NPxP 15 PxP.
White's gain in freedom would be offset by the
knight file being opened against his king.

14 . . .   P-KR3

15 P-KR4   R-KN1

16 P-R3   Q-K2

17 PxP   PxP

18 Q-Q2   N-Q2

19 P-B3   0-0-0

20 PxP   See diagram on page 151.

20 . . .   KPxP!

This way of capturing clears the square K4, a fine
spot for Petrosian's pieces.

21 P-QN4!

Fischer opens fire on the Q-side.

21 . . .   K-N1

Petrosian sidesteps such ventures into the unknown
as might result from 21 . . . PxP 22 PxP QxNP

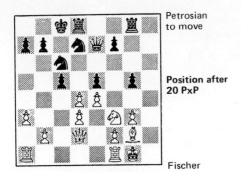

Petrosian
to move

**Position after
20 PxP**

Fischer

23 QxQ NxQ 24 RxP NxP 25 NxQP, and White calls the tune.

22 KR-B1   N(B3)-K4

Petrosian is not tempted by the gain of a pawn, as after 22 . . . PxP 23 PxP QxNP, White seizes the initiative with 24 Q-R2.

23 NxN   QxN

24 R-B4

The plausible 24 P-B4 exposes White to sudden attack by 24 . . . PxBP 25 PxKBP (on 25 QxP, RxP wins a pawn) Q-R1!! 26 K-B1 RxB 27 QxR (27 KxR loses in a hurry after 27 . . . R-N1ch) R-N1 28 Q-KB2 (nothing else avails) Q-R6ch 29 K-K1 R-N7, and Black wins the queen.

24 . . .   R-QB1

25 QR-QB1   P-N5

This ends any freeing attempts by P-B4.

26 Q-N2   KR-Q1!

27 P-R4   Q-K2

28 R-N1

Good moves are hard to find. Almost anything succumbs to the entrance of the knight at K4. For example,

If 28 PxP N-K4 29 RxP NxP, and Black wins the exchange.

If 28 P-K5 NxP 29 RxBP RxR 30 RxR NxP, and Black wins the exchange.

If 28 B-B1 (to come to the aid of the delicate queen pawn) N-K4 29 RxBP RxR 30 RxR N-B6ch 31 K-N2 R-R1 32 B-K2 R-R7ch 33 K-B1 R-R8ch 34 K-N2 R-N8 mate.

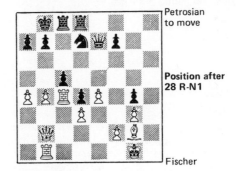

Petrosian
to move

**Position after
28 R-N1**

Fischer

28 . . .   N-K4!

The knight is magnificently posted in the center.

29 RxBP   RxR

Not at once 29 . . . NxP, as White turns on his tormentor with 30 RxRch RxR (or 30 . . . KxR 31 Q-B2ch, and White picks up the errant knight) 31 QxP, and White has gained a pawn.

30 PxR   NxP

31 Q-Q2   NxQBP

32 Q-B4ch   Q-B2

33 QxNP   NxRP

Black is now a pawn up, and has three passed pawns. The win will not be easy though, as every advance of the Q-side pawns increases the exposure of the king.

34 P-K5

All of a sudden the Bishop comes to life!

34 . . .   N-B4

35 Q-B3   P-Q6

36 Q-K3   P-Q7

The advanced position of this pawn, on the verge of becoming a queen, is bound to tie down one or two of White's pieces.

37 B-B3   N-R5
38 Q-K4
Winning the queen is worse than useless, as after
38 RxPch QxR   39 BxQ P-Q8(Q)ch Black comes
out a rook and a knight ahead.

38 . . .   N-B4
39 Q-K2   P-R3
40 K-N2   K-R2
41 Q-K3   R-Q6
42 Q-B4   Q-Q2
43 Q-B4
Fischer defends carefully, as 43 Q-QN4 instead would
offer Petrosian an opportunity to wind up the game
neatly by 43 . . . Q-N4   44 QxQ PxQ   45 B-K2 P-N5!
46 BxR NxB   47 R-Q1 P-N6   48 RxP P-N7, and
White must give up his rook at once for the pawn.

43 . . .   P-N3
44 R-Q1
What else is there?
If 44 B-Q1 Q-Q4ch forces an exchange of queens,
simplifying the position.
    Or if 44 Q-B2 Q-B4   45 Q-Q1 RxB   46 QxR
QxR, and Black wins easily.

44 . . .   P-R4
45 Q-B4   R-Q5
46 Q-R6   P-N4
47 Q-K3
If 47 Q-B8, to penetrate behind the lines, Q-B2
48 Q-R8ch K-N3, and White has run out of checks.

47 . . .   K-N3
Begins an original king wandering, to escort the
Q-side pawns.

48 Q-R6ch   N-K3
49 Q-K3   K-R3
50 B-K2   P-R5
51 Q-QB3   K-N3

52 Q-K3   N-B4
53 B-B3   P-N5
54 Q-R6ch   N-K3
55 Q-R8   Q-Q1
56 Q-R7   Q-Q2
57 Q-R8   P-N6!
This had to be calculated carefully, as the king had
to be sure of having a place of refuge.

58 Q-N8ch   K-R4
59 Q-R8ch
Watch it, Tigran! If 59 . . . K-N5   60 B-B6
followed by 61 QxPch wins a pawn for White.

59 . . .   K-N4
60 Q-N8ch   K-B5
61 Q-N8   K-B6
62 B-R5   N-Q1
Petrosian holds on to every button.

63 B-B3   P-R6
64 Q-B8   K-N7
Away from the madding crowd.

65 Q-R8   N-K3
A blockade that puts an end to any ambitions the
pawn might have entertained.

66 Q-R8   P-R7
67 Q-R5   Q-R5!
68 RxPch   K-R6
69 Resigns

58

White **T. Petrosian**   Black **J. Barendregt**
Benoni Defence
Beverwijk, 1960

Petrosian is a master of the switch attack! His pieces
dart to one side of the board and then the other, as

Barendregt is kept on tenterhooks, wondering where disaster will strike.

Petrosian applies a few deft touches here and there, and Barendregt's game just falls apart!

1   P-QB4   P-KN3

2   P-Q4   B-N2

3   N-QB3   P-Q3

4   P-K4   P-QB4

This attack on the center seems safe enough, as after 5 PxP Q-R4 6 PxP BxNch 7 PxB QxPch 8 B-Q2 Q-Q5, and Black recovers one of the pawns.

5   P-Q5   P-K4

6   B-K2   N-KR3

Evidently with the idea of supporting the thrust 7 . . . P-B4.

There is nothing wrong with 6 . . . N-KB3, except that Black might not have cared to allow 7 N-B3 0-0 8 B-N5, and he is into the Petrosian Variation.

7   P-KR4

The players of an earlier generation would regard this move with horror. It initiates a premature attack, moves a pawn instead of a piece, and makes castling (for White) on the K-side hazardous.

7   . . .   P-B4

This seems more inviting than castling, when 8 P-R5 sets up problems.

8   B-N5   Q-N3

9   R-N1

And this makes Q-side castling impossible, but that does not bother Petrosian.

9   . . .   N-B2

10   B-Q2   P-QR4

A preventive measure against the threat of 11 P-R3 followed by 12 P-QN4, but it weakens his game ever so slightly, and Petrosian will see to that little weakness.

11   N-B3   P-R3

Now Black is concerned about White's knight coming in at KN5, when 12 . . . NxN 13 PxN opens the rook file against him.

12   P-KN3

Ever cautious, Petrosian stops 13 . . . P-B5 followed by 14 . . . P-N4.

12   . . .   N-R3

13   P-R3   Q-Q1

14   Q-B2

Now intending 15 P-R5, to attack the base of the pawn chain (as per Nimzowitsch's recipe).

14   . . .   P-R4

15   PxP   PxP

This is preferable to 15 . . . BxP 16 B-Q3, and the square K4 will be available to White's pieces.

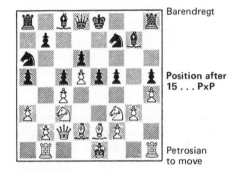

Barendregt

Position after 15 . . . PxP

Petrosian to move

16   N-KN5

This knight attacks on the K-side . . .

16   . . .   Q-B3

17   N-R4

. . . and the other knight attacks on the Q-side.

17   . . .   P-B5

If 17 . . . Q-Q1 (to save the queen rook pawn) 18 N-K6 BxN 19 PxB N-R3 20 BxPch K-K2 21 BxN BxB 22 QxP, and White wins.

18   N-N6   B-B4

19   B-Q3   BxB

20 QxB   R-QN1

21 N-K4   Q-Q1

22 BxRP   0-0

This is the position:

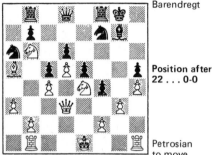

Barendregt

Position after
22 . . . 0-0

Petrosian
to move

23 Q-Q1

The queen retreats—in order to attack!

23 . . .   P-B6

The king rook pawn could not be saved either.
Black offers his bishop pawn to get some counterplay after 24 QxP by 24 . . . N-N4   25 Q-K2 N-B6ch.

24 P-QN4

Switch attack—once more. White supports his bishop,
in order to free the queen knight, and prepares to
bring his queen rook into the game.

24 . . .   N-R3

25 R-N3   N-N5

26 0-0

Long delayed (and unexpected) castling—the hallmark
of Petrosian.

26 . . .   B-B3

'Hope springs eternal,' as someone once said. There
is a wee bit of a chance that he might break in by
27 . . . BxP.
    But Petrosian nips that little idea in the bud.

27 QxP!

Again unexpected, and superior to 27 RxP. Now if

27 . . . BxP   28 Q-R1 B-K2   29 QxP, and the queen
comes strongly into the adverse position. A plausible
continuation could be   29 . . . N-B3   30 Q-N6ch K-R1
31 K-N2, and check by the rook will be fatal.

27 . . .   Q-K2

If 27 . . . R-B2 (to protect the rook pawn) 28 Q-B5
R-R2   29 P-B3, and White wins a piece.

28 Q-B5   R-B2

29 QxRP   R-N2

30 P-B3

Steals the knight.

30 . . .   BxP

31 PxN   R-R2

32 Q-B5

And now the bishop.

32 . . .   Resigns

59

White **T. Petrosian**   Black **W. Unzicker**
Queen's Gambit Declined
U.S.S.R.-West Germany, Hamburg, 1960

So subtle is the Petrosian strategy as to induce white-
squared weaknesses on one side of the board, and black-
square weaknesses on the other!
    His control of the queen bishop file has a paralyzing
effect on his opponent, whose pieces dare not leave that
area.
    But Petrosian's pieces can and do! They switch to the
K-side, and seize control of the rook file, ready to launch
an attack.
    The attack, when it does come, involves so many
threats that it quickly breaks down Unzicker's resistance.

1 P-Q4   N-KB3

2 N-KB3   P-K3

3 B-N5

The Torre attack, with which the young Mexican star won some beautiful games, one of his victims being Dr. Lasker, who got entangled in a windmill combination.

3 ...   P-Q4

If Black wants to wrest the initiative, he should try 3 . . . P-B4   4 P-K3 Q-N3.

4 P-B4   P-B3

Here, too, bolder spirits might venture on 4 . . . B-N5ch   5 N-B3 PxP   and into the complexities of the Vienna Variation. It has its dangers, though, as this pretty little game will show:
1 P-Q4 N-KB3   2 N-KB3 P-K3   3 B-N5 P-Q4
4 P-B4 B-N5ch   5 N-B3 PxP   6 P-K4 P-B4   7 BxP
PxP   8 NxP Q-R4   9 BxN BxNch   10 PxB QxPch
11 K-B1 QxBch   12 K-N1 0-0   (12 . . . PxB
13 R-B1 is ruinous)   13 Q-N4 P-KN3   14 Q-B4
N-Q2   15 P-K5 NxB   16 PxN (still threatening
17 Q-R6 and mate) 16 . . . K-R1   17 R-QB1 Q-Q4
18 Q-R6 R-KN1   19 N-B3 (threatens 20 N-N5)
19 . . . Q-KR4   20 N-N5! QxQ   21 NxBP mate.

5 Q-B2

On 5 P-K3, Black might reply with 5 . . . Q-R4ch followed by 6 . . . N-K5, whereas now the bishop can interpose on the queen check.

5 ...   B-K2

6 P-K3   0-0

7 N-B3   P-KR3

8 B-B4   QN-Q2

If 8 . . . N-R4   9 B-K5 N-Q2 (but not 9 . . . P-B3 10 BxN RxB, when 10 P-KN4 catches the wayward knight) 10 P-KN4, and the consequent opening of the knight file when the pawn advances.

9 PxP   BPxP

More natural seems 9 . . . KPxP, to facilitate the development of the queen bishop. Did Black fear the minority attack, beginning with 10 R-QN1 and 11 P-QN4?

10 B-Q3   P-R3

11 0-0   P-QN4

Understandably, Black wants to develop his queen bishop, but this weakens the Q-side pawns. Safer might have been 11 . . . N-N1 and 12 . . . N-B3.

12 P-QR4!

Very strong! This move interferes with Black's plan to increase the activity of his pieces by 12 . . . B-N2, 13 . . . R-B1, 14 . . . N-N3, and 15 . . . N-B5.

It is just as important, as Petrosian demonstrates, to hinder the opponent from carrying out his strategic plans, as it is to carry out your own.

12 ...   P-N5

13 N-R2

Much superior to 13 N-K2. The knight is on its way to N3 (via B1) where it will bear down strongly on QR5 and QB5, two important squares.

Meanwhile, there is a threat of 14 B-B7 followed by 15 B-R5, and the capture of the knight pawn.

13 ...   N-K1

14 N-B1   P-QR4

15 N-N3

A beautiful spot for the knight; it can do its job there without being disturbed.

15 ...   B-R3

Black is anxious to exchange his bad bishop, hemmed in as it is by its own pawns, but its removal will create weaknesses on the white squares.

You may be sure that Petrosian's eagle eye will spot the weaknesses in a flash, and exploit them to the fullest.

16 BxB   RxB

17 Q-Q3   R-R2

18 KR-B1   N-Q3   See diagram on page 156.
On 18 . . . B-Q3, the response 19 R-B6, threatening 20 R-R6, is strong.

19 BxN!

The knight must be eliminated! Otherwise it anchors itself at QB5, where it blocks the open file.

Unzicker

Position after 18 . . . N-Q3

Petrosian to move

19 . . .   BxB

20 R-B6!

A cunning move. The attack on the bishop, combined with the threat of 21 R-R6, forces Black's knight to retreat.

20 . . .   N-N1

The plausible 20 . . . N-N3 is met by 21 KN-Q2 (to prevent any intrusion at his B4) followed by 22 Q-N5.

21 R-B2   N-Q2

22 QR-B1

The first part of the plan is completed—pressure on the bishop file. It will take patience to exploit Black's weaknesses (his QB3 square, and his rook pawn, which requires constant attention) but Petrosian has a plentiful supply of patience.

22 . . .   N-N3

23 Q-N5   N-B5

24 KN-Q2

It's important to dispose of Black's active knight.

24 . . .   NxN

25 RxN   Q-R1

26 R(Q2)-B2   R-Q1

Passive resistance, but energetic measures might be dangerous. If, for example, 26 . . . Q-N2 27 QxQ RxQ 28 R-B6 followed by 29 R-R6 wins a pawn.

27 R-B6   P-N3

Sooner or later he must provide against P-B4 and P-B5.

28 P-N3   K-N2

29 K-B1

Petrosian has subdued his opponent on the Q-side, and prepares to break through on the K-side. First he must spirit his own king away to a place of safety.

29 . . .   K-N1

Meekly awaiting the turn of events, but he has little choice. Opposing rooks leads to this: 29 . . . R-N1 30 R-N6 R-Q1 (on 30 . . . B-B2, the reply 31 RxB wins a piece) 31 R(B1)-B6, and Black is worse off than before.

30 P-R4   P-R4

31 R(B1)-B2

Clears the road for the king's journey.

31 . . .   K-R2

32 K-K1   K-N1

33 K-Q1   K-R2

34 K-B1   K-N1

35 K-N1   K-R2

36 Q-K2

Threatens P-N4, when the time is ripe for the advance—but Petrosian is never impetuous.

36 . . .   Q-N2

37 R-B1   K-N2

The position at this point:

Unzicker

Position after 37 . . . K-N2

Petrosian to move

38 Q-N5!

Petrosian suddenly switches to the Q-side!

38 ...   Q-R1

Black does not dare accept the offer to exchange queens, as Petrosian would effect this pretty win:

38 . . . QxQ   39 PxQ P-R5   40 P-N6 R(R2)-Q2 (if 40 . . . R-R1   41 P-N7 R(R1)-N1   42 N-R5, and White wins)   41 N-R5 R-QR1   42 RxB! RxR 43 P-N7 R-QN1   44 R-B8 R-Q1   45 RxR(Q8) RxR 46 N-B6!, and Black will have to give up his rook for the passed pawn.

39 P-B4   K-R2

40 Q-K2

On revient toujours à ses premiers amours.

Black must have been plagued with doubts at this point. If he plays 40 . . . P-B4 to stop 41 P-N4, his king pawn becomes shaky. This would add another weak pawn to his present collection, and accentuate as well the weakness of his black squares.

So he waits for the blow to strike!

40 ...   Q-N2

41 P-N4!

It isn't long in coming!

Black's defence is hampered by his pieces being tied down to the Q-side.

41 ...   PxP

42 QxP   Q-K2

43 P-R5   Q-B3

All is not yet lost. If Petrosian hastily plays 44 PxPch, he captures by 44 . . . QxPch, and forces an exchange of queens, leaving him drawing chances.

44 K-R2

But Tigran is wary, and tucks the king away in a corner.

44 ...   K-N2

45 PxP   QxNP

Or 45 . . . PxP   46 N-B5, with new terrors.

46 Q-R4   B-K2

The impulsive 46 . . . R-KR1 loses on the spot by 47 Q-B2, when White threatens to win a piece by 48 RxB, or to win the queen by 48 R-KN1.

47 Q-B2   K-B1

The king gets out of the line of fire.

48 N-Q2

The knight seems headed for K5, but Petrosian changes his mind—or is he toying with Unzicker?

48 ...   R-N2

Carefully, the knight retraces its steps. On 49 N-B3 instead, 49 . . . P-N6ch followed by 50 . . . R-N5 might cloud the issue.

49 N-N3   R-R2

50 Q-R2!

This is the position:

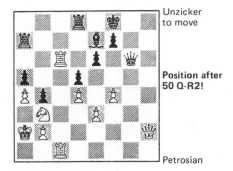

Unzicker to move

Position after 50 Q-R2!

Petrosian

Black must guard against 51 P-B5, which could be painful.

50 ...   B-B3

This secures the K-side (temporarily) at the cost of leaving his QB4 square unguarded—but the bishop cannot be in two places at once.

The alternative 50 . . . B-Q3 leads to 51 RxB! RxR 52 P-B5 PxP   53 R-B8ch K-K2   54 Q-R8, and Black is lost.

51 R-B8!

Intending this finish: 52 RxRch BxR   53 R-B8
K-K2   54 RxB KxR   55 P-B5! QxP   56 Q-N8ch,
and White wins the rook.

51 ...   R-Q2

Or he could choose this death: 51 . . . RxR
52 RxRch K-K2   53 P-B5 QxP   54 Q-N8 R-Q2
55 R-K8 mate.

52 N-B5!   P-N6ch

If 52 . . . RxR   53 NxRch K-K2   54 RxR wins the
exchange, or if 52 . . . R-Q3   53 P-B5 QxP   54 QxRch
wins a whole rook.

53 KxP   R-Q3

54 P-B5!

At last! This has been hanging over Unzicker's head as
the Sword of Dionysius hung over that of Damocles.

The threats are 55 PxQ and 55 QxRch (no mean
threats!).

54 ...   R-N3ch

55 K-R2   Resigns

There is no defence. Black's queen is attacked, and
56 N-Q7ch winning a rook is in the air.

A masterly performance by Petrosian.

60

White **T. Petrosian**   Black **L. Aronin**
Réti Opening
Moscow, 1961

Petrosian's style is inimitable! Other masters may rush to
develop their pieces, but Petrosian has them retreat to
accomplish his ends.

Here is a game where Petrosian's originality (such as
winning the game with only one piece in play!) might
have impressed even the great Nimzowitsch, and made
him pause to wonder.

1 N-KB3   P-QB4

2 P-KN3   N-QB3

3 B-N2   P-Q4

4 0-0   N-B3

5 P-Q3   B-N5

6 P-B4   P-K3

7 Q-R4

Threatens 8 N-K5 Q-N3   9 NxB NxN   10 PxP, and
both Black's knights are *en prise.*

7 ...   Q-Q2

8 N-B3   P-Q5

9 N-QN5   B-K2

10 P-KR3   BxN

11 PxB   0-0

12 Q-Q1

The queen undevelops. This is the first retreat. There
will be more!

12 ...   KR-K1

13 P-B4   B-Q1

14 N-R3

Now the knight returns.

14 ...   B-R4

15 N-B2

The knight continues its retreat.

15 ...   B-B2

16 P-R3   P-QR4

This prevents 16 P-QN4, with Q-side activity.

17 R-QN1   B-Q3

Again with the same object in view.

18 B-Q2   P-K4

Rather than remain passive, Black creates a diversion
in the center.

19 PxP   NxP

20 P-B4   N-B3

Black discovers, to his dismay, that 20 . . . NxQP is

immediately penalized by 20 . . . Q-B3, and the knight has no escape.

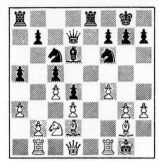

Aronin

Position after 20 . . . N-B3

Petrosian to play

21 Q-B3   P-R4
To stop 22 P-KN4. Note how Black has been forced to weaken his pawn position on both sides of the board.

22 KR-K1   RxRch

23 RxR   R-K1

24 RxRch   QxR

25 N-K1
The knight is now happily posted on the back rank!

25 . . .   Q-Q1

26 Q-Q1
Now the queen comes back (again!) from her aggressive position.

26 . . .   Q-N3

27 B-QB1
Another piece returns home!

27 . . .   N-K2

28 Q-B3   Q-N6

29 P-N4
An attacking move?

29 . . .   PxP

30 PxP   P-KN3

31 B-B1
Now the king bishop returns to its home base. Petrosian (unlike any other player in the world) can prepare a decisive attack by posting most of his pieces on the back rank!
   What would Morphy think?

31 . . .   Q-N3

32 P-B5   PxP

33 PxP   K-B1
Would you believe that White, with only one piece in play, now wins this in about half a dozen moves?
   Here is the position:

Aronin

Position after 33 . . . K-B1

Petrosian to move

34 B-N2   N-B3

35 Q-R3   N-KN1

36 Q-R8
Threatens 37 B-R6ch, winning the knight.

36 . . .   B-N6
If 36 . . . P-B3   37 B-Q5 N(B3)-K2   38 B-R6ch, and White wins a piece.
   Black's idea (with 36 . . . B-N6) is to force 37 N-B3, blocking the bishop. This would allow Black time to defend by 37 . . . N-K2.

37 P-B6!
But Petrosian doesn't bother to save his knight!

37 . . .   BxN

38 Q-N7ch   K-K1

39 QxNch   K-Q2

40 B-R3ch   Resigns

The continuation would be: 40 . . . K-Q3 41 B-B4ch
N-K4 42 Q-N8ch K-B3 (if 42 . . . Q-B2 43 BxNch
wins the queen) 43 Q-K8ch K-B2 44 Q-B8ch K-Q3
45 Q-Q7 mate—a pretty exploitation of the pin motif.

61

White **T. Petrosian**   Black **S. Schweber**
King's Indian Defence
Interzonal Tournament, Stockholm, 1962

Petrosian's opponents often seem to be hypnotized into
passive resistance.

Petrosian starts a K-side attack, abandons it only two
moves later, and makes that area the quietest on the board.

He has two long-range bishops, but exchanges one of
them for a knight standing peacefully on the back rank.

Much later in the game, as though suddenly reminded
that he still has that privilege, Petrosian decides to castle.

Throughout the whole game he increases his superiority so imperceptibly as to lull his opponent into a state
of inactivity.

No wonder that Petrosian's strategy can be bewildering!

1 P-Q4   N-KB3

2 P-QB4   P-KN3

3 N-QB3   B-N2

4 P-K4   P-Q3

5 B-K2   0-0

6 B-N5   P-KR3

This weakens the pawn position near the king, but
Black may have feared an exchange of his king bishop
by 7 Q-Q2 followed by 8 B-R6.

7 B-K3   P-K4

8 P-Q5   P-B3

Black misses the opportunity to play 8 . . . N-K1, to
get in the thematic 9 . . . P-KB4 as soon as possible.
Petrosian does not give him another chance!

9 P-KR4!

Apparently with the intention of prying open the
file leading to the king's residence.

Strange! Petrosian rarely goes in for a direct
K-side attack.

9 . . .   PxP

10 BPxP   QN-Q2

This seems tame, but it's too late to effect the
customary breakthrough by . . . P-KB4. If 10 . . .
N-K1 11 Q-Q2! K-R2 (protects the rook pawn)
12 P-R5 P-N4 (on 12 . . . P-B4 13 PxPch KxP
14 PxPch BxP 15 BxP wins a pawn) 13 P-KN4,
and White stifles any attempt to counter-attack on
the K-side.

11 P-R5!

Petrosian is evidently out to win by direct assault!

In reality, it's nothing of the sort. It's the prelude
to strategy of a high order, the strategy of encirclement.

11 . . .   P-KN4

12 P-B3   P-R3

A preparatory move for 13 . . . P-N4, to gain
some space on the Q-side.

13 P-KN4

Clearly, Petrosian has no interest in opening up files
for an attack. What he prefers is a nice quiet game,
where he can gently and methodically crush his
opponent to death.

A glance at the board shows that White enjoys a
considerable advantage, even at this early stage.

He has two active bishops, aimed menacingly at
the Q-side. Black's, by comparison, are impotent.
One has little mobility, being hampered by pawns of
the same color, while the other is still waiting to
make its entrance to the game.

White's king knight has the prospect of occupying

the marvellous square KB5, while Black's knight can not possibly reach the corresponding square.

Lastly, White may double his rooks on the queen bishop file to advantage.

All these are intangibles, but Petrosian thrives on intangibles. It's the equivalent of winning a pawn.

13 ...   P-N4

14 P-R4   P-N5

15 N-N1   P-R4

16 N-Q2   N-B4

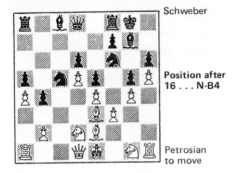

Schweber

Position after 16 ... N-B4

Petrosian to move

17 BxN!

Brilliant! Petrosian not only exchanges a bishop for a knight (enough to make most chess players shudder) but keeps the ill-favoured bishop, the one whose freedom is restricted by so many of his pawns standing on white squares.

17 ...   PxB

18 B-N5   B-N2

19 N-K2   N-K1

20 BxN!

'Off with his head!,' in the immortal words of the Red Queen in *Alice in Wonderland.* Petrosian destroys the knight before it can blockade his passed pawn by moving to Q3.

20 ...   RxB

Black is left with the two bishops, but they are rather ineffectual.

21 N-QB4   B-R3

22 Q-N3   Q-B3

Black could have played 22 ... BxN, avoiding Scylla, only to fall into Charybdis, his remaining bishop being completely imprisoned by the half-dozen of his pawns occupying black squares.

23 R-QB1   B-KB1

24 N-N3   B-B1

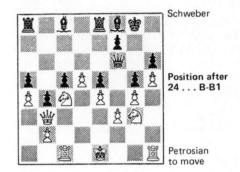

Schweber

Position after 24 ... B-B1

Petrosian to move

25 0-0

Petrosian often castles late in the game, as though it were an afterthought.

25 ...   R-Q1

26 K-N2   R-R2

27 R-KB2   K-R2

28 R(B2)-B2

All according to plan. The rooks are now doubled on the bishop file, bearing down on their victim, the queen bishop pawn.

28 ...   Q-R3

Tiring of all this inactivity, Schweber sacrifices a pawn, to allow his bishop some freedom.

29 NxKP   R-B2

Not at once 29 ... B-KN2, as the reply 30 N-B6 wins the exchange.

30 N-B4   B-KN2

31 Q-Q3   K-N1

32 R-Q2   R-K2

Prevents 33 P-K5—or does it?

33 P-K5!

Petrosian returns the pawn, as he foresees a win in the ending.

33 ...   BxKP

34 NxB   RxN

35 QxQ   BxQ

36 RxP   B-B1

Attacking the passed pawn by 36 ... B-N2 is refuted by 37 N-K4 R(K4)xP 38 R(Q2)xR RxR 39 RxR BxR 40 N-B6ch, and White wins a piece.

Or if in this 37 ... K-B1, then 38 P-Q6 RxR 39 NxR, and the simplified position should offer no difficulties.

37 RxP   P-B4

Rather than submit to slow death, Black tries a breakthrough.

38 PxP   BxP

39 NxB   RxN

40 R-N5   R(Q1)-KB1

41 P-Q6!   RxR

Capturing the pawn is out of the question, as the reply 42 P-Q7 would cost a rook at once.

42 PxR   K-B2

43 P-Q7   Resigns

The win is easy:

If 43 ... K-K2 44 P-Q8(Q)ch RxQ 45 RxR KxR 46 K-N3, and the king advances to N4, B5, and N6, captures the two pawns, and queens his rook pawn. Black meanwhile captures both knight pawns, and advances his pawn to N7. White captures the pawn, and queens his last pawn.

Or if 43 ... R-Q1 44 P-N6 K-K2 45 P-N7 R-QN1 (on a king move, White wins by 46 P-N8(Q) RxQ 47 P-Q8(Q), and Black must give up his rook) 46 P-Q8(Q)ch RxQ 47 RxR KxR, and the knight pawn moves on to the last square to win.

Years ago, when Petrosian's name was little-known, Santasiere made this comment in annotating a Petrosian game, 'All I can say is that if, on a dark and stormy night, I meet Mr. Petrosian on a chessboard, even though fortified with ambrosia, I shall offer him a draw.'

62

White **T. Petrosian**   Black **P. Benko**
Grünfeld Defence
Los Angeles, 1963

Petrosian is unperturbed by the fact that his opponent has acquired four connected passed pawns before the fifteenth move.

To tame the threats of these wicked-looking pawns, Petrosian initiates an attack which keeps Benko far too busy defending to undertake any aggressive action.

The skillful blending of attack and defence by Petrosian makes this one of his most attractive games.

1 P-Q4   N-KB3

2 P-QB4   P-KN3

3 N-QB3   P-Q4

4 Q-N3

Botvinnik's move, an effective means of inducing Black to give up the center.

4 ...   PxP

5 QxBP   B-K3

6 Q-N5ch   N-B3

7 N-B3

Of course not 7 QxP NxP, and White faces mate on the move (to say nothing of the danger to his rook).

7 ...   N-Q4

An improvement on 7 ... R-QN1, played by Alekhine against Euwe in the second game of their 1935 match, a game which Euwe won by beautifully precise play.

8 P-K4

The tempting 8 QxP leads to this pretty possibility:
8 . . . N(Q4)-N5 (threatens to trap the queen by
9 . . . R-QN1) 9 B-B4 (on 9 Q-N5 N-B7ch 10 K-Q1
NxP is in Black's favour) 9 . . . B-R3! 10 BxP
NxQP! 11 BxQ N(Q5)-B7ch 12 K-Q1 RxBch, and
Black wins.

8 . . . N-N5

9 Q-R4   B-Q2

10 Q-Q1   P-K4

11 P-QR3

White avoids 11 NxP, as the recapture 11 . . . NxQP
is strong for Black, while 11 PxP is met by 11 . . .
B-N5 12 B-KN5 BxN 13 BxQ BxQ 14 B-B6 B-R4
15 BxR B-R3!, and White has his difficulties.

11 . . . PxP

12 N-QN1   N-R3

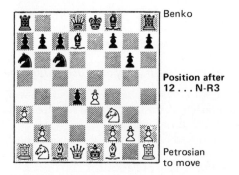

Benko

**Position after
12 . . . N-R3**

Petrosian
to move

13 P-QN4   N(R3)xP

This sacrifice is practically forced, as after 13 . . .
N(R3)-N1 14 P-N5 N-K2 15 QxP is to White's
advantage.

14 PxN   BxPch

Incredible, but Black has four connected passed
pawns! What's more, only one white piece is off its
original square.

15 B-Q2   Q-K2

16 B-Q3   BxBch

17 QNxB   N-N5

18 Q-K2   P-QB4

19 O-O   O-O

20 P-K5!

Petrosian must start things humming on the K-side,
before the passed pawns become menacing. His
intention now is to play 21 N-K4, and establish the
knight at B6.

20 . . . K-N2

Black can try to exchange pieces, to lessen the force
of the attack, by 20 . . . NxB 21 QxN B-B3, but
after 22 N-K4 BxN 23 QxB, White can still stir up
trouble by playing P-R4 next move.

21 N-K4   B-B3

22 P-R4   P-QR3

23 KR-B1

The pawns must be restrained, and this prevents
23 . . . P-QN4 followed by 24 . . . P-B5.

23 . . . P-N3

24 P-R5   QR-Q1

25 Q-Q2

Planning to drive a wedge into Black's position by
26 P-R6ch.

25 . . . P-R3

26 R-K1   P-QN4

27 N-Q6

Threatens 28 NxQP PxN (but not 28 . . . NxB, when
29 N(Q4)-B5ch wins the queen) 29 QxN, and White
has won a pawn.

27 . . . BxN

28 PxB   Q-N4ch

Black reduces it to an ending, as the lesser of the
evils. Otherwise he has to contend with the continuation 29 P-B4 followed by 30 P-B5, which will add
to his worries.

29 QxQ   PxQ

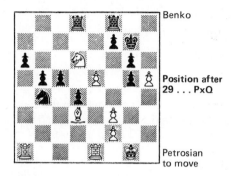

Benko

Position after
29 . . . PxQ

Petrosian
to move

30 B-K4

New threats by the indefatigable Petrosian. This one
is 31 KR-QB1 P-B5   32 KR-N1, and Black must part
with a pawn.

30 . . .   PxP

31 KR-QB1   P-B3

Here, too, if 31 . . . P-B5   32 KR-N1 N-Q6   33 BxN
PxB   34 RxP, and the rest of Black's pawns are not
long for this world.

32 N-B5ch   K-B2

Restrains the king pawn, as 32 . . . K-R1 would allow
33 P-K6 to good effect.

33 RxBP   PxP

34 R-N1   N-R7

Away from it all!

35 R-B7ch   K-B3

36 R-QR7   N-B6

37 RxPch   K-B2

38 R(N1)-R1

Threatens all sorts of mates, beginning with
39 R-R7ch. If then

(a) 39 . . . K-K1   40 R-K7 is an epaulet mate.

(b) 39 . . . K-K3   40 R(R1)-R6ch, and mate next
move.

(c) 39 . . . K-N3   40 R(R1)-R6ch R-B3   41 R-N7
mate.

(d) 39 . . . K-N1   40 N-R6ch K-R1   42 R-R7 mate.

38 . . .   P-KN5

The king must have a flight square!

39 B-B2   PxP

40 B-N3ch   N-Q4

Black must interpose, as 40 . . . K-K1 is fatal, viz:
41 R-K6ch K-Q2   42 R-R7ch K-B1   43 N-K7ch
K-N1   44 N-B6ch K-B1   45 R(K6)-K7, and mate is
inevitable.

41 R-K1   R-N1ch

If 41 . . . R(B1)-K1, to protect the pawn, 42 N-Q6ch
wins the exchange.

42 K-B1   R-N3

43 BxNch   Resigns

After 43 . . . RxB   44 RxR KxR   45 N-K7ch wins
a whole rook.

63

White **T. Petrosian**   Black **B. Spassky**
Yugoslav System
World Championship Match, Moscow, 1966, 10th game

In one of the most brilliant games ever played in a world
championship match, Petrosian springs a surprise by two
sudden sacrifices of the exchange.

After several forced moves, he hurls a thunderbolt
which winds up the game in a blaze of glory.

This is The Bright Side of Petrosian!

1 N-KB3   N-KB3

2 P-KN3   P-KN3

3 P-B4   B-N2

4 B-N2   0-0

5 0-0   N-B3

6 N-B3   P-Q3

7 P-Q4   P-QR3

8 P-Q5   N-QR4

Black plays a defence based on Q-side expansion, combined with the influence of his powerful king bishop.

It abounds in 'Quips and Cranks and wanton Wiles.'

9 N-Q2   P-B4

10 Q-B2   P-K4

The customary continuation is 10 . . . R-N1   11 P-N3 P-QN4, to obtain more space on the Q-side.

Kashdan ventured on 10 . . . P-K3 against Gligorić at Hollywood in 1952, but was quickly subdued by the Yugoslavian star.

11 P-N3   N-N5

This or 11 . . . N-K1 is essential, as the king bishop pawn must be mobilized *tout de suite.*

12 P-K4

Petrosian must have satisfied himself that Black's queen knight was out of play, or he would have driven it further back by 12 P-QR3 P-N3   13 P-QN4 N-N2 .

12 . . .   P-B4

13 PxP   PxP

Black prefers this to 13 . . . BxP, which allows White the square K4 for his knights.

14 N-Q1

With three objects in mind:

(a) It clears the long diagonal for the queen bishop.

(b) It prepares to deploy the knight to K3, a vital square.

(c) It encourages Black into embarking on a premature attack.

For example, if Black becomes ambitious, and plays 14 . . . P-K5, there follows 15 B-N2, and if 15 . . . B-Q5, then 16 BxB PxB   17 P-N4 wins the stranded knight.

14 . . .   P-N4

15 P-B3

The safer move was 15 B-N2, but Petrosian may have been in the mood to stir up complications.

15 . . .   P-K5

Spassky too could play safe by retreating his knight to R3, but he too may have been caught up in the excitement, and plunges into the melee.

16 B-N2

Petrosian apparently considered that the position resulting from 16 PxN BxR   17 PxBP BxP   18 NxP did not warrant sacrificing the exchange.

16 . . .   KPxP

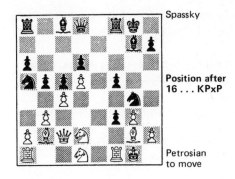

Spassky

Position after 16 . . . KPxP

Petrosian to move

17 BxP

The proper recapture. If 17 NxP instead, 17 . . . BxB 18 QxB (on 18 NxB, N-K6 wins the exchange) PxP 19 PxP NxBP wins a pawn. (Strange that the pawn falls which a moment ago was protected three times!)

17 . . .   BxB

18 QxB   N-K4

19 B-K2!

Excellent! The bishop helps protect the queen bishop pawn, covers Q3, and clears the king bishop file for the rook.

19 . . .   P-B5

Spassky decides to complicate matters before White can blockade his isolated pawn by 20 N→K3→N2→B4.

20 PxBP

Petrosian had a good alternative in 20 RxP RxR 21 PxR N-N3   22 N-K4 NxKBP   23 N-K3! R-R2

24 N-B6ch K-B2   25 R-KB1 QxN   26 QxQch KxQ
27 RxNch, and White has the better chances in the
endgame.

The text move gambles a bit, on the chance of
luring Spassky into a cleverly-concealed trap.

20 ...   B-R6

Spassky leaps in, as the move is tempting.

Preferable was 20 ... RxP   21 RxR Q-N4ch
22 K-R1 QxR, and Black's queen is enabled to take
part in the action.

Spassky may have expected 21 R-B2 in reply.
when 21 ... RxP   22 RxR Q-N4ch gains a tempo.

21 N-K3!

Petrosian happily sacrifices the exchange, as his
pieces will spring to life.

21 ...   BxR

Black must accept the gift, as after 21 ... RxP
22 RxR Q-N4ch   23 R-N4! BxR   24 NxB NxN
25 BxN QxBch   26 K-R1 White, with even pieces
and a strong attack, has a won game.

22 RxB   N-N3

The forced departure of the knight from its beautifully centralized position is White's bonus for the
exchange sacrifice.

23 B-N4!

Seizes control of the white squares. It would be
petty to play 23 N-N4 with a one-move threat of
mate.

23 ...   N(N3)xP

24 RxN!

One good sacrifice deserves another!

24 ...   RxR

25 B-K6ch!   R-B2

On 25 ... K-B1, White has this pretty win, pointed
out by Kmoch: 26 Q-R8ch K-K2   27 QxPch, and

(a) 27 ... K-K1 (if 27 ... K-B1   28 Q-R6ch catches
the rook) 28 Q-N6ch K-K2   29 Q-N5ch R-B3

30 N-B5ch K-K1   31 Q-N8ch R-B1   32 Q-N6ch, and
mate next move.

(b) 27 ... K-B3   28 N-N2 (the finesse!) R-Q5
29 Q-B7ch K-N4   30 Q-N7ch K-R4   31 B-B7 mate.

(c) 27 ... K-B3   28 N-N2 K-K4   29 Q-R5ch K-Q5
30 NxR K-K6   31 N-B1ch KxN   32 Q-B5 mate.

26 N-K4   Q-R5

27 NxQP   Q-N4ch

Black would lose after 27 ... Q-K8ch   28 K-N2 QxN
by 29 BxRch K-B1   30 Q-R8ch K-K2   31 N-B5ch
K-Q2 (if 31 ... KxB   32 QxPch followed by
33 NxQ) 32 B-K6ch K-B2   33 QxPch, and Black's
queen comes off next move.

28 K-R1   R(R1)-R2

29 BxRch   RxB

Now comes a spectacular finish!

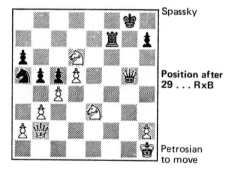

Spassky

Position after
29 ... RxB

Petrosian
to move

30 Q-R8ch!

The thunderbolt!

30 ...   KxQ

31 NxRch   K-N2

32 NxQ

And wins

'It must be an advantage to Petrosian,' says Purdy,
'that his opponents are never expecting him to play
like Tal.'

Botvinnik

Botvinnik has been the god of Soviet chess for most of his life. Gifts have been showered on him, garlands of flowers have adorned him, honours have been bestowed on him, and praises have been sung to him. For his great deeds brought fame and glory to him and his country.

His achievements have been many. These are some of the high points:

At the age of 16, Botvinnik's first performance in a Soviet Championship tourney earned him the title of master. This was in 1927, and the next few years showed Botvinnik increasing so greatly in strength as to dominate Soviet chess until the middle sixties.

In 1933 Botvinnik caught the eye of the chess world by drawing a 10-game match with Salo Flohr, Champion of Czechoslovakia, then at the height of his powers. In the course of the match, incidentally, the contestants attended a performance of the ballet at the Bolshoi Theatre. To Flohr's surprise (as he had no idea of Botvinnik's popularity) their entrance was greeted with applause by the entire audience.

Two years after the match with Flohr, Botvinnik gave striking evidence of his enormous talent, in a tournament held at Moscow, where 12 Soviet players and 8 foreign masters were to take part, the latter being Lasker, Capablanca, Flohr, Spielmann, Pirc, Stahlberg, Lilienthal, and Vera Menchik. Botvinnik tied with Flohr for first and second, ahead of former World Champions Lasker and Capablanca. His performance impressed Euwe, who paid tribute to the new star by saying, 'The Soviet leader fully deserved his success. He must now be ranked among the best players in the world.'

Botvinnik was awarded the title of Soviet Grandmaster, the first player to be so distinguished. (He was also given an automobile by the Ministry of Heavy Industry.)

Botvinnik has won the Championship of the U.S.S.R. seven times, a feat which puts all other title-holders in the shade, as no one else has ever come close to that record.

In 1936 (a good year for Botvinnik—and for Capablanca) a double-round tournament was arranged at Moscow, in which 5 Soviet masters (Botvinnik, Kan, Levenfisch, Ragozin, and Riumin) measured their strength against 4 Western masters (Lasker, Capablanca, Flohr, and Lilienthal). While Capablanca came in first, Botvinnik's second (a point behind) was a distinct triumph, as he came in ahead of the mighty Lasker, who was still a dangerous old lion.

In the same year one of the strongest tournaments ever was held at Nottingham. The entry list included four World Champions (Euwe, Alekhine, Lasker, and Capablanca) and four rising stars (Flohr, Fine, Reshevsky, and Botvinnik—a future world champion). Botvinnik did himself proud by finishing in a tie for first and second with Capablanca, without loss of a game.

Two years later, at the Avro tournament, Botvinnik came in third after Keres and Fine, but ahead of a powerful field which included Alekhine, Capablanca, Euwe, and Reshevsky. Botvinnik had the unique and enviable distinction of beating Alekhine and Capablanca in one event, the latter game (No. 66) being, according to Botvinnik, 'the game of my life.'

A first prize at Groningen in 1946 added to Botvinnik's laurels, but the crowning achievement occurred in 1948 when he won first prize and with it the title of Chess Champion of the World, in the Hague-Moscow Tournament to pick a successor to Dr. Alekhine. Botvinnik finished three points ahead of his nearest competitor Smyslov, the other contestants being Keres, Reshevsky, and Euwe.

The subsequent matches for the title form a remarkable chapter in the history of chess, for this is briefly what happened:

In 1951 Botvinnik and Bronstein drew a 24-game match.

In 1954 Botvinnik and Smyslov drew a 24-game match.

In 1957 Smyslov defeated Botvinnik for the title by 6 wins to 3.

In 1958 Botvinnik regained his title by beating Smyslov 7 wins to 5.

In 1960 Tal beat Botvinnik in a title match by 6 wins to 2.

In 1961 Botvinnik recaptured his title by beating Tal 10 wins to 5.

In 1963 Petrosian defeated Botvinnik in a title match by 5 wins to 2.

Botvinnik made no further attempts to regain his title, one reason being, as he said, 'A match takes a year off your life.'

Botvinnik has the proud distinction of having a plus score against the nine world championships he has played in his life, these being Lasker, Capablanca, Alekhine, Euwe, Smyslov, Tal, Petrosian, Spassky, and Fischer, his 32 wins exceeding their 28 wins. (I hasten to add that he did not beat all the nine World Champions; these are total wins for his rivals.)

Botvinnik's accomplishements gained him another signal honour. In 1957 he was awarded the Order of Lenin for his achievements in chess.

Botvinnik's great strength is in the opening, in the midgame, and in the ending.

Botvinnik plays few openings, but he plays those few superbly. His theoretical knowledge is immense, and to this he adds profound analytical discoveries of his own. This makes for a formidable opening repertoire, limited though it may be. ('Chess is the art of analysis,' says Botvinnik).

Botvinnik's midgames are often complicated, but he thrives on difficult positions, as they stimulate his faculties to the utmost. He actually seems to enjoy positions which call for endless patience, and nerves of steel. Long positional struggles do not dismay him, nor complications which call for combinative play, for he is a skilled tactician.

Botvinnik's versatility extends to the endgame, where his superlative technique has accounted for many victories.

One reason for Botvinnik's continual improvement was his rigid self-criticism, for his annotations show that he was just as severe on himself as on his opponents. As a result, Botvinnik's play early in his career, reached a point where he could say, without fear of seeming conceited, '1930 marked a turning point; I learned the art of winning regularly against masters.'

Vasiliev, in his absorbing book on Petrosian, calls Botvinnik 'a fearless fighter with an iron will. His strategy is deep and original, and his analytical powers unequalled. Whole generations of Soviet chess players learned from his creations, and among that number the present challenger Petrosian. 'I studied Botvinnik's games,' said Petrosian on the eve of his match with Botvinnik, 'when I was twelve years old, and I am still learning from them.'

William Winter says, 'Botvinnik's best games have the smoothness of a lyric poem, rolling on grandly to their appointed end.'

In 1960 I wrote, 'Select a quartet of the greatest players that ever lived, and you would have to include Botvinnik. He is the master most qualified to join the immortal trio of Capablanca, Alekhine, and Lasker.' But this was before the advent of the super-star Fischer; so the quartet of immortals has grown to a quintet.

I consider Botvinnik the fifth greatest chess player of all time.

64

White **I. Rabinovich**   Black **M. Botvinnik**
Dutch Defence
Moscow, 1927

This game, from Botvinnik's first appearance in master chess, brought him instant recognition as a player of brilliance and imagination, to say nothing of 'a style characterized by colossal energy and patience, and theoretical knowledge on a par with the great analysts of Western Europe.'

1	P-Q4	P-K3
2	P-QB4	P-KB4
3	P-KN3	N-KB3
4	B-N2	B-K2
5	N-QB3	0-0
6	N-B3	P-Q4
7	0-0	P-B3

The drawback in the Stonewall Defence, which Botvinnik has built up, is that Black's black squares are weak. In compensation though, he gets the opportunity to attack on the K-side.

8 Q-B2   Q-K1

Heading for R4, a good spot for the queen.

9 B-B4

Rather tame; more to the point was 9 B-N5 Q-R4 10 BxN BxB   11 PxP KPxP   12 P-K3 N-Q2 13 P-QN4, with the Minority Attack in view.

9 ...   Q-R4

10 QR-Q1   QN-Q2

11 P-N3

Creates a tiny weakness at QB3—which of course will not escape Botvinnik's eagle eye.

11 ...   N-K5

12 N-K5!

Both players have stationed their knights at K5,

White's with perhaps more effect, as no pawn can drive it off, whereas Black's can be dislodged by 13 P-B3.

White threatens to gain a positional advantage by 14 N(K5)xN BxN   15 P-B3, or more simply by 15 P-B3 followed by 15 P-K4.

12 ...   N-N4

Clearly intending to eliminate one of White's bishops by 13 ... N-R6ch.

13 P-KR4

This compromises White's K-side. Black's threat was purely psychological, for after 13 P-B3! N-R6ch 14 BxN QxB   15 P-K4, White would obviously have a good game, the Stonewall variation being sufficiently weak to allow White the luxury of a few inaccurate or second-best moves.

13 ...   N-K5

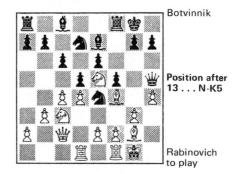

Botvinnik

Position after 13 ... N-K5

Rabinovich to play

14 B-B3

Botvinnik says, 'Irresolute. With 14 N(B3)xN BPxN 15 P-B3 White would get a better game, as the sacrifice of the exchange 15 ... RxB   16 PxR gave Black no prospects.'

Botvinnik might be mistaken though, as this continuation shows: 16 ... P-K6!   17 Q-Q3 BxP   18 QxP B-N6   19 N-N4 N-B3!, and wins, a likely sequel being 20 R-B2 (the alternative is 20 NxNch PxN 21 R-B2 Q-R7ch   22 K-B1 P-K4!   23 BPxP B-R6 and wins) 20 ... P-K4!   21 QxP BxN   22 PxB

Q-R7ch   23 K-B1 R-K1   24 Q-B5 (forced) BxR
25 KxB N-K5ch, winning the queen or mating.

14 ...   Q-K1

15 N(K5)xN   BxN

16 K-N2   B-N5!

Strikes at the weak spot!

17 BxN

An error on two counts: it parts with the bishop, a
stout defender of the K-side, and the recapture
offers interesting possibilities to Black's rook along
the bishop file.

Simply 17 N-N1 was the better move.

17 ...   BPxB

18 R-KR1   Q-R4

The queen returns, and the threat of winning a
pawn by 19 ... BxN   20 QxB QxP will force a
further weakening in the neighborhood of the king.

19 P-B3   Q-N3

Black summons up new threats: 20 ... PxPch
winning the queen, or 20 ... RxB winning a piece.

20 K-B1   P-K4!

Spurning the win of a mere pawn, (by 20 ... KPxP
21 QxQ PxQ   22 R-B1 PxPch) Botvinnik, going
after bigger stakes, rips the game wide open.

21 QPxP

White did not care to go in for this line: 21 BxP
KPxP   22 QxQ PxP dbl.ch   23 KxP PxQ   24 R-QB1
B-N5ch   25 K-K1 R-B6   26 K-Q2 B-KB4!, and Black
wins easily.

He could put up a tough struggle with 21 P-R5
Q-B4   22 QPxP KPxP   23 QxQ BxQ   24 R-B1 P-Q5
25 N-Q1 B-K5, but Black should win the ending.

21 ...   RxB!

This sacrifice has been in the air for some time.

22 PxR

Now comes a quiet but powerful move!

22 ...   Q-N6!

This confronts White with five terrifying threats:

(1) 23 ... P-K6 and 24 ... Q-B7 mate.
(2) 23 ... B-QB4 and 24 ... Q-B7 mate.
(3) 23 ... KPxP and 24 ... Q-N7ch winning a rook.
(4) 23 ... B-R6ch   24 RxB QxRch   25 K-B2
(on 25 ... K-K1, P-K6 wins) 25 ... B-B4ch
26 P-K3 Q-R7ch, winning the queen.
(5) 23 ... R-KB1, and a breakthrough on the king
bishop file.

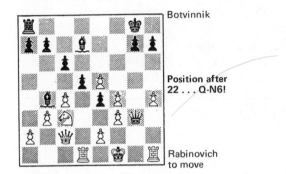

Botvinnik

**Position after
22 ... Q-N6!**

Rabinovich
to move

23 NxKP

There is nothing better. If instead
(a) 23 PxQP B-QB4   24 NxKP B-R6ch   25 RxB
Q-N8 mate.

(b) 23 PxKP B-QB4   24 P-K3 Q-B6ch   25 K-K1
(or 25 K-N1 BxPch   26 K-R2 Q-R6 mate) 25 ...
QxKRch   26 K-Q2 Q-R7ch wins.

23 ...   PxN

24 RxB

White avoids this pretty way of losing: 24 QxP B-QB4
25 P-K3 B-B4   26 QxB QxBPch, and White must
(unhappily) choose which rook to give up.

Despite the few pieces left on the board, Black can
still ruin all his good work by making one natural,
impulsive (yea, almost irresistible) move.

If he should play 24 ... P-K6, there would come
like a shot 25 RxPch!, and, after the recapture by
king or queen, 26 R-N1, a pin that wins the queen and
the game.

Eternal vigilance is the price that the goddess Caissa exacts from her worshippers.

24 ...   B-B4!

Botvinnik is always on the alert!

25 P-K3   QxBPch

26 Q-B2

Disaster results from 26 K-N1 BxPch   27 K-R2 B-B7   28 R-KN1 BxRch (picking up one rook) 29 KxB Q-N5ch (and now the other).

26 ...   QxRch

27 K-K2   Q-R6!

Ready to meet 28 RxP with 28 . . . R-Q1, and control of the queen file will win quickly.

28 P-B5   Q-N5ch

29 K-Q2   R-KB1

30 P-K6

Trappy to the last. White hopes to elicit the plausible capture 30 . . . RxP, when 31 R-Q8ch B-B1 (if 31 . . . R-B1   32 Q-B7ch forces mate) 32 QxR! QxQ 33 P-K7 follows, and the threat of 34 P-K8(Q) compels Black to take the draw by perpetual check.

30 ...   QxBP

31 QxQ   RxQ

32 RxQNP

The desperate 32 R-Q8ch yields to 32 . . . R-B1, but not to 32 . . . B-B1, when 33 P-K7 wins for White.

32 ...   R-B7ch

33 K-K1   R-B3

34 P-N4   BxKP

35 K-K2   B-N8

36 P-K7   K-B2

37 P-K8(Q)ch   KxQ

38 RxNP   R-N3

39 RxKRP   B-Q5!

Centralization is the magic key to winning chess—in the opening, in the midgame, and in the ending.

40 P-B5   R-N7ch

41 K-B1   R-B7ch

42 K-K1   P-K6

43 Resigns

65

White **M. Botvinnik**   Black **V. Chekover**
Réti Opening
Moscow, 1935

The longest combination ever seen in master play is this 22-mover by Botvinnik. In the course of it he sacrifices two knights and a rook to start his opponent's king on a long journey from which he never returns.

It surpasses in length the 20-move combination conceived by Alekhine against Treybal at Pistyan in 1922 (which incidentally appears only in Alekhine's notes to the game).

It is typical of Botvinnik's modesty that he did not enter the game for a brilliancy prize, nor did he include it in his *One hundred selected games.*

1 N-KB3   P-Q4

2 P-B4   P-K3

3 P-QN3   N-KB3

4 B-N2   B-K2

5 P-K3   O-O

Modern masters rarely begin with turbulent openings such as Muzio, Danish, or Evans Gambits.

They start out quietly with positional openings, such as the Queen's Pawn, the Réti, or the Ruy López —and yet they produce masterpieces that far outshine the old-time brilliancies.

6 B-K2   P-B3

This is meant to strengthen the pawn center. A more vigorous defence was 6 . . . P-B4   7 O-O N-B3   8 P-Q3 P-QN3 followed by 9 . . . B-N2 and 10 . . . R-B1.

7 0-0   QN-Q2

8 N-B3   P-QR3

9 N-Q4   PxP

Preferable to this voluntary surrender of the center was 9 . . . P-B4 10 N-B3 P-QN3 and the fianchetto of the bishop.

10 PxP   N-B4

Evidently planning to continue with 11 . . . P-K4 followed by 12 . . . N-Q6.

11 P-B4

Prevents 11 . . . P-K4, and gets a grip on the center.

11 . . .   Q-B2

Supports the intended pawn push.

12 N-B3

And White once again restrains the advance.

12 . . .   R-Q1

13 Q-B2

With this move White puts a stop to any ideas of intrusion by 13 . . . N-Q6 or 13 . . . N(B4)-K5.

Despite its innocent appearance, the position is deceptive. If Black were to play so normal a developing move as 13 . . . B-Q2, the reply 14 P-Q4 unexpectedly wins a piece.

13 . . .   N(B4)-Q2

Still fighting to enforce 14 . . . P-K4.

14 P-Q4

This ends the argument. White is in full control of K5.

14 . . .   P-B4

15 N-K5

A powerful outpost for the knight! Black dares not exchange knights, as the recapture with the bishop pawn opens up a wonderful file for the king rook.

15 . . .   P-QN3

16 B-Q3   PxP

17 PxP   B-N2

White now has the notorious hanging pawns. Strangely enough they do not look weak. Could it

be because Botvinnik is watching over them?

18 Q-K2

A subtle move. The queen over-protects the squares K4 and QB4, and is poised for action that may take place on the K-side.

18 . . .   N-B1

Threatens 19 . . . RxP. If White hastily protects the pawn by 19 Q-KB2, the rook takes it anyway!

19 N-Q1

The knight starts out on a long trip. Clearly its destination is KN5, but why go to all this trouble when Black can always keep the knight out by . . . P-R3?

19 . . .   R-R2

20 N-B2   Q-N1

Black misses an opportunity to defend his king bishop pawn by 20 . . . B-B3 and 21 . . . B-K1.

21 N-R3   P-R3

Black stops the knight from reaching N5—or does he?

Chekover

Position after 21 . . . P-R3

Botvinnik to move

22 N-N5!

This move which begins a long and accurately calculated combination, must have come as a shock to Black, who thought he had discouraged the knight from moving to this square.

22 . . .   PxN

23 PxP

The sacrifice paves the way for—another sacrifice!

23 ...   N(B1)-Q2

The other knight, though under attack, must not move! If 23 . . . N(B3)-R2   24 NxP NxP   25 Q-R5 N(N4)-R2   26 P-Q5 PxP   27 N-R6ch K-R1   28 Q-B7 N-B3   29 Q-N8ch! NxQ   30 N-B7 mate.

24 NxP!

Very pretty, this second surprise for Chekover. Instead of regaining his piece, Botvinnik gives away a second knight!

24 ...   KxN

25 P-N6ch   K-N1

Against the alternative 25 . . . K-K1, Botvinnik had prepared this neat finish: 26 QxP N-B1   27 Q-B7ch K-Q2   28 B-R3 R-K1   29 RxN PxR   30 P-N7, and White wins.

26 QxPch   K-R1

27 Q-R3ch   K-N1

28 B-B5

Threatens 29 B-K6ch and mate next move.

28 ...   N-B1

If 28 . . . B-Q3 instead, there is a mate in four by 29 B-K6ch K-B1   30 Q-R8ch K-K2   31 QxPch KxB 32 Q-B7 mate. Or if 28 . . . B-N5 (to give the king more room) White wins nicely by 29 B-K6ch K-B1 30 BxN Q-Q3 (or 30 . . . RxB   31 QxR Q-K1 32 RxNch PxR   33 P-N7ch, and Black loses his queen) 31 Q-R8ch K-K2   32 QxP mate—a neat self-block.

29 B-K6ch!   NxB

30 QxNch   K-R1

31 Q-R3ch   K-N1   See diagram at top of next column.

32 RxN!

A third sacrifice!

32 ...   BxR

Forced, as 32 . . . PxR allows a mate in two.

33 Q-R7ch   K-B1

34 R-K1!

Chekover

Position after 31 . . . K-N1

Botvinnik to move

Cuts off the king's escape, and so threatens instant mate.

34 ...   B-K4

Black must close the king file.

35 Q-R8ch!

Brilliant and more forceful than 35 RxB QxR 36 PxQ R-Q8ch   37 K-B2 R-Q7ch, though that wins too.

35 ...   K-K2

The king sets out unwillingly on what proves to be his last long journey.

36 QxPch   K-Q3

There is no turning back, as 36 . . . K-K1 runs into 37 Q-B7 mate.

37 QxBch   K-Q2

38 Q-B5ch   K-B3

Or 38 . . . K-B2   39 R-K7ch K-B3   40 Q-K4ch, and mate next move.

39 P-Q5ch   K-B4

40 B-R3ch   KxP

41 Q-K4ch   K-B6

The king must march down to his doom, as 41 . . . K-N4 permits 42 Q-N4 mate.

42 B-N4ch   K-N7

43 Q-N1 mate

Strange that the three black pieces huddled in the corner have not stirred for the last 22 moves!

66

White **M. Botvinnik**   Black **J.R. Capablanca**
Nimzo-Indian Defence
AVRO, 1938

Botvinnik was justifiably proud of his magnificent victory over Capablanca in this great tournament.

He said of it, 'It is the game of my life!'

The game is of absorbing interest throughout, its high point being the particularly elegant closing combination, which brought about resignation from the man who so rarely turns down his king in surrender.

It is Botvinnik's Immortal, and deserves to be ranked among the greatest masterpieces in the literature of chess.

1 P-Q4   N-KB3

2 P-QB4   P-K3

3 N-QB3   B-N5

4 P-K3

White's aim is to build up a strong center by 5 B-Q3 6 KN-K2 7 P-B3 and 8 P-K4.

4 . . .   P-Q4

A popular alternative is 4 . . . P-QN3 and 5 . . . B-N2, to fight for control of K5.

5 P-QR3   BxNch

6 PxB   P-B4

7 BPxP   KPxP

The recapture by the pawn makes it difficult for White to enforce P-K4.

8 B-Q3   0-0

9 N-K2   P-QN3

10 0-0   B-R3

Black wants to eliminate his opponent's most dangerous attacking piece.

11 BxB   NxB

Botvinnik is willing, since the recapture displaces the knight. It will take the knight four more moves to reach the ideal outpost QB5.

12 B-N2

Botvinnik criticizes this, suggesting instead 12 Q-Q3, which would force 12 . . . Q-B1 in reply.

12 . . .   Q-Q2!

Now 13 Q-Q3 would be strongly met by 13 . . . Q-R5.

13 P-QR4   KR-K1

Botvinnik calls this 'a surprising mistake,' and suggests instead 13 . . . PxP 14 BPxP KR-B1, with pressure on the queen bishop file.

14 Q-Q3   P-B5

And this move is 'a positional blunder,' according to Botvinnik.

But the fact is that Capablanca was playing for a win, intending the maneuver N→N1→B3→R4→N6, eventually isolating and winning the queen rook pawn. He expected to prevent the advance of the king pawn, after which his Q-side majority would prevail.

The alternative 13 . . . N-B2, suggested by Botvinnik, was certainly not attractive, as there could follow 14 PxP PxP 15 P-QB4 with advantage to White.

15 Q-B2   N-N1

The knight returns home, to start anew on a long journey.

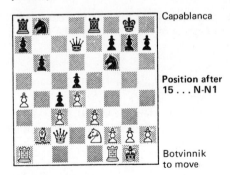

Capablanca

Position after
15 . . . N-N1

Botvinnik
to move

16 QR-K1

Botvinnik accepts the challenge! He could save the life of the rook pawn by 16 B-R3 N-B3   17 B-N4, but plays for an all-out attack, beginning with a break-through in the center.

If he can win, it will be in the grand manner!

16   ...   N-B3

More cautious was 16 . . . N-R4. Then if 17 N-N3, to support the infantry, an exchange by 17 . . . NxN would weaken White's attack.

17   N-N3   N-QR4

18   P-B3   N-N6

19   P-K4   QxP

Both players have achieved their objectives: Black has won a pawn, while White has advanced in the center.

20   P-K5   N-Q2

Now there is a threat of 21 . . . N(N6)-B4, after which White must exchange queens, or allow the knight to come in powerfully at Q6.

21   Q-B2

This evades the threat, and lends additional support to the attack.

The next part of Botvinnik's plan is to anchor the knight at Q6 (by way of B5) and to advance to B6 with the bishop pawn.

21   ...   P-N3

Capablanca plans to open the king file, confident that simplification of the position will be to his advantage.

22   P-B4   P-B4

He must stop 23 P-B5, if only for the moment.

23   PxP *en passant*

The only way to maintain the attack. Any respite would allow 23 . . . N-B1 and 24 . . . N-K3, stifling all attempts to break through.

23   ...   NxBP

24   P-B5   RxR

Black exchanges to cut down the number of attack-ing pieces. Unfortunately he still has two pieces away from the scene of action.

25   RxR   R-K1

Botvinnik refutes 25 . . . R-KB1 with 26 Q-B4 Q-R7 27 PxP QxB (if 27 . . . PxP   28 Q-N5)   28 P-N7 KxP 29 N-B5ch K-R1   30 Q-R6 R-B2   31 QxNch RxQ 32 R-K8ch and mate next.

26   R-K6!   RxR

Black must exchange rooks, the alternatives succumb-ing as follows:

(a) 26 . . . N-K5   27 NxN PxN   28 PxP! R-KB1 (if 28 . . . PxP   29 RxPch, and mate in two) 29 PxPch, and White wins a rook.

(b) 26 . . . N-N5   27 Q-K2, and White wins quickly.

(c) 26 . . . K-B2   27 RxNch KxR   28 PxP dis.ch KxP   29 Q-B5ch K-N2   30 N-R5ch K-R3   31 P-N4 Q-B3   32 B-R3!, and the bishop's entry is irresistible, thus: 33 B-B8ch RxB   34 QxRch K-N4 (34 . . . K-N3 allows 35 Q-N7 mate)   35 Q-B5ch K-R5 (here if 35 . . . K-R3   36 P-R4 forces mate)   36 N-B6, and Black will have to surrender his queen to prevent 37 Q-R5 mate.

27   PxR

Now White has acquired a formidable passed pawn, with a 'lust to expand.'

27   ...   K-N2

28   Q-B4

The queen comes closer, bringing with her new designs on the king, such as 29 N-B5ch PxN 30 Q-N5ch K-B1   31 QxNch K-K1, and mate by 32 Q-B7ch K-Q1   33 P-K7ch K-B2 (if 33 . . . K-Q2 34 P-K8(Q) dbl.ch K-Q3   35 Q(B7)-K7 mate) 34 P-K8(Q) dis.ch K-Q3   35 Q(B7)-K7 mate.

28   ...   Q-K1

29   Q-K5   Q-K2

There is no holding back the barbaric hordes by 29 . . . N-QR4   30 B-B1 N-B3   31 B-R6ch KxB 32 QxN (threatens 33 N-B5ch) N-K2   33 P-R4 P-R4

34 N-R5!, and mate at N5 by the queen is inevitable.

Capablanca's actual move seems to smother the attack:

(a) The passed pawn is blockaded.

(b) the bishop is prevented from moving to R3, and seizing a long diagonal.

(c) Black's king knight is doubly protected.

This is how the board looks:

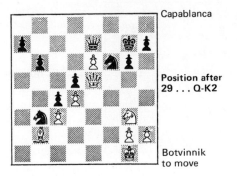

Capablanca

**Position after
29 . . . Q-K2**

Botvinnik
to move

30 B-R3!

Marvelous! Botvinnik begins a twelve-move combination with a stunning double sacrifice!

This particular move would have gladdened Nimzowitsch's heart, as it complies with his dictum, 'Remove the blockader!' Notice too that it is the modest queen bishop, hidden away at N2, that suddenly assumes an important part in the proceedings by offering up its life!

30 . . .   QxB

Black must accept the bishop, as after 30 . . . Q-K1 31 Q-B7ch K-N1   32 B-K7 N-N5   33 Q-Q7, White has an easy win.

31 N-R5ch!

One sacrifice after another!

31 . . .   PxN

This capture is forced too, as after 31 . . . K-R3 32 NxN Q-B8ch   33 K-B2 Q-Q7ch   34 K-N3 QxBPch

35 K-R4 QxQPch and the interposition 36 N-N4ch!, costs Black his queen.

32 Q-N5ch   K-B1

33 QxNch   K-N1

There is no choice, as 33 . . . K-K1   34 Q-B7ch K-Q1 35 Q-Q7 is mate.

34 P-K7!!

Two exclamation points for this move. It would be so easy to play precipitously 34 Q-B7ch K-R1 35 P-K7, only to fall into 35 . . . Q-B8ch   36 K-B2 Q-Q7ch   37 K-N3 QxBPch   38 K-R4 QxPch 39 KxP Q-K4ch, and the draw is inevitable.

34 . . .   Q-B8ch

35 K-B2   Q-B7ch

36 K-N3   Q-Q6ch

37 K-R4   Q-K5ch

38 KxP   Q-K7ch

No better is 39 . . . Q-N3ch   40 QxQch PxQch 41 KxP, and White mates next move.

39 K-R4   Q-K5ch

40 P-N4   Q-K8ch

41 K-R5   Resigns

67

White **I. Bondarevsky**   Black **M. Botvinnik**
French Defence
U.S.S.R. Absolute Championship, Leningrad, 1941

This elegant little game deserves to be better known.

Played in a tournament where Botvinnik was at the top of his form, its merits have been overshadowed by a half dozen other masterpieces that he produced in the course of the competition.

The clever way in which Botvinnik gains control of the center is by itself a delight, two amusing queen moves being reminiscent of a similar subtle strategy employed by Nimzowitsch in his famous encounter with Johner at Dresden in 1926.

Those two moves alone are worth the price of admission.

1 P-K4   P-K3

2 P-Q4   P-Q4

3 P-K5

The Nimzowitsch variation, wherein White drives a wedge into the opponent's position.

3 . . .   P-QB4

The proper response, an attack on the center.

4 N-KB3

Nimzowitsch advocated over-protection of the wedge (the king pawn) with pieces, even if it meant loss of the queen pawn.

He recommended 4 Q-N4, though, as he said, it was 'a move that would appeal only to the few; it is not everybody's fancy to give up a pawn, and afterwards—not to play for an attack.'

4 . . .   N-QB3

5 B-Q3

A temporary loan of a pawn, in the spirit of the gambit.

5 . . .   PxP

6 0-0   B-B4

7 P-QR3

This seems slow, for gambit play. White should develop (and over-protect) by 7 B-KB4.

7 . . .   KN-K2

8 QN-Q2

This is routine play, whereas proper timing required 8 B-KB4. If then 8 . . . N-N3 in reply, the bishop can settle down nicely at N3.

8 . . .   N-N3

Initiates an attack on the all-important king pawn.

9 N-N3   B-N3

10 R-K1   B-Q2

11 P-N3

Preparation for an attack by 12 P-KR4 and 13 P-R5, but the king knight loses a pawn support—a circumstance that will not escape Botvinnik's notice.

Less chances were offered by 11 BxN RPxB (opens the rook file)   12 N(N3)xP NxN   13 NxN Q-R5, and Black wins a pawn.

Botvinnik to move

Position after 11 P-N3

Bondarevsky

11 . . .   P-B3

A third attack on the king pawn. White must now either give up the center by 12 PxP, or part with his precious king bishop.

12 BxNch   PxB

The open rook file is bound to benefit Black.

13 Q-Q3

White can win back his pawn, only to run into other troubles, thus: 13 N(N3)xP NxN   14 NxN PxP 15 RxP Q-B3   16 P-KB4 P-N4   17 P-B3 PxP 18 BxP B-B2, and White's position will quickly crumble.

13 . . .   K-B2!

14 P-KR4

A necessary provision for 15 B-B4, which if played at once meets with 14 . . . P-N4 in reply.

Botvinnik's next move is a profound one. It deserves a diagram, and an exclamation point or two.

Botvinnik
to move

Position after
14 P-KR4

Bondarevsky

14 ...   Q-KN1!!

This beautiful queen maneuver crosses up White's plan to regain his pawn without losing hold of the center.

White intended to protect his king pawn by 15 B-B4 (now that ... P-N4 has been prevented) and then capture the queen pawn at his leisure.

15 B-Q2

White abandons 15 B-B4, realizing that he is in for trouble after a few moves, the continuation being 15 ... Q-R2 16 N(N3)xP NxN 17 NxN P-N4, and the threats of 18 ... PxB, or 18 ... QxQ followed by 19 ... BxN, force 18 QxQ RxQ 19 B-K3, when 19 ... PxP wins a pawn, and in short order the game itself.

15 ...   Q-R2!

16 B-N4

So the bishop tries another tack! It is headed either for Q6, to bolster the king pawn, or for B5, in an attempt to eliminate one of Black's potentially dangerous bishops.

16 ...   P-N4

Now we begin to see the depth of Botvinnik's strategy. He will force the removal of White's annoying king pawn, and then build up a strong pawn center of his own, even though it costs him a pawn.

17 QxQ   RxQ

18 KPxP

There was no way to maintain the center. If 18 RPxP PxKP 19 NxPch NxN 20 RxN B-B2 21 R-K2 P-K4, and threats (one such being 22 ... B-N5 followed by 23 ... B-B6) begin to spring up.

18 ...   PxBP

19 PxP   P-K4!

20 PxP   KxP

As a result of his thoughtful planning, Botvinnik has a powerful pawn center, two bishops eagerly waiting in the background, and open files at the disposal of his rooks.

In contrast, his opponent's pieces have no opportunity of obtaining a foothold in the center.

21 B-Q6   R-K1

22 N-R4   R-KN1!

Threatens to remove the knight.

23 K-R2

The poor creature may not even return, as after 23 N-B3 there comes 23 ... P-Q6!, and the threat of 24 ... RxPch wins quickly.

23 ...   B-KB4

24 R-K2   P-Q6

25 R-Q2

Or 25 PxP BxQP 26 R-Q2 B-B5 27 N-B1 N-Q5 (threatens the rook by 28 ... N-B6ch) 28 R-Q1 (if 28 K-R3 B-B8ch wins) 28 ... N-B6ch 29 K-R3 BxP, and White can stop struggling.

25 ...   PxP

26 P-B4   B-K6

27 BxPch

Moving the rook to K2 instead, loses like a shot by 27 ... BxP!

27 ...   NxB

28 PxNch   K-K2

29 R-KB1

On 29 R-K2 B-B5 admits of no reply.

29 ...   P-B8(Q)!

This breaks down all resistance: if 30 NxQ BxR
31 RxB BxN wins a rook. Or if 30 RxQ RxNch
31 PxR B-B5ch 32 K-R1 B-K5ch, and Black wins
both rooks.

30 Resigns

An impressive performance by Botvinnik.

68

White **M. Botvinnik**   Black **I. Boleslavsky**
French Defence
Moscow, 1941

There are original touches in the opening of this game
that assure Botvinnik of domination of the black squares.
This leads to an interesting midgame situation that is
resolved by an elegant combination. The resulting clearance leaves a rook-and-pawn ending that is handled by
Botvinnik with flawless precision. It is an ending that
offers pleasure to the reader, and also serves as a priceless
lesson in technique.

The whole game is a Botvinnik masterpiece on a grand
scale.

1 P-K4   P-K3

2 P-Q4   P-Q4

3 N-Q2

This line, advocated by Tarrasch, avoids the Winawer
variation (3 . . . B-N5) and permits support of the
queen pawn by P-QB3.

3 . . .   P-QB4

Black attacks the center—the best course of action.

4 PxQP   KPxP

While this capture might leave Black with an isolated
queen pawn, it is probably preferable to 4 . . . QxP,
when something like this might follow: 5 KN-B3!
PxP 6 B-B4 Q-Q3 7 0-0 N-KB3 8 N-N3 N-B3
9 R-K1 P-QR3 10 P-QR4 B-K2 11 KNxP, with
White for choice.

5 B-N5ch   N-B3

6 KN-B3   B-Q3

7 0-0   KN-K2

8 PxP   BxP

9 N-N3   B-N3

10 B-K3!

An original concept! White offers an exchange which
will saddle him with a sickly-looking king pawn—but
in return he will have other benefits.

10 . . .   BxB

11 BxNch!

This *zwischenzug* is the first point of the Botvinnik
combination.

11 . . .   PxB

Black must recapture this way, as after 11 . . . NxB
12 R-K1 P-Q5 13 N(B3)xP, White has won a pawn.

12 PxB

As compensation for his isolated king pawn, White
exerts unmistakable, if invisible, pressure on the
critical squares Q4 and QB5, whose strategical signifi-
cance will later be evident.

12 . . .   0-0

13 Q-Q2!

The queen too will exert her influence on the all-
important black squares in the center.

13 . . .   Q-N3

14 Q-B3!

This prevents Black from freeing himself by 14 . . .
P-QB4.

The next step in the plan consists in anchoring the
knights on Q4 and QB5, squares from which they
cannot be dislodged by pawns.

14 . . .   R-N1

15 QR-N1

The knight pawn must be guarded once again before
White can play N-B5.

15 . . .   R-K1

16 KR-K1   N-N3

Black will of course try to equalize the situation by centralizing his knight.

17 N-B5   B-N5

18 N-Q4   N-K4

Both players have carried out their designs, and this is the situation:

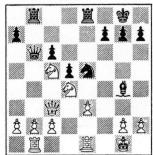

Boleslavsky

**Position after
18 . . . N-K4**

Botvinnik
to move

19 P-N4   QR-Q1

20 P-K4!   PxP

21 RxP

With one blow White has rid himself of the isolated pawn and activated one of his rooks.

21 . . .   P-QR4

22 P-QR3   PxP

23 PxP   P-B3

This adds support to the knight, and helps guard against the effects of 24 Q-KN3—threats against the loose pieces.

24 R(N1)-K1   K-R1

Black's best defence was 24 . . . B-R4 (adding protection to the king rook) followed by 25 . . . B-B2, making the square K3 unavailable to an enemy knight.

25 K-R1

After this, Black can lose in a number of ways.

(a) 25 . . . R-Q4   26 RxB, and White wins a piece.

(b) 25 . . . B-B1   26 N-R4 Q-R3   27 QxP QxQ 28 NxQ, and White wins a pawn.

(c) 25 . . . B-R4 (recommended by a host of annotators) 26 N(Q4)-K6 R-QN1 27 RxN! PxR 28 QxP (threatens mate) RxN 29 NxR, and Black must give up his bishop or suffer mate.

25 . . .   B-Q2

26 NxB   RxN

27 QxP!

This wins a pawn, thanks to the vulnerable last rank, and begins a delightful combination.

27 . . .   Q-Q1

The penalty for 27 . . . NxQ is instant mate.

28 N-B3   R-QB2

After this plausible move, Botvinnik unfolds a startling combination which clears away most of the pieces like magic, and leaves a rook-and-pawn ending, with Botvinnik a pawn ahead.

This is the board, before the fireworks:

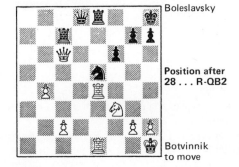

Boleslavsky

**Position after
28 . . . R-QB2**

Botvinnik
to move

29 NxN!   PxN

If 29 . . . RxQ   30 N-B7ch K-N1   31 NxQ RxN 32 P-B4 P-B4   33 R-B4, and White wins. Or if 29 . . . RxN   30 RxR PxR (on 30 . . . RxQ 31 R-K8ch forces mate)   31 Q-K4, and White should win.

30 QxRch!   QxQ

31 RxP   Q-KN1

Willy-nilly, Black must return his queen for a rook.

32 R-K8   RxP

33 RxQch   KxR

34 R-QN1!

The ideal place for the rook in this type of ending is behind the passed pawn. The rook not only supports the pawn, but its own power increases with every forward step taken by the pawn.

34 ...   K-B2

35 P-N5   K-K3

36 P-N6

The pawn will tie up Black's king and rook. White meanwhile can bring up his king and terrorize the K-side pawns.

36 ...   R-B1

37 P-R3

Advancing the passed pawn would be premature, as Botvinnik shows: 37 P-N7 R-QN1   38 K-N1 K-Q3   39 K-B2 K-B2   40 K-N3 RxP   41 RxRch KxR   42 K-B4 K-B3   43 K-K5 K-Q2, and White's advantage has been dissipated.

37 ...   R-QN1

38 K-R2   K-Q4

39 K-N3   K-B3

40 K-N4   K-N2

The king blockades the pawn, and frees the rook for counterplay.

The capture 40 . . . RxP is of course fatal, as after 41 RxRch KxR   42 K-B5 the king gets to the pawns and removes them.

41 R-K1!

Indirectly protects the passed pawn, while threatening 42 R-K7ch, followed by 43 RxP, and the capture a few moves later of the remaining pawn.

41 ...   R-N1

Here, too, 41 . . . KxP loses by 42 R-N1ch, and the exchange of rooks.

42 R-K6!

Combines attack and defence.

42 ...   K-R3

About as good a move as there is. 42 . . . P-R3 lets the king in by 43 K-R5, while 42 . . . P-N3 allows 43 K-N5 and 44 K-R6.

43 K-N5   K-N2

44 P-R4   K-R3

45 P-R5   K-N2

46 P-N4   K-R3

47 K-R4   K-N2

48 P-R6!

This will do the trick!

48 ...   PxP

Or 48 . . . P-N3   49 R-K7ch KxP   50 RxP K-B4   51 R-KN7 R-KR1   52 RxP, and Black may as well resign.

49 RxP   R-N2

50 K-R5   K-R3

If 50 . . . R-KB2   51 R-K6 R-N2   52 P-N5 K-R3   53 K-R6 R-Q2   54 R-K8 KxP   55 R-KR8, and White wins.

51 R-QB6   R-K2

Or 51 . . . K-N2   52 R-B7ch RxR   53 PxR KxP   54 K-R6, and White wins easily, Black's king being too far away to cause any trouble.

52 R-B7   R-K4ch

53 P-N5   KxP

54 RxP   K-B3

55 K-R6   K-Q3

56 P-N6   R-K8

57 R-KB7   K-K3

58 R-B2

Draws an invisible line, beyond which the king may not approach.

58 ...   R-QR8

59 P-N7   R-R8ch

60 K-N6   R-N8ch

61 K-R7   R-R8ch

62 K-N8   K-K2

63 R-K2ch   K-Q2

Or 63 . . . K-B3, and 64 K-B8 settles it.

64 R-K4!

The Lucena specific, discovered in 1497, and still effective today.

64 . . .   R-R7

65 K-B7   Resigns

The dénouement, though Boleslavsky did not care to see it: 65 . . . R-B7ch   66 K-N6 R-N7ch   67 K-B6 R-B7ch   68 K-N5 R-N7ch   69 R-N4, and the pawn cannot be headed off from the queening square.

69

White **V. Makogonov**   Black **M. Botvinnik**
Slav Defence
Sverdlovsk, 1943

Combinations have a way of interrupting the best-laid plans of strategians.

In this game, which seems to be devoted to the exploitation of white-square weaknesses, combinations suddenly spring up to interrupt (or is it adorn?) the sober strategy.

Some of them make their appearance in the actual play, while others 'slumber beneath a thin coverlet,' in Nimzowitsch's apt phrase.

Which of the combinations are the more beautiful?

1 P-Q4   P-Q4

2 P-QB4   P-K3

3 N-QB3   P-QB3

4 P-K3   N-B3

5 N-B3   QN-Q2

6 N-K5

Makogonov avoids 6 B-Q3, as he wants to get out of the books.

6 . . .   NxN

7 PxN   N-Q2

8 P-B4   B-N5

9 PxP

This is premature, as it facilitates the development of Black's queen bishop.

9 . . .   KPxP

10 B-Q3   N-B4

11 B-B2

White evidently suspects no danger in this innocent-looking position.

He should quietly castle, dull though that might be.

11 . . .   Q-R5ch!

Hoping to provoke the automatic response 12 P-N3, which would enable Botvinnik to carry out his insidious designs.

12 P-N3

One can appreciate that White found little appeal in 12 K-B1.

12 . . .   Q-R6

After only a dozen moves, Botvinnik has so maneuvered as to saddle his opponent with white-square weaknesses.

Now his threat of 13 . . . Q-N7 will give him the necessary time to effect an exchange of bishops.

13 K-B2   BxN

Kills off the knight, one of the guardians of the vital K4 square.

14 PxB   B-B4

And this is the next step in securing control of that square.

15 BxB   QxB

16 P-N4!

Beautifully played! (Even the loser is entitled to some exclamation points.) He sets the queen some problems.

For example, if 16 . . . Q-K5   17 B-R3! N-Q6ch
18 K-N3 QxKPch   19 Q-B3 QxQch   20 KxQ P-QB4
21 KR-Q1 P-B5   22 QR-N1 0-0-0   23 B-Q6, and
White has a certain amount of initiative for the pawn.

Botvinnik
to move

Position after
16 P-N4!

Makogonov

16 . . .   Q-K3

17 B-R3   N-K5ch

At last! The knight places itself securely on an ideal
square.

18 K-B3   P-KR4

Botvinnik resists the temptation of winning a pawn,
as after 18 . . . NxP   19 Q-N3 N-N4   20 B-N2 0-0-0
21 P-B5, and White has wrested the initiative.

19 P-R3   P-B3!

Obviously this is to rip away the pawns surrounding
the king, and expose him to wintry blasts.

20 P-B4   PxPch

The purpose of this and the next move is to divert
White's queen from the center.

21 PxP   RxR

22 QxR   0-0-0

Safeguards the king, and threatens 23 . . . N-Q7ch,
winning a pawn.

23 R-Q1   PxKP

24 PxQP   PxQP

25 R-B1ch   K-N1

26 Q-R4   R-K1

Institutes a threat against the king and the queen,
thus: 27 . . . PxP   28 PxP (28 KxP is immediately
fatal, as Black mates in two beginning with 28 . . .
Q-B2ch)   28 . . . N-Q7ch   29 K-N2 Q-K5ch!, and
White must choose the manner of his finish: if
30 K-R2(or N1) N-B6ch wins the queen; if 30 K-B2
Q-K7ch wins the queen or mates next move; if
30 K-N3 Q-B6ch followed by 31 . . . R-K7ch forces
mate; finally, if 30 K-R3 Q-B6ch   31 Q-N3 R-R1 is
checkmate.

27 P-B5   Q-B2

28 R-B2   P-KN3

29 B-N2

With his bishop pawn unable to receive further protection (if 29 Q-R3 N-N4ch wins the queen) White
evolves a little plot. He intends to meet 29 . . . PxP
with 30 BxPch (the bishop is safe, as capturing it
allows mate on the move) K-R1   31 P-N5.

29 . . .   P-R3

Two can play at this game! This is Botvinnik's
counter-combination: if 30 BxPch RxB   31 Q-Q8ch
K-R2   32 R-B8 RxPch!, and Black mates first
(33 PxR QxPch   34 K-K2—or 34 K-N2 Q-B7ch
35 K-R1 N-N6 mate—34 . . . Q-B7ch   35 K-Q3
Q-Q7 mate).

30 K-K2

White in turn is ready to reply to 30 . . . PxP with
31 BxPch! RxB   32 Q-Q8ch K-R2   33 R-B8, and
this time he does the mating!

30 . . .   K-R2!

The king quietly leaves the eighth rank, and its
attendant anxieties.

The position is shown on page 187.

31 Q-R2   Q-B3

32 PxP   QxP

33 Q-N2

Capturing the pawn would allow Botvinnik to win
in problem-like style, thus:

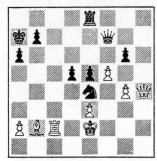

Botvinnik

Position after
30 . . . K-R2!

Makogonov
to move

33 BxP QxPch   34 K-K1 (if 34 K-B1 or K-Q3, Q-Q8ch wins) 34 . . . RxB! (forces a self-block) 35 QxR Q-N8ch   36 K-K2 Q-B7ch   37 K-Q3 (or 37 K-Q1 Q-B8 mate)   37 . . . Q-B8ch   38 K-Q4 (or 38 R-K2 Q-Q8ch and mate next move)   38 . . . Q-Q8ch   39 R-Q2 QxR mate.

33 . . .   R-KB1

34 BxP

White sees a combination that involves a sacrifice of his queen. Will it succeed, or does it have a hidden flaw?

34 . . .   R-B7ch

35 QxR   NxQ

36 B-Q4ch   P-N3

37 R-B7ch   K-N1

38 B-K5

Now it appears that White will regain his queen. On 38 . . . K-R1   39 R-B8ch K-N2   40 R-B7ch enables White to draw by perpetual check.

38 . . .   NxP

This first move in the counter-combination. Botvinnik is ready to refute 39 R-N7 dis.ch with 39 . . . NxB, after which 40 RxQ NxR leaves him a piece ahead.

39 B-B4   N-K4!

The second move, one that White had overlooked when he started his combination.

40 R-K7

Realizing of course that 40 BxN Q-R4ch followed by 41 . . . QxB is fatal, he contents himself with winning the knight, and fighting on.

40 . . .   Q-B7ch

41 K-K1   K-B1

42 BxN   QxP

Theoretically, Black has an easy win, but Makogonov manages to set up an ingenious trap whereby Botvinnik can lose—beautifully.

43 R-B7ch   K-Q1

44 R-B1   P-R4

45 B-Q4

White can win a pawn by 46 B-B7ch K-Q2   47 BxP, but after 47 . . . Q-N7   48 R-B7ch K-Q3   49 R-QN7 K-B3   50 R-N8 QxB ends the struggle.

45 . . .   P-N4

46 R-R1   Q-N6

Here too White can win a pawn by 47 B-N6ch K-Q2 48 BxP, whereupon Black wins the rook by this pretty zig-zag combination:
    48 . . . QxPch   49 K-B1 Q-B5ch   50 K-N1 Q-N4ch 51 K-R1 Q-R3ch   52 K-N1 Q-N2ch, and the rook comes off the board.

47 K-B2   P-R5

48 K-B3   Q-B7

49 K-B4   K-Q2

50 K-K5   Q-K5ch

51 K-B6   Q-K2ch

52 K-N6   P-R6

53 R-KB1   P-N5

Botvinnik lets White win his queen!

54 R-B7

One hasty move at this point, and Botvinnik can lose this game, and several nights of sleep afterwards. The instinctive pawn push by 54 . . . P-N6 falls into 55 RxQch KxR   56 B-B5ch followed by 57 BxP, and White wins.

54 . . .   QxRch!

The proper caper!

55 KxQ   P-N6

56 Resigns

The loser deserves credit too for contributing to the pleasure offered by this game.

70

White **M. Botvinnik**   Black **M. Vidmar**
Catalan System
Groningen, 1946

From the very beginning, the originality of this game is enough to hold one's attention.

The midgame strategy, with its unusual twistings and turnings, maintains it.

The climax is reached though in the cleverly-staged ending, where the highlight is a *pas de deux* between a light-footed knight and a lumbering rook.

The whole performance is one of the finest in the Botvinnik repertoire.

1 P-Q4   P-Q4

2 N-KB3   N-KB3

3 P-B4   P-K3

4 P-KN3   PxP

5 Q-R4ch   Q-Q2

Preferable is 5 . . . B-Q2 or 5 . . . QN-Q2, but Vidmar is anxious to simplify, and offers an exchange of queens.

6 QxBP   Q-B3

Now he becomes insistent, and allows no choice, as White's queen bishop is unprotected.

7 QN-Q2   QxQ

8 NxQ   B-N5ch

More of the same tactics, but more to the point was 8 . . . P-B4, attacking the center pawn.

9 B-Q2   BxBch

10 KNxB!

Obviously (after one sees it!) the best way to recapture. The knight is brought to the Q-side, where it can be more usefully employed, the long diagonal is cleared for the bishop, and there are prospects of setting up a strong pawn center by P-K4.

10 . . .   N-B3

11 P-K3   N-QN5

Vidmar's threat of 12 . . . N-B7ch gains a tempo in the re-grouping of his pieces by . . . B-Q2 and . . . B-B3.

12 K-K2!

Excellent! The king disposes of the threat by coming to the center, the proper strategy when queens are off the board.

12 . . .   B-Q2

13 B-N2   B-B3

14 P-B3

Rather than exchange bishops, Botvinnik prepares the foundation for building an imposing pawn center.

This, with the open queen bishop file, and the centralization of his king, should yield a slight advantage.

14 . . .   N-Q2

15 P-QR3   N-Q4

16 P-K4   N(Q4)-N3

17 N-R5   B-N4ch

18 K-K3   0-0-0

Protects the knight pawn, and simultaneously safeguards the king.

Black will next try to evict the annoying knight at R5 by . . . N-N1 and . . . N-B3.

19 KR-QB1!

The right rook, the queen rook being needed just where it is, to support the advance of the rook pawn. This pawn will help disorganize Black's forces.

19 ...   N-N1

20 P-QN3   B-Q2

Vidmar senses the danger in his somewhat tangled position, and avoids such possibilities as 20 ... N-B3 21 P-QR4 NxN   22 PxB, and the knight at R4 is caught in the web.

21 B-B1

The bishop, heretofore a quiescent spectator, is recalled for active duty.

21 ...   N-B3

22 NxN   BxN

Vidmar

Position after 22 ... BxN

Botvinnik to move

23 P-QR4!

Threatens an irruption on the Q-side by 24 P-R5 N-R1   25 P-R6 and   26 PxPch, which would split up Black's pawns and make them vulnerable to attack.

23 ...   B-K1

24 P-R5   N-R1

Sad, but necessary, as the knight guards the bishop pawn from the corner. If 24 ... N-Q2 instead, the sequel, according to Botvinnik, would be 25 P-R6 P-QN3   26 R-B3 K-N1   27 QR-B1 R-QB1   28 N-B4 (threatens 29 N-Q6) R-Q1   29 N-R3 R-QB1 30 N-N5, and White wins.

   All Black pieces now occupy the first rank, and while the position might have pleased Steinitz, it would take the skill and patience of a Steinitz to keep it intact.

25 P-R6   P-QN3

26 P-QN4   K-N1

This is necessary before Black can move ... P-B3 to clear a square for the knight. If at once 26 ... P-QB3, there follows 27 B-N5 K-B2 (blocks the knight, but how else to save the pawn?) 28 R-R3 R-Q3   29 QR-B3, and after 30 P-K5 the pawn will fall.

27 R-B3

'The threat is stronger than the execution.' If at once 27 P-N5 P-QB3   28 PxP R-Q3   29 B-N5 N-B2 30 P-K5 R-Q1   31 B-B1 N-Q4ch   32 K moves R-QB1, and Black wins back the pawn with good chances of defence.

27 ...   P-QB3

This may be weakening, but it's better than being smothered to death. Too, the knight must be brought back into the game.

28 QR-B1   P-B3

And this pawn move is intended to prevent 29 N-B4 and 30 N-K5.

   For Black to mobilize his knight now would be premature, as after 28 ... N-B2   29 P-N5 NxNP 30 BxN PxB   31 R-B7 B-Q2   32 R-N7ch K-R1 33 R(B1)-B7, the doubled rooks on the seventh rank assure White of a win.

   At this point, believing his position to be proof against direct assault, Vidmar offered Botvinnik a draw—but the offer was refused.

29 N-N1!

Retreat is sometimes the best way to make progress, or as the French say, '*Reculer pour mieux sauter.*'

29 ...   B-Q2

30 N-R3

Intending to break in by 31 P-N5 PxP   32 BxP BxB 33 NxB, with unremitting pressure.

   Black could avoid this by playing 30 ... P-QN4, but then comes 31 N-N1 N-B2   32 R-R3, followed by a tour of the knight to Q2, N3, and B5. Once the knight is established on this strong outpost, the position would be definitely won for White.

30 ...   N-B2

31 P-N5

Cheerfully sacrificing a pawn to get a rook on the seventh rank.

31 ...   NxNP

32 BxN   PxB

33 R-B7!

This is the position:

Vidmar
to move

Position after
33 R-B7

Botvinnik

The immediate threat is 34 R-N7ch K-R1 35 R(B1)-B7, and the rest is child's play.

The situation is critical, and could lead to checkmate for Black. For example, if 33 ... P-N5 34 R-N7ch K-R1 35 R(B1)-B7 (threatens 36 RxPch K-N1 37 R(B7)-N7ch K-B1 38 R-R8 mate) 35 ... B-B1 36 RxPch K-N1 37 N-N5, and Black must give up a piece to prevent 38 R(B7)-N7ch BxR 39 RxBch K-B1 40 N-R7 mate.

33 ...   R-QB1

Black might have saved the game with 33 ... B-B1 34 NxP R-Q2! 35 RxR BxR 36 NxP KxN 37 R-B7ch KxP 38 RxB R-QB1!, with a probable draw, since he dominates the open file, and has a dangerous passed pawn.

34 R-N7ch   K-R1

35 RxB!

So strong is the power of the rook on the seventh rank, that White can give up the exchange, and still maintain the pressure.

None the less, the sacrifice requires that Botvinnik have the courage of his convictions.

35 ...   RxR

36 NxP

The first fruits; White is sure to pick off more of the helpless pawns on the seventh rank.

36 ...   KR-QB1

Both rooks are needed to keep guard over the queen bishop file. If Black tries instead 36 ... R-KN1 (to protect his knight pawn) there follows 37 RxPch K-N1 38 R-N7ch K-B1 (on 38 ... K-R1 39 N-B7ch regains the exchange, with a winning position for White) 39 N-Q6ch K-Q1 40 P-R7 R-QR8 41 R-N8ch K-B2 (if 41 ... K-Q2 or 41 ... K-K2 42 RxR RxP 43 RxPch wins the other rook too) 42 RxR RxP 43 N-N5ch, and White removes the second rook.

37 RxNP   P-R3

38 RxPch   K-N1

39 R-N7ch   K-R1

40 R-R7ch   K-N1

41 R-N7ch

This gains time on the clock, and sometimes shakes up the opponent, who is made to feel helpless—a favourite device of Tarrasch's.

41 ...   K-R1

42 P-N4

Prepares to fix Black's rook pawn by 43 P-R4 and 44 P-R5.

42 ...   P-K4

Black in desperation allows White a passed pawn on the queen file. It is the only means he has of obtaining the square QB4 for one of his rooks, so that he can dislodge the troublesome knight.

43 P-Q5   R(B8)-B4

44 R-R7ch   K-N1

45 R-N7ch   K-R1

46 RxP   R-QN1

Vidmar must have sighed with relief at the prospect of being left with a rook against Botvinnik's knight, after this forced exchange of rooks.

47 RxRch   KxR

48 P-R7ch

The position, with Black to play:

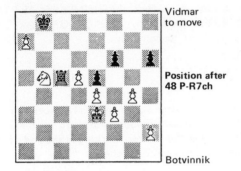

Vidmar
to move

**Position after
48 P-R7ch**

Botvinnik

48 ...   K-N2!

Vidmar puts up stout resistance. If instead 48 . . . K-R1   49 P-Q6 R-B1 (forced, as getting behind the pawn by 49 . . . R-B8 loses at once by 50 P-Q7 R-Q8   51 N-B7ch KxP   52 N-Q5, and the rook is cut off from the pawn)   50 K-Q3! K-N2 (on 50 . . . R-B8   51 N-B3 wins instantly)   51 N-B7 KxP   52 K-B4 K-N3   53 K-Q5 and wins, a plausible continuation being   53 . . . R-Q1   54 N-K6 R-Q2 (other rook moves permit 55 P-Q7 and Q8)   55 N-B5 R-Q1   56 P-Q7 K-B2   58 N-K6ch, and the rest plays itself.

49 N-Q6ch!

Much better than 49 P-Q6 R-B1   50 K-Q3 R-B8   51 N-B3 R-QR8, and the win, if any, is not too evident.

49 ...   KxP

50 N-K8   K-N3

51 NxP   R-B6ch

52 K-B2   R-B2

Black guards against loss of the king pawn by 53 N-Q7ch, or of the rook pawn by 53 N-N8.

53 P-R4   R-B2

54 N-R5   K-B2

55 P-N5!   PxP

56 PxP   R-R2

57 N-B6   R-R7ch

Black tries to restrain the knight pawn by getting behind it, as other means fail. For example, if 57 . . . R-B2 (of course not 57 . . . R-N2   58 N-K8ch, and the rook falls)   58 P-B4! PxP (or 58 . . . K-Q3 59 P-B5)   59 P-K5, and White wins easily.

58 K-N3   R-R8

59 K-N2!

Domination! The rook has only one decent square left to it on the file.

59 ... · R-R1

Last chance to stop the pawn! If 59 . . . R-R8 instead, the continuation   60 P-N6 R-R1   61 P-N7 K-Q3 62 P-N8(Q) wins the rook.

60 P-N6

Now if 60 . . . R-R3   61 P-N7 R-N3ch   62 K-B2 RxP   63 N-K8ch, and the knight fork which spears the rook is a nice finishing touch.

60 ...   Resigns

71

White **M. Botvinnik**   Black **M. Tal**
Nimzo-Indian Defence
World Championship Match, Moscow, 1961, 7th Game

Even a World Champion must not go pawn-hunting.
   Lured by the looks of a likely-looking pawn, Tal yields to temptation, and goes after it.

Punishment comes quickly when his opponent, by a series of clever moves, weaves a mating net which entangles the enemy king in its strands.

1 P-QB4   N-KB3

2 N-QB3   P-K3

3 P-Q4   B-N5

4 P-QR3   BxNch

5 PxB   P-QN3

Tal, in search of a win, tries a little-known (and perhaps an inferior) line.

6 P-B3   B-R3

The idea is to exchange bishops, and then gain control of the white squares.

7 P-K4   P-Q4

Better for Black is 7 . . . N-B3. Then if 8 P-K5 N-KN1 9 N-R3 N-R4   10 Q-R4 N-K2   11 B-Q3 0-0 12 B-N5 Q-K1, and Black has a fairly good game.

8 BPxP   BxB

9 KxB   PxP

10 B-N5   P-KR3

Tal puts the question to the bishop, thereby avoiding such perplexities as   10 . . . QN-Q2   11 P-K5 N-N5 12 Q-Q2 (12 BxQ N-K6ch) P-KB3   13 P-K6 N-B1 14 B-B4 N-R3   15 BxN PxB   16 R-K1, and White has the upper hand.

11 Q-R4ch!

Botvinnik could win a pawn (at the cost of position) by 11 BxN QxB   12 PxP 0-0, but prefers this, which could lead Tal astray.

11 . . .   P-B3

For Tal it is a choice of evils. After 11 . . . Q-Q2 12 QxQch QNxQ   13 BxN NxB   14 P-K5, the queenless position is not to his taste, as it offers no opportunities to complicate matters.

He could hardly have foreseen that the road he chose was no less thorny.

12 B-R4   PxP

13 R-K1   P-KN4

14 B-B2

A little finesse, as Botvinnik points out. After the routine reply 14 B-N3, Black gets a fair game by 14 . . . Q-Q4. After White's actual move, the queen pawn is protected, and 14 . . . Q-Q4 is countered by 15 P-QB4 Q-K3   16 Q-B2 and 17 PxP, with a decisive advantage to White.

If White plays 16 PxP in this line (instead of 16 Q-B2) there is a pretty refutation (suggested by Botvinnik) by 16 . . . NxP   17 Q-B2 P-KB4   18 P-N4 K-Q1!   19 PxP QxQBPch   20 QxQ N-Q7ch, and Black regains his queen nicely.

14 . . .   Q-K2

15 N-K2   P-N4

16 Q-B2   QxP

Tal rarely chases after pawns, generally dispensing them lavishly himself. Evidently after 16 . . . P-K6 17 BxP, the sight of the rook lurking at the end of the king file was not a welcome one.

17 P-KR4

The pawn makes way for the rook's entrance into the game.

17 . . .   PxRP

No better is 17 . . . R-N1   18 RPxP RPxP, and White controls the rook file.

18 BxP   QN-Q2

19 N-N3   0-0-0

The king flees the scene, his position being none too secure in the center, or on the K-side.

20 NxP   KR-K1

This involves the offer of a piece, but the alternative is even more costly, thus: 20 . . . NxN   21 QxN P-B3 (if the queen rook moves, the reply 22 QxPch is immediately fatal) 22 QxPch K-N1   23 B-N3ch N-K4   24 RxN!, and the threat of 25 RxP dbl.ch and mate is more than mortal can cope with.

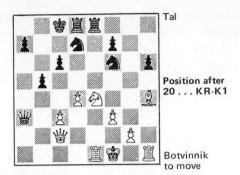

Tal

**Position after
20 . . . KR-K1**

Botvinnik
to move

21 K-B2!

A quiet little move, but an effective one. The king
steps out of the way, so that the rooks can be united.
Botvinnik rejects his opponent's kind gift, as the
sequel to 21 NxN RxRch 22 KxR Q-R8ch
23 Q-Q1 QxPch 24 K-B1 N-K4 leaves him with no
appreciable advantage.

So he plays for an attack!

21 . . .   NxNch

This is practically forced, as 21 . . . R-K3 (to protect
the knight) fails after 22 NxN NxN 23 RxR PxR
24 BxN, and White has won a piece.

22 PxN   P-B3

23 R-R1   Q-K2

24 RxP   QxP

Hoping that an exchange of queens might take the
edge off White's attack.

25 QxQ   RxQ

Now, with very little material, Botvinnik weaves a
net to ensnare the king.

26 R-R8ch   N-N1

The only move, as 26 . . . K-B2 loses a piece after
27 B-N3ch N-K4 28 RxR.

27 B-N3   K-N2

The only way to save the knight.

28 KR-R1

Threatens 29 R(R8)-R7ch K-B1 30 R-B7 mate.

28 . . .   R-QB1

29 R(R8)-R7ch   K-N3

30 BxN

To which Black may not reply 30 . . . RxB, on
account of mate on the move.

30 . . .   P-N5

31 B-Q6   PxP

32 B-B5ch   K-N4

33 R(R1)-R4   Resigns

As mate will follow at N4 by one rook, or at R5 by
the other.

72

White **M. Botvinnik**   Black **L. Portisch**
English Opening
Monaco, 1968

Even in his later years, Botvinnik was a dangerous man
to tangle with.

Known primarily as a strategian of the highest order,
Botvinnik is perfectly at home in the realm of combination play.

Here, in no time at all (or so it seems) he manages to
get a rook on the seventh rank, and uncorks a sparkling
combination that bowls Portisch over.

The game, strangely enough does not appear in the
book *Botvinnik's best games, 1947-1970*, though it was
voted the best game of the year by a jury of eight grandmasters.

1 P-QB4   P-K4

2 N-QB3   N-KB3

3 P-KN3

Instead of the customary 3 N-B3 N-B3 4 P-Q4,
Botvinnik turns the opening into a King's Indian
Reversed, a popular idea nowadays.

3 . . .   P-Q4

4 PxP   NxP

5 B-N2   B-K3

Duckstein tried 5 . . . N-N3 against Botvinnik in the 1958 Olympiad, but got the inferior game after 6 N-B3 N-B3   7 P-QR3 B-K2   8 P-Q3 0-0   9 P-QN4, and eventually lost.

6 N-B3   N-QB3

7 0-0   N-N3

8 P-Q3   B-K2

9 P-QR3!

Prepares for 10 P-QN4 and Q-side expansion, as in the game against Duckstein.

9 . . .   P-QR4

Black prevents this maneuver, but weakens his own Q-side. Perhaps the noncommittal 9 . . . P-B3 10 P-QN4 P-QR3 was a more prudent defence.

10 B-K3   0-0

11 N-QR4!

The elimination of Black's knight at N3 (which is badly placed there, according to Tarrasch) is a far-sighted move.

11 . . .   NxN

Against 11 . . . N-Q4, White has the strong reply 12 B-B5!, which, sooner or later, will provoke . . . P-QN3, or . . . P-QN4, with a consequent loosening of support for Black's queen knight.

12 QxN   B-Q4

13 KR-B1

Botvinnik puts pressure immediately on the open file, which will be augmented by the doubling of his rooks.

Then if he can drive the knight off . . .

13 . . .   KR-K1

Black wants to retreat his knight, and set up (by . . . P-QB3) a pawn barricade. To accomplish this, he must first defend the king pawn—which explains his rook move.

How was Black to know at this stage, when there

was no hint of danger in the air, that his king bishop pawn needed the rook's additional protection?

14 R-B2   B-KB1

15 R(R1)-QB1   N-N1

Black still had some chances, either with 15 . . . B-Q3 followed by 16 . . . N-K2, or with the bold 15 . . . P-K5   16 PxP BxP   17 R-Q2 Q-B3, though White has the edge after 18 R-B4!

Portisch's last move is a necessary preliminary to blockading the position by 16 . . . P-QB3.

For the moment, his queen bishop pawn is *en prise*, but capturing it would land the rook in a trap.

Or would it?

This is the state of affairs:

Portisch

Position after 15 . . . N-N1

Botvinnik to move

16 RxP!

This falls in with Portisch's designs, but Botvinnik, seeing more deeply into the position than his worthy opponent, has prepared a refutation that is brilliant.

16 . . .   B-B3

Surrounds the rook, and apparently cuts it off from all aid.

17 R(B1)xB!

Not entirely unexpected, as thousand of masters have sacrificed the exchange, but it's the next move of Botvinnik's that is breath-taking.

17 . . .   PxR

18 RxKBP!

Sacrificing the exchange is one thing, but giving up a whole rook as well is something else!

Only now does Black realize he must not touch the rook. After 18 . . . KxR there follows 20 Q-B4ch, and he is faced with these choices:

(a) 19 . . . K-B3 20 B-N5ch, and White wins the queen.

(b) 19 . . . Q-Q4 20 N-N5ch, and White wins the queen by discovered attack.

(c) 19 . . . K-N3 20 Q-N4ch K-B2 21 N-N5ch K-N1 (if 21 . . . K-K2 22 Q-K6 is mate, or if 21 . . . K-N3 22 N-K6 dis.ch wins the queen) 22 Q-B4ch K-R1 23 N-B7ch K-N1 24 N-R6 dbl.ch K-R1 25 Q-N8 mate.

(d) 19 . . . R-K3 20 N-N5ch K-N3 (instant mate follows 20 . . . K-K2 or 20 . . . K-B3, by 21 QxR) 21 QxRch Q-B3 (or 21 . . . K-R4 22 B-B3 mate) 22 B-K4ch K-R4 23 Q-R3 mate.

(e) 19 . . . R-K3 20 N-N5ch, and Black may give up his pieces by 20 . . . K-K1 21 QxRch Q-K2 22 Q-B8ch Q-Q1 23 BxPch NxB 24 QxNch Q-Q2 25 QxRch, and White wins easily.

If in this 21 . . . B-K2, there is a pretty win by 22 Q-N8ch K-Q2 (on 22 . . . B-B1 23 Q-B7 is mate) 23 B-R3ch, and Black loses his queen by a knight fork—23 . . . K-Q3 24 N-B7ch, or 23 . . . K-B2 24 N-K6ch.

(Strange that all of Black's pieces stand so help-lessly on the back row!).

18 . . .   P-R3

Gives his king a little air, and also prevents intrusion by the knight.

19 R-N7   Q-B1

20 Q-B4ch   K-R1

Black could resist longer after 20 . . . Q-K3 21 NxP QxQ 22 NxQ—but to no avail, as White has the superiority in material and position.

21 N-R4   QxR

22 N-N6ch   K-R2

23 B-K4

Threatens 24 N-K7dis.ch, and mate at N8.

23 . . .   B-Q3

24 NxP dis.ch   P-N3

Or 24 . . . K-R1 25 N-B7ch, and Black must give up his queen at once.

25 BxPch   K-N2

26 BxPch!

The *coup de grâce!*

26 . . .   Resigns

After 26 . . . KxB 27 Q-R4ch K-N2 28 Q-R7ch K-B3 29 N-N4ch K-K3 30 QxQ (threatens 31 Q-B7 mate) N-Q2 31 Q-N3ch K-K2 32 Q-B7ch K-Q1 33 QxRch, followed by removing the second rook.

Refusing the bishop leads to this neat finish: 26 . . . K-B3 27 Q-B4ch K-K3 28 B-B7ch K-K2 29 Q-N5 mate!

Fischer

Fischer is the greatest living chess master. In tournament and match play he has no equal, and in blitz (five-minute chess) he stands head and shoulders above the competition.

Fischer's chess is tough and hard-hitting. He is fiercely determined to crush his opponent to the wall. Playing for a draw does not enter his mind, and as for losing—the very thought of it is repellent.

Fischer's attitude reminds one inevitably of his friend Evans's adage, 'The chess master today must have courage, a killer instinct, stamina, and arrogance.'

Fischer's play from the very beginning has been astonishingly mature. Where most youngsters revel in tactics (the witty interplay of chess pieces), Fischer preferred sober position play—less glamorous perhaps, but infinitely more rewarding. He learnt the grand strategy of the game, the art of the seasoned master.

While Fischer limits himself in his choice of openings (for years he never strayed from 1 P-K4) he knows the openings that he does play better than the man who wrote them. Unlike those other geniuses Morphy and Capablanca, Fischer studies the openings assiduously, and is familiar with every new wrinkle of the countless lines of play employed by the hierarchy of the chess world. Even as a high-school student, he was an omnivorous reader of chess literature, one who studied and constantly analyzed published play, and who could be seen carrying copies of *Schachmatny bulletin* in his back pocket. Fischer supplements his opening knowledge by independent analysis, and the Fischer analysis is high-grade indeed.

Fischer has Lasker's fighting spirit, and technique that is reminiscent of Capablanca's. He knows how to obtain a positional advantage, and pursue it in classic style. He is familiar with the fine art of transferring a minimal advantage into an endgame, which he handles with consummate mastery.

Fischer is a tactician who can be as brilliant as Tal, if the occasion warrants combination play. But again, like Capablanca, he prefers the triumph of logical strategy to a show of fireworks.

Perceptively commenting on the Fischer-Stein game played at Sousse in 1967 (No. 60 in Fischer's *My 60 memorable games*) Purdy says, 'By ordinary standards, playing chess like White in this game requires nerves of steel. Fischer's powers of calculation and confidence in his judgment make it possible for him to conduct vital contests in a style which nobody else would venture over the board, except in games played for fun. Tal certainly has played with at least equal daring, but it seems to me that he deliberately speculates. Fischer gives the impression of having everything sewn up. The game, which in the tournament doesn't officially exist and yet was its masterpiece, symbolizes the triumph of genius over schooled mastery.'

Let's look at some of Fischer's amazing performances:

At the age of 13, Fischer gave the world an immortal game in his brilliancy against Byrne (No. 73).

At 14, Fischer became Chess Champion of the United States, the youngest ever to win that title.

At 15, Fischer became an International Grandmaster, the youngest ever to acquire that rating.

Fischer has won the title of Chess Champion of the United States eight times in succession. This despite the frequent participation of Reshevsky, a five-times title holder.

Fischer racked up 11 victories in a row in the 1963 U.S. Championship Tournament, not allowing a single draw to be scored against him.

Fischer came in first in the 22-round Interzonal Tournament at Stockholm in 1962, without losing a game. Fischer came in ahead of such seasoned veterans as Petrosian, Geller, Korchnoi, Gligorić, and Stein.

At Palma de Mallorca in 1970, Fischer finished first in a 23-round tournament, leading the runner-up Larsen by 3½ points! The rest of the field included such stalwarts as Geller, Portisch, Smyslov, Gligorić, and Reshevsky.

In 1971 Fischer accomplished the seemingly impossible in the series of Candidates' Matches.

He won six straight from Taimanov.

He won six straight from Larsen.

He trounced Petrosian (the hardest man in the world to beat) to the tune of 6½ points to 2½.

Then in 1972 Fischer played Spassky for the proud title of Chess Champion of the World. Despite losing the first game and having the second one forfeited, Fischer defeated Spassky decisively by a score of 12½ points to 8½, thereby winning the match and acquiring the title of Champion.

Three more noteworthy achievements:

In 1970 Fischer won the *Blitz Tournament of the Century* by a fantastic score of 19 points out of the 22 possible maximum. He came in 'way ahead of Tal, Korchnoi, and Petrosian, who are world-famous for the speed and accuracy of their play. Fischer's score was 4½ points ahead of that of Tal, the runner-up. Fischer's play was phenomenally fast, most of his games being finished in far less than the alloted five minutes. After the tournament, Fischer called off from memory the scores of all his 22 games, involving more than 1000 moves!

Fischer wrote and annotated *My 60 memorable games*, a work worthy to be classed with Alekhine's *My best games of chess*.

Finally, Fischer's exploits have popularized chess to an undreamed-of extent. The whole world has become chess-conscious, a development for which we are all grateful.

I consider Fischer the fourth greatest chess player of all time.

73

White **D. Byrne**   Black **R. Fischer**
Grünfeld Defence
Rosenwald Tournament, New York, 1956

Bobby Fischer's inspired play in this game must have made the audience gasp with 'Oh's' and 'Ah's' of awe and admiration.

From his 11th move on, the 13-year old master unfolds one startling move after another, in a combination that is as profound as it is brilliant.

It is a remarkable game, and the only one by a chess prodigy worthy of being classed with the Capablanca-Corzo masterpiece.

Both games are wonderful.

1	N-KB3	N-KB3
2	P-B4	P-KN3
3	N-B3	B-N2
4	P-Q4	0-0
5	B-B4	P-Q4
6	Q-N3	

Fischer's offer of a pawn is turned down, as after 6 PxP NxP   7 NxN QxN   8 BxP N-R3   9 B-N3 B-B4 10 P-QR3 (to stop 10 . . . N-N5) QR-B1, Black has the initiative.

6	. . .	PxP
7	QxBP	P-B3
8	P-K4	QN-Q2

Instead of the popular Smyslov maneuver of 8 . . . KN-Q2, Fischer's move lays a little trap: If 9 P-K5 N-Q4 10 NxN PxN   11 QxQP NxP   12 QxQ NxNch 13 PxN RxQ, and Black wins a pawn.

9	R-Q1	N-N3
10	Q-B5	B-N5
11	B-KN5	

The old convention still holds good: Do not move a piece twice in the opening. Naturally, it is worth doing so, if it interferes with the opponent's development.

Here, White's idea is simply to put pressure on the king pawn, and thereby prevent an attack on the queen by 11 . . . KN-Q2.

A preferable procedure was 11 B-K2 followed either by 12 0-0, or by 12 B-K3 to strengthen the center.

Fischer's reply to this move must have given Byrne the shock of his young life!

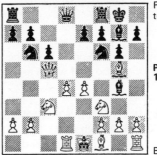

Fischer to move

Position after 11 B-KN5

Byrne

11 . . .   N-R5!
A spectacular move, which sets off a display of fireworks.

12 Q-R3
If 12 NxN NxP   13 QxKP Q-R4ch   14 P-N4 (on 14 N-B3 KR-K1 wins) QxN   15 QxN KR-K1 16 B-K7 (not 16 N-K5, when 16 . . . QxR is mate) BxN   17 PxB B-B3, and Black wins.

Or if 12 NxN NxP   13 Q-B1 Q-R4ch   14 N-B3 BxN   15 PxB NxB, and Black regains his piece, and wins a pawn as well.

12 . . .   NxN

13 PxN   NxP!
Now this knight makes a surprise move! Black offers the exchange in order to pry open the king file.

14 BxP   Q-N3!
An ingenious reply, and superior to the attractive

14 . . . Q-K1, which allows White the resource of 15 R-Q3 followed by 16 R-K3.

15 B-B4

White spurns the kind offer of the exchange, as after 15 BxR BxB 16 Q-N3 NxQBP 17 QxQ (if 17 QxN B-N5 pins the queen) 17 . . . PxQ 18 R-Q3 RxP. Black has a winning attack.

15 . . .   NxQBP!

Black comes up with one beautiful move after another.

Clearly Black is ready to meet 16 QxN with 16 . . . KR-K1, with an extra pawn as bonus, but there is more to Bobby's move than meets the eye.

16 B-B5   KR-K1ch

17 K-B1

But what does Bobby Fischer do now? How does he rescue his queen and knight, both of which are under attack?

Counter-attack on the queen by 17 . . . N-N4 fails after 18 BxPch KxB 19 Q-N3ch B-K3 20 N-N5ch K-N1 (or 20 . . . K-B3 21 Q-B3ch wins) 21 NxB Q-R4 22 N-N5 dis.ch K-R1 23 N-B7ch, and mate in three more moves by the smothered mate idea.

Fischer to move

Position after 17 K-B1

Byrne

17 . . .   B-K3!

The shot that was heard 'round the world!

This magnificent offer of the queen must have thrilled the most blasé spectator.

18 BxQ

Byrne decides to accept the queen sacrifice. Two other possibilities were: 18 QxN QxB 19 PxQ BxQ, and 18 BxB Q-N4ch 19 K-N1 N-K7ch 20 K-B1 N-N6 dbl.ch 21 K-N1 Q-B8ch 22 RxQ N-K7 mate —the well-known but always pleasing smothered mate.

18 . . .   BxBch

This begins one of the longest king hunts in the literature of chess.

19 K-N1   N-K7ch

20 K-B1   NxP dis.ch

21 K-N1

Interposing the rook allows this pretty finish: 21 R-Q3 PxB 22 Q-B3 NxN! 23 QxB R-K8 mate!

21 . . .   N-K7ch

22 K-B1   N-B6 dis.ch

23 K-N1   PxB

After this, White must abandon his rook, for 24 Q-B1 loses both queen and rook by 24 . . . N-K7ch 25 K-B1 NxQ dis.ch 26 K-N1 N-K7ch 27 K-B1 N-B6 dis.ch followed by 28 . . . NxR.

White has a seductive defence of the rook by 24 Q-Q6, but then comes the cunning 24 . . . QR-Q1 25 QxR N-K7ch 26 K-B1 N-Q5 dis.ch followed by 27 . . . RxQ.

24 Q-N4   R-R5

25 QxP

Or 25 Q-Q6 NxR 26 QxN RxP, and Black continues 27 . . . R-R8, with ruinous effect.

25 . . .   NxR

Fischer is now ahead in material, and 'the rest is a matter of technique.' Byrne plays on though, apparently unconvinced that a thirteen-year-old boy could beat him so brilliantly, until he is forced into a mating net.

26 P-KR3   RxP

27 K-R2   NxP

28 R-K1   RxR

29 Q-Q8ch   B-B1

30 NxR   B-Q4

Black could win by queening a pawn, but he prefers to play for mate.

31 N-B3   N-K5

32 Q-N8   P-QN4

33 P-R4   P-R4

34 N-K5   K-N2

Frees the bishop, with a threat—35 . . . B-Q3 36 Q-K8 B-K3, and Black wins the knight.

35 K-N1   B-B4ch

36 K-B1

Mate in three comes after 36 K-R1, by 36 . . . N-N6ch   37 K-R2 N-B8ch   38 K-R3 BxP check and mate.

36 . . .   N-N6ch

37 K-K1   B-N5ch

Fischer is enjoying himself, or he would shorten the agony by 37 . . . R-K7ch   38 K-Q1 B-N6ch   39 K-B1 B-R6ch   40 K-N1 R-K8 mate.

38 K-Q1   B-N6ch

39 K-B1   N-K7ch

40 K-N1   N-B6ch

41 K-B1   R-B7 mate

74

White **C. Guimard**   Black **R. Fischer**
King's Indian Defence
Buenos Aires, 1960

Fischer's play is simply delightful throughout this fascinating game.

Right from the start, Fischer is thrown on the defence by an opponent who wants to sweep him off his feet. Fischer stays cool, and finds all sorts of devilishly ingenious moves to stave off the attack.

After the excitement has simmered down, the players reach a rook-and-pawn ending. Fischer handles it with the facility of one who is giving a lesson in endgame play.

1 P-Q4   N-KB3

2 N-KB3   P-KN3

3 B-N5   B-N2

4 QN-Q2   P-Q3

5 P-K4   P-KR3

6 BxN

Unusual at this point, and probably a departure from published play.

6 . . .   BxB

7 B-N5ch   P-B3

8 B-Q3   0-0

Fischer does not hinder the king pawn from advancing, but . . .

9 P-K5   B-N2

10 Q-K2   P-QB4

. . . proceeds to undermine the center pawns.

11 P-KR4

This seems premature, but Guimard is bent on attacking at all costs.

11 . . .   PxQP

12 P-R5   P-KN4

13 Q-K4

Threatens nothing less than mate on the move!

13 . . .   P-B4

14 PxP *en passant*

Were it not for the genius who invented this form of capture, the game would be over at this point, with a win for Black.

14 . . .   RxP

15 NxNP   P-Q4!

Black cannot afford 15 . . . PxN, as after 16 Q-R7ch K-B1   17 P-R6, his prospects would be bleak.

Fischer's actual move does three things.

(1) It takes the pressure off the knight pawn, permitting the development of his queen bishop.

(2) It clears the third rank for his rook (though the utility of this was almost impossible to foresee).

(3) It forces White's queen to commit herself to a definite course of action.

All this from moving a pawn one square forward!

16 Q-R7ch   K-B1

17 0-0-0   N-B3

18 P-KB4

Prevents the knight from occupying K4.

18 ...   N-N5

19 P-R3

The bishop must allow its exchange, as 19 B-N6 places White's pieces in a hopeless tangle.

19 ...   NxBch

20 QxN   PxN

21 P-R6

This offers problems to the defender, but Fischer (like all truly great players) can summon up marvelous resources to his command.

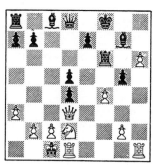

Fischer to move

Position after 21 P-R6

Guimard

21 ...   BxP!

22 PxP   B-B4

23 RxB   BxQ

24 R-R8ch   K-N2

25 RxQ

But not 25 PxRch, as Black does not touch the checking pawn, but plays 25 . . . KxR and wins. Now all three black pieces are *en prise*.

25 ...   R-B3!

Beautiful! White is forced to capture the rook that is offered him, or lose his own rook!

26 RxR   RxPch

27 K-N1   RxN dis.ch

28 K-B1

The king is caught in the windmill, a tactical device as effective as it is amusing.

28 ...   R-B7ch

29 K-N1   R-B1 dis.ch

30 RxB   RxR

31 RxP   R-Q1

The win should present no difficulties, as Black has two connected passed pawns in the center.

Nevertheless, Fischer's procedure to attain his objective is interesting.

32 K-B2   K-N3

33 R-KB4   KxP

34 R-B7   R-Q2

35 K-Q3   K-N3

36 R-B8   K-N2

37 R-QR8   P-N3

38 K-Q4   K-B3

39 R-B8ch   K-K3

40 R-KN8   K-Q3

41 P-N4

Nothing is to be gained by 42 R-N6ch P-K3, after which Black's rook switches to one of the open files, and dislodges the king—blockader of the passed pawns.

41 ...   P-K4ch

42 K-Q3   R-R2

43 P-N5   K-K3

44 P-N6   R-R6ch

45 K-B2   R-R7ch

46 K-N3   R-N7

Quite properly, the rook gets behind the passed pawn.

47 P-N7   K-B3

48 R-Q8   RxP

49 RxP   R-QB2

This of course, is to cut off the king.

50 P-R4   P-K5

51 R-KR5   P-K6

52 R-R3   R-K2

53 R-R1   P-K7

54 R-K1   K-B4

55 K-B3   K-B5

56 K-Q2   K-B6

57 R-KR1   R-Q2ch

58 K-B2   K-N7

59 Resigns

After 59 R-K1 K-B7 forces Black to give up his rook.

75

White **R. Letelier**   Black **R. Fischer**
King's Indian Defence
Team Tournament, Leipzig, 1960

Brilliancies in miniature are a rarity in present-day play.

Fischer concocts a little beauty, adds some original touches of his own, and embellishes it with a queen sacrifice.

The startling sacrifice is the sting (reminiscent of Alekhine) that Fischer provides at the end of the combination.

1 P-Q4   N-KB3

2 P-QB4   P-KN3

3 N-QB3   B-N2

4 P-K4   0-0

Fischer varies from the book move 4 . . . P-Q3.

5 P-K5

Letelier accepts the challenge to dislodge the knight, while building up an imposing pawn center at the same time.

Tempting—but is the pawn center strong by virtue of its very existence, or is it weak, since it is a target for attack, and may be destroyed?

Time (and Fischer) will tell.

5 . . .   N-K1

6 P-B4   P-Q3

7 B-K3   P-QB4

Begins the process of undermining.

8 PxBP   N-B3

Black rushes the development of his pieces.

9 BPxP

White, on the other hand, neglects his development, preferring to remove anything that is not nailed down.

9 . . .   PxP

10 N-K4

And now (horrors!) he moves the same piece twice in the opening! Does he expect Fischer to play 10 . . . PxP, and lose the exchange by 11 B-B5?

10 . . .   B-B4!

11 N-N3

White avoids the difficulties attendant on 11 NxP NxN 12 QxN (if 12 PxN BxP snags the rook) QxQ 13 PxQ BxP 14 R-Q1, and Black can pursue the attack by 14 . . . B-B7, or by 14 . . . N-N5, when the threat of 15 . . . B-B7, winning the exchange, will regain the pawn with advantage.

11 . . .   B-K3

12 N-B3   Q-B2

13 Q-N1

A strange place for the queen, but from this square she protects the knight pawn, and supports a possible pawn push at KB5.

13 ...   PxP

14 P-KB5

This looks good, but Fischer is not unprepared.

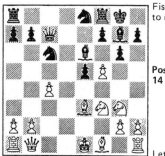

Fischer to move

Position after 14 P-KB5

Letelier

14 ...   P-K5!

'An example of the proverbial combination,' as Sergeant says in his Charousek book, 'expected by the stronger player, who sees farther than his opponent.

15 PxB

White goes ahead with the planned combination, the alternatives not being appetizing: If 15 NxP BxKBP is strong, while 15 QxP PxP 16 Q-R4 (on 16 NxP Q-R4ch wins the silly knight) 16 ... BxNP, and Black has a winning advantage.

15 ...   PxN

16 NPxP   P-B4!

On with the attack! The pawn can be picked up later.

17 P-B4

Practically forced, to avert loss of a piece by 17 ... P-B5.

17 ...   N-B3

18 B-K2

The attractive 18 B-N2 succumbs to 18 ... N-KN5 19 B-Q2 Q-N3, and the threats of winning a piece by 20 ... Q-B7ch, or the exchange by 20 ... BxP, are overwhelming.

18 ...   KR-K1

19 K-B2   RxP

Regains the pawn without abating the pressure.

20 R-K1   QR-K1

21 B-B3

White seems to have reorganized his forces to good effect, but he is in for a rude awakening.

This is the situation:

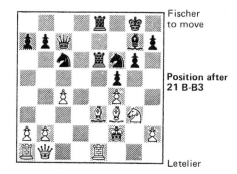

Fischer to move

Position after 21 B-B3

Letelier

21 ...   RxB!

22 RxR   RxR

23 KxR   QxPch!

This must have been a stunner!

23 ...   Resigns

In view of

(a) 23 KxQ B-R3 mate,

(b) 23 K-K2 N-Q5ch wins,

(c) 23 K-B2 N-K4   24 Q-Q1 N(B3)-N5ch, and Black wins the queen or forces mate.

White gives up the struggle.

76

White **R. Fischer**   Black **M. Tal**
Sicilian Defence
Bled, 1961

Fischer is at his brilliant best in this smashing win over Tal.

The fact that Fischer had never beaten Tal, in their six earlier encounters, sweetened this victory.

World Champion Botvinnik, not one to give praise lightly, said of Fischer's performance, 'Fischer played with great inventiveness and with great technical perfection.'

To this I may add that he played the whole game in the fiery style characteristic of Tal himself, his formidable opponent.

1 P-K4   P-QB4

2 N-KB3   N-QB3

3 P-Q4   PxP

4 NxP   P-K3

5 N-QB3   Q-B2

6 P-KN3!

A double-edged move! At one stroke Fischer prepares the development of both bishops!

The king bishop can be fianchettoed at N2, while the queen bishop (with the support of the knight pawn) can enter the game at KB4, there to make the opposing queen uncomfortable.

6 . . .   N-B3

So refined is chess technique nowadays, that it can describe this normal developing move, in a conventional enough position, as a losing move.

Of it, Botvinnik says, 'It is evident that after 6 . . . N-B3 Black's game is objectively lost. 6 . . . P-QR3 was a *must*,' while Fischer himself says, 'Probably a losing move.'

Yet there are many who think that the masters know all the good moves in the opening, and simply play the first fifteen or twenty moves mechanically.

7 N(Q4)-N5   Q-N1

8 B-KB4   N-K4

Preferable to 8 . . . P-K4, relinquishing his Q4 square. The sequel to this could be 9 B-N5 P-QR3 10 BxN PxB 11 N-R3 BxN 12 PxB N-Q5 13 N-Q5!, and White stands better.

Now White must not be hasty and attack the pinned knight by 9 Q-Q4, as the response 9 . . . N-B6ch, winning a piece, is an unpleasant surprise.

9 B-K2

Unexpected, and stronger than the anticipated fianchetto by 9 B-N2.

The bishop, keeping watch in two directions, guards against sorties by a knight to any white squares in the vicinity.

9 . . .   B-B4

The attempt to dislodge the menacing knight by 9 . . . P-QR3 leads to this: 10 Q-Q4 P-Q3 11 0-0-0 PxN 12 BxN, and Black loses a pawn, as he dare not recapture by 12 . . . PxB on pain of instant mate.

10 BxN!

A stunning move (Who gives up a bishop for a knight?) which must have been a shock to Tal.

10 . . .   QxB

11 P-B4

Fischer's pawns now advance and rip up Black's position.

11 . . .   Q-N1

12 P-K5   P-QR3

The retreat by 12 . . . N-N1 was unthinkable, in view of the continuation 13 N-K4, followed by anchoring one of the knights at Q6, with crushing effect.

13 PxN   PxN

14 PxP   R-N1

15 N-K4   B-K2

Black's last few moves have been forced.

16 Q-Q4   R-R5

17 N-B6ch   BxN

The alternative 17 . . . K-Q1 allows White the pleasant choice of winning by 18 Q-N6ch Q-B2 19 QxQch KxQ   20 NxR, or by 18 NxR RxQ 19 NxB KxN   20 P-N8(Q).

18 QxB

Disaster now looms in the air in various forms: (a) by 19 B-R5, or (b) by 19 B-Q3 followed by 20 BxRP, or (c) by 19 Q-R6 and 20 QxRP.

18 . . .   Q-B2!

Black is prepared to meet 19 B-R5 with 19 . . . P-Q4, while the alternative attack by 19 B-Q3 lets him escape by 19 . . . Q-B4   20 BxRP Q-K6ch   21 K-B1 Q-B6ch   22 K-N1 Q-K6ch   23 K-N2 Q-K7ch 24 K-R3 RxNP!   25 QxR Q-R4ch, and Black draws by perpetual check.

19 0-0-0   RxRP

20 K-N1   R-R3

Black hopes to get in 21 . . . P-K4, and bring about a simplifying exchange of queens.

On 20 . . . Q-R4 instead, White replies 21 P-N3, disposes of the mate threat, and in turn he menaces 22 B-R5 or 22 B-Q3, either of which would have a deadly effect.

Finally, if Black tried 20 . . . R-R4, it would lead to disaster by 21 B-R5 P-Q4   22 RxP! PxR   23 R-K1 check.

21 BxP   R-N3

22 B-Q3   P-K4   See diagram.

Tal hopes for 23 QxPch QxQ   24 PxQ RxP, when he can still fight, though a pawn down.

But Fischer has other ideas!

23 PxP!

If this queen sacrifice is not particularly profound, it deserves an exclamation point or two for artistry.

It received this mark of approbation from every annotator but Botvinnik.

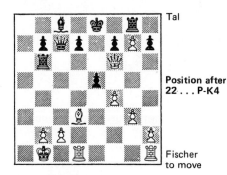

Tal

Position after 22 . . . P-K4

Fischer to move

23 . . .   RxQ

24 PxR   Q-B4

Black must get rid of those two advanced pawns! If he plays 24 . . . Q-N3 instead, there follows 25 KR-B1 (threatening 26 BxP) RxP   27 PxR, and the pawn moves on to become a queen.

After Black's actual move, there is no point in 25 KR-B1 as 25 . . . RxP   26 PxR Q-KN4 stops the pawn dead in its tracks.

25 BxP   Q-KN4

26 BxR   QxBP

27 KR-B1   QxP

28 BxPch   K-Q1

29 B-K6

Threatens 30 R-B7 Q-N3   31 BxP!, winning easily.

29 . . .   Q-R3

The position at this point is fantastic.

Tal has only two pawns on the board, but they imprison his unfortunate bishop!

The scene is shown on page 207.

30 BxP   BxB

The bishop emerges, but only for a moment: his career is short-lived.

31 R-B7   QxP

32 R(Q1)xBch

How does Fischer always manage to get his rooks onto the seventh rank?

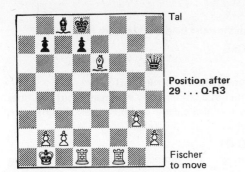

Tal

Position after
29 . . . Q-R3

Fischer
to move

32 ... K-K1

33 R(Q7)-K7ch K-Q1

34 R-Q7ch K-B1

35 R-B7ch K-Q1

36 R(KB7)-Q7ch K-K1

37 R-Q1 P-N4

38 R-QN7 Q-R4

If 38 . . . QxP 39 R-R1 (threatens mate at R8)
Q-K4 40 R-R8ch! (why let the queen stop you?)
QxR 41 R-N8ch, and White wins.

39 P-KN4 Q-R6

On 39 . . . QxP 40 R-R1 wins the queen in the
fashion of the previous note.

40 P-N5 Q-B6

41 R-K1ch K-B1

42 RxP K-N2

43 R-N6

Threatens 44 R-K7ch K-B1 45 R-B6ch, winning
the queen.

43 ... Q-KN6

44 R-Q1 Q-B2

45 R(Q1)-Q6 Q-B1

On 45 . . . Q-B4, White wins either by 46 R-Q7ch,
or by 46 R-N7ch.

46 P-N3 K-R2

47 R-QR6!

White threatens to double rooks on the seventh
rank, beginning with 48 R-R7ch. If Black prevents
this by 47 . . . Q-N2, there follows 48 R-R6ch K-N2
49 R(QR6)-N6ch K-B1 50 R-R8ch K-B2
51 R-R7ch, and White wins the queen. Therefore . . .

47 ... Resigns

77

White **R. Fischer**   Black **J. Bolbochan**
French Defence
Interzonal Tournament, Stockholm, 1962

Fischer's outstanding technique conveys the impression
that he can win with the White side of the Sicilian
Defence—or with the Black side!

Clever strategy in this game enables Fischer to establish
a knight securely at Q5, after which it's a matter of finding
the right 'petite combinaison,' as Capablanca called it,
to force capitulation.

Fischer does evolve a combination, and it proves to be
pretty enough to earn him a brilliancy prize.

1 P-K4 P-QB4

2 N-KB3 P-Q3

3 P-Q4 PxP

4 NxP N-KB3

5 N-QB3 P-QR3

6 P-KR3 N-B3

Developing a piece may be the best reply to Fischer's
bayonet attack.

If instead 6 . . . P-K4, a plausible continuation
could be: 7 KN-K2 B-K3 8 P-KN4 P-Q4 9 P-N5
NxP (other moves by the knight lose the queen pawn)
10 NxN PxN 11 QxQch KxQ 12 N-N3 B-Q4
13 B-K3 (threatens to win a piece by castling) 13 . . .
K-B2 14 0-0-0 B-B3 15 B-N2, after which White
regains his pawn, with a superior position.

7 P-KN4   NxN

8 QxN   P-K4

9 Q-Q3   B-K2

10 P-N5!

Dislodging this knight is necessary if Fischer's knight is to occupy the outpost at Q5, 'a consummation devoutly to be wish'd,' as Hamlet observed.

10 . . .   N-Q2

11 B-K3   N-B4

An alternative was 11 . . . BxP 12 BxB QxB 13 QxP Q-K2 14 QxQch KxQ 15 N-Q5ch, and White has the edge.

12 Q-Q2   B-K3

13 0-0-0   0-0

Black might have played 13 . . . Q-R4, to induce the weakening 14 P-R3, the natural 14 K-N1 losing a pawn immediately by 14 . . . NxP!

14 P-B3   R-B1

15 K-N1   N-Q2

The knight seeks greener pastures at QB5, by way of N3.

An expedition by the queen to R4 would not now be fruitful, as the reply 16 N-Q5! Q-Q1 17 NxBch QxN 18 QxP would lose a valuable pawn.

16 P-KR4   P-N4

17 B-R3!

An excellent move, as it eliminates both Black's best minor piece, and its pressure on White's Q5 square.

17 . . .   BxB

This will give Fischer what he wants—the Q5 square for his knight. But what else was there?

If 17 . . . N-N3 18 BxN QxB 19 N-Q5! Q-Q1 20 NxBch, and the queen pawn falls.

Or if 17 . . . R-K1 18 N-Q5 B-B1 19 Q-N2 followed by 20 P-R5 will make the going difficult for Black.

18 RxB   N-N3

19 BxN!

The knight must be destroyed, ere it reaches B5.

19 . . .   QxB

20 N-Q5

A dream square for the knight!

White has a strategically won game, but this does not mean that the game will play itself. Fischer must still exercise care—much care . . .

20 . . .   Q-Q1

. . . even as at this moment, he can quickly go down to defeat (and negative immortality) by carelessly playing 21 NxBch QxN 22 QxP, when 22 . . . QR-Q1 would force him to give up his queen or be mated.

21 P-KB4   PxP

Otherwise 22 P-B5 puts on intolerable pressure.

22 QxP   Q-Q2

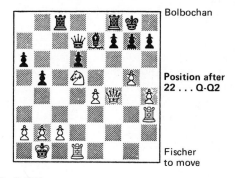

Bolbochan

Position after
22 . . . Q-Q2

Fischer
to move

23 Q-B5!

Beautifully simple and simply beautiful!

Fischer leaves his opponent a choice of losing moves:

(a) 23 . . . QxQ 24 NxBch wins a piece.

(b) 23 . . . Q-Q1 24 QxR QxQ 25 NxBch wins a rook.

(c) 23 . . . KR-Q1 24 QxQ RxQ 25 N-N6 wins the exchange.

23 . . .   QR-Q1

24 R-R3!

Fischer's rook swings over from KR3 to QR3, as Morphy's queen did in his celebrated Philidor's Defence against Bird at London in 1858, a game I commend to your attention.

24 . . .   Q-R2

25 R-QB3!

Threatens strongly 26 R-B7.

Black cannot defend by 25 . . . Q-Q2, as 26 R-B7 wins a piece. Nor is 25 . . . R-Q2 (protecting the bishop) security against loss, as Fischer would win neatly by 26 N-B6ch BxN   27 PxB P-N3   28 Q-N5 K-R1   29 Q-R6 R-KN1   30 R-B8!, and mate cannot be staved off.

25 . . .   P-N3

This weakens the K-side position, but the queen must be driven off.

26 Q-N4   Q-Q2

27 Q-B3   Q-K3

Opposing rooks by 27 . . . R-B1 runs into loss by 28 RxR RxR   29 N-N6, and White wins the exchange.

28 R-B7   QR-K1

Protecting the bishop by 28 . . . R-Q2 meets with the brusque rejoinder 29 N-B4, and the rook falls victim to the theme 'removing the guard.'

29 N-B4   Q-K4

30 R-Q5   Q-R1

Bolbochan's pieces are now huddled together in a tragi-comic position.

31 P-R3

The pause that refreshes. White takes time (his opponent being helpless) to give his king some air.

31 . . .   P-R3

32 PxP   QxRP

33 P-R5   B-N4

34 PxP   PxP

Or 34 . . . BxN   35 PxPch RxP   36 RxR KxR 37 R-B5ch, and White wins easily.

But what now? Does White lose the knight which is pinned and triply attacked?

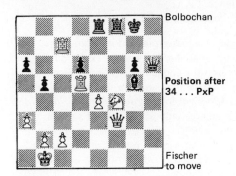

Bolbochan

Position after
34 . . . PxP

Fischer
to move

35 Q-QN3!

Brilliant! Fischer's threat of discovered check creates new problems for Black. He may not play 35 . . . R-B2, as 36 RxB wins instantly; nor 35 . . . BxN when R-R5 dis.ch wins the queen.

Finally if 35 . . . K-R1   36 NxPch QxN   37 RxB R-B8ch   38 K-R2 QxR   39 Q-KR3ch K-N1   40 QxR! winning, but not (as many annotators have suggested) 40 Q-R7ch K-B1   41 Q-R8ch Q-N1   42 Q-R6ch, and mate next move, the flaw being that Black's 41st move (41 . . . Q-N1) is an interposition *with check*, forcing 42 QxQch KxQ, after which Black would win instead of losing.

35 . . .   RxN

36 R-K5 dis.ch   K-B1

37 RxRch   Resigns

For after 37 . . . KxR   38 Q-N8ch Q-B1   39 Q-K6ch B-K2   40 R-B8 mate.

78

White **R. Fischer**   Black **M. Tal**
Sicilian Defence
Candidates' Tournament, Curaçao, 1962

Fischer produces a masterpiece of endgame play.

After an unusual opening, and an exciting midgame, the players reach the endgame stage, with Fischer a pawn down. Despite the handicap, Fischer skillfully inveigles his opponent into a *zugzwang* position, from which he can emerge only at the cost of a pawn.

The method being so effective, Fischer applies it once again with even happier results, as the former World Champion can do nothing but surrender to the future World Champion.

1 P-K4   P-QB4

2 N-KB3   N-QB3

3 P-Q4   PxP

4 NxP   P-K4

Named after the master who tried it in his sixth match game against Morphy, the Lowenthal Variation is an attempt to wrest the initiative at the cost of weakening the square Q4.

5 N-N5

This improves the Morphy line 5 NxN BPxN, which provides protection to the weak square. (Though I hasten to add that Morphy won the game beautifully.)

5 ...   P-QR3

6 N-Q6ch   BxN

7 QxB   Q-B3

8 Q-Q1

Nothing is to be gained by exchanging queens, as after 8 QxQ NxQ 9 N-B3 P-Q4! 10 PxP N-QN5, and Black regains his pawn with a good game.

8 ...   Q-N3

Attacks the king pawn and exerts pressure on the knight pawn, thereby preventing White's king bishop from entering into the game.

9 N-B3   KN-K2

10 P-KR4!

This move, which endeavors to create weaknesses in the enemy's black squares, and also clears a path for the rook, would not even have been dreamed of in the days of Morphy and Anderssen.

10 ...   P-KR4

11 B-KN5   P-Q4!

Bold, but Tal had to do something about his backward pawn.

12 BxN

Rather intricate is the pawn capture, as Levy and Keene indicate: 12 PxP N-N5 13 BxN KxB! (not 13 ... NxPch 14 K-Q2 NxR 15 B-KN5, and White emerges with two pieces for a rook) 14 B-Q3! NxBch 15 QxN QxQ 16 PxQ P-QN4 17 0-0-0 R-Q1 18 KR-K1, and White has the advantage.

12 ...   P-Q5!

13 B-KN5   PxN

14 PxP   QxPch

Tal has transformed the scene, so that it is White who has the weak pawns.

15 B-K2   P-B3

Naturally, Black does not snap at the knight pawn, as 16 B-B3 catches his queen.

16 B-K3

Sets a clever little trap. If Black plays 16 ... QxNP, there follows 17 BxPch P-N3 (king moves allow a winning attack) 18 B-B3, and the queen is caught.

16 ...   B-N5

17 Q-Q3   QxQ

18 PxQ

The exchange of queens has straightened out White's pawns.

18 ...   BxB

19 KxB   0-0-0

20 QR-Q1   N-K2

21 P-Q4   N-Q4

22 R-QB1   KR-K1

23 KR-Q1   P-B4

Somewhat risky, as it opens new vistas for White's bishop. Safer (but why should a Tal play safe?) was 23 . . . PxP   24 PxP dis.ch K-N1.

24 B-N5   R-Q2

Less promising was 24 . . . PxP dis.ch   25 K-Q3! PxP ·26 BxR RxB   27 K-B4 P-N4ch   28 K-B5.

25 PxP   RxPch

26 K-B3   R-K5

27 R-Q3   R-QB5

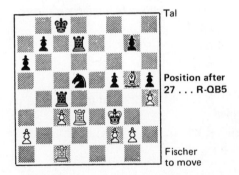

Tal

Position after 27 . . . R-QB5

Fischer to move

28 R(B1)-Q1!

Skilful play! Fischer offers a pawn to enable his king to invade the enemy K-side by way of B4 and N5.

28 . . .   RxBP

29 RxR   NxR

30 R-QB1   R-QB2

Probably best, as 30 . . . R-Q6ch   31 K-B4 K-Q2 (not 31 . . . P-KN3, when 32 B-B6 wins the knight) is hard going.

31 B-B4   R-B3

32 B-K5!

Ideal centralization, as the bishop attacks the knight in one direction, and a pawn in another.

32 . . .   N-Q4

But not 32 . . . NxP (decentralization) when 33 RxRch PxR   34 BxP P-B4   35 K-B4 P-B5   36 KxP P-B6 37 P-N4! P-B7   38 B-N2 PxP   39 P-R5, and White wins, as Chistiakov shows in the Tournament book.

33 R-Q1!

Fischer could win a pawn by 33 RxRch PxR 34 BxP, but after 34 . . . K-Q2, his king is kept at bay, and Black has a bit the better of it.

33 . . .   N-B3

It was certainly hard to foresee, but holding on to the pawn loses eventually, whereas giving it up by 33 . . . R-B4   34 BxP K-Q2 offered drawing chances.

34 K-B4!

Fischer's play from now on could go under the heading, *How to win an ending with a pawn down.*

34 . . .   P-KN3

If 34 . . . R-B7   35 B-Q4 secures White's K-side pawns, while Black's are left defenceless.

35 P-B3!

Just a safeguard against any ideas the knight might have of occupying K5 or KN5.

35 . . .   N-Q2

36 B-Q6   R-B7

37 P-N3   R-K7

It was dangerous to take the pawn, as after 37 . . . RxP, White can choose between 38 R-K1 K-Q1 39 R-K6, and 38 K-N5 followed by 39 KxNP and 40 KxRP, and the passed pawn will effectuate the win.

38 K-N5   R-K3

39 B-B4   N-B1

40 R-Q6   P-R4

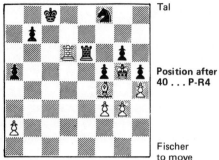

Tal

**Position after
40 . . . P-R4**

Fischer
to move

41 K-R6!

The key to the win, and far superior to the exchange of rooks, which leads at best to a draw.

41 . . .   R-K7

42 R-Q2   R-K2

Returning to K3 would be catastrophic, thus:
42 . . . R-K3   43 K-N7 N-Q2   44 R-B2ch K-Q1
45 B-N5ch K-K1   46 R-B8 mate.

43 B-Q6   R-R2ch

44 K-N5   R-KB2

Passive resistance, but an attempt to counter-attack would let Fischer win in beautiful style. If 44 . . . N-Q2   45 KxP R-R1   46 K-N7 R-K1   47 K-B7! R-K6 (on 47 . . . R-R1   48 R-B2ch K-Q1   49 B-K7 is mate)   48 R-B2ch K-Q1   49 B-B7ch K-B1 50 B-B4 dis.ch, and White picks up the rook.

45 R-QN2!   P-B5

Gives up a pawn, but Black is in *zugzwang*, and there just aren't any moves!

If 45 . . . P-R5   46 P-R3 leaves Black in the same fix, or if 45 . . . K-Q2   46 RxPch K-K3   47 RxR KxR 48 BxN KxB   49 KxP, and ruin, absolute ruin!

The reader will note that up to this point, Black has been a pawn ahead! But, as Capablanca once said, 'Position comes first; material next.'

46 BxP   R-B4ch

47 K-R6   P-QN4

48 B-Q6   P-N5

Or 48 . . . RxP   49 RxP, and White has an easy win.

49 P-N4   RxP

50 P-N5!

Threatens 51 BxN, and the consequent removal of the K-side pawns.

50 . . .   N-K3

51 KxP   R-Q6

52 B-K5   R-K6

53 K-B5   N-B1

The knight is ready to snap the pawn off, if it makes a move.

54 R-N2   R-B6ch

55 B-B4   K-Q2

56 P-N6   N-K3

Tal wins a piece, but it's only a temporary loan.

57 P-N7!   RxBch

58 K-K5   R-B1

59 PxR(Q)   NxQ

60 K-Q5   P-R5

Or 60 . . . N-K3   61 R-KB2, and the king rook pawn is doomed.

61 R-N7ch   K-K1

62 K-Q6   P-N6

63 P-R3!

Black is in *zugzwang* again. His knight may not move on pain of instant capture, while a king move is met by 64 R-QR7, and the threat of mate wins the rook pawn. Therefore:

63 . . .   Resigns

79

White **R. Fischer**   Black **B. Larsen**
French Defence
Candidates' Match, First Game, Denver, 1971

Fischer does not waste a move (he rarely does) in an attack that could be called vicious—if it were not so beautiful.

Suffice it to say that at one point Fischer's king is threatened with mate on the move, while his queen is threatened with capture. The move that saves the situation is startling, for Fischer deliberately lets his king walk into a double check.

If further recommendation be needed, Fischer considers this game one of the best in his life.

1 P-K4   P-K3

2 P-Q4   P-Q4

3 N-QB3   B-N5

The Winawer Variation of the French requires bold, enterprising play, but bold, enterprising play is Larsen's *métier*.

4 P-K5   N-K2

5 P-QR3   BxNch

6 PxB   P-QB4

7 P-QR4

This prevents a sortie by Black's queen to R4 and R5, which puts a clamp on White's Q-side development, a strategy which accounted for some fine wins by Botvinnik.

7 . . .   QN-B3

8 N-B3   B-Q2

9 B-Q3!

Sharper than the routine 9 B-K2, this induces Black to commit himself, sooner or later, by . . . P-B5.

9 . . .   Q-B2

But definitely not 9 . . . 0-0, when 10 BxPch would come like a shot, and Fischer would win by a sacrificial idea first executed by Paulsen against Schwarz, away back in 1879.

10 0-0   P-B5

This releases the tension in the center, but poses other problems.

11 B-K2   P-B3

12 R-K1

Protects the pawn from a distance. If 12 . . . PxP 13 PxP NxP (fatal) 14 NxN QxN 15 B-R5ch, and Black loses his queen.

12 . . .   N-N3

13 B-R3!

Fischer prefers to sacrifice a pawn, rather than have the knight file opened against his king by 13 PxP PxP.

13 . . .   PxP

14 PxP   QNxP

15 NxN   NxN

It was too dangerous to venture on 15 . . . QxN, when 16 BxP QxP 17 BxP opens up the position in White's favour.

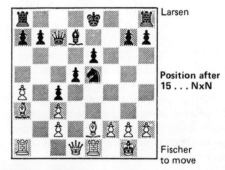

Larsen

Position after
15 . . . NxN

Fischer
to move

16 Q-Q4   N-N3

On 16 0-0-0 17 QxRP regains the pawn with advantage, while 16 . . . N-B3 loses in a hurry by 17 B-R5ch K-Q1 18 QxNP.

17 B-R5   K-B2

This parries White's threats of 18 QxQP and 18 QxNP.

The alternative, 17 . . . 0-0-0, allows Fischer to pursue the attack with 18 QxRP, or with 18 P-R5 followed by 19 B-B5.

18 P-B4!

With the fearsome threat of 19 P-B5 PxP 20 R-K7ch and mate next move.

18 . . .   KR-K1

19 P-B5   PxP

20 QxQPch

Presents a little problem. If 20 . . . B-K3 21 RxB
RxR 22 QxPch R-B3 23 Q-Q5ch R-K3 24 R-B1ch,
and White wins a piece, as the king must abandon the
rook, while 20 . . . R-K3 succumbs to 21 QxPch
R-B3 22 R-K7ch, and the bishop falls victim.

20 . . .   K-B3

21 B-B3

Life is not simple, even for the player who is doing
the attacking. Before making this move, Fischer had
to consider all the ramifications it involved, as well
as those offered by such attractive alternatives as
(a) 21 P-N4, or (b) 21 B-Q6, or (c) 21 B-B5.

21 . . .   N-K4

Larsen decides on giving up two pieces for a rook, as
the least of his evils.

After the straightforward 21 . . . B-K3, there
comes 22 Q-Q4ch K-B2 23 QR-N1 (or perhaps
23 B-Q6 first) and it's hard going for Black.

White must not be precipitate now, but heed
the order of moves. If, for example, he plays 22 RxN
RxR 23 Q-Q4 (pinning the rook, and threatening to
win it by 24 B-Q6) he discovers to his horror that
Black can extricate himself from the pin by 23 . . .
Q-N3!, clamping on a pin of his own!

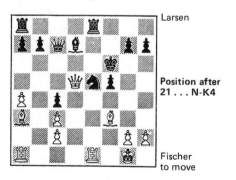

Larsen

**Position after
21 . . . N-K4**

Fischer
to move

22 Q-Q4!

Threat: 23 B-Q6.

22 . . .   K-N3

'This must be the next step in the plan initiated by
his previous move,' says Byrne, 'but in any event it
was impossible to play 22 . . . QR-Q1 23 B-Q6 Q-R4
24 B-Q5, curtain.'

23 RxN   QxR

This is less costly than 23 . . . RxR 24 B-Q6 Q-N3
25 BxR.

24 QxB   QR-Q1

Larsen hopes to post a rook on the seventh rank,
with a chance to counter-attack.

He resists the temptation of playing 24 . . . QxP,
as retribution would follow in the form of 25 Q-Q6ch
K-N4 26 P-R4ch KxP 27 Q-B4 mate.

25 QxP   Q-K6ch

26 K-B1   R-Q7

The sight of the heavy pieces closing in for the kill
is enough to terrorize anybody.

27 Q-B6ch   R-K3

And now the queen is under attack! How will Fischer
rescue the royal family? If 28 Q-B5 R-B7ch 29 K-N1
RxB dis.ch, and Black emerges the exchange ahead.

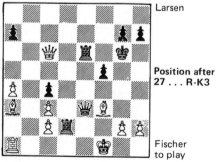

Larsen

**Position after
27 . . . R-K3**

Fischer
to play

28 B-B5!

Beautiful play! Fischer's dramatic move adds to the
excitement.

28 . . .   R-B7ch

29 K-N1

Fischer's king still seems to be in mortal danger, but strangely enough, Black does not have a worthwhile discovered check!

29 . . . RxNP dbl.ch

There is nothing in 29 . . . RxB dis.ch 30 BxQ RxQ 31 PxR, and White has an extra bishop.

30 KxR Q-Q7ch

31 K-R1 RxQ

32 BxR QxP(B6)

33 R-N1ch K-B3

34 BxP

Now the passed pawn becomes a powerful weapon.

34 . . . P-B5

35 B-N6 QxP

36 P-R5 Q-N7

37 B-Q8ch K-K3

38 P-R6 Q-R6

39 B-N7 Q-B4

The attempt to queen his own pawn loses in this way: 39 . . . P-QB6 40 B-N6 P-B7 41 P-R7 P-B8(Q) 42 RxQ QxRch 43 B-N1, and there is no defence against the queening of the pawn.

40 R-N1 P-QB6

41 B-N6 Resigns

After 41 . . . P-B7 42 R-K1ch Q-K4 43 RxQch KxR 44 P-R7 P-B8(Q)ch 45 B-N1, and White wins.

80

White **R. Fischer**   Black **B. Larsen**
Sicilian Defence
Candidates' Match, Fifth Game, Denver, 1971

Fischer illustrates in clear-cut style the validity of Capablanca's dictum: Position comes first; material next.

Fischer sacrifices a pawn, and then the exchange, in almost casual style. In return for the investment, his pieces obtain an advantage in position.

The advantage carries over into the ending, where Fischer demonstrates that it is no trouble at all for a king and three pawns to overcome a king and three pawns.

1 P-K4 P-QB4

2 N-KB3 P-Q3

3 P-Q4 PxP

4 NxP N-KB3

5 N-QB3 N-B3

6 B-QB4

Bobby puts pressure immediately on the delicate bishop pawn.

6 . . . P-K3

Safest, as 6 . . . P-KN3 is strongly met by 7 NxN PxN 8 P-K5! N-N5 (not of course 8 . . . PxP, when 9 BxPch wins the queen) 9 B-B4 Q-N3 10 Q-B3 B-B4 (if 10 . . . PxP 11 BxPch) 11 PxP PxP 12 0-0, with advantage to White.

7 B-N3 B-K2

8 B-K3 0-0

9 0-0 B-Q2

10 P-B4 Q-B1

Larsen's idea is to prevent (or at least discourage) 11 P-B5.

11 P-B5!

A fine sacrifice of a pawn, to open lines for White's pieces.

11 . . . NxN

12 BxN PxP

13 Q-Q3 PxP

14 NxP NxN

On 14 . . . B-B4 instead, the winning line is not the palpable 15 NxNch followed by capturing the bishop (which loses), but 15 RxB QxR 16 NxNch (which wins).

15 QxN   B-K3

16 R-B3   Q-B3

Black would love to simplify, and eliminate some of the dangers facing him, but if 16 . . . BxB   17 R-N3 (threatens mate in two)   17 . . . P-KN3   18 QxB Q-K3 (to stop 19 Q-B6)   19 Q-R4 B-Q4   20 R-K3 Q-B4 (the queen must guard the KB3 square) 21 R-KB1 QxP (indirect protection by virtue of the mate threat)   22 QxPch! KxQ   23 R-R3ch K-N1 24 R-R8 mate.

17 R-K1   QxQ

After 17 . . . BxB, White does not play 18 QxB KR-K1   19 Q-R4 BxBP!, but continues instead with 18 Q-N4 P-KN3   19 RxB(K7) B-K3   20 RxB Q-B1 21 R-K4 P-B4   22 Q-R4 PxR   23 Q-K7, with mate to follow, as Gipslis indicates.

18 RxQ   P-Q4

19 R-N3   P-KN3

Naturally, Black does not bite on 19 . . . PxR, when he gets slaughtered by the windmill attack, thus: 20 RxPch K-R1   21 RxBP dis.ch B-B3   22 BxBch K-N1   23 R-N7ch K-R1   24 B-B3 QR-B1 25 R-QB7 dis.ch, and White wins.

20 BxQP   B-Q3

Larsen disdains the draw by 20 . . . BxB   21 RxB KR-K1, and tries for a win.

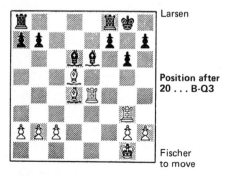

Larsen

Position after 20 . . . B-Q3

Fischer to move

21 RxB!   BxR

Obviously, 21 . . . PxR   22 BxPch R-B2   23 R-B3

cuts down most of the pieces, and leaves an easy White win.

22 R-K7   B-Q3

23 RxNP

Fischer has bishop and pawn for his rook, but his rook is posted on the seventh (as usual), his bishops look menacing, and his Q-side pawns are ambitious.

23 . . .   QR-B1

24 P-B4   P-QR4

25 R-R7   B-B2

The only way to defend the pawn: If instead 25 . . . B-B4   26 BxB RxB   27 K-B2, and the king moves on to Q4, and dislodges the rook. Or if 25 . . . B-N5 26 P-QR3 B-Q7   27 K-B2, when QR-K1 (to prevent 28 K-K2) loses the exchange by 28 B-B5.

26 P-KN3   KR-K1

27 K-B1   R-K2

28 B-KB6   R-K6

29 B-QB3   P-R4

Hoping to push on to R5, and stir up some trouble.

30 R-R6!

Threatens 31 RxPch, as well as 31 R-QB6. This is the position:

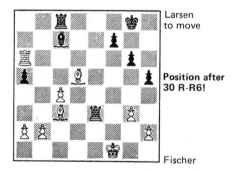

Larsen to move

Position after 30 R-R6!

Fischer

30 . . .   B-K4

31 B-Q2!   R-Q6

32 K-K2   R-Q5

There was no saving the game by 32 ... RxBch
33 KxR BxQNP   34 RxPch K-B1   35 R-QR6.

33 B-QB3   R(B1)xP

The ending after 33 . ... RxB   34 PxR BxB   35 PxB
RxP   36 P-Q6 R-B7ch   37 K-K3 is a win for White.

34 B(Q5)xR   RxB

35 K-Q3

Of course not 35 BxB R-K5ch, and Black draws the
game.

35 ...   R-B4

36 RxP   RxR

37 BxR   BxQNP

Material is even, but the outside passed pawn is as
good as the ace of trumps.

38 P-QR4   K-B1

39 B-B3   BxB

Avoiding the exchange would lead to this: 39 ...
B-R6   40 P-R5 B-B4   41 P-R6 B-Q3 (otherwise
42 B-Q4 wins)   42 B-N4, and White gets a queen.

40 KxB   K-K2

41 K-Q4   K-Q3

42 P-R5   P-B3

43 P-R6   K-B3

44 P-R7   K-N2

45 K-Q5   P-R5

46 K-K6   Resigns

The rest is elementary. The king removes the two
pawns, and his knight pawn marches through to
become a queen.

81

White **R. Fischer**   Black **T. Petrosian**
Sicilian Defence
Candidates' Match, Seventh Game, Buenos Aires, 1971

The spectators at a chess match thrill to surface brilliancies—the sudden sacrifice of a queen or a rook. Rarely
do they react to a move that is modest, but none the less
deadly.

In this game, Fischer played a move that took everybody, from amateur to grandmaster, by complete surprise.
It was a sacrifice, but of a different sort. Fischer gives up
a definite advantage for one that seems nebulous. It may
not sound exciting, but it was enough to make this game
outstanding.

That this was the best game of the match, was the
opinion of all the commentators—and Fischer as well.

And if Petrosian, as Botvinnik said, 'was unrecogniz-
able in this game,' it is something that happens to all
great players when they are on the losing side.

Even the mighty tiger can be made to look like a
kitten.

1 P-K4   P-QB4

2 N-KB3   P-K3

3 P-Q4   PxP

4 NxP   P-QR3

The Paulsen-Kan system, introduced by Morphy's
rival in the First American Chess Congress in 1857,
and refined by a present-day master, aims at Q-side
pawn expansion, pressure on the center by a fianchettoed bishop, and control of the queen bishop file.

5 B-Q3   N-QB3

Black had a good alternative in 5 ... B-B4, to drive
the knight away from the center.

6 NxN   NPxN

7 0-0   P-Q4

8 P-QB4!

Fischer attacks the center at once! This vigorous
move is probably an improvement on 8 N-Q2, Spassky's
placid developing move.

8 ...   N-B3

At first glance 8 ... PxBP   9 BxP QxQ   10 RxQ
seems unthinkable, as Black is left with two isolated

pawns, but continue on with 10 . . . N-B3 11 N-B3
B-B4 12 B-KN5 P-K4, and, as Botvinnik points out,
the weak queen bishop pawn plays a useful role, as it
defends the weak square at Q4.

9 BPxP   BPxP

10 PxP   PxP

Black avoids 10 . . . NxP, when 11 B-K4 B-K2
12 N-B3 B-N2 13 Q-R4ch Q-Q2 14 QxQch KxQ
15 R-Q1 followed in the game Averbach-Taimanov,
and White won a pawn.

Safest is probably 10 . . . QxP 11 N-B3 Q-Q2,
when the position is less open than after the text
move.

11 N-B3!

Fischer took twenty minutes on this move, either
regarding it as an improvement on the recommended
line 11 B-K3 B-K2 12 B-Q4 0-0, or simply to get
Petrosian out of the books.

11 . . .   B-K2

12 Q-R4ch   Q-Q2

Petrosian was apparently dissatisfied with 12 . . .
B-Q2, when White obtains a slight advantage with
13 Q-Q4 (better than 13 Q-B2 0-0 14 B-KN5 P-Q5)
13 . . . B-K3 14 B-KB4 0-0 15 QR-B1, though it
still may have been his best reply to the check.

13 R-K1!

Simple and strong. Fischer refuses the offer of the
exchange, as after 13 B-QN5 PxB 14 QxR 0-0
15 Q-R5 P-Q5 16 NxP B-N2, and the threats of
17 . . . R-R1, and 17 . . . BxP, give Black attacking
chances.

So Fischer plays it in Capablanca style, as several
annotators (Averbach, Byrne, Bisguier & Soltis, and
Wade & O'Connell) have observed.

13 . . .   QxQ

14 NxQ

The knight now menaces several black squares in the
neighborhood.

14 . . .   B-K3

15 B-K3   0-0

Petrosian has his troubles. If 15 . . . N-Q2 (to protect
his weak QN3 and QB4 squares) there comes 16 P-B4
P-N3 17 B-Q4 0-0 18 QR-B1, and White has the
better position.

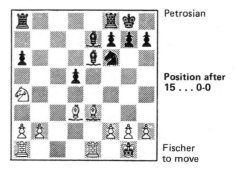

Petrosian

Position after
15 . . . 0-0

Fischer
to move

16 B-QB5!

Straight as an arrow, and right to the point!

Fischer eliminates the defender of the critical
black squares.

16 . . .   KR-K1

17 BxB   RxB

18 P-QN4!

It is important to get this move in, fixing Black's
rook pawn, before playing N-B5. Now if 18 . . .
P-QR4, the reply is 19 P-N5, and Black has a passed
pawn to contend with.

18 . . .   K-B1

19 N-B5   B-B1

Protects the doubly-attacked rook pawn.

20 P-B3

Takes away squares from the enemy knight, and
simultaneously clears a path for the king's entrance
into the game.

20 . . .   R(K2)-R2

Good moves are in short supply, but better chances
were offered by 20 . . . RxRch 21 RxR N-K1

followed by 22 ... N-B2, with a position not happy, but perhaps tenable.

21 R-K5!

Excellent! This paralyzes the knight, which is tied to the defence of the queen pawn, and prevents it from completing the defensive maneuver 21 ... N-K1 and 22 ... N-B2. From there the knight could protect both weak, isolated pawns.

21 ...   B-Q2

Fischer's next move is a profound one.

This is the position:

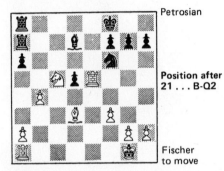

Petrosian

**Position after
21 ... B-Q2**

Fischer
to move

22 NxBch!

This move took everybody by surprise, and 'everybody' includes all the grandmasters watching the game, and analyzing its progress.

None of them suggested this move, or even took it into consideration!

Fischer sacrifices his beautifully-posted knight for a bishop that is practically useless! This transforming of one advantage into another shows that Fischer has a deep appreciation of the art of position play.

22 ...   RxN

23 R-QB1

Fischer seizes the open file, and poses a threat (24 BxQRP) at the same time.

23 ...   R-Q3

A nice move, which accomplishes three things:
  (1) It protects the rook pawn.
  (2) It prevents 24 R-B6.
  (3) It vacates the square Q2 for the knight.
  A nice move, but not good enough, for Fischer (like love) will find a way.

24 R-B7   N-Q2

25 R-K2   P-N3

26 K-B2   P-KR4

27 P-B4   P-R5

28 K-B3   P-B4

Prevents loss of his rook pawn by 29 K-N4, but the cost (the weakened state of his K-side pawns) is great.

29 K-K3   P-Q5ch

Plausible, as it interferes with the king's progress to the center, but it opens a splendid diagonal for the bishop.

30 K-Q2   N-N3

Lets the king rook reach the seventh, but other moves allow 31 B-B4 followed by K-Q3 and R-K6, and the collapse of his game is inevitable.

31 R(K2)-K7   N-Q4

A knight fork that extends artistically in four directions, but perfectly harmless.

32 R-B7ch   K-K1

33 R-QN7   NxNP

34 B-B4   Resigns

The threat of mate by 35 R-KR7 R-KB3 36 R-R8ch R-B1 37 B-B7ch K-Q1, and 38 RxR is unanswerable.

Lasker

Lasker was the first great master to be thoroughly at home in both position and combination play. In his understanding of strategy, he was far ahead of his time. We find such modern concepts as exploitation of weaknesses on the white squares, as far back as 1909, in his games against Mieses and Tartakover at St. Petersburg. The continual switching of attack from one weak point to another, in his game against Salwe in the same tournament was unheard of at the time, while his use of *zugzwang* as an endgame weapon, notably in his first match game against Marshall in 1907 (No. 85) shows complete familiarity with this device.

Lasker's games bristle with all sorts of combinative ideas. But where others used their gifts for combination play to bring about sensational climaxes, Lasker was content to strew combinations freely about in games that were really strategical in essence. 'It is no easy matter,' said Pollock despairingly, 'to reply correctly to Lasker's bad moves.' Acute too was George Marco's observation, 'It is remarkable and deserves special mention, that the great masters, such as Pillsbury, Maroczy, and Janowsky, play against Lasker as though hypnotized.'

Reuben Fine says of Lasker's play, 'To me, many of his games are bottomless wells. I have been through them a dozen times, and each time I have unearthed new ideas in them which I had not seen before. In Lasker I see, above all, the supreme tactical genius.'

Capablanca pays high tribute to Lasker's skills with, 'No other great master has been so misunderstood by the vast majority of chess amateurs and even by many masters, as has Emanuel Lasker. It was often said of Lasker that he had rather a dry style, that he could not play brilliantly, and that his victories were chiefly the result of his uncanny endgame skill and of his opponent's mistakes. That he was a great endgame player is unquestionable; in fact, he was the greatest I have ever known. But he was also the most profound and the most imaginative player I have ever known.'

Perhaps the most appropriate summing-up of Lasker's play lies in the quote, 'Lasker's style is like limpid clear water—with a dash of poison in it!'

Lasker's record is marvelous in both match and tournament play. Here are some outstanding exploits:

Lasker engaged in 22 matches, of which he won 19, drew 2, and lost 1 (to Capablanca).

In the course of these matches Lasker defeated Mieses 5 to 0, Blackburne 6 to 0, Bird 5 to 0, Marshall 8 to 0, Janowsky 8 to 0, and Tarrasch 5 to 0.

Lasker assumed the title of World's Champion by defeating the title-holder Steinitz (Champion for 28 years) in a match in 1894, by a score of 10 to 5, and in a return match a few years later by 10 to 2.

He retained the title until 1921 (27 years) when he lost it to Capablanca in a match, the latter scoring 4 wins to no losses, 10 games being drawn.

In tournaments, Lasker's deeds were equally glorious, these being some of the high spots:

In 1893 at New York, Lasker won 13 games in a row, permitting no draw to be scored against him.

At St. Petersburg in 1895-6, Lasker took first prize in a strong tournament, the entries being restricted to the world's leading masters, these being (besides Lasker) Pillsbury, Steinitz, and Tchigorin.

Another strong tournament was held at Nuremberg in 1896, and in this Lasker came in first ahead of Pillsbury, Maroczy, Tarrasch, Schlechter, and Steinitz.

Lasker ran away with the double-round tournament held at London in 1899, scoring 23½ points, which was 4½ points ahead of runners-up Pillsbury, Janowsky, and Maroczy.

The following year at Paris, Lasker's first was a comfortable 2 points ahead of Pillsbury.

A four-star achievement was Lasker's winning first prize at St. Petersburg in 1914, ½ point ahead of Capablanca and 3½ points ahead of Alekhine.

Another four-star triumph was the winning of first prize at New York in 1924, again ahead of his great rivals Capablanca and Alekhine, by 1½ points and 4 points respectively.

Lasker took third prize at Moscow in 1935, ½ point behind Botvinnik and Flohr, but ½ point ahead of Capablanca. A third prize, but sensational withal, as Lasker was 67 years old at the time!

I consider Lasker the third greatest chess player of all time.

82

White **E. Lasker**   Black **J. Bauer**
Bird's Opening
Amsterdam, 1889

It takes only one game, early in a chess master's career, to show the world that a new talent has burst upon the scene.

Here is Lasker in his first master tournament, demolishing the castled K-side with an explosive two-bishop sacrifice that made chess history.

Other masters have adapted this brilliant pattern of combination (notably Tarrasch against Nimzowitsch at St. Petersburg in 1914, Schlechter against Maroczy at Vienna in 1907, and Alekhine against Drewitt at Portsmouth in 1922) but none has executed it with the flair and panache of Lasker.

It is still the classic game of the genre.

1	P-KB4	P-Q4
2	P-K3	N-KB3
3	P-QN3	P-K3
4	B-N2	B-K2
5	B-Q3	

The conventional move is 5 N-KB3, but Lasker intends to launch (early in the game) a K-side attack—something he would not have dreamed of doing later in his career.

5	. . .	P-QN3
6	N-QB3	B-N2
7	N-B3	QN-Q2
8	0-0	0-0
9	N-K2	

All units are to be aimed at the K-side; so this knight swings over to K2, on its way to N3 and points North.

9 . . .   P-B4

Routine, mechanical, unimaginative. A modern master would unhesitatingly move 9 . . . N-B4, and snap off one of the dangerous bishops.

10	N-N3	Q-B2
11	N-K5	NxN
12	BxN	

At this point, so natural a move as 12 . . . B-Q3 could be ruinous. There would follow 13 BxN PxB   14 Q-R5 P-B4 (on 14 . . . KR-K1   15 Q-R6 holds the king, and 16 N-R5 finishes him off) 15 Q-N5ch K-R1   16 Q-B6ch K-N1   17 N-R5, and it's all over with Black.

12 . . .   Q-B3

13 Q-K2

An all-round move. This is what it does:

(a) It develops a piece.

(b) It unites the rooks.

(c) It guards the square N2 against incipient threats of mate.

(d) It prevents 13 . . . R(either one)-B1, when 14 B-N5 wins the queen.

Remarkable how much great players can get out of their pieces with one little move!

13 . . .   P-QR3   See diagram on page 224.
Intending to continue with 13 . . . P-QN4, to acquire more Q-side space.

The last chance to save the game was by 13 . . . N-Q2, after which White could not afford to be overly ambitious.

A plausible sequel could be: 14 B-N5 Q-B1 15 BxN QxB   16 N-R5 P-B3   17 Q-N4 P-N3 18 B-N2 P-B4   19 Q-N3 K-B2   20 N-N7 R-KN1, and the knight does not get out alive.

14 N-R5!

After this, there is no saving move. For example, these possibilities:

(a) 14 . . . N-K1   15 BxNP NxB   16 Q-N4 and *finis.*

(b) 14 . . . K-R1   15 NxP KxN   16 Q-N4ch K-R1 17 Q-N5 R-KN1   18 BxNch BxB   19 QxBch R-N2 20 R-B3, and White wins.

(c) 14 . . . P-B5   15 NxNch PxN   16 BxPch KxB

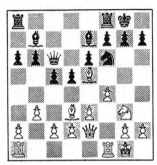

Bauer

Position after
13 . . . P-QR3

Lasker
to move

17 Q-R5ch K-N1   18 Q-N4ch K-R2   19 R-B3,
and 20 R-R3 will mate.

14 . . .   NxN

Expecting the simple recapture of the knight (and
who wouldn't?) but Lasker inserts a brilliant *zwischenzug.*

15 BxPch!   KxB

16 QxNch   K-N1

17 BxP!

Beautiful! The second sacrifice complements the
first one.

17 . . .   KxB

Black must accept the offer, as 17 . . . P-B4   18 R-B3
Q-K1   19 Q-R6 is an easy White win.

18 Q-N4ch   K-R2

Of course not 18 . . . K-B3, when 19 Q-N5 is mate.

19 R-B3   P-K4

Black must part with his queen—and then one of his
vulnerable bishops.

20 R-R3ch   Q-R3

21 RxQch   KxR

22 Q-Q7!

The point of the combination!
    Lasker wins one of the bishops, while still retaining
the attack.

22 . . .   B-KB3

23 QxB

Lasker has a won game, but the way in which he
forces resignation is an interesting lesson in tactics.

23 . . .   K-N2

If 23 . . . PxP   24 QxNP K-N2   25 R-KB1 should
convince Black.

24 R-KB1   QR-N1

25 Q-Q7

Picking off pawns instead would be petty.

25 . . .   KR-Q1

Provides a flight square for his king. White was
threatening mate by 26 Q-N4ch followed by 27 R-B3.

26 Q-N4ch   K-B1

27 PxP   B-N2

But not 27 . . . BxP   28 Q-K6, and the threat of
mate wins the bishop.

28 P-K6   R-N2

Here if 28 . . . P-B3,   29 P-K7ch forces the king to
unprotect the bishop.

29 Q-N6   P-B3

30 RxPch

The final *coup.*

30 . . .   BxR

31 QxBch

There still remains a rook to be removed—and Lasker
proceeds to do so.

31 . . .   K-K1

32 Q-R8ch   K-K2

33 Q-N7ch   Resigns

Although this game is famous for the two-bishop
sacrifice, it is also a fine example of forceful queen
play.

    A leading critic said at the time, 'From his conduct
of this game, one sees something of the extraordinary
talent of the rising generation of chess players.'

    Strangely enough, despite Lasker's success with
Bird's Opening, he never again played it in his life!

83

White **H.N. Pillsbury**   Black **E. Lasker**
Queen's Gambit Declined
St. Petersburg, 1895-6

Lasker and Pillsbury must have felt
   'The stern joy which warriors feel
   In foemen worthy of their steel.'
   In this particular tournament, they had already faced each other three times, with disastrous results for Lasker. Pillsbury had won two games and drawn the third. Anyone but Lasker would have felt the shadow of defeat hovering over him. But Lasker was calm and unruffled, and produced a game that was truly a masterpiece.
   The young genius Pillsbuty simply never had a chance against Lasker's inspired combination, whose high point was a brilliant sacrifice of a rook at QR6, followed later by the sacrifice of his second rook at QR6!
   No higher praise can be given to this game than to say that Lasker himself considered it to be the finest he ever played in his life!

1 P-Q4   P-Q4

2 P-QB4   P-K3

3 N-QB3   N-KB3

4 N-B3   P-B4

5 B-N5   BPxP

6 QxP   N-B3

7 Q-R4
   Pillsbury improved on this move when he played 7 BxN against Lasker at Cambridge Springs in 1904, and won in spectacular style.

7 ...   B-K2

8 0-0-0   Q-R4!
   Lasker starts an attack against White's somewhat exposed king.

9 P-K3   B-Q2

10 K-N1   P-KR3!
   This will force the bishop to a decision, sooner or later.

11 PxP   PxP

12 N-Q4   0-0

13 BxN
   The exchange increases the effectiveness of Black's king bishop, but there was little choice. The sacrifice by 13 BxP PxB 14 QxP accomplishes nothing after 14 . . . N-K4.

13 ...   BxB

14 Q-R5
   An aggressive move, Pillsbury being intent on attack. Later analysis showed that he should have been content with the modest 14 Q-N3.
   But how could Pillsbury have anticipated the diabolical combination that Lasker conjures up out of a harmless-looking position?

14 ...   NxN

15 PxN   B-K3

16 P-B4
   Pillsbury plans one of his famous breakthroughs, this one by 17 P-B5, followed by P-KN4 P-KR4, B-R3, and P-N5.

16 ...   QR-B1

17 P-B5   See diagram on page 226.
   Blissfully unaware that the scene is now set for a magnificent combination, Pillsbury proceeds with his plan.

17 ...   RxN!

18 PxB
   The attempt to win a rook by 18 PxR QxP 19 PxB would be disastrous because of 19 . . . Q-N5ch 20 K-B2 (if 20 K-R1 R-B1! wins because of the threats of 21 . . . R-B8ch!, or 21 . . . BxPch!, or 21 . . . R-B7!) R-B1ch, winning easily.
   It is true that 18 PxR QxP 19 Q-B3 Q-N5ch 20 Q-N3 offers a fair defence, but 20 . . . BxPch

Lasker
to move

**Position after
17 P-B5**

Pillsbury

leaves Black with a strong game, as well as two pawns for the exchange.

18 ...   R-QR6!

One of the most inspired moves ever made on a chessboard! If now 19 PxR Q-N3ch   20 K-R1 BxPch 21 RxB QxRch, with a winning attack.

The post-mortem analysis of these two great players showed this interesting possibility: 19 P-K7 R-K1   20 PxR Q-N3ch   21 K-B2 R-B1ch   22 K-Q2 BxP   23 P-K8(Q)ch RxQ   24 B-Q3 Q-R4ch 25 K-B1 and now 25 ... QxPch (overlooked by both Lasker and Pillsbury!) forces mate next move!

19 PxPch   RxP

20 PxR   Q-N3ch

21 B-N5!

Practically forced, as after 21 K-R1 BxPch 22 RxB QxRch 23 K-N1 Q-K5ch 24 K-B1 R-B7, and Black wins.

Or if 21 K-B2 R-B2ch   22 K-Q2 QxPch   23 B-Q3 R-B7ch   24 KxR Q-N7 mate!

21 ...   QxBch

22 K-R1   R-B2

Threatens mate in three, beginning with 23 ... R-B8ch.

Certainly a strong-looking move, but Lasker chastises himself for not finding one that was even stronger. As he explains it, 'Fifteen moves an hour were prescribed and I had consumed nearly two hours. Thus I had to make these moves in a hurry. The logical

continuation was 22 ... Q-B5. It would have made it impossible for White to guard his second rank.'

23 R-Q2   R-B5

24 KR-Q1   R-B6

25 Q-B5

If 25 Q-K2 R-B8ch!   26 RxR BxPch   27 RxB QxQ 28 R-KN1 Q-KB7   29 R(Q4)-Q1 P-Q5, and Black should win.

25 ...   Q-B5

Threatens (once again) 26 ... R-B8ch   27 RxR QxRch   28 Q-N1 QxR, winning easily.

26 K-N2

Lasker says, 'A mistake. 26 K-N1 was indicated.' Black should win though after 26 K-N1 by 26 ... RxP   27 Q-QB2 R-B6   28 Q-N2 P-QN4.

26 ...   RxP!

The first sacrifice having astonished the natives, Lasker offers a sacrifice of his second rook at QR6—the same square!

27 Q-K6ch   K-R2

28 KxR   Q-B6ch

and Black mates in four moves: 29 K-R4 P-N4ch 30 KxP Q-B5ch   31 K-R5 B-Q1ch   32 Q-N6 BxQ mate.

Lasker gives the score of this game in his great work *Manual of Chess*, but does not adorn even one of his brilliant moves with an exclamation mark.

84

White **M. Porges**   Black **E. Lasker**
Ruy López
Nuremberg, 1896

Lasker rarely fought for the initiative early in the game. Like Steinitz, Nimzowitsch, and Petrosian, he was content with equality, and unperturbed by positions that restricted the free movements of his pieces.

Strange though how often Lasker's pieces, seemingly quiescent, could suddenly spring into action and bring about the threat of checkmate.

You will enjoy, I am sure, watching Lasker let loose with ten moves in a row, each move containing a threat!

1 P-K4   P-K4

2 N-KB3   N-QB3

3 B-N5   N-B3

Modern theory recommends that 3 . . . P-QR3 be interpolated before developing the king knight. Lasker said though, 'We can now announce our final judgment. The defence considered, initiated by 3 . . . N-B3, yields, in all respects a satisfactory game to the second player.'

4 O-O   NxP

Regarding the capture of a pawn early in the game, Lasker gives this advice, 'When you are conscious not to have violated the rules laid down, you should accept the sacrifice of an important pawn, as the king pawn, queen pawn, or one of the bishop pawns. If you do not, as a rule, the pawn which you have rejected will become very troublesome to you. Do not accept the sacrifice, however, with the idea of maintaining your material advantage at the expense of development. Such a policy never pays in the end. By far the better plan is to give the pawn up after your opponent has made some exertion to gain it.'

It is worthy of note that the unauthorized 'revised' edition of Lasker's *Common sense in chess* changes Lasker's comment to read: 'This move exposes Black to some danger, because he loses valuable time guarding or retreating the knight.'

5 P-Q4   B-K2

6 Q-K2   N-Q3

7 BxN   NPxB

8 PxP   N-N2

Tarrasch says at this point, 'When a knight makes four out of the first eight opening moves, to land at this unbelievable post, I find it so absurd, that I cannot comprehend how this manner of development could be considered normal after so many years.

One inherits not only rules and principles, as Mephistopheles says, but also bad moves, which remain like a perpetual illness.'

It is true that Black's development is backward and the knight is badly placed; but this state of affairs is only temporary, for after he castles, he can bring his knight to the excellent square K3 (via B4) where he will strike effectively at the center squares. Furthermore, Black may play . . . P-B3 to force the exchange of the enemy king pawn, after which the pressure on his pawns would be relieved. In addition the exchange would enable him to bring the queen rook to the king file (embarrassing White's queen) while the open king bishop file in conjunction with the two sweeping bishops would give him good attacking chances.

9 P-QN3

The fianchettoed bishop is not particularly well placed, as it exerts no pressure on Black's game. A better line is 9 N-B3 O-O   10 N-Q4! B-B4   11 R-Q1 BxN   12 RxB P-Q4   13 PxP *en passant* PxP   14 P-QN4!, as in the game Schlechter-Réti at Vienna in 1914.

9 . . .   O-O

10 B-N2   P-Q4!

Once he gets . . . P-Q4 in, Black can equalize in nearly all king pawn openings.

11 PxP *en passant*

This dissipates any advantage White might have had. Preferable was 11 QN-Q2, but after N-B4   12 N-Q4 B-R3   13 P-QB4 Q-Q2 followed by 14 . . . N-K3 Black has excellent prospects.

11 . . .   PxP

12 QN-Q2   R-K1

Indirectly threatens White's queen. It is interesting to see how quickly Black obtains a decisive advantage.

13 KR-K1   B-Q2

Additional protection is provided for the rook, while developing a piece.

14   N-K4

An aggressive-looking move, but it simply wastes time. The queen is in danger facing the enemy rook, and should leave the file without delay—say to B1 (a sorry retreat, but a safe one).

14 ...   P-Q4

Once more Black plonks down a pawn in the center —and with gain of time!

15   N(K4)-Q2

The knight must return to this square to avoid material loss.

If 15 N-N3, B-N5 wins the exchange for Black, or if 15 N-B3 B-QR6 wins a piece.

15 ...   B-QR6

16   B-K5

This is forced, the seductive 16 Q-R6 (attacking two pieces) being defeated by 16 ... BxB   17 QR-N1 N-B4, and Black emerges a piece ahead.

16 ...   P-B3

17   Q-R6

Unable to save his pinned bishop, White retaliates by a double attack on knight and bishop. Will that get him out of his troubles?

17 ...   PxB

18   QxB

White removes the fleet-footed bishop (the better course) as 18 QxN loses by 18 ... P-K5   19 Q-R6 (if 19 N-Q4 B-N7 is a painful attack on two pieces) B-N7   20 QR-N1 B-B3, and Black wins the unfortunate knight, who lacks a flight-square.

18 ...   P-K5

19   N-Q4   Q-B3!

Black has attained his objective. All his pieces are admirably placed for a K-side attack, while White's pieces are disorganized and ineffective.

20   P-QB3   R-KB1

21   P-B3

On 21 R-KB1 Q-N4 (attacks the knight)   22 Q-B1 B-R6, and Black wins the exchange, as mate must be prevented.

Lasker
to move

Position after
21 P-B3

Porges

21 ...   Q-N4!

'One attacking move after another! Lasker plays this very strongly,' says Tarrasch admiringly of his great rival's play.

22   Q-B1

The knight (at Q2) must not move, as 22 ... P-B4 in reply, followed by 23 ... PxP wins, while if 22 QR-Q1 P-B4   23 N-K2 PxP initiates three dire threats: 24 ... QxP mate, or 24 ... PxN, winning a piece, or 24 ... P-B7ch, winning a rook.

22 ...   N-B4

The somnolent knight awakes and leaps to action, and displays his might with an immediate threat of 23 ... N-Q6, attacking queen and rook.

23   N-B1   Q-N3

24   R-K3   N-Q6

25   Q-Q1   N-B5

Threatens the king by 26 ... QxP mate, and the queen by 26 ... N-R6ch   27 K-R1 N-B7ch.

26   N-N3   P-KR4

The knight must be ousted!

27   N(Q4)-K2   NxP

Begins an elegant combination.

28 KxN   PxPch

29 RxP   B-R6ch

30 KxB

Or 30 K-B2 B-N5 31 RxRch RxRch 32 K-K3
P-R5 33 N-KB1 Q-K5ch 34 K-Q2 R-B7, and White
is lost.

30 . . .   Q-N5ch

31 K-N2   QxRch

32 K-N1

If 32 K-R3 Q-N5ch 33 K-N2 P-R5, and the poor
knight is pinned.

32 . . .   P-R5

33 N-R1

If 32 N-KB1, P-R6 forces mate quickly.

33 . . .   Q-K6ch

34 Resigns

For 34 K-N2 allows 34 . . . P-R6 mate, a pretty
finish.

85

White **F.J. Marshall**   Black **E. Lasker**
Ruy López
World Championship, First Match Game, New York, 1907

Lasker paid little attention to the openings. He was content to play sound, developing moves, instead of searching
assiduously (as other masters did) for sharp moves that
might yield an advantage.

Midgame complications held no terrors for him. He
did not seek them out, nor did he avoid them. Lasker's
confidence never wavered, even if he went astray in the
tortuous mazes, and realized that he was lost. For Lasker
was a supreme fighter—a characteristic that enabled him
to turn more lost games into wins than did any other man
who ever lived!

It was in the endgame, though, that Lasker displayed
skill that was legendary. In this game with Marshall, he

turns out an ending that is one of the most remarkable
ever seen on a chess-board. It is conducted with the care,
thought, and finesse that are the hallmarks of Lasker at
his best.

1 P-K4   P-K4

2 N-KB3   N-QB3

3 B-N5   N-B3

Lasker practised what he preached. In *Common
sense in chess*, he said, 'According to principle, either
3 . . . P-Q3 or 3 . . . N-B3 should be done. Both of
these moves very frequently are made, and, on the
whole, with satisfactory results. Personally, I favour
the immediate development of the king knight, as
3 . . . P-Q3 deprives the king bishop of the possibility
to occupy the file from QB4.'

4 P-Q4

Highly recommended by Henry W. Barry, this continuation is considered inferior to the customary
4 0-0.

Pillsbury was of a different opinion, and indicated
his readiness to play Barry a match, to prove his
views. Unfortunately nothing came of it, and we, who
have been deprived of some Pillsbury masterpieces,
are the losers by it.

4 . . .   PxP

This is better than 4 . . . NxQP 5 NxN PxN 6 P-K5
P-B3 7 0-0 PxB 8 B-N5 B-K2 9 PxN BxP
10 R-K1ch K-B1 11 BxB QxB 12 P-QB3 P-Q4
13 PxP B-K3 14 N-B3 P-QR3 15 R-K5 R-Q1
16 Q-N3 Q-K2 17 QR-K1 P-N4 18 Q-Q1 Q-B3
19 R(K1)-K3 R-KN1 20 RxB, and wins—which is
how Morphy beat Anderssen in their third match
game at Paris in 1858.

5 0-0   B-K2

6 P-K5   N-K5

7 NxP   0-0

8 N-B5   P-Q4

Of course not 8 . . . NxKP 9 Q-Q5, and White wins one of the stranded knights.

Lasker's actual move establishes a pawn in the center, and enables the queen bishop to make its début.

9 BxN

'Unfortunately Marshall uses his own head,' says Tarrasch, 'instead of relying on eminent authority. Zukertort (in this position) continued with 9 NxBch NxN 10 P-KB3 N-B4 11 P-QN4 N-K3 12 P-KB4, whereby White has something to show for his efforts —a strong pawn center, the two bishops, and attacking chances. After the text move White has nothing.'

9 . . .   PxB

10 NxBch   QxN

Now, after ten moves of one of the most formidable openings, White does not have a single piece in active play!

11 R-K1

Indirectly protects the king pawn, as 11 . . . QxP loses a piece after 12 P-KB3.

Protecting the pawn directly by 11 B-B4 fails after 11 . . . P-N4, and Black wins a pawn.

Counter-attack by 11 P-KB3 is even less satisfactory, when 11 . . . Q-B4ch 12 K-R1 N-B7ch forces White to give up his rook for the knight.

11 . . .   Q-R5

Réti says of this move, 'The positional requirement here was 11 . . . P-KB3; and it would have been simplest and best to make this move at once. Chess today however has reached a stage of development where it has become very difficult to win a game with the best and simplest moves, though the often positionally incorrect combination of an Anderssen would even be less effective these days. Lasker however is a master of the art of creating complications, and of blending the requirements of a position with these complications. It is the same method which has led Alekhine and Nimzowitsch from success to success.

In the present position Lasker evolves an idea from the fact that White has played 11 R-K1, thus depriving KB2 of a guard, and that it is Black's intention of playing P-KB3 in order to open the king bishop file, and so begins a complicated attack against point KB7.'

(Another consideration was that this sort of move is annoying to Marshall, who likes to attack, and is uncomfortable on the defence).

12 B-K3   P-B3

13 P-KB3

This is the position, with Black to play:

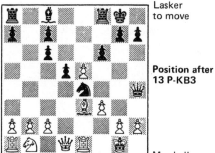

Lasker
to move

Position after
13 P-KB3

Marshall

13 . . .   PxP!

A true sacrifice, as it involves an element of risk. For the moment, all Lasker gets in return for the knight is an open file for his king rook, and the prospect of maintaining a troublesome pawn at Q5.

14 PxN

On 14 P-KN3 instead, 14 . . . NxP 15 PxN QxPch 16 K-R1 RxP, with (says Tartakover) ineluctable threats.

14 . . .   P-Q5

Attacks the bishop—and the bishop may not run away!

If 15 B-B1 Q-B7ch 16 K-R1 B-N5 17 Q-Q2 Q-B8ch 18 RxQ RxR mate.

Or, should White retreat the bishop to Q2 (adding its protection to the rook) a decisive attack would

follow by 15 . . . B-N5 (not the suggestive
15 . . . Q-B7ch) 16 Q-B1 R-B7 (threatens 17 . . .
B-B6) 17 B-N5 RxPch 18 KxR B-R6ch 19 K-B3
(if 19 K-R1 Q-B7 20 R-N1 Q-B6ch forces mate)
Q-N5ch 20 K-B2 Q-N7 mate—a pretty Lasker combination.

15 P-KN3 Q-B3

16 BxP

Marshall decides to return the piece, fearing that he
might otherwise lose by something like this: 16 B-Q2
Q-B7ch 17 K-R1 B-R6 18 R-N1 P-KR4! (threatens
19 . . . B-N5 followed by 20 . . . B-B6ch) 19 QxP
QxRch 20 KxQ R-B8 mate.

16 . . . PxB

17 R-B1

One move too late, as Marshall discovers to his sorrow.

17 . . . QxRch

18 QxQ RxQch

19 KxR

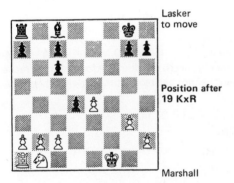

Lasker
to move

Position after
19 KxR

Marshall

The position is apparently even. Black can develop
his pieces somewhat faster—say his bishop with check.
White has an isolated pawn, against which Black has a
doubled pawn. Black's bishop in the ending is superior
to his opponent's knight, but again the knight can
reach N3 (by way of Q2), and from there attack the
queen pawn, or seize control of QB5, a fine station.

19 . . . R-N1!

How many players could resist the temptation to
gain time by developing the bishop with check?

Lasker's cool, accurate endplay, beginning with
this move, is outstanding.

His rook move forces the knight pawn to advance,
taking the square N3 away from the knight. In addition, the rook is poised for another unusual *coup*.

The bishop meanwhile is quite effectively posted
right where it is, at QB1!

20 P-N3 R-N4!

Another surprising move, and a decisive one! The rook
controls the fourth rank, free and clear, and is in
position to attack all of the white pawns.

21 P-B4

Thereby Black acquires a passed pawn, but what
else was there? If 21 N-Q2 R-QB4 22 R-B1 (or
22 N-B4 B-R3, and Black wins a pawn) B-R3ch
23 K-K1 R-B6, and the king pawn is not long for this
world, the threat against it being 24 . . . R-K6ch
25 K-Q1 B-K7ch 26 K-K1 B-Q6 dis.ch 27 K-Q1
BxKP.

21 . . . R-KR4

22 K-N1 P-B4!

Multum in parvo, as my grandfather used to say.

The pawn moves one step forward, and accomplishes these things:

(a) It strengthens the queen pawn, turning it into a
protected passed pawn.

(b) It clears the third rank, for the benefit of the rook.

(c) It increases the scope of the bishop, now that
most of the pawns occupy black squares.

23 N-Q2 K-B2

Very important, as otherwise 24 R-B1 prevents the
king from coming into the game.

24 R-B1ch

'Here we have the difference between Marshall and
Lasker,' says Tarrasch. Lasker refrained from check-

ing with the bishop at his 19th move, tempting though it was! Marshall cannot resist the rook check, though it is obviously bad! He goes by the old saying, 'One check can never hurt,' or, as Mackenzie used to say jokingly, 'Never miss a check!'

Black's king will be more effectively placed, while the rook (which should be concerned with the protection of the queen rook pawn) much less so. One can hardly expect more of a move than that it help the enemy, and at the same time hinder one's own game!

24 . . .   K-K2

25 P-QR3   R-R3

The rook prepares to swing over to the Q-side, to terrorize the pawns in that area.

26 P-KR4

Counterplay by 26 P-QN4 fails after 26 . . . R-R3 27 PxP RxP 28 N-B3 B-R6, and Black wins the exchange, as 29 R-B2 runs into 29 . . . R-R8ch and quick mate.

26 . . . R-R3

27 R-R1   B-N5

Paralyzes the knight, and fixes White's entire K-side.

28 K-B2   K-K3

29 P-R4

To release the rook from guard duty. If instead 29 N-B3 BxN 30 KxB K-K4, and Black will win a pawn after a rook check.

29 . . .   K-K4

The king advances whenever he can, ready to support the passed pawn.

30 K-N2   R-KB3

31 R-K1   P-Q6

'The passed pawn's lust to expand,' enables the king to come in at Q5, and pick off some pawns, or simply take up a commanding post at the sixth rank.

32 R-KB1   K-Q5

33 RxR

Marshall does not even try for the swindle 33 N-B3ch KxP (on 33 . . . K-K6 34 R-K1 is mate!) 34 R-K1ch K-B4 35 R-K5ch K-N3 36 R-N5ch followed by 37 RxB. The refutation (after 33 N-B3ch) would be simple: 33 . . . BxNch 34 RxB P-Q7, and it's all over.

33 . . .   PxR

34 K-B2   P-B3

Played to exhaust White's pawn moves, after which a move by his king will enable further inroad by . . . K-K6.

Tarrasch suggests, as more efficient, 34 . . . K-B6, followed by removing the knight pawn and the bishop pawn, as the knight must eventually move and unguard the pawns.

35 P-QR5   P-QR3

36 N-B1   KxP

Here too, Tarrasch prefers 36 . . . K-B6 followed by 37 . . . B-K7, to cut down resistance.

37 K-K1   B-K7

38 N-Q2ch   K-K6

39 N-N1   P-B4

Not at once 39 . . . K-B6 40 N-B3 KxP 41 N-K4ch, and White still needs subduing. After the text move, the knight cannot get to K4 (until it's too late).

40 N-Q2

But not 40 N-B3 P-Q7 mate.

40 . . .   P-R4

41 N-N1   K-B6

42 N-B3   KxP

43 N-R4   P-B5

44 NxP   P-B6

45 N-K4ch   K-B5

46 N-Q6   P-B4

Ready to meet 47 N-N7 with 47 . . . K-K6 and mate with either pawn.

47 P-N4   PxP

48	P-B5	P-N6
49	N-B4	K-N6
50	N-K3	P-N7
51	Resigns	

86

White **F.J. Marshall**   Black **E. Lasker**
Queen's Gambit Declined
World Championship, Third Match Game, New York, 1907

Some players are made to order for their opponents. Capablanca regarded Vidmar as an easy mark, and referred to him as his meat. Alekhine would beat Tarrasch early and often, usually in spectacular style.

Lasker had a good customer in Marshall, whom he dispatched with easy efficiency. It is worthy of note, though, that Marshall did manage to win two games from his redoubtable opponent in a lifetime of tournament and match play. The first was in their first encounter at Paris in 1900, and the second in their last encounter at New York in 1940—40 years later!

Here is a little-known victory of Lasker's, which deserves to be rescued from obscurity.

1	P-Q4	P-Q4
2	P-QB4	P-K3
3	N-QB3	N-KB3
4	B-N5	B-K2
5	P-K3	N-K5

A simplifying defence, named after Lasker, though it was played as far back as 1902 by Atkins. Strangely enough this was also against Marshall, in the Anglo-American Cable Match. Atkins won the game by a vigorously conducted K-side attack.

6	BxB	QxB
7	B-Q3	

Better procedure is 7 PxP NxN 8 PxN PxP 9 Q-N3,

and White has pressure on the queen pawn and on the knight file.

White also has the opportunity to follow up with P-QB4, thereby playing the Queen's Gambit a second time in one game.

7	...	NxN
8	PxN	N-Q2
9	N-B3	

Tarrasch recommends instead 9 PxP PxP 10 Q-N3 followed by 11 P-QB4, with the better game.

9	...	0-0
10	0-0	R-Q1
11	Q-B2	

Marshall plays this move as consistently, in Queen's Gambits, as Pillsbury does N-K5.

11	...	N-B1
12	N-K5	P-QB4
13	QR-N1	Q-B2

A necessary precaution against the knight's coming in at B6, after Black plays . . . P-QN3.

14	Q-N3	P-QN3
15	BPxP	KPxP
16	Q-R4	B-N2
17	Q-Q1	

After several wavering queen moves, Marshall decides that his best chances lie in a K-side attack, so he switches the queen to that area.

17	...	R-Q3

A fine all-round move, but then Lasker always handled his rooks expertly. (See as instances his 4th match game against Tarrasch in 1908, his game against Steinitz in the fourth round at St. Petersburg in 1895-6, and his first match game against Marshall in 1907).

18	Q-N4	R-K1

And this move restrains any such ambitious attempts as 19 P-KB4, when 19 . . . P-B3 wins the king pawn.

19 Q-N3

Marshall intends to continue with 20 N-N4, when he would then have a beautiful threat in 21 N-B6ch (taking advantage of the double pin to win a rook or more) 21 . . . K-R1   22 NxR, and now the knight not only attacks queen and rook, but also supports his own queen in a threat of mate on the move.

Unfortunately this delightful little combination appears only in the notes to the game.

19 . . .   R(Q3)-K3

20 B-B5   R(K3)-K2

21 P-KB4

Marshall avoids the exchange of queens ensuing from 21 . . . P-B3   22 N-B3. But now his king pawn is backward, and his K4 square weakened.

21 . . .   B-B1!

Clever strategy! It is important to eliminate a guardian of White's K4 square, so that Black's knight can settle there undisturbed.

22 BxB

The exchange is forced, as after 22 B-B2 P-B3 wins the king pawn.

22 . . .   RxB

The proper recapture, as 22 . . . QxB allows 23 P-B5 in reply.

23 Q-B3

Now the advance 23 P-B5 would be met by 23 . . . P-B3   24 N-N4 QxQ   25 PxQ P-KR4, and the king pawn falls.

23 . . .   Q-Q3

24 KR-B1

Lasker now has choice of three methods of procedure:

(1) Double the rooks on the king file, dislodge the knight, and win the king pawn.

(2) Double rooks on the bishop file, play . . . PxP, and after the recapture by the king pawn,

maneuver the knight over to K5, to bear down on, and finally remove, the queen bishop pawn.

(3) Move 24 . . . P-B5 followed by advancing the queen knight pawn, (supported by the queen rook pawn) to N5, and create a passed pawn.

24 . . .   R(K2)-B2

25 P-KR3   P-KR3

Clears a square for the knight, whose goal is K5.

26 K-R2   N-R2

27 Q-R5

Marshall is ready to meet 27 . . . PxP with 28 BPxP, as 28 . . . RxR   29 RxR RxR is neatly refuted by 30 QxPch K-R1   31 N-N6ch, and Black must give up his queen.

27 . . .   N-B3

28 Q-B5   PxP

29 KPxP

This is the picture on the board:

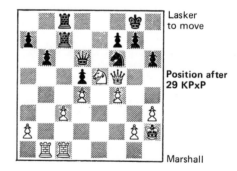

Lasker to move

Position after 29 KPxP

Marshall

Marshall sets an insidious trap here: If 29 . . . RxP 30 QxRch! RxQ   31 RxRch K-R2   32 R-R8ch KxR 33 NxPch, and White not only regains the queen, but emerges with an extra rook.

But Lasker, himself a master of tactical tricks, is not easily lured into a trap.

29 . . .   N-K5

'The combination conceived with this move is brilliant, subtle, and sound,' says John F. Barry. 'Rarely does the opportunity present itself when these three qualities can be combined in play, and when it does, only the true master is able to perceive and seize it.'

Tarrasch sees things in a different light! He says, 'All commentators give this move one or two exclamation marks, though it is based on an oversight that hands over a well-deserved win. Lasker, absorbed in evading the trap set by his resourceful opponent, overlooked the fact that his bishop pawn could be captured. Had he given it thought, he would have realized that the continuation he chose led to a draw, not a win.

The win was still there, but by this means: 29 . . . P-N3 30 Q-Q3 (but not 30 NxNP PxN 31 QxPch R-N2, and the queen dare not take the third pawn on pain of a knight check combined with a discovered attack on the queen) N-K5 31 R-N3 P-B3 32 NxP K-N2, and Black wins the knight, which dare not move, as 33 N-R4 QxPch followed by 34 . . . QxR is even more costly.'

30 NxP RxN

'Lasker makes a virtue of necessity,' says Tarrasch. 'Through the sacrifice of the exchange he obtains an attack that assures him of a draw at least.'

31 QxR(B8)ch R-B1

32 Q-N7

The queen is cut off from the K-side, as after 32 Q-N4, RxP threatens an inescapable discovered check winning the queen.

32 . . . QxPch

33 K-N1

If 33 K-R1 N-B7ch 34 K-N1 NxPch 35 PxN (on 35 K-R1 N-B7ch 36 K-N1 N-N5 wins for Black) 35 . . . Q-N6ch 36 K-R1 QxPch 37 K-N1 Q-N5ch 38 K-R1 R-B7 and Black wins.

33 . . . Q-K6ch

34 K-R2!

But not 34 K-R1 N-B7ch 35 K-R2 Q-B5ch 36 K-N1 (or 36 P-N3 Q-B4 and Black wins) 36 . . . NxPch, and Black wins—the mixture as before!

34 . . . Q-N6ch

35 K-N1 N-Q7

Threatens a neat finish by 36 . . . N-B6 37 K-B1 N-K8 dis.ch 38 K-K2 Q-Q6ch, and mate next move.

36 QxPch K-R1

37 K-R1

If 37 R-B1 Q-K6ch wins a rook.

37 . . . N-B6

38 PxN QxRPch

39 K-N1 Q-N6ch

40 K-R1 R-B5

41 Q-Q8ch

'With this check and the following move,' says Tarrasch, 'Marshall thinks that he can not only save himself, but win the game. He is dreadfully mistaken. The simplest move was 41 Q-R5, after which Black had nothing better than to force the draw by 41 . . . R-R5ch, and the perpetual.'

41 . . . K-R2

42 R-B1

Plausible enough, but it loses in a hurry! The move to save the game was 42 R-B2, when Black could hardly hope to win the ending (after 42 . . . R-R5ch 43 QxR) of queen against two rooks.

42 . . . R-B4!

This little move does the trick! If now 43 Q-K8, to cover the rook's mating square, Black forces the win by 43 . . . Q-R5ch 44 K-N2 R-N4 mate.

87

White **E. Lasker**   Black **S. Tarrasch**
Queen's Gambit Declined
St. Petersburg, 1914

Chess authorities are not in complete agreement on the strength or weakness of an isolated queen pawn.

Philidor, almost 200 years ago, said, 'A pawn, when separated from his fellows, will seldom or never make a fortune.'

Tartakover said, 'An isolated pawn spreads gloom over the entire chessboard.'

Nimzowitsch championed both sides when he commented, 'The strength of an isolated queen pawn lies in its lust to expand, and in its creation of the outpost stations K5 and QB5. On the other hand, the pawn tends to become a weakness in the ending.'

Tarrasch said simply and unequivocally, 'He who fears an isolated queen pawn should give up chess.'

Here Tarrasch defends his views (and the isolated queen pawn) against the assaults of the mighty Dr. Lasker, Champion of the World.

1 P-Q4   P-Q4

2 N-KB3   P-QB4

3 P-B4   P-K3

Tarrasch considered this to be the best defence to the Queen's Gambit, since . . . P-QB4 is the freeing move for Black, and must be made as soon as possible.

4 BPxP   KPxP

5 P-KN3   N-QB3

6 B-N2   N-B3

7 0-0   B-K2

8 PxP

Tarrasch is quite pleased with his position. 'White has no positional equivalent,' he says, 'for the centralized pawn.'

8 . . .   BxP

9 QN-Q2

The customary 9 N-B3 allows Black to gain a tempo by 9 . . . P-Q5. White's idea is to swing the knight over to N3 and then Q4, where it will blockade the isolated pawn.

9 . . .   P-Q5

Tarrasch admits this move to be an error, as he could have developed a piece instead.

Nimzowitsch's wry comment on this move was, 'The isolated pawn has the choice of becoming weak at Q4 or Q5.'

10 N-N3   B-N3

11 Q-Q3!

Blockade! This fixes the pawn so that it cannot move. Now Lasker threatens to play 12 R-Q1, attacking the hapless pawn with four pieces.

11 . . .   B-K3

12 R-Q1   BxN

Black is forced to remove one of the attacking pieces, and leave his opponent with the advantage of the two bishops. This must have been annoying to Tarrasch, who once said, 'He who has the two bishops holds the future in his hands.'

13 QxB

Now there is a threat against the queen pawn by 14 P-K3, which accounts for Black's reply.

13 . . .   Q-K2

14 B-Q2!

A subtle move, and superior to the anticipated 14 B-B4.

14 . . .   0-0

15 P-QR4!!

Tarrasch himself awards this move two exclamation points. (How can I do less?)

'An unusually fine move,' says Tarrasch, 'The pawn is to be advanced to R5 and then R6, where it will undermine the position of the Q-side pieces, especially that of the knight.'

15 . . .   N-K5

Obviously, capturing the king pawn would be fatal. After 15 . . . QxP   16 R-K1 Q-R3   17 B-KB1, the queen is cornered.

16 B-K1   QR-Q1

17 P-R5

The brash pawn has the support of the bishop, which was shrewdly developed at Q2.

17 . . . B-B4

18 P-R6!

En avant! Undermines the support of the knight, one of the defenders of the isolated pawn.

18 . . . PxP

White also gains the advantage after 18 . . . P-QN3 by 19 Q-R4 R-B1 20 QR-N1, and the advance by 21 P-QN4 will dislodge the bishop and win the queen pawn.

19 QR-B1

The advance and then the immolation of the rook pawn has accomplished two things: it has loosened the position of Black's minor pieces so that they now hang in the air, and it has increased the potential activity of White's king bishop.

19 . . . R-B1

This is the picture on the board:

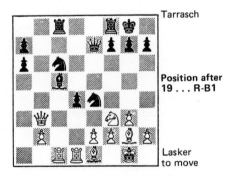

Tarrasch

Position after
19 . . . R-B1

Lasker
to move

20 N-R4!

Poses some threats, mainly against the overworked queen, the immediate one being 21 BxN QxB 22 RxB, winning a piece for White.

20 . . . B-N3

Probably as good as there is.

If 20 . . . N-Q1 21 N-B5 Q-K4 22 BxN QxB

23 N-Q6, and White wins the exchange by a pretty pin and knight fork.

Or if 20 . . . B-Q3 21 N-B5 attacks the queen, which protects the knight, which protects the bishop. If then 21 . . . Q-K4 22 BxN, and Black does not dare recapture by 22 . . . QxB as 23 NxB wins a piece, and then the exchange!

21 N-B5 Q-K4

22 BxN QxB

23 N-Q6 QxP

24 NxR RxN

Black has a knight and two pawns for the rook he lost, but ironically enough, his heretofore weak isolated pawn has suddenly blossomed into a passed pawn—a potentially dangerous one!

25 Q-Q5 Q-K3

The attempt to save the knight by other means would have provided a beautiful illustration of five tactical themes, as follows:

If 25 . . . N-K2 (unpinning) 26 RxRch NxR 27 Q-R8 (pinning) Q-K1 28 R-B1 (double attack on a pinned piece) N-Q3 (unpinning) 29 QxQch NxQ 30 R-B8 (pinning) K-B1 31 B-N4ch (driving off the protecting piece) K-N1 32 RxN mate (the vulnerable last rank).

26 Q-B3 P-R3

27 B-Q2!

This convinces Tarrasch that he should offer to exchange rooks. Otherwise, this is what could happen:

28 R-K1 Q-Q2 29 R-B4 (to double rooks on the file) N-R4 (or 29 . . . N-K2 30 RxN, and White wins a piece) 30 R-K7 QxR 31 RxRch K-R2 32 BxN BxB 33 Q-B5ch, and White picks up the luckless bishop.

27 . . . N-K4

28 RxRch QxR

29 Q-K4 N-Q2

30 R-QB1 Q-B1

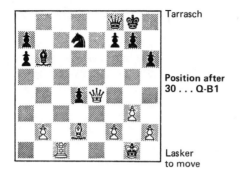

Tarrasch

Position after
30 . . . Q-B1

Lasker
to move

31 BxP!
Lasker picks up a pawn, benefitting by the exposed
state of Black's knight.

31 . . .   N-B4
On 31 . . . PxB   32 Q-N4ch regains the piece.

32 Q-N4   P-B4

33 Q-N6
Lasker's threat of 34 P-QN4 N-Q2   35 R-B8 QxR
36 QxP mate compels an exchange of queens—and
all exchanges are to his advantage.

33 . . .   Q-B2

34 QxQch   KxQ

35 B-N5   N-Q6

36 R-N1
'A miserable move!' says Tarrasch jokingly. 'Much
prettier is 36 R-B2, protecting the pawn, when
Black can reply 36 . . . N-K8, followed by 37 . . .
N-B6ch winning the bishop.'

36 . . .   K-K3

37 P-N3
This move and the next prevent the king from pene-
trating further and helping the queen pawn.

37 . . .   K-Q4

38 P-B3   P-R4

39 P-R4   N-B4

40 P-R5   P-Q6

41 K-B1   P-R5
Tarrasch intends to follow 42 PxP NxP with an
advance by his king to B5, B6, and B7, when the
passed pawn (née the isolated pawn) could become
a real menace.

42 PxP   NxP

43 B-B6!
A little surprise for Tarrasch! It wins a pawn, and
clears a pathway for the rook pawn.

43 . . .   K-K3
Capturing by 43 . . . PxB loses instantly by 44 P-R6,
and the pawn advances to the queening square. Nor
is there salvation by 43 . . . B-Q5, as 44 BxB KxB
45 R-N4ch wins the offside knight.

44 BxP   K-B2

45 B-K5   N-B4

46 R-Q1   Resigns
For 47 B-Q4 followed by 48 BxN will finally win
the queen pawn (which has had a charmed life, considering the high mortality rate of isolated pawns).
   Both Alekhine and Tarrasch had unqualified
praise for the elegance of Lasker's positional and
tactical play in this game.

88

White **E. Lasker**   Black **J.R. Capablanca**
Ruy López
St. Petersburg, 1914

This is Lasker's most glorious victory, and worthy of a
great occasion.
   The game was won against Capablanca, when Lasker
needed a win desperately. For it was the 18th round of
the great St. Petersburg Tournament, with three more
rounds to go, and both masters were tied at 11 points
each. Capablanca had already had his bye, and had four
games (including this one) to play, while Lasker had only
three games left. A loss, or even a draw, might put Lasker

out of the running for first prize; so he had to stake everything on this one effort.

And he had the toughest opponent in the world in Capablanca! Here was a man with nerves of steel, fiercely ambitious, possessed of incomparable technique, and (as if that were not enough) a man who lost fewer games than any other master who ever lived!

Lasker chose as his weapon the exchange variation of the Ruy López, a favourite line that had brought him nine wins against only one loss in the past.

It was a wise choice, as it brought Lasker victory, and added another to an already illustrious collection of masterpieces.

1 P-K4   P-K4

2 N-KB3   N-QB3

3 B-N5   P-QR3

4 BxN

This line of play may not seem enterprising, but with it Lasker had defeated Pillsbury, Steinitz, Tarrasch, Tchigorin, and Janowsky.

Capablanca had tried the exchange variation only once in his career. Strangely enough, it was in this very tournament, where he beat Janowsky in a classic game.

4 . . .   QPxB

5 P-Q4   PxP

6 QxP   QxQ

7 NxQ

Despite the exchange of queens, there is plenty of fight in this position. White has a clear, unimpeded pawn majority on the K-side; Black's corresponding pawn majority on the other wing is practically worthless because of the doubled pawn, but he has two bishops. So Lasker has what he wants: a position full of tension, uncertainty, and complex possibilities.

It may have been games such as this one which evoked the comment, 'Lasker played 1 P-K4 with a view to the endgame.'

7 . . .   B-Q3

The recommended procedure is 7 . . . B-Q2 followed by castling Q-side. Or 7 . . . P-QB4   8 N-K2 B-Q2   9 P-QN3, as in Lasker-Tarrasch 1908, but now instead of Tarrasch's reply 9 . . . B-B3, the forceful 9 . . . P-B5! led to a brilliant win by Alekhine against Verlinski in 1909.

Capablanca explains his reasons for choosing 7 . . . B-Q3 as follows: Black's idea is to castle K-side; the king ought to remain on the weaker side to oppose later the advance of White's pawns. Theoretically there is very much to be said in favour of this reasoning, but whether in practice that would be the best system would be rather difficult to prove. The student should notice that if now all the pieces were exchanged White would practically be a pawn ahead, and would therefore have a won ending.

8 N-QB3   N-K2

Capablanca develops the knight here in order not to obstruct Black's pawns, and in some eventualities to bring the knight to KN3.

9 0-0   0-0

Tarrasch prefers 9 . . . P-KB4 instead, in order to remove, or isolate, the king pawn, the strong point of White's position. If then 10 R-K1 0-0   11 P-K5 B-B4   12 N-N3 B-R2, and eventually . . . P-B5.

10 P-B4

Lasker plays to realize his advantage—the K-side majority of pawns.

Capablanca says: This move I considered weak at the time, and I do so still. It leaves the king pawn weak, unless it advances to K5, and it also makes it possible for Black to pin the knight by B-QB4.

10 . . .   R-K1

Capablanca says of this move: Best. It threatens 11 . . . B-QB4   12 B-K3 N-Q4. It also prevents 11 B-K3 because of 11 . . . N-Q4 or 11 . . . N-B4.

11 N-N3

'Parries the threat,' says Lasker. 'Now 12 P-K5 might be a strong move, as the bishop has only one flight square. After brief consideration, Capablanca made his move.'

11 ...   P-B3

Opinion is divided on the merits of this move.

Réti says: An absolutely unnecessary defensive move, for White's P-K5 would be of advantage only to Black, since he would then have the points Q4 and KB4 for his pieces.

Tarrasch agrees, with: Black parries the non-existent threat of 12 P-K5, as such an advance would only benefit Black. He should simply develop by 11 ... B-Q2 and 12 ... QR-Q1. Also 11 ... N-N3 was better than the move chosen.

Capablanca, in support of his move, says: This is preparatory to ... P-QN3 followed by ... P-QB4 and ... B-N2 in conjunction with ... N-N3, which would put White in great difficulties to meet the combined attack against the two center pawns.

Brinckmann, agreeing with Capablanca, says: The move 11 ... P-B3 was not made out of fear of 12 P-K5, but to fix the king pawn where it stands, and later concentrate an attack against it. It is the first step in a clear strategic concept.

The position at this point:

Capablanca

**Position after
11 ... P-B3**

Lasker
to move

12 P-B5!

Chernev: Very daring; Lasker disregards the weakening of his king pawn, and the fact that Black gets a strong square for his pieces at K4.

Lasker: A piece of finesse which Capablanca did not expect. This advance seemingly makes the king pawn a candidate for death. Upon closer inspection, however, one sees that the pawn can nevertheless stand, and the move, notwithstanding all these surface weaknesses, has much in compensation. It hinders the king bishop pawn, the queen bishop, as well as the king knight, and in addition, forces the exchange of the strong king bishop.

Capablanca: It has been wrongly claimed that this wins the game, but I would like nothing better than to have such a position again. It required several mistakes on my part finally to obtain a lost position.

12 ...   P-QN3

An unfortunate plan, as the bishop is withdrawn from the defence of the point K3. A simple alternative was 12 ... B-Q2   13 B-B4 BxB   14 RxB P-QN3   15 P-KN4 N-B1, followed by bringing the knight over to Q3, initiating play against the king pawn.

13 B-B4   B-N2

Tarrasch says: Black must exchange bishops, and then develop by ... B-Q2 and ... QR-Q1. The knight could then come strongly into play at Q3, by way of B1. After the text move, Black's game is completely crippled.

Capablanca's comment on his move is illuminating: Played against my better judgment. The right move of course was 13 ... BxB. Dr. Lasker gives the following variation: 13 ... BxB   14 RxB P-B4   15 QR-Q1 B-N2   16 R-B2 QR-Q1   17 RxR RxR   18 R-Q2 RxR   19 NxR, and he claims that White has the best of it. Taking Dr. Lasker's variation, however, whatever advantage there might be disappears at once if Black plays 19 ... N-B3, threatening 20 ... N-N5 and also 20 ... N-Q5, neither of which can be stopped. In fact, after 19 ... N-B3, Black threatens so many things that it is difficult to see how White can prevent the loss of one or more pawns.

14 BxB   PxB

The exchange undoubles the pawns, but saddles Black with a weak queen pawn.

Lasker now plans the following:

(a) To anchor a knight at K6.

(b) To attack the queen pawn, thereby tying Black's pieces down to its defence.

(c) To start his K-side pawns rolling by P-KN4 and P-KN5.

15 N-Q4   QR-Q1

Lasker says: Black here played very thoughtfully. He did not wish to delay his development with 15 . . . B-QB1 and planned, with regard to the knight which forces its way to K6, to drive it off later. For the time being, however, he attacked nothing.

16 N-K6

Anderssen's comment seems appropriate here, 'Once get a knight firmly posted at K6, and you may go to sleep. Your game will then play itself.'

16 . . .   R-Q2

17 QR-Q1   N-B1

Capablanca tells us his thoughts when he made this move: I now was on the point of playing 17 . . . P-B4, to be followed by 18 . . . P-Q4, which I thought would give me a draw, but suddenly I became ambitious and thought that I could play the text move, 17 . . . N-B1, and later on sacrifice the exchange for the knight at K6, winning a pawn for it, and leaving White's pawn still weaker. Now let us analyze: 17 . . . P-B4. If 18 N-Q5 BxN   19 PxB P-QN4, and a careful analysis will show that Black has nothing to fear. Black's plan in this case would be to work his knight around to K4, via QB1, QN3, and QB5 or Q2. Again 17 . . . P-B4   18 R-B2 P-Q4   19 PxP BxP   20 NxB (best, since if 20 R(B2)-Q2 BxN gives Black the advantage) RxN   21 RxR NxR, and there is no good reason why Black should lose.

Brinckmann not only agrees with Capablanca, but says: Let's carry the analysis a bit further: 22 R-Q2 N-K6   23 R-Q6 NxKBP   24 RxP N-Q5   25 NxN

PxN   26 RxRP R-QB1!, and we must go along with Capablanca.

18 R-B2   P-QN4

Capablanca makes room for his knight to swing over to K4, by way of N3 and B5.

Unfortunately, he is given no time to carry out this project. He still had drawing chances by playing 18 . . . K-B2 and then 19 . . . RxN, giving up his rook for a knight and a pawn.

19 R(B2)-Q2

Nails the knight down, as it must defend the pawn.

19 . . .   R(Q2)-K2

20 P-QN4!

Lasker says: And now the queen bishop pawn is crippled. Strategically, Black is beaten, for he plays without the co-operation of the queen bishop. This bishop can be brought into action only through loss of some sort.

Lasker's move created a hole at his QB4, but it is of no consequence, as Black cannot possibly deploy his knight to that square.

20 . . .   K-B2

21 P-QR3   B-R1

Of this, Capablanca says: Once more changing my plan, and this time without good reason. Had I now played 21 . . . RxN   22 PxRch RxP, as I intended to do when I went back with the knight to B1, I doubt very much if White would have been able to win the game. At least it would have been extremely difficult.

22 K-B2   R-R2

23 P-N4

Prepares a possible breakthrough on the K-side.

23 . . .   P-R3

24 R-Q3   P-QR4

Black tries to get some air.

25 P-KR4   PxP

'Here,' says Lasker, 'Capablanca moved with nervous haste. He was in fear of White's attack, but saw no possibility of escaping it.'

26 PxP   R(R2)-K2

27 K-B3   R-N1

28 K-B4

Lasker: The break with P-N5 requires the most careful preparation. First of all, the rooks must be doubled on the king knight file.

28 ...   P-N3

Lasker: Not to permit White time for these preparations.

29 R-N3   P-N4ch

Tarrasch recommends 29 . . . PxP, when 30 NPxP in reply allows an exchange of rooks, and the seizure of the knight file by Black's rook. Or if 30 KPxP. P-Q4 advances the backward queen pawn.

Brinckmann's analysis disagrees: if 29 . . . PxP 30 KPxP P-Q4 31 R(Q1)-KN1 N-Q3 32 P-N5 RPxPch 33 PxP PxPch 34 NxPch K-K1 35 N-K6 RxR 36 RxR R-QR2 37 R-N8ch K-K2 38 R-N7ch N-B2 39 N-N5 K-B1 40 RxNch RxR 41 NxR KxN 42 K-N5, and White wins.

30 K-B3

Not 30 PxP RPxPch 31 K-B3 R-R1, and the open file offers Black some counterplay, whereas after the text-move 30 . . . PxP is met by 31 R-R3, winning two rook pawns for one.

30 ...   N-N3

The knight emerges, and offers a Greek gift. If now 31 RxP N-B5 32 R-Q1 N-K4ch 33 K-K2 PxP, and Black has a good game.

31 PxP   RPxP

32 R-R3!

Far better to seize the open file, than to capture the queen pawn. After 32 RxP N-B5 33 R-Q1 N-K4ch 34 K-K2 R-R1, Black has some positional compensation for his pawn.

32 ...   R-Q2

Reti says: More natural, but not so good, would be

32 . . . N-B5, as the following continuation will show: 32 . . . N-B5 33 R-R7ch K-K1 34 R-QR1 B-N2 35 N-B7ch K-Q2 36 RxRch KxR 37 R-R7 R-QN1 38 N-R6, and White wins.

33 K-N3

The king leaves the diagonal, as a discovered check would interfere with his planned combination, which is: 34 P-K5! QPxP (if 34 . . . BPxP 35 N-K4 with a winning position) 35 RxRch NxR 36 R-R7ch K-K1 37 N-K4 and mate in two moves.

33 ...   K-K1

34 R(Q1)-KR1   B-N2

Black is running out of moves. If 34 . . . R-QR2 35 R-R8 wins a rook; if 34 . . . N-B5 35 R-R8 wins the bishop hiding in the corner; and if 34 . . . P-Q4 35 PxP NxP 36 N-K4 followed by 37 R-R8 wins for White.

This is the position:

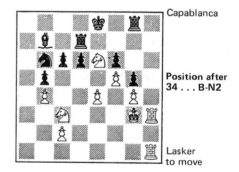

Capablanca

Position after 34 . . . B-N2

Lasker to move

35 P-K5!

An artistic vacating sacrifice. It enables the queen knight (Lasker's one inactive piece) to take powerful part in the concluding attack.

35 ...   QPxP

There are various ways that Black can lose:

(a) 35 . . . P-B4 36 R-R8 RxR 37 RxRch K-B2 38 R-B8ch K-K2 39 PxBP mate.

(b) 35 . . . P-Q4 36 N-B5 R-K2 37 R-R8 RxR

38 RxRch K-B2   39 R-R7ch K-K1   40 RxRch KxR
41 PxPch KxP   42 NxB and wins.

(c) 35 . . . BPxP   36 N-K4 N-Q4   37 R-R8 RxR
38 RxRch K-K2   39 N(K6)xP N-B3   40 NxN KxN
41 R-R6ch K-K2 (on 41 . . . KxN   42 R-N6 is mate)
42 P-B6ch K-Q1   43 P-B7 and wins.

36 N-K4

Threatens 37 NxPch, attacking king and both rooks.

36 . . .   N-Q4

37 N(K6)-B5

Wins the exchange, as 37 . . . R-K2 (for example)
allows 38 NxB RxN   39 N-Q6ch, and White wins
a whole rook.

37 . . .   B-B1

38 NxR   BxN

39 R-R7   R-B1

40 R-R1

Complete encirclement!

40 . . .   K-Q1

41 R-R8ch   B-B1

42 N-B5

In view of the three threats of mate in two, beginning
with 43 R-Q7ch, or 43 N-K6ch, or 43 N-N7ch, Capablanca resigned.

Lasker described the scene at the finish, thus:
The spectators had followed the final moves breath-
lessly. That Black's position was in ruins was obvious
to the veriest tyro. And now Capablanca turned over
his king. From the several hundred spectators there
came such applause as I have never experienced in all
my life as a chess player. It was like the wholly spontaneous applause which thunders forth in the theatre,
of which the individual is almost unconscious.

89

White **Réti**   Black **E. Lasker**
Réti Opening
New York, 1924

Emanual Lasker was 56 years old, and no longer Champion
of the World, when he won the first prize at the great
International Chess Tournament held at New York in
1924.

Although he lost a game to Capablanca, Lasker still
finished ahead of his great rival, and out-distanced too
the young Hypermodern masters whose new, dynamic
concepts were changing the face of chess.

Lasker disposed of Alekhine with a win and a draw,
of Tartakover with a win and a draw, and of Bogolyubov
with two wins.

As for Réti . . .

Their first game had been won by Lasker, who with
White made short work of Réti's French Defence.

In this, their 16th round game, Réti began naturally
enough with the Réti Opening, an opening that he
originated, and with whose finesses he was thoroughly
familiar.

Réti built up his position in approved Hypermodern
style—the bishops stationed in the wings, center pawns
modestly in the background, rooks doubled on an open
file, and the queen (Réti's own touch) artfully placed at
QR1, bearing down on the enemy center.

Lasker developed his game in simple, classical style—
pawns at K4 and Q4, bishops on important diagonals,
other pieces watching over activities in the center.

All this had so strong an effect, as to compel Réti to
sacrifice the exchange. Réti did win a pawn in the process
and could have won another by means of a pretty combination (pointed out by Alekhine in his magnificent
Book of the Tournament). But he missed his chance, the
opportunity of a lifetime!

Lasker assumed control, and in a few moves clamped
an unbreakable pin on a knight. Shortly after he forced
an exchange of queens, to bring it to an ending. This he
handled with his usual merciless efficiency.

A most enjoyable game, and one of Lasker's best.

1 N-KB3   P-Q4

2 P-B4   P-QB3

This lets White transpose into the Slav Defence by
3 P-Q4.

3 P-QN3

True to his principles, Réti develops à la fianchetto.

3 . . .   B-B4

Lasker's method is to bring his pieces out the
traditional way.

4 P-N3   N-B3

5 B-KN2   QN-Q2

6 B-N2   P-K3

7 0-0   B-Q3

8 P-Q3   0-0

9 QN-Q2   P-K4

Considering that he is on the black side of a Réti,
Lasker's position is more than satisfactory.

10 PxP   PxP

11 R-B1   Q-K2

12 R-B2   P-QR4!

Threatens a further advance, a danger which must
be prevented.

13 P-QR4

Practically forced, but now White's queen knight pawn
is weak, and so is his QN4 square.

13 . . .   P-R3

Prepares a flight square for the queen bishop, a
necessary preliminary to the advance of the king
pawn.

Black could not proceed at once with 13 . . . P-K5
and 14 . . . P-K6, on account of the intervening reply
14 N-Q4, attacking the bishop.

14 Q-R1

Echt Réti! This arrangement of queen and bishop had
been successful against Yates in the sixth round, so
why not try it against Lasker?

An alternative course was to play 14 N-N1,
15 N-B3, and 16 N-N5, benefiting by the weakness
of that square, to establish a knight strongly there.

14 . . .   KR-K1

15 KR-B1

Réti has achieved an ideal formation for this opening
—control of the bishop file, and pressure on the center
from the wings.

15 . . .   B-R2

Black is prepared to break open the king file by
16 . . . P-K5 and 17 . . . P-K6.

16 N-B1   N-B4

Puts pressure at once on the knight pawn.

Lasker could have gained the exchange by 16 . . .
P-K5   17 PxP PxP   18 N-Q4 P-K6   19 NxP BxR
20 RxB, but at the risk of contending with two powerful bishops.

17 RxN

Réti decides that giving up a rook for knight and pawn
offers the most resistance. Other defences are not
quite satisfactory. For example, if 17 Q-R3 (forfeiting
the initiative) 17 . . . N-R3 with the threat of 18 . . .
N-N5 would be fatal. Or if 17 N(B3)-Q2 R-R3 followed
by 18 . . . R-N3 is hard to meet.

17 . . .   BxR

18 NxP

This removes a valuable pawn; so it is not all one-sided.

It is worth noting at this point that:
No position is completely innocuous!

If White had captured by 18 BxP, then 18 . . .
BxPch   19 KxB N-N5ch followed by 20 . . . NxB
wins for Black.

18 . . .   QR-B1

19 N-K3

White has an eye on the isolated queen pawn, which
would make a nice addition to his collection of Black
pawns.

19 . . .   Q-K3

20 P-R3   B-Q3

Instead of this, Alekhine suggests 20 . . . P-QN3, to
bolster up the bishop and the Q-side.

Another, perhaps simpler course, was 20 . . . BxN 21 PxB RxRch 22 QxR R-QB1, though it meant allowing the advantage of the two bishops.

After the actual move, Lasker might have run into serious trouble.

21 RxR   RxR

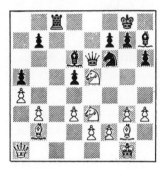

Lasker

Position after
21 . . . RxR

Réti
to move

22 N-B3

'White is not aware that Dame Fortune smiles at him,' says Alekhine. By means of the obvious 22 N(K5)-N4 NxN 23 PxN he could have won a second pawn for the exchange and thereby have avoided the danger of loss. After 23 . . . B-B1 (if 23 . . . BxNP 24 BxQP, etc.) 24 BxQP Q-Q2 25 KB-B3, it would have been for Black, possibly through 25 . . . P-QN4, to strive for a difficult draw. After the not easily understood text-move, Black holds fast until the end.'

Réti's move 22 N-B3 (back to Chernev again) was not merely indecision. He was apparently trying to lure Lasker into playing 22 . . . BxNP, after which Réti had two interesting continuations:

(1) 23 BxN PxB 24 N-N4 B-K4 25 N(B3)xB PxN 26 BxP!

(2) 23 N-Q4 Q-K1 24 N(Q4)-B5 BxN 25 NxB B-N1 26 BxN PxB 27 QxP.

22 . . .   B-K2

23 N-Q4   Q-Q2

24 K-R2

Réti must have been in time-pressure, or he would have rearranged his pieces by 24 N-N5, 25 B-Q4, and 26 N-B3, to bear down on the queen pawn.

24 . . .   P-R4!

Lasker intends to break through the pawn barrier surrounding the enemy king, even at the cost of a pawn or two.

25 Q-R1

Win or lose, this is a delightful move!

25 . . .   P-R5

Lasker proceeds with his plan, though he still might have changed his mind and played 25 . . . R-Q1, to save his queen pawn.

26 NxP   PxPch

27 PxP   NxN

28 BxN   B-B3

The point! Black pins and paralyzes the knight, and threatens to win a piece by this: 29 . . . R-B4 30 P-K4 BxN 31 BxB R-B7ch, and White must give up his bishop or lose his queen.

29 BxP   R-B4

30 B-R6

Ingeniously holding Black at bay, as 30 . . . BxN wins a piece, but loses the game after the reply 31 Q-R8ch.

30 . . .   B-N3

So Lasker renews the threat!

31 Q-N7

Protecting the knight instead by the natural move 31 P-K3 is fatal, as after 31 . . . BxN 32 BxB R-B7ch nets the queen for Black.

31 . . .   Q-Q1

32 P-QN4

Here too White dare not play 32 P-K3, as 32 . . . BxN 33 BxB R-B7ch 34 K-N1 Q-Q3 35 Q-R8ch K-R2 36 Q-B3 (he must defend against capture of the pawn and then mate) 36 . . . QxB(R3) wins for Black. Nor is there a saving move by 32 N-B6, when

32 . . . Q-K1 attacks two pieces, and 33 BxB allows mate in two, while 34 N-Q4 succumbs to 33 . . . BxN 34 BxB QxKPch 35 K-R1 Q-B8ch 36 B-N1 QxPch 37 B-R2 R-B8 mate.

32 . . .   R-B2

33 Q-N6   R-Q2

This forces White to exchange queens, as his knight is under a triple attack.

34 QxQch   RxQ

35 P-K3

White is still unable to break the pin by 35 N-B6, as 35 . . . R-Q3   36 BxB RxN will cost him one of the unprotected bishops.

35 . . .   PxP

This little pawn is the last straw that breaks the camel's back!

36 K-N2   BxN

37 PxB

Bitter necessity, as 37 BxB RxB   38 PxR P-N6 39 B-B4 P-N7   40 B-R2 BxP wins Réti's last piece and the game.

37 . . .   B-B4

38 B-N7   B-K3

Stops the rook pawn in its tracks! If 39 P-R5 B-Q4ch 40 BxB RxB and 41 . . . R-QR4 wins the pawn.

39 K-B3   B-N6

40 B-B6   R-Q3

41 B-N5   R-B3ch

42 K-K3   R-K3ch

43 K-B4

White has no good moves left. If 43 K-B3 B-Q8ch enables the rook to get behind the lines, or if 43 K-Q2 R-KN3   44 P-N4 R-KR3, and Black wins a pawn.

43 . . .   R-K7

44 B-B1   R-QB7

45 B-K3   B-Q4

46 Resigns

90

White **F. J. Marshall**   Black **E. Lasker**
Queen's Gambit Declined
Moscow, 1925

Despite some imperfections, this is a thoroughly fascinating game.

Imperfections? Regrettably, yes. Lasker may even have missed a win (a rare enough occurrence) and Marshall, hypnotized by a brilliant move that attacks queen and rook and threatens mate, misses a chance to force a neat draw.

Nevertheless, the game is delightful enough to justify a critic's remark that playing it over is like walking through a beautiful garden.

1 P-Q4   P-Q4

2 P-QB4

It is one of the mysteries of life that Frank Marshall, a genius of attack, who liked wide-open positions that gave scope to his pieces, preferred Queen's Gambits (Closed Games) to K-side openings (Open Games).

2 . . .   P-K3

3 N-QB3   N-KB3

4 B-N5   QN-Q2

5 P-K3   P-B3

6 PxP   KPxP

Both sides gain by this exchange: White has the bishop file for his rook, while Black will have less difficulty in developing his queen bishop.

7 B-Q3   B-Q3

Spielmann tried 7 . . . B-K2 in a previous round

against Marshall—to his sorrow. Marshall tore into his position with all the pieces in sight, and they left ruin and desolation in their wake.

8 N-B3   0-0

9 Q-B2   P-KR3

10 B-R4   R-K1

11 0-0   N-B1

12 P-K4

Marshall starts an attack. Very few players would allow the isolation of the queen pawn—attack or no attack.

Most masters would be more than content to apply slow but steady pressure by 12 P-QR3, 13 P-QN4, 14 N-R4, and 15 N-B5.

12 ...   PxP

13 NxP   B-K2

No time is lost by this retreat, as Black threatens 14 . . . NxN, winning a piece.

14 BxN   BxB

15 KR-K1

His queen pawn being indirectly defended, Marshall goes about his business. If Black tries 15 . . . BxP, then 16 NxB QxN   17 N-B6ch costs him the exchange.

15 ...   B-N5

16 NxBch QxN

17 N-K5   B-K3

Marshall must have been pleased with his prospects. His knight occupies a fine outpost at K5, and his king rook is ready to enter the fray, by way of K3.

Black's reward for sound, unassuming position play is his control of Q4.

18 R-K3   KR-Q1!

The right rook!—though it might seem to be a loss of time to move the king rook twice.

19 Q-B3   B-Q4

20 B-K4

Marshall, always aggressive, prepares to pursue the attack with 21 R-B3.

Lasker
to move

Position after
20 B-K4

Marshall

20 ...   N-K3!

21 R-B3

And continues with his plan, not realizing that he might be the one to be in danger.

21 ...   Q-R5!

22 BxB   RxB

White's double attack on the king bishop pawn is counterbalanced by the triple attack on his queen pawn.

23 R-K1

Unfortunately, he may not capture the pawn with either piece, as 23 RxP loses by 23 . . . RxN, and 23 NxKBP succumbs to 23 . . . NxP.

23 ...   NxP

24 R(B3)-K3

His first scheme having failed, White pins his hopes on the power of his doubled rooks on the king file.

24 ...   QR-Q1

25 R-K4   Q-B3

After 25 . . . QxR!   26 RxQ N-N4   27 Q-B1 R-Q8ch should win, with queens off the board and Black a pawn ahead (theoretically, anyway).

But Lasker may have been playing for more, per-

haps preferring to out-combine Marshall in the complications.

26 N-N4   Q-N3

27 P-KR3!

White avoids 27 N-K5, which would offer Lasker
another chance to win by 27 . . . QxR.

27 . . .   P-KR4

28 N-K5   Q-Q3

29 N-B4   Q-N1

30 N-K5   P-QB4

31 Q-B1   Q-B2

32 P-QN4   N-K3

Finally, vistas are opened along the queen file for the
black rooks.

33 Q-R3

If 33 NxP QxN   34 RxN QxR   35 RxQ R-Q8ch
36 R-K1 RxQ   37 RxR PxP, and Black has a won
game.

33 . . .   R-Q8

Any attempts at the life of the black rook pawn
would find quick retribution thus: 34 QxP P-B5
35 Q-K3 P-B6   36 R-QB4 QxR   37 NxQ P-B7, and
Black wins.

34 PxP   QxP

35 Q-KB3!

This threatens about everything on the board—a rook,
two pawns, and to draw by perpetual check.

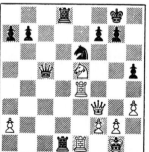

Lasker
to move

**Position after
35 Q-KB3!**

Marshall

35 . . .   N-N4

Lasker retaliates by defending his bishop pawn,
meanwhile attacking queen and rook.

36 QxRP

Very clever! Marshall is ready to meet 36 . . . NxR
with 37 QxPch K-R2   38 Q-R5ch, and perpetual
check. Or if 36 . . . Q-Q4   37 QxN QxR   38 QxRch
RxQ   39 RxQ, and White wins.

36 . . .   R(Q1)-Q7!

This diversion, a threat of mate in two, requires immediate attention.

37 N-Q3

This seems to be a tremendous move! It defends
against mate, attacks the queen, threatens to win a
rook, and also threatens a devastating check at K8.

Had Marshall not been seduced by the power and
beauty of this move, he would have searched for the
draw instead of a win. The draw (which Alekhine
pointed out) was as follows:

37 QxN! ('Capture first and philosophize later!'
says Tartakover) QxPch   38 K-R2 RxR   39 RxR
P-B3 (not 39 . . . QxR   40 N-B3, and White wins the
rook)   40 Q-N4 QxR   41 Q-K6ch K-R2   42 Q-B5ch
with a draw by perpetual check.

Marshall's actual move (37 N-Q3) is pretty, but it
loses!

Lasker had forseen it, and prepared a little surprise
himself.

37 . . .   NxR!

38 NxQ

This move is forced, as White's own queen is *en prise*.

38 . . .   RxRch

39 K-R2   NxP

Much stronger than 39 . . . RxBP   40 NxN RxN
41 Q-Q5, and the threats of 42 QxNP or 42 Q-Q8ch
assure White of equality.

40 Q-B5   R-K1

Lasker now forces a quick win in efficient, economical
style.

41 NxP   N-Q8

42 Q-B5   R-K3

This has three purposes—to stop the knight from coming in at Q6, to prevent perpetual check, and to attack on the king knight file.

43 Q-B1   N-K6!

44 Q-B8ch

Not of course 44 QxR, when 44 . . . N-B8ch wins the queen.

44 . . .   K-R2

45 Q-B3   R-KN3!

The rooks stage a neat finish.

46 QxN   R(Q7)xPch

47 K-R1   R(N7)-N6

48 Resigns

The mate threat will cost White his queen.

The secret of Lasker's success, according to Réti, is that 'He studies the game, the manner of playing, the strong and the weak points of the masters whom he is to meet. He is not so much interested in making the objectively best moves as those most disagreeable to his opponent; he turns the game in a direction not suitable to the style of his opponent, and on this unaccustomed road leads him to the abyss, often by means of intentionally bad moves. This is why Lasker's opponent never has a chance of playing a position that suits him, that, objectively speaking, he often stands to win, but is again and again confronted by new and for him difficult problems. And thus much precious time is lost, awkward difficulties appear to become overwhelming, and then all of a sudden Lasker begins to play magnificently and to show his real strength. There follows the nervous collapse, the psychic catastrophe, the direct consequence of which is a catastrophe on the chess board.'

Another aspect of his attitude to chess is well exemplified by his game against Winter in the Nottingham International Tournament of 1936. 'After over half an hour's thought,' says Winter, 'I placed a knight on a square on which it could be taken by a pawn. Lasker replied instantaneously with a quiet defensive move, and I soon found that all I had gained by my "brilliancy" was the loss of valuable thinking time.'

At the end of the game, Lasker was asked what would have occurred had he taken the knight. 'I do not know,' he answered. 'I was playing a strong master, and if a strong master thinks for half an hour and then plays a piece where I can take it, I think that it will not be healthy to take it, and I let it alone.'

'Other masters,' says Winter, 'always concerned to make the objectively best move, would have examined every variation of the sacrifice before rejecting it. All Lasker considered was that he had gained valuable time on the clock.'

Alekhine

Alekhine is the most brilliant, the most imaginative player in chess history. His achievements are enormous.

Alekhine won more first prizes in international tournaments than has any other master; he was Champion of the World for eighteen years, until his death; he was an annotator who had few equals and no superiors; he was one of the truly great blindfold players in history; his contributions to chess theory are of such importance as to justify saying, 'The openings consist of Alekhine's games, with a few variations.'

Alekhine's games can be described in one word—wonderful! They form a collection of masterpieces imbued with artistry, originality, imagination, and brilliance. In the field of combination play, Alekhine is unsurpassed. His creations, rich in colour and variety, are always of absorbing interest. At his best, and that was often, Alekhine astounded the world with a wealth of inspired combinations dazzling in their beauty and splendour.

Alekhine's fiery play has always inspired raves, such as these:

'At his best, Alekhine may have had equals, but he did not have any superiors,' says Reuben Fine, 'For sheer originality, profundity, and technical perfection he was never surpassed. He ranks among the really great artists of the chessboard.'

Elsewhere Fine says, 'Mirror, mirror on the wall, who was the strongest of them all? The Capablanca-Alekhine controversy will remain a fascinating subject for speculation for a long time to come.'

Stahlberg says, 'Alekhine stands out for all lovers of the game of chess as one of the few really great masters, perhaps as the greatest of all. Alekhine has been called the incomparable tactician. This is true with some modifications. He has created many a strategic masterpiece, and his tactics, in contrast to Lasker's, reside less in the utilization of his opponent's weak points, and more in the expression of his own genius and great faculties. Alekhine was not Lasker's equal as a psychologist, but as a fighting and creative spirit he surpassed all his rivals.'

Beheim says, 'If some fairy were to grant me the ability to play like one of the World Champions— Steinitz, Lasker, Capablanca, Alekhine, Euwe, Botvinnik, Smyslov, or Tal—I would ask her to let me play like Alekhine.'

Alekhine played chess as if his life depended on it. He had to win, win, win, and live up to what he once said, 'I dominate them all!'

What was behind this burning ambition? Rueben Fine takes us behind the scenes with this account of his first encounter with Alekhine, 'When I first met him, at Pasadena, in 1932, I began to under-stand the secret of his genius. He was showing a game with Euwe played at Berne a few months earlier, and his eyes and bearing had a strange intensity which I had never seen before. The man loved chess; it was the breath of life to him. At the bridge table he would suddenly start talking about an obscure variation in the Scotch; on the train to Mexico he assiduously devoted four hours a day to the analysis of new lines; any game, played by anybody, was good enough to sit him down and evolve new ideas for hours on end; on off days and periods he amused himself by playing rapid transit. He lived for chess, and chess alone.'

Alekhine had enormous confidence in his abilities. On the eve of his Championship match with Capablanca, he said, 'Yes it is difficult to picture Capablanca losing six games, but I find it more difficult picturing Capablanca beating me six games'.

Alekhine *was* a hard man to beat. In order to win a game from Alekhine, it was said that he had to be beaten three times: once in the opening, once in the midgame, and once in the ending.

Now to some of the deeds of the mighty Alekhine:

Alekhine won more brilliancy prizes than any other man has ever done.

Alekhine competed in 87 tournaments, winning first prize outright 50 times, and finishing in a tie for first and second 12 times.

Alekhine played 23 matches, of which five were for the World's Championship. Alekhine won the crown by beating Capablanca in 1927 by six wins to three losses, defended it twice successfully against Bogolyubov in 1929 and 1934, lost it to Euwe in 1935 and regained it in 1937.

Of the remaining 18 matches, Alekhine won 13, lost one match to Nenarokov, and drew four matches, with Fahrni, Nimzowitsch, Teichmann, and Bernstein.

Two tournament triumphs deserve particular mention. At San Remo in 1930, in a field which in-cluded such notables as Nimzowitsch, Rubinstein, Bogolyubov, Yates, and Spielmann, Alekhine scored 13 wins and 2 draws—more than 90 per cent!

At Bled the following year, Alekhine finished 5½ points ahead of Bogolyubov, the second-prize winner. Alekhine went through 26 rounds without losing a game, though he had such tough oppon-ents as Bogolyubov, Nimzowitsch, Flohr, Kashdan, and Stoltz to encounter.

In the field of blindfold play, only Pillsbury was in his class when it came to the profundity of his concepts in the planning of his strategy, and the flow of brilliant ideas that inspired his combination play. The record of conducting 32 boards simultaneously blindfold which he established at Chicago in 1933 has since been broken in number by Koltanowski and then by Najdorf, but not in quality of performance.

Alekhine's annotations are marvelous! His masterpiece *My best games of chess 1908-1923* is a book of magnificent games matched by magnificent notes. What more could you ask for? I have gone through it a dozen times, and still enjoy it as much as when I first looked at it in 1927.

Another peak of annotating skill is *The Book of the New York International Chess Tournament 1924.* The games are great, but the notes by Alekhine add so much to their flavour as to make this the No.1 tournament book.

These two books alone are enough to give you years of pleasure (and of course improve your game immeasurably), after which you can go on to more of Alekhine's writings, such as *My best games of chess 1924-1937,* and *The New York International Tournament of 1927.*

I consider Alekhine the second greatest chess player of all time.

91

White **A. Nimzowitsch**   Black **A. Alekhine**
Queen's Pawn Opening
Vilna, 1912

From the moment I first saw this remarkable game, I went quietly mad about it—and about all Alekhine games.

Not only were they bursting with beautiful combinations, but there were combinations in the notes—the things that could have happened, but didn't—that were equally beautiful.

I call your attention to Nimzowitsch's elegant queen sacrifice early in the game, and to one by Alekhine of equal elegance later on, both (alas!) hidden away in the notes.

1 P-Q4   P-Q4

2 N-KB3   P-QB4

3 B-B4   N-QB3

4 P-K3   N-B3

5 N-B3   B-N5

6 B-QN5   P-K3

7 P-KR3   B-R4

This allows White to take the initiative. A preferable course was 7 . . . PxP (freeing the bishop) 8 PxP B-R4 9 P-KN4 B-N3   10 N-K5 Q-N3   11 P-QR4 B-N5, with easy equality.

8 P-KN4   B-N3

9 N-K5

Black has to be careful now, as it is easy to make the most natural move on the board—and lose!

If 9 . . . R-B1   10 NxN PxN   11 B-QR6 R-R1 12 B-N7, and the rook is caught in a barrage of bishops.

9 . . .   Q-N3

10 P-QR4!

An energetic advance! The threat of 11 P-R5 forces Black to weaken his QN4 square.

10 . . .   P-QR4

11 P-R4   P-R4

Those who, like me, cannot resist curious chess facts, please note that P-R4 has been played four times in succession.

12 NxB   PxN

13 PxRP

Nothing is to be gained by driving the knight back, as after 13 P-N5 N-N1   14 Q-Q3 K-B2, the knight comes into good play by . . . N-K2 and . . . N-B4.

13 . . .   PxRP

14 Q-K2   0-0-0

15 0-0-0!

Nimzowitsch sets a pretty trap, including, believe-it-or-not, a queen sacrifice!

This is the position, with Black to move:

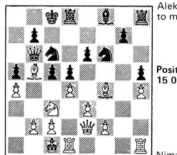

Alekhine to move

Position after 15 0-0-0!

Nimzowitsch

This is the plot: If 15 . . . PxP   16 PxP NxP   17 RxN QxR   18 QxKPch N-Q2   19 Q-B6ch! PxQ   20 B-R6 mate.

If, in this, 18 . . . R-Q2   19 BxRch K-Q1 (or 19 . . . NxB   20 Q-K8 mate) 20 B-B7ch KxB   21 N-N5ch, and White wins the queen.

15 . . .   B-Q3!

Alekhine avoids the trap, subtle though it is.

16 BxB   RxB

17 B-Q3

The bishop relinquishes N5 for the knight, who might accomplish more than the bishop did.

17 . . .   P-B5!

This not only dislodges the bishop, but interferes as well with White's plans for the knight. For, on 18 N-N5, there follows 18 . . . PxB   19 NxRch K-Q2 and White must give up the knight to save his queen, who is under attack.

18 B-N6   N-K2

19 KR-N1   Q-N5

20 K-Q2

A strange game, chess! The king protects the knight pawn by abandoning it! If now 20 . . . QxNP 21 R-N1 Q-R6   22 N-N5, and the double attack on queen and rook wins the exchange.

20 . . .   R-N3!

The position, with White to move:

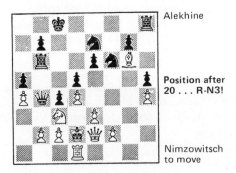

Alekhine

Position after 20 . . . R-N3!

Nimzowitsch to move

Now it is Alekhine who matches Nimzowitsch's effort by concocting a combination, including, believe-it-or-not, a queen sacrifice!

This is the idea: 21 . . . NxB   22 RxN QxNP 23 R-QN1 QxNch!   24 KxQ N-K5 mate!

21 P-B3!

This prophylactic move of Nimzowitsch's deserves an exclamation point.

It is the mark of a great player to anticipate the combinations of an opponent, as well as devise them himself.

21 . . .   R-KR3

Now begins a pursuit of the bishop.

22 B-B7   N-B4

The attack on the pawn is incidental to clearing K2 for the queen.

23 Q-R2   Q-K2

24 N-N5

On 24 B-N6 instead, the reply 24 . . . NxRP wins the bishop (25 QxN losing the queen by 25 . . . N-K5ch).

Reconciling himself to the loss of the bishop, Nimzowitsch tries to invade with knight and queen, and work up an attack.

24 . . .   QxB

25 N-R7ch   K-Q2

26 Q-N8   N-Q3

Black wants to surround and then capture the queen, and begins by cutting off her retreat.

27 R-N5   N(B3)-K1

And this further circumscribes the queen's activities.

28 R(Q1)-KN1   R-KB3

29 P-B4   P-N3

30 K-B1   Q-R2

31 P-B3   Q-B2

32 K-N1   Q-K2

The knight pawn is safe from capture, as 33 RxNP is penalized by 33 . . . Q-R2, pinning the rook.

33 K-R1   R-B1

34 N-N5

The knight tries to help the queen escape.

34 . . .   NxN

35 PxN   N-B2

36 Q-R7   Q-Q3

The queen is trapped! If 37 QxRP R-QR1 is a pin by

the king rook, or if 37 RxNP NxP 38 R-N7ch K-B3[·]
39 QxP R-R3 is a pin by the queen rook.

37 Resigns

92

White **A. Alekhine**   Black **K. Sterk**
Queen's Gambit Declined
Budapest, 1921

Alekhine had the faculty of conjuring up startling moves
out of nowhere.

In this game, the Q-side is the scene of spirited fencing,
when suddenly, out of a clear blue sky, there comes a
bolt of lightning on the K-side.

So electrifying was the move made by Alekhine that it
must have been enough by itself to persuade the judges
to award the game a prize for brilliancy.

1 P-Q4   P-Q4

2 N-KB3   N-KB3

3 P-B4   P-K3

4 N-B3   QN-Q2

5 P-K3   B-Q3

Quiet development by 5 . . . B-K2 was more to the
point.

6 N-QN5

An original move, but not commendable, as it impels
the bishop to retreat to a better square.

Alekhine could have put on the pressure immediately by 6 P-B5 B-K2 7 P-QN4 and 8 B-N2.

6 . . .   B-K2

7 Q-B2   P-B3

8 N-B3   0-0

9 B-Q3   PxP

10 BxP   P-B4!

This just about equalizes the position.

11 PxP

After 11 0-0 N-N3 12 B-Q3 PxP 13 PxP, White's
position is free and full of promise, but he does have
an isolated pawn to nurture.

11 . . .   BxP

12 0-0   P-QN3

13 P-K4

Alekhine, being Alekhine, does not fear any complications that might arise from this move. A Rubinstein,
I imagine, would be content with such a continuation
as 13 P-QN3 B-N2 14 B-N2 R-B1 15 Q-K2, with a
quiet, respectable game.

Alekhine's move has its attractions, as the pawn
occupies a central square, and releases the bishop.

13 . . . B-N2

14 B-KN5

Alekhine avoids precipitate action, which could
plunge him into disaster, thus: 14 P-K5 N-N5
15 N-KN5 P-N3 16 NxKP (certainly a tempting
prospect!) Q-R5 17 P-KR3 Q-N6!, and mate is
inevitable.

14 . . .   Q-B1!

But this changes the picture! Black releases his queen
from the influence of the bishop, and threatens to
win a pawn by 15 . . . BxPch followed by 16 . . . QxB.

15 Q-K2   B-N5!

Another fine move, this threatens to win the king
pawn by removing one of its defenders.

How shall White deal with the threat? The natural
16 QR-B1 is found wanting after 16 . . . BxN 17 B-Q3
N-B4! 18 RxB BxP 19 BxN BxB, with an attack
on the king rook.

Alekhine finds a way, though, to involve his opponent in complications on the Q-side, and then suddenly
—well, we'll see!

16 B-Q3   BxN

This is the position with White to move:

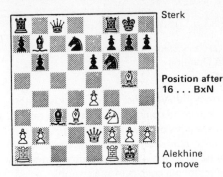

Sterk

**Position after
16 . . . BxN**

Alekhine
to move

17 KR-B1!

A profound move, and one that shows that Alekhine
is not bound by tradition. Usually, it is the queen
rook that moves to QB1, while the king rook moves
to Q1, but Alekhine has his own ideas.

Alekhine is now prepared for this continuation:
17 . . . N-B4   18 RxB BxP   19 BxN BxB   20 Q-K3
(note that the king rook is no longer under attack)
20 . . . PxB   21 P-QN4 B-N3   22 PxN PxP   23 RxP
Q moves   24 P-KR4, and White has attacking
chances to make up for the pawn he gave up.

17 . . . NxP

Black, not content with the line of play indicated,
goes into a combination which will enable him to un-
pin the bishop.

18 BxN   BxB

19 QxB   N-B4

The point of Black's combination. This *zwischenzug,*
an attack on the queen, will allow the bishop the
necessary time to flee the rook's clutches.

Sterk now expected Alekhine to play 20 Q-N1,
when 20 . . . B-N5 (other moves by the bishop allow
an attack on the pinned knight by 21 P-QN4)
21 P-QR3 Q-N2   22 PxB N-N6 lets him put up stout
resistance.

20 Q-K2!

Very strong, and the prelude to some fascinating
combination play.

20 . . .   B-R4

21 QR-N1

Suddenly Black is faced with the problem of saving
the lives of two pieces, both of which are threatened
by the imminent 22 P-QN4.

21 . . .   Q-R3

The only defence, as it unpins the knight, and attacks
White's unprotected queen. If now 22 QxQ, the recapture by 22 . . . NxQ nullifies the threat of P-QN4.

22 R-B4

But this revives it!

22 . . .   N-R5

Sterk's response is just as ingenious! Sterk is prepared
to meet 23 P-QN4 with 23 . . . N-B6 (exploiting the
circumstance that the rook is pinned) to win the
exchange.

This is the position:

Sterk

**Position after
22 . . . N-R5**

Alekhine
to move

23 B-B6!!

Magnificent! This unexpected shot on one side of
the board after all the thrust and parry on the other,
is enough to scare one out of a year's growth!

Alekhine now threatens 24 R-KN4! QxQ
25 RxPch K-R1   26 R-N6 dis.ch and mate.

There is no escape by 23 . . . P-R4, as after
24 R-KN4! QxQ   25 RxPch K-R1   26 N-N5!, there
is no way to avoid the impending 27 R-R7 dbl.ch
K-N1   28 R-R8 mate.

23 ...   KR-B1

Since 23 . . . PxB loses the queen by 24 R-N4ch, and other defences fail, Black tries this, his only chance to survive. With his double attack on the rook, Black might induce 24 RxRch QxR, and his queen is out of danger.

But he reckons without his host, who this time is the resourceful Alekhine.

24 ...   Q-K5!!

Another startling move! Alekhine continues the attack, meanwhile leaving two pieces *en prise*.

Here are some of the combinations evolved by *The King of Combination Play:*

(a) 24 . . . PxB   25 R-N4ch K-B1 (if 25 . . . K-R1 26 QxP mate)   26 Q-Q6ch K-K1   27 R-N8 mate.

(b) 24 . . . QxR   25 Q-KN5 K-B1   26 QxNPch K-K1 27 Q-N8ch K-Q2   28 N-K5ch K-B2   29 QxPch, and White wins the queen.

(c) 24 . . . RxR   25 Q-KN5 K-B1 (or 25 . . . R-KN5 26 QxR P-N3   27 QxN)   26 QxPch K-K1   27 N-K5!, and Black cannot avoid being mated.

24 ...   R-B4

25 Q-N3!

Simple, but effective.

25 ...   P-N3

26 RxN

Removes an innocent bystander.

26 ...   Q-Q6

27 R-KB1   R(R1)-QB1

Black is moving out of sheer inertia. But one does hate to resign!

28 R-Q4   Q-B4

29 Q-B4   Q-B7

30 Q-R6   Resigns

One of Alekhine's most brilliant games.

93

White **S. Tarrasch**   Black **A. Alekhine**
Queen's Pawn Opening
Pistyan, 1922

This is a brilliancy by Alekhine, which crackles with original ideas. Even the combinations in the notes—those that never see the light of day—are dazzling.

There is one combination wherein Alekhine dreams up a 'staircase' mate in which a queen sacrifice is the prelude to three double checks in succession!

1 P-Q4   N-KB3

2 N-KB3   P-K3

3 P-B4   P-B4

4 P-Q5   P-QN4

5 PxKP

Tarrasch disregards his own stern admonitions, and plays to win a pawn. He said, 'Never give up the birthright of attack for the mess of potage of a pawn. To be a pawn ahead at the cost of position and development is generally dangerous.'

Preferable is 5 B-N5, continuing development.

5 ...   BPxP

6 PxP   P-Q4

Look at that beautiful pawn center!

7 P-K3

Prevents Black from regaining his pawn by 7 . . . Q-R4ch, but is inferior to 7 QN-Q2 followed by 8 P-KN3 and 9 B-N2, when the bishop has a strong influence on the center.

7 ...   B-Q3

8 N-B3   0-0

9 B-K2   B-N2

10 P-QN3   QN-Q2

11 B-N2   Q-K2

Alekhine puts every piece to work, before starting any definite action.

12 0-0   QR-Q1

13 Q-B2   P-K4

Black's position becomes more menacing with every move he makes.

Behind the center pawns, who stand like the three musketeers, are pieces charged with potential power, beautifully placed for attack or defence.

14 KR-K1

In order to protect his K-side pawns, White prepares to post one knight at B1 to guard his rook pawn, and the other at Q1 to guard his bishop pawn.

14 ...   P-K5

15 N-Q2   N-K4

16 N-Q1   N(B3)-N5

17 B(K2)xN

If 17 N-B1 directly, then 17 ... N-B6ch   18 PxN PxP   19 B-Q3 Q-R5, and White is helpless against the coming ... Q-R6 and ... Q-N7 mate! As we shall see, the congestion of White's forces is an important factor in the success of Black's attack.

17 ...   NxB

18 N-B1   Q-N4!

Taking advantage of the absence of White's best defender, a knight at KB3, Alekhine now intends the maneuver ... N→R3→B4→R5 forcing the ghastly weakening move P-N3. To avoid this, Tarrasch makes R-KN1 possible; but he weakens himself all the same.

19 P-KR3   N-R3

20 K-R1   N-B4

21 N-R2   See diagram.

21 ...   P-Q5!

Instead of the anticipated 21 ... N-R5, Alekhine strikes at KN7 in a finer and subtler way: if now 22 PxP P-K6! (Black's long-range bishop comes to

Alekhine to move

Position after 21 N-R2

Tarrasch

life!) 23 NxP NxN   24 PxN Q-N6!   25 N-B3 RxN!, and Black wins.

Another pretty win (after 21 ... P-Q5) is 22 PxP P-K6!   23 KR-N1, and now instead of Alekhine's intended 23 ... Q-N6 (which is not convincing after the reply 24 N-KB3) simply 23 ... KPxP, which attacks the rook and also threatens a smothered mate.

22 B-B1   P-Q6

23 Q-B4ch   K-R1

24 B-N2   N-N6ch

Releases the pent-up energy.

25 K-N1

Clearly 25 PxN QxNP, with the queen threatening two mates, is out of the question.

25 ...   B-Q4

Alekhine can win the exchange after 25 ... P-Q7, but he is after bigger game.

26 Q-R4

If 26 Q-B3 N-K7ch   27 RxN PxR, and Black wins a knight that is rooted to the spot.

26 ...   N-K7ch

27 K-R1   R-B2

28 Q-R6   P-R4!

A necessary preliminary to a bishop sacrifice several moves later.

29 P-N6

White hopes for 29 . . . PxP, when he can sacrifice the exchange by 30 RxN PxR 31 QxKP, and get his queen back into play on the K-side.

But even that small wish is denied him, as Alekhine swings into the final attack.

29 . . . N-N6ch

30 K-N1 PxP

31 QxNP P-Q7!

Decisive! The advance of this pawn wins the exchange —as a start!

32 R-KB1 NxR

33 NxN B-K3!

The position, with White to play:

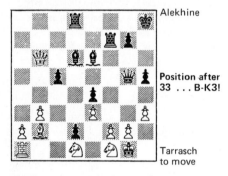

Alekhine

Position after
33 . . . B-K3!

Tarrasch
to move

34 K-R1

If White had tried to protect the square KN2 by 34 Q-B6 followed by 35 QxKP, he would have succumbed to a spectacular zigzag combination planned by Alekhine, as follows: 34 Q-B6 R-B6! 35 QxKP B-Q4 36 Q-QR4 QxPch! 37 KxQ R-N6 dbl.ch 38 K-R2 R-N7 dbl.ch 39 K-R1 R-R7 dbl.ch 40 K-N1 R-R8 mate. Exquisite!

34 . . . BxRP!

Alekhine storms the bastions.

35 PxB R-B6

36 N-N3 P-R5

Now we see the point of 28 . . . P-R4.

37 B-B6

The ingenuity of despair. If 37 . . . P(or R)xB 38 QxRch saves White.

37 . . . QxB

38 NxP RxPch

If now 39 K-N1 B-R7ch wins the queen, while 39 K-N2 Q-B6ch 40 K-B1 R-R8 checkmates the king.

39 Resigns

94

White **A. Alekhine**   Black **H. Wolf**
Queen's Pawn Opening
Pistyan, 1922

Alekhine once said, 'There must be no reasoning from past moves, only from the present position.'

In the opening stages of this justly celebrated game, Alekhine moves his queen four times, and his king knight three times.

Despite the dazzling originality of his play, his surprise moves were not an attempt to be eccentric, or to astonish the natives. The more surprising his moves seemed, the more logical they were!

1 P-Q4 P-Q4

2 N-KB3 P-QB4

3 P-B4 BPxP

4 PxP N-KB3

5 NxP P-QR3

Black avoids the logical 5 . . . NxP, as he fears the continuation 6 P-K4 followed by 7 B-N5ch.

Moves of this nature are dangerous though,

against an Alekhine, who is always on the alert to punish artificial maneuvers.

6 P-K4!

Astonishing! The idea of this move, which is original and typifies Alekhine's genius, is to sacrifice the king pawn, in order to preserve the queen pawn. Alekhine foresees that this pawn, which becomes isolated and presumably weak will be a strong factor in delaying his opponent's development.

6 ...   NxKP

7 Q-R4ch!

Only beginners (and great players) bring their queens out so early in the game. The check seems time-wasting, as it lets Black develop a piece, driving the queen away. Note though that the check forces a blocking of the queen file, which shields the queen pawn from attack.

7 ...   B-Q2

Interposing the queen (7 . . . Q-Q2) loses the exchange after 8 B-N5.

8 Q-N3!   N-B4

The knight seems to gain a tempo by this reply: it attacks the queen and protects the knight pawn at the same time.

There is a drawback, though. The knight is un-protected at B4, and subject to various threats.

9 Q-K3!

This is superior to the plausible 9 Q-KB3, with its concealed attack on the queen knight pawn. The pretty sequel to that would be: 9 . . . P-K4! 10 PxP *en passant* NxP 11 NxN BxN 12 QxNP B-Q4!, and White must give up a piece to extricate his queen.

9 ...   P-KN3

Black was not happy about developing by 9 . . . P-K3 as 10 N-QB3 maintains the pressure, so he plans to fianchetto his bishop.

10 N-KB3!

Again he moves an already developed piece, but this gain of time (an attack on the knight) allows him to prevent the contemplated 10 . . . B-N2 followed by 11 . . . 0-0.

10 ...   Q-B2

11 Q-B3

This attack on the rook, and threat to the knight (by 12 P-QN4) forces Black to abandon any idea of castling.

11 ...   R-N1

12 B-K3   P-N3

13 QN-Q2

Against further attack on the pinned knight, Black wriggles out of his troubles by clamping on a pin of his own, this way: 13 P-QN4 B-N2 14 N-Q4 (on 14 B-Q4 BxB 15 NxB Q-K4ch releases the knight) Q-R2! 15 PxN PxP, and Black regains his piece.

White therefore brings another piece into play.

13 ...   B-N2

14 B-Q4   BxB

15 QxB

White's position is incontestably superior to his opponent's. In two moves (B-K2 and 0-0) he can complete his development, and bring his rooks into operation on the open files. His isolated queen pawn too, is a thorn in the flesh.

Black has lost the right to castle on one side, and dare not on the other. The position of his king in the center will be none too secure.

15 ...   B-N4

Strange-looking, but if he tries to develop his Q-side by 15 . . . B-B4 16 B-K2 QN-Q2, then 17 P-KN4 B-B7 18 R-QB1 B-R5 leaves his pieces awkwardly placed (though 19 P-N4 does not gain a piece, nor does 19 QxB, as 19 . . . N-Q6ch is a rude awakening).

16 BxBch   PxB

17 0-0   R-R5

18 P-QN4   Q-Q1

19 P-QR3

Tarrasch too used to play these quiet waiting moves, to demoralize his opponent by demonstrating how powerless he was.

19 . . .   QN-Q2

20 KR-K1   K-B1

Wolf

Position after
20 . . . K-B1

Alekhine
to move

21 P-Q6!   N-K3

On 21 . . . P-K3 there follows 22 Q-K3 N-N2 23 Q-Q3 R-QR1 24 N-K4 (preserves the invaluable queen pawn) and White wins the queen knight pawn—as a start.

22 RxN!

A Spielmann or a Marshall would likewise have sacrificed the exchange, but could they have so brilliantly created the opportunity for the sacrifice?

22 . . .   PxR

23 N-N5   Q-N1

On 23 . . . P-K4, there is a neat forced win: 24 Q-Q5 (threatens the king with mate, and the queen with loss by a knight fork) Q-K1 25 N-K6ch K-B2 26 N-B7 dis.ch P-K3 27 Q-B3ch, and White wins the queen.

24 NxPch   K-B2

On 24 . . . K-K1, 25 N-K4 brings another piece into the fray.

25 N-N5ch   K-B1

Here if 25 . . . K-K1   26 R-K1 applies more pressure.

26 Q-Q5   R-N2

27 N-K6ch   K-N1

28 NxR dis.ch   KxN

29 PxP   N-B3

30 QxP   R-R2

31 R-K1   Q-Q3

32 P-K8(N)ch

A neat promotion, after which the board is quickly cleared of all three knights, to set the stage for the finale—a mating attack.

32 . . .   NxN

33 QxN   QxN

34 Q-K5   K-B2

35 P-KR4

Prepares for 36 R-K3 followed by 37 R-B3ch, and quick mate.

35 . . .   RxRP

The pawn will not make him rich, but Black is setting an ingenious trap, as a last desperate resort.

36 Q-K8ch   K-N2

But not 36 . . . K-B3, which allows instantaneous mate.

37 R-K7ch   K-R3

38 Q-B8ch   K-R4

39 R-K5ch   K-N5

Black hopes for 40 P-B3ch K-N6 41 R-N5ch, when he turns the tables with 41 . . . QxR 42 PxQ R-R8 mate.

But Alekhine is on the *qui vive,* and not to be caught by traps, ingenious though they may be.

40 R-N5ch!   Resigns

95

White **A. Alekhine**   Black **F.D. Yates**
Queen's Gambit Declined
London, 1922

Steinitz used to say, 'I play my king all over the board. I make him fight!'

Steinitz would have loved this Alekhine game, and the combination in which the king plays such an important part. In the very midgame Alekhine's king takes a walk to the middle of the board, and attacks a rook. The unfortunate piece can retreat, or stay to be defended, but either way it results in checkmate.

As in many an Alekhine combination, there is a kick at the tail-end of it!

1 P-Q4   N-KB3

2 P-QB4   P-K3

3 N-KB3   P-Q4

4 N-B3   B-K2

5 B-N5

It was Pillsbury who discovered the strength of this continuation (instead of the customary 5 B-B4), a sort of Ruy López on the K-side.

5 ...   0-0

6 P-K3   QN-Q2

7 R-B1   P-B3

8 Q-B2   R-K1

9 B-Q3   PxP

10 BxP   N-Q4

The Capablanca maneuver, which lets Black breathe a bit.

11 N-K4

Alekhine himself considered this inferior to 11 BxB, but it creates complications, and Alekhine thrived on complications.

11 ...   P-KB4

A serious strategical error on three counts:

(1) It leaves Black with a backward king pawn.

(2) It shuts the white-squared bishop in permanently.

(3) It weakens the black squares, especially K4, a favourable square for an enemy knight to settle on.

12 BxB   QxB

13 N(K4)-Q2   P-QN4

Now a similar error on the other side! Now Black's QB4 is weakened irretrievably, and will soon be under White's control.

14 BxN!

Alekhine eliminates the strongly-posted knight, and prepares to exploit his command of the open file.

14 ...   BPxB

15 0-0   P-QR4

16 N-N3!

White hastens to get this move in, before 16 ... P-R5 renders it impossible. The knight is of course headed for QB5, the magic square.

16 ...   P-R5

17 N-B5   NxN

18 QxN

The proper recapture, and in accordance with Tarrasch's precept, 'Weak points or holes in the opponent's position must be occupied by pieces, not by pawns.'

18 ...   QxQ

19 RxQ

The exchanges have left White with just the position he wanted: he has control of the open queen bishop file, and will eventually play to the seventh rank and double his rooks on it; he dominates the black squares, and will post his knight unassailably on K5; he has easy play against Black's weak pawn position; finally, his opponent has the bad bishop, which is limited to purely defensive functions.

19 ...   P-N5

20 KR-B1   B-R3   See diagram on page 264.

21 N-K5!

This giant of a knight dominates the center!

The knight prevents Black from trying to dispute the bishop file: If 21 ... KR-B1   22 RxRch RxR

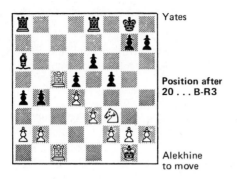

Yates

Position after
20 . . . B-R3

Alekhine
to move

23 RxRch BxR   24 N-B6, and the attack on the
knight pawn as well as the threat of winning the
bishop by 25 N-K7ch would gain a pawn for White.

21 . . .   KR-N1

22 P-B3

A new advantage: White can bring his king into
aggressive play, while the opponent's must stay put.

22 . . .   P-N6

23 P-QR3   P-R3

Here too, Black dare not exchange rooks, as after
23 . . . R-QB1   24 RxRch RxR   25 RxRch BxR
26 K-B2 K-B1   27 K-K1 K-K2   28 K-Q2 K-Q3
29 K-B3, and Black cannot save his queen rook pawn.

24 K-B2!

The starting point of mate threats, in which the king
himself takes part!

24 . . .   K-R2

25 P-R4   R-KB1

Black still comes to grief if he tries to clear the rooks
off the board, thus: 25 . . . R-QB1   26 RxR RxR
27 RxR BxR   28 N-Q3 B-Q2   29 N-B5, and Black
loses either his king pawn or his queen rook pawn.

26 K-N3   KR-QN1

Black can do nothing but sit tight, and await develop-
ments.

27 R-B7

Seizing the seventh rank is usually the prelude to the

final movement of the symphony.

An Alekhine win seems inevitable, but his method
is inimitable.

27 . . .   B-N4

28 R(B1)-B5

Threatens 29 R-K7 R-K1   30 R-KB7, and the attack
on the bishop gives White the needed tempo to play
31 R(B5)-B7, doubling rooks on the seventh rank.

28 . . .   B-R3

29 R(B5)-B6

Step by step White approaches his goal. Black must
protect his king pawn, as an attempt to exchange
rooks by 29 . . . R-QB1 loses instantly by 30 RxB!,
and White wins a piece.

29 . . .   R-K1

30 K-B4

Now that the doubling of his rooks on the seventh
cannot be prevented, Alekhine takes time to bring
his king closer to the center.

30 . . .   K-N1

31 P-R5!

Tightens the mating net around the king.

31 . . .   B-B8

32 P-N3   B-R3

The bishop can do little harm. If 32 . . . B-K7,
White guards the pawn by moving his knight to KN6
and R4, and then comes in at K5 with his king, to
win the king pawn—as a start.

33 R-B7

Prepares to double rooks. Black cannot oppose this
by playing either rook to B1, as one rook must protect
the bishop, and the other the king pawn.

33 . . .   K-R2

34 R(B6)-B7

This doubling of rooks on the seventh nearly always
means disaster.

34 . . .   R-KN1

35 N-Q7

Threatens 36 N-B6ch winning the exchange.

35 ...   K-R1

The scene is now set for Alekhine, who finishes with a display of Chessboard Magic!

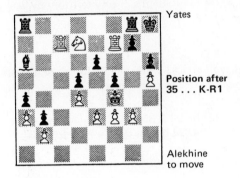

Yates

Position after 35 . . . K-R1

Alekhine to move

36 N-B6!   KR-KB1

Obviously, if 36 . . . PxN   37 R-R7 is instant mate.

37 RxP!

Simply elegant.

37 ...   RxN

38 K-K5!

The king is a strong piece: White wins a whole rook! If Black moves 38 . . . R-KB1 (either rook!) he is mated in two moves by 39 R-R7ch K-N1 40 R(B7)-N7 mate.

38 ...   Resigns

96

White **E. Bogolyubov**   Black **A. Alekhine**
Dutch Defence
Hastings, 1922

This is the Alekhine game that has everything!

There is attack and counter-attack, and subtleties of position play, leading up to *zugzwang*, and threats of smothered mate.

There are sacrifices galore!

Queens and rooks are given away with a lavish hand by Alekhine. He lets Bogolyubov capture a queen and two rooks in three successive moves—the last with check!

The strategy is on a grand scale, and the whole board sparkles with rare, original combinations.

It is the writer's deeply considered opinion, based on a lifetime of study of master chess, that this brilliant effort of Alekhine's is the greatest masterpiece ever created on a chessboard.

1 P-Q4   P-KB4

Alekhine considered this defence risky, but he needed a win at all costs to make sure of first prize.

2 P-QB4   N-KB3

3 P-KN3   P-K3

4 B-N2   B-N5ch

5 B-Q2   BxBch

6 NxB

The better recapture was by 7 QxB, followed by developing the knight at QB3, its natural square.

Bogolyubov's move decentralizes the knight, and blocks the queen file.

6 ...   N-B3

7 KN-B3   0-0

8 0-0   P-Q3

9 Q-N3   K-R1

10 Q-B3

Bogolyubov may have thought he was preventing 10 . . . P-K4, as he had three pieces trained on that square.

10 ...   P-K4!

Black insists on his share of the center.

The king pawn is indirectly protected, as after 11 PxP PxP 12 NxP, there would follow 12 . . . NxN 13 QxN QxN, and Black has won a piece.

11 P-K3   P-QR4!

This restrains counteraction on the Q-side by
12 P-QN4.

12 P-N3

Customary preparation for advancing the rook
pawn. If at once 12 P-QR3, then 12 . . . P-R5 ends
that demonstration.

12 . . .   Q-K1!

13 P-QR3   Q-R4!

Black mobilizes his forces with a view to a K-side
attack. He does not fear 14 PxP PxP   15 NxP, as
after 15 . . . NxN   16 QxN N-KN5!, the threat of
mate by 17 . . . QxP wins the queen.

　　Or if 14 P-QN4 P-K5   15 N-K1 PxP   16 PxP RxR
wins the knight pawn.

14 P-KR4

Renews the threat of 15 PxP, winning a pawn.

14 . . .   N-KN5

15 N-N5

Clearly to follow up with 16 P-B3, evicting the
unwelcome knight.

15 . . .   B-Q2

16 P-B3   N-B3

17 P-B4

Compulsory, to prevent the break by 17 . . . P-B5.

17 . . .   P-K5

18 KR-Q1

Clears the square KB1, making it possible for the
knight to help defend the shaky knight pawn from
there.

　　White should first have closed the center by
18 P-Q5!

18 . . .   P-R3

19 N-R3   P-Q4!

Alekhine intends to consolidate his center before
embarking on a flank attack.

20 N-B1   N-K2

In order by 21 . . . P-R5 to weaken the pawn support

of the bishop pawn. If then 22 P-QN4 PxP   23 QxP
N(K2)-Q4, and Black's knight dominates the center,
as no pawns can drive it away.

21 P-R4   N-B3!

Now that White's queen rook pawn is at R4, Black's
knight is free to invade the enemy territory by way
of QN5 and Q6.

22 R-Q2   N-QN5

23 B-R1   Q-K1!

Virtuosity in attack! White will be forced to give up
a pawn or the strategic Q5 square.

24 R-KN2

The blockade by 24 P-B5 is not satisfactory, as the
reply 24 . . . P-QN4 breaks open a file for Black.

24 . . .   PxP

25 PxP

White chooses the lesser evil, and gives up a pawn.
The consequences of 25 QxP N(B3)–Q4 followed by
26 . . . P-QN4 were bound to be calamitous.

25 . . .   BxP

26 N-B2

White is trying desperately to get in 27 P-N4, and break
things up a bit.

26 . . .   B-Q2

'But even this weak counterchance will not be vouch-
safed him,' says Alekhine.

27 N-Q2   P-QN4!

Alekhine tries to undermine the annoying pawn that
prevents his king knight from reaching Q4.

28 N-Q1

Clearly, if 28 P-B5, KN-Q4 is devastating.

28 . . .   N-Q6

29 RxP

The position is now ripe for Black.

29 . . .   P-N5!

The beginning of a magnificent combination, in
Alekhine's most imaginative style.

Alekhine

**Position after
29 . . . P-N5!**

Bogolyubov
to move

It is not the heavy pieces (the queen and the rooks) but this little pawn that breaks into White's position!

30 RxR

If 30 Q-R1 RxR 31 QxR Q-R1! 32 QxQ RxQ, and the rook will swoop down to the seventh or the eighth rank with telling effect.

30 . . . PxQ!

It is not often that one distinguishes the capture of a queen by awarding it an exclamation mark, but in this case Black sacrifices his queen and both rooks in return!

31 RxQ P-B7!!

The point of Alekhine's wondrous combination. The pawn cannot be prevented from queening, and a new phase begins.

32 RxRch K-R2

33 N-B2

Any other move loses a piece.

33 . . . P-B8(Q)ch

34 N-B1 N-K8!

Threatens 35 . . . N-B6—a picturesque smothered mate!

35 R-R2 QxBP

Now the threat is 36 . . . B-N4 37 N-Q2 (or 37 B-N2 NxB winning a piece) Q-QB8 38 N-B1 N-B6ch and mate next move.

36 R-QN8 B-N4

37 RxB QxR

38 P-N4

White struggles to loose his bonds.

38 . . . N-B6ch!

Another surprise move, and there's more where that came from!

39 BxN PxB

40 PxP

Forced, for on 40 P-N5 N-N5 41 NxN (or if 41 R-R3 Q-K7 wins) 41 . . . PxN, and Black has two connected passed pawns.

40 . . . Q-K7!!

Ties White up completely. Any move by one of his pieces loses. If, for example, 41 N-R3 N-N5 42 RxQ PxR, and Black gets a new queen (White being unable to move his king to B2).

Or if 41 R-R3 N-N5! is again the winning move.

This is the position:

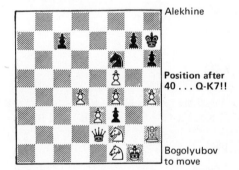

Alekhine

**Position after
40 . . . Q-K7!!**

Bogolyubov
to move

41 P-Q5

His pieces being held by the force of *zugzwang*, White is left with pawn moves.

41 . . . K-N1

Care is needed when you have a won game—especially if you have a won game! The natural continuation 41 . . . P-R4 allows White to escape cleverly by 42 N-R3 N-N5 43 N-N5ch K-N1 44 RxQ PxR 45 N-B3!

42 P-R5   K-R2

Alekhine waits for Bogolyubov's pawn moves to be exhausted.

43 P-K4   NxKP

44 NxN   QxN

45 P-Q6   PxP

46 P-B6

Unable to save his pawns, White sells their lives dearly, by breaking up his opponent's pawns.

46 ...   PxP

47 R-Q2   Q-K7!

'A pretty finish, worthy of this fine game,' says Alekhine himself, pardonably proud of a great creation.

The queen's occupation of the fatal square forces a delightful simplification, and offers a fine illustration of the dictum, 'Pawn endings are the easiest to win.'

The sign of a great master is his ability to win a game quickly and painlessly.

48 RxQ   PxR

49 K-B2   PxN(Q)ch

50 KxQ   K-N2

51 K-B2   K-B2

52 K-K3

On 52 P-B5, there follows 52 ... K-K2   53 ... K-K3 P-Q4   54 K-Q3 K-Q3   55 K-Q4 K-B3, and Black wins easily.

52 ...   K-K3

53 K-K4   P-Q4ch

54 Resigns

Bogolyubov does not care to see the continuation: 54 K-Q4 K-B4   55 KxP KxP   56 K-Q4 P-B4 57 K-Q3 K-N6, and Alekhine will soon have a fourth queen on the board!

97

White **E. Grünfeld**   Black **A. Alekhine**
Queen's Gambit Declined
Carlsbad, 1923

'The essence of beauty in chess lies in three points: first, profundity, with which is linked the element of surprise, the latter coming preferably at the end of a movement; for in the perfect chess combination, as in a first-rate short story, the whole plot and counter-plot should lead up to a striking finale, the interest not being allayed until the very last moment. Secondly, elegance of maneuvering, the rhythm of appropriate move and counter-move; and, thirdly, economy, both of force and time, which unifies the whole into a chess poem.

These three qualities are exhibited to a particularly high degree in the game against Grünfeld, which is perhaps the finest game ever played.'

Yates & Winter

1 P-Q4   N-KB3

2 N-KB3   P-K3

3 P-B4   P-Q4

4 N-B3   B-K2

5 B-N5   QN-Q2

6 P-K3   0-0

7 R-B1   P-B3

8 Q-B2   P-QR3

Black waits for B-Q3 to be played, before taking the pawn, so that the bishop wastes a move in its recapture.

9 P-QR3   P-R3

10 B-R4   R-K1

Improves a Grünfeld-Maroczy game played at Vienna in 1922, which took this course: 10 ... PxP   11 BxP P-QN4   12 B-R2 R-K1   13 B-N1 B-N2   14 N-K5

N-B1   15 0-0 P-B4   16 PxP BxBP   17 KR-Q1 Q-K2
18 N-N4 QR-B1   19 BxN! PxB   20 R-Q7!, and
Black must decide whether to lose his queen by 20 . . .
QxR   21 NxPch, or his king by 20 . . . NxR
21 Q-R7ch.

11 B-Q3   PxP

12 BxP   P-QN4

13 B-R2   P-B4!

Black usually equalizes if he can get this move in
safely. There is no danger in White's attack by
14 PxP NxP   15 B-N1, as after 15 . . . B-N2!   16 BxN
BxB   17 Q-R7ch K-B1   18 NxP PxN   19 RxN BxP,
the position favours Black.

14 R-Q1

Instead of playing for a trap, Grünfeld should complete
his development by 14 0-0, reserving the square Q1 for
his king rook.

14 . . .   PxP

15 NxQP   Q-N3

Alekhine avoids the trap easily. For one thing, he
would not leave his queen on a file facing an enemy
rook.

The trap: 15 . . . B-N2   16 NxKP PxN   17 BxPch
K-R1   18 B(R4)xN BxB   19 BxN, and White has
gained two pawns.

16 B-N1

A wily move, the idea being to prevent 16 . . . B-N2,
which would be answered by 17 N(Q4)xNP PxN
18 RxN!, when Black could not recapture on pain of
mate in two.

16 . . .   B-N2!

Alekhine has seen further ahead, and goes about the
business of developing his pieces.

If White tries 17 N(Q4)xNP, there follows 17 . . .
Q-B3!   18 N-Q4 QxP, and Black has a strong attack.

17 0-0   QR-B1

Black has completed his development in exemplary
fashion, and already threatens the annoying 18 . . .
B-K5 or 18 . . . N-K5.

Q-Q2   N-K4!

The knight has his eye on the beautiful square QB5.
This knight bears watching as it plays a heroic part
in the dénouement.

19 BxN

This is part of a subtle plot to gain control of K4, and
eliminate Black's long-range bishop.

19 . . .   BxB

20 Q-B2

The immediate 20 B-K4 loses by 20 . . . RxN   21 BxB
(if 21 QxR (or PxR) BxB wins two pieces for a rook)
R-Q6, and Black wins a piece.

20 . . .   P-N3

This is less a precaution against 21 Q-R7ch (which
would be harmless enough) but to provide a secure
retreat for the king bishop.

21 Q-K2   N-B5

The knight, strongly posted here, already makes its
presence felt by threatening 22 . . . NxRP, winning
a pawn.

22 B-K4

An ingenious defence of the pawn. If now 22 . . .
NxRP   23 Q-B3! (attacks three of Black's pieces) BxB
24 NxB (now White attacks two pieces) BxN   25 PxB
(Black's knight is still *en prise*) N-B5   26 N-B6ch,
and White emerges from the melee the exchange
ahead.

22 . . .   B-N2!

With this quiet reply, Black retains the advantage, and
maintains his threats.

23 BxB   QxB

24 R-B1

The rook returns, to prevent loss of the rook pawn.

24 . . .   P-K4!

The idea of this, and the next move, is to secure a
base at Q6 for the knight, where its effectiveness will
be increased immeasurably.

25 N-N3   P-K5

26 N-Q4   KR-Q1!

27 KR-Q1   N-K4!

28 N-R2

Some beautiful pinning combinations would result from 28 R-B2 (to answer 28 . . . N-Q6 by 29 NxKP) as follows:

28 R-B2 N-Q6! 29 NxKP QxN 30 RxN (if 30 QxN QxQ 31 RxQ RxR wins a rook) 30 . . . RxR 31 QxR RxN! (but not the plausible 31 . . . BxN, when the counterpin 32 Q-Q1 wins the bishop) and White is helpless to recapture.

If in this 30 RxR RxR 31 RxN BxN 32 RxB Q-N8ch 33 R-Q1 R-B8 34 RxR QxRch 35 Q-B1 QxNP, and Black has a winning ending.

28 . . .   N-Q6

A powerful invasion, and the prelude to a remarkable final combination.

29 RxR   QxR

This is the situation:

Alekhine

Position after 29 . . . QxR

Grünfeld to move

30 P-B3

Now this move comes too late, but getting the off-side knight back into play is refuted by this beautiful conception:

30 N-QB3 P-B4 31 P-B3 RxN! 32 PxR BxPch 33 K-B1 N-B5 34 Q-Q2 Q-B5ch 35 N-K2 (on 35 K-K1, P-K6 wins: e.g. 36 QxB NxP mate) P-K6! 36 Q-K1 BxP 37 R-Q8ch K-B2 38 Q-Q1 BxP 39 Q-Q7ch B-K2 40 Q-K8ch K-B3 41 Q-R8ch

K-N4 42 P-R4ch K-R4 43 P-N4ch PxP 44 Q-K5ch P-N4! and Black wins (Alekhine).

30 . . .   RxN!

Alekhine is in his element!

31 PxP

Apparently a clever way out of his troubles. Against 31 PxR Alekhine intended 31 . . . BxPch 32 K-B1 N-B5 33 Q-Q2 (if 33 QxKP Q-B5ch 34 K-K1 NxPch 35 K-Q2 B-K6ch, and White must give up his queen) 33 . . . Q-B5ch 34 K-K1 P-K6 35 QxB NxP mate.

The text move looks good, as Black must clearly lose a piece, but it does not catch him off-guard.

Alekhine is ready, even for moves that seem to break up his combinations.

31 . . .   N-B5!

This move must have given Grünfeld a jolt! It affects all his pieces, even the knight hiding at R2.

32 PxN

Forced, of course.

32 . . .   Q-B5!

Attacks two loose pieces, the queen and the knight. If now 33 N-B3 (attempting to protect both pieces) 33 . . . QxQ 34 NxQ RxRch wins a rook.

33 QxQ

Grünfeld avoids one disaster—only to plunge into another.

33 . . .   RxRch

34 Q-B1   B-Q5ch!

And Black mates next move.

98

White **R. Réti**   Black **A. Alekhine**
King's Fianchetto
Baden-Baden, 1925

Alekhine says, 'I consider this, and the game against Bogolyubov at Hastings in 1922, the most brilliant games of my chess career. By a peculiar coincidence they both remained undistinguished, as there were no brilliancy prizes awarded in either of these contests.'

C.J.S. Purdy, whose writing is witty and perceptive, called this game, 'the gem of gems,' and commented further, 'Alekhine's chess is like a god's. One can revere, but never hope to emulate.'

Former World Champion Euwe said, 'A peerless example of Alekhine's attacking skill. The position is incredibly complicated and everything is suspended in mid-air; but Alekhine dominates the proceedings. He pulls the wires, and it is to his bidding that the marionettes dance.'

C.S. Howell in his introduction to the game in *The American Chess Bulletin* said, 'The game is a wonderful one, and the amateur who fails to study it, or studying it learns naught, would do well to give up chess and try another game—say Mah Jong.'

To these songs of praise, I can only add my own voice. It is truly a game of bewildering beauty, one of the greatest masterpieces in the entire literature of chess.

1 P-KN3   P-K4

2 N-KB3   P-K5

3 N-Q4   P-Q4

Alekhine was satisfied with this move which offered free scope to his pieces. But he could obtain more (as he says) by 3 . . . P-QB4! 4 N-N3 P-B5 5 N-Q4 B-B4 6 P-QB3 N-QB3, 'thus bringing *ad absurdum* White's "development."

4 P-Q3   PxP

5 QxP   N-KB3

6 B-N2   B-N5ch

7 B-Q2   BxBch

8 NxB   0-0

9 P-QB4   N-R3

This is preferable to 9 . . . P-QB4, when 10 N(Q4)-N3 in reply attacks both center pawns.

10 PxP   N-QN5

11 Q-B4   N(N5)xQP

12 N(Q2)-N3   P-B3

13 0-0   R-K1

14 KR-Q1   B-N5

15 R-Q2

On 15 P-KR3, Black brings his bishop to K5, by way of R4 and N3.

15 . . .   Q-B1

16 N-QB5   B-R6!

A brilliant offer of a pawn. If 17 BxB QxB 18 NxNP N-KN5 19 N-B3 N(Q4)-K6 20 PxN NxKP (threatens mate at N7, and attacks the queen as well) 21 QxPch K-R1! (not 21 . . . KxQ 22 N-N5ch) 22 N-R4 R-KB1, and Black wins the queen, as a queen move is answered by 23 . . . R-B8ch, forcing mate.

17 B-B3   B-N5

18 B-N2   B-R6

19 B-B3   B-N5

Here Alekhine erroneously claimed a draw by recurrence of position. The position had occurred only twice, and even had it occurred three times, Black could not claim a draw because a draw by recurrence can be claimed only by the 'Player': i.e., the one whose turn it is to move. Had Réti now played 20 B-N2, Black could then have claimed successfully. Having a slight superiority in position, Réti decides to evade the draw. Not, of course, by allowing the exchange of his fianchetto bishop, as that would seriously weaken his white squares.

Alekhine may have made the absurd claim deliberately, to make Réti overconfident. (Purdy)

20 B-R1

Heaven be praised for this move! Had Réti played 20 B-N2 instead, the game could have been called a draw by repetition of position, and we should have been deprived of a masterpiece of combination play.

20 . . .   P-KR4!

Now that Réti has refused his offer of a draw, Alekhine begins his K-side attack. His immediate intention is to advance his king rook pawn to weaken White's KN3.

21 P-N4   P-R3

22 R-QB1   P-R5

23 P-R4   PxP

24 RPxP   Q-B2

The start of Alekhine's second combination.

25 P-N5

The prudent course was 25 P-K4! N-N3   26 Q-N3 N(N3)-Q2, with equal chances.

25 . . .   RPxP

26 PxP

Never suspecting Black's next move—a spectacular one!

Alekhine to move

Position after 26 PxP

Réti

26 . . .   R-K6!

Startling, to say the least. White must not take the rook, as after 27 PxR QxPch   28 B-N2 (if 28 K-B1 NxP is mate) NxP, and White cannot prevent mate, let alone save his queen.

Meanwhile, Black threatens 27 . . . RxPch.

27 N-B3   PxP

28 QxP   N-B6!

The fireworks continue. Most of the pieces on the board will soon be *en prise*.

29 QxQ   QxQ

30 NxQ   NxPch

31 K-R2

If 31 K-B1 NxPch   32 PxN BxN   33 BxB RxBch 34 K-N2 R(R1)-R6   35 R-Q8ch K-R2   36 R-R1ch K-N3   37 R-R3 R(B6)-N6, and White must give up the knight, or be mated in two moves by the rooks.

31 . . .   N-K5!

Putting a third rook *en prise*, Black begins a new combination which ends a dozen moves later in winning the knight at White's QN7, a piece far away from the scene of the fighting!

32 R-B4

White loses after 32 PxR N(K5)xR   33 R-B2 (or 33 NxN NxR) NxNch   34 BxN (34 K-N2 N-K8ch is even worse) 34 . . . BxB, when Black has gained a piece.

32 . . .   NxBP

Alekhine does not fall into 32 . . . NxR   33 NxN!, and two of Black's pieces are attacked, nor into 32 . . . BxN   33 R(B4)xN RxR   34 BxB N-B6 35 BxR NxB, and White is out of the woods.

33 B-N2

Avoids Black's threat of 33 . . . NxB   34 KxN BxNch followed by 35 . . . BxN.

33 . . .   B-K3

Gains a decisive tempo, the bishop vacating a square for the knight's use.

34 R(B4)-B2   N-N5ch!

35 K-R3

Obviously, 35 . . . K-R1 allowing 35 . . . R-R8ch is fatal.

35 . . .   N-K4 dis.ch

36 K-R2   RxN!

37 RxN

Taking the rook loses a piece at once: 37 BxR NxBch 38 K-N2 NxR.

37 . . .   N-N5ch!

38 K-R3   N-K6 dis.ch

39 K-R2   NxR

40 BxR   N-Q5!

The final move takes your breath away! If now
41 R-K3 NxBch   42 RxN B-Q4, and Black wins the
knight, which unfortunately cannot be protected by
the rook.

41 Resigns

A wonderful combination, marked by fantastic
maneuvering of the minor pieces.

99

White **A. Alekhine**   Black **N. Schwartz**
King's Indian Defence
London, 1926

The highlight of this remarkable game, one of fifteen
played blindfold simultaneously, is a scintillating
combination wherein Alekhine sacrifices a rook in
order to queen two pawns—both of which are immediately captured!

It's all part of the plot though, in this impressive
ending, which Alekhine himself considered one of his
best achievements in blindfold chess.

The pleasing, graceful blending of profound strategy
and lively tactics moves me to nominate it to occupy the
niche reserved for *The Immortal Blindfold Game* in
Caissa's Hall of Fame.

1 P-Q4   N-KB3

2 P-QB4   P-KN3

3 P-KN3   B-N2

4 B-N2   0-0

5 N-QB3   P-Q3

6 N-B3   N-B3

7 P-Q5   N-QR4

Two of Alekhine's opponents (in tournament play)
had tried 7 . . . N-N1 at this point—to their sorrow.

Sir George Thomas had been beaten in beautiful
style at Carlsbad in 1923, and so was Réti at New
York in 1924.

The text move is an improvement (for one move
only!) which could lead into the Yugoslav Variation.

8 Q-Q3   P-N3

Black intends to bring his knight to QB4, by way of
N2.

A better way to rescue the knight (which was
threatened by 9 P-QN4) was either by 8 . . . P-B4,
or by 8 . . . P-K4, after which 9 P-QN4 could be met
by 9 . . . P-K5.

9 N-Q4   N-N2

10 N-B6

What an outpost!

10 . . .   Q-Q2

11 0-0   P-QR4

12 P-N3   N-B4

13 Q-B2   B-N2

14 P-KR3

A preventive move against Black's knight swinging
over to K4 via N5.

14 . . .   QR-K1

15 P-R3

White prepares to evict the obtrusive knight by
16 P-QN4.

15 . . .   BxN

16 PxB   Q-B1

17 P-QN4   PxP

18 PxP   N-R3

'After this the knight will be buried alive,' says
Alekhine, 'but also 18 . . . QN-K5   19 N-QN5 was
anything but pleasant.'

19 R-R4   N-N1

20 P-N5

This stalemates the unlucky creature.

20 . . .   P-R3

21 R-R7

Notice how the great masters aim to get a rook on the seventh? There must be a valuable lesson in this!

21 . . .   P-K4

22 K-R2

More of this preventive stuff; after P-B4, White does not want to be bothered by . . . N-R4 in reply.

22 . . .   K-R2

23 P-B4   R-K2

24 PxP   RxP

25 B-B4   R(K4)-K1

After 25 . . . R-R4   26 N-Q5 NxN   27 PxN, the rook never gets out alive.

26 N-Q5   NxN

27 BxN   Q-Q1

28 P-R4   Q-K2

29 P-K3   K-R1

Unpins the knight pawn, and so threatens to win a piece by 30 . . . P-N4.

There is always a chance that the blindfold player will overlook the threat, assuming the king to have made a simple, waiting move.

30 K-N2

Two can play at that game! If now 30 . . . P-N4 31 PxP PxP 32 R-R1ch, and White wins at once.

30 . . .   P-B4

31 R-K1   K-R2

32 P-K4   B-K4

33 PxP   PxP

Now comes a brilliant twelve-move combination which wins a piece and the game.

The position, before the fireworks display, is shown in the next column.

34 P-B5!   NPxP

The pawn must be captured, as White threatened

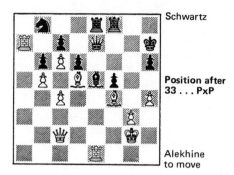

Schwartz

Position after
33 . . . PxP

Alekhine
to move

35 PxNP. Taking by 34 . . . QPxP is out of the question because of 35 RxB in reply.

35 P-N6   R-B1

36 Q-B3   KR-K1

Capturing the queen is disastrous: 36 . . . BxQ 37 RxQch K-N3 38 P-R5ch KxP (or 38 . . . K-B3 39 R-K6ch K-N2 40 BxRPch) 39 R-K6 K-N5 40 B-B3 mate.

37 BxB   PxB

38 QxKP!

This continuation, involving a rook sacrifice, had to be 'seen' earlier, or else the previous moves had no meaning.

38 . . .   QxQ

39 RxQ   RxR

40 RxPch   RxR

41 PxR   R-K1

The knight must stay put.

42 PxN(Q)   RxQ

43 B-K6!

This is the star move! White controls the queening square, and so wins the rook for a pawn. This is the kick which so often comes at the end of an Alekhine inspiration.

43 . . .   K-N3

44 P-B7   R-KB1

45 P-B8(Q)   RxQ

46 BxR   P-QB5

47 B-R6   P-B6

48 B-Q3   K-B3

Black could resign, but he has a little trap in reserve.

49 K-B3   K-K4

50 K-K3   P-R4

51 B-B2   K-B3

52 K-B4   K-N2

53 KxP   K-R3

Does he think that Alekhine, even with his eyes closed, will play 54 K-B6, allowing a stalemate?

54 K-B4!   Resigns

100

White **A. Kevitz** and **A. Pinkus**   Black **A. Alekhine**
Réti's Opening
New York, 1929

The artistry and dramatic richness of Alekhine's play is best described in the German word *ideenreich*.

Not the least attractive feature of this game, is the king's journey from one end of the board to the other, before Alekhine embarks on the final combination.

This is a beautiful, beautiful game, and a particular favourite of mine.

1 N-KB3   N-KB3

2 P-B4   P-QN3

3 P-KN3   B-N2

4 B-N2   P-K4

5 N-B3   B-N5

6 0-0   BxN

7 NPxB

Both sides are content with the exchange of pieces:

White, that he has the two bishops; Black, that his opponent is left with a doubled pawn.

7 ...   P-Q3

With so many pawns controlling black squares, Alekhine had little use for his king bishop.

8 P-Q4   P-K5

9 N-R4   0-0

10 P-B3   PxP

11 BxP

This way of recapturing activates White's pieces, but renders his king pawn backward.

11 ...   N-K5

12 Q-Q3   R-K1

13 P-Q5

This interrupts the pressure of Black's bishop along the long diagonal, but in return Black has the use of the splendid QB4 square for his knight.

From this spot (ideal, since there is no fear of being annoyed by pawns) the knight remains a constant menace to the opponent.

13 ...   N-B4

14 Q-Q4   QN-Q2

15 B-R5   N-K4

Of course not 15 . . . P-N3, as Alekhine does not voluntarily create organic weaknesses in his pawn structure.

16 B-KB4   Q-Q2

The queen seizes an important diagonal, meanwhile adding her protection to the delicate bishop pawn.

The attempt to win a piece instead by 16 . . . P-N3 17 B-B3 P-KN4 could be disastrous, as Alekhine shows, the continuation being: 18 BxN PxB 19 Q-N4 P-KR4 20 QxRP PxN 21 B-K4! NxB 22 QxBPch K-R1 23 Q-R5ch K-N1 24 R-B7, and White wins!

17 N-B3   N-N3

18 N-Q2   Q-R6

19 BxN

If 19 B-R6 (hoping to catch the queen by 19 . . . PxB 20 B-N4) the reply 19 . . . R-K4 ruins that little scheme.

19 . . .   RPxB

20 P-K4   P-KB3

Stops the king pawn dead in its tracks. Black will next double rooks on the king file, and bring enormous pressure on the pawn.

21 QR-K1   P-KN4

This placing of all seven pawns on black squares increases the effectiveness of Alekhine's white-squared bishop.

22 B-K3   R-K2

23 K-R1   QR-K1

24 B-N1   B-B1

Alekhine is in no hurry to capture the king pawn, as after 24 . . . NxP   25 NxN RxN   26 RxR RxR   27 QxR QxR   28 Q-K8ch K-R2   29 Q-R5ch, White draws by perpetual check.

25 R-B3   B-N5

26 R(B3)-K3   Q-R4

Alekhine could have won the king pawn by concentrating all his fury on it, say by . . . Q-R2, then . . . B→R4→N3, and then force an ending where he had the advantage of an extra pawn.

But in the light of White's weaknesses—the doubled pawns, the backward king pawn, and the weak light-colored squares—he felt justified in adopting more decisive measures.

'The preliminary maneuver takes, true enough, fifteen more moves,' says Alekhine, 'but the success of the scheme gives the game an artistic touch it would otherwise lack.'

Black's last move, incidentally, threatens 27 . . . NxP   28 N(or R)xN B-B6ch, and mate next move.

27 K-N2   B-R6ch

28 K-R1   Q-N5

29 B-B2   P-QR4

30 B-N1   P-R5

Prevents 31 N-N3, and a possible exchange of knights.

31 B-B2   R-K4

32 B-N1   R(K1)-K2

33 B-B2

This is the position, with Black to move:

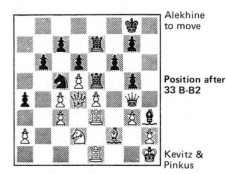

Alekhine
to move

Position after
33 B-B2

Kevitz &
Pinkus

33 . . .   K-B2!

Who but an Alekhine would have seen the necessity for moving the king over to the opposite end of the board, before starting the final combination? The combination that this piece of strategy initiates is one of the most attractive in the Alekhine repertoire.

34 B-N1   K-K1

35 B-B2   K-Q1

36 B-N1   K-B1

37 B-B2   K-N2

38 B-N1   K-R3

39 B-B2   Q-R4

Another bit of strategy: the queen and bishop must exchange places.

40 B-N1   B-N5

41 K-N2   Q-R6ch

42 K-R1   P-N3

43 B-B2

The preparations are complete; so Alekhine starts the wheels of the combination going.

This is the position, with Black to play:

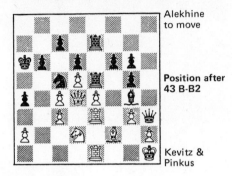

Alekhine
to move

Position after
43 B-B2

Kevitz &
Pinkus

43 ...   P-B4!

44 PxP   PxP

45 RxR

On 45 B-N1 N-K5, threatening 46 . . . NxN   47 QxN B-B6ch forces the win. If White (after 45 . . . N-K5) tries 46 NxN, then 46 . . . RxN   47 RxR B-B6 is mate, or if 46 N-B1, P-B5, and Black pauses for a reply.

45 ...   PxR

And now if White takes the king pawn, he loses by this fascinating combination: 46 RxP RxR   47 QxR B-B6ch!   48 NxB Q-B8ch   49 N-N1 (or 49 B-N1

QxN mate!) N-Q6!, and the knight's attack on the queen, together with the threat of 50 . . . NxB mate, will exact a resignation.

46 Q-K3   P-K5

47 P-Q6!

This gives Black a chance to go wrong.

The alternative 47 QxNP loses after 47 . . . R-R2 48 B-N1 N-Q6 (threatens 49 . . . N-B7ch   50 BxN QxRP mate)   49 R-KB1 QxR!   50 NxQ B-B6 mate.

47 ...   PxP

48 B-N1!

Very ingenious! If Black wins a rook by force, he gets mated!

After 48 . . . B-B6ch   49 NxB PxN   50 QxBP RxR 51 Q-R8 is mate!

48 ...   P-B5!

But Alekhine is not caught so easily!

49 Resigns

After 49 PxP B-B6ch   50 NxB PxN (now the pawn is protected)   51 Q-B2 RxR, and White must yield.

This was one of three games, played simultaneously against teams of consulting masters. Despite the difficulties he faced, Alekhine managed to turn out a masterpiece of the highest order, worthy of his imprimatur.

When he tried to cross the Polish border in 1935, Alekhine was asked to produce proofs of his identity. Lacking these documents, Alekhine said to the Guard, 'I am Alexander Alekhine, Chess Champion of the World. This is my cat. Her name is *Chess.* I need no passport!'

This was characteristic of Alekhine, and reminiscent of Oscar Wilde's arrival in America. When he was asked by the Customs Officer if he had anything to declare, he responded, 'I have nothing to declare but my genius.'

Capablanca

Capablanca was a genius, the greatest ever produced by chess.

He handled every phase of the game with equal facility. He was superb in the opening, marvelous in the midgame, and wonderful in the ending.

He could see complicated combinations in a flash, and work out the details with astonishing speed and accuracy. 'What others could not see in a month's study, he saw at a glance,' says Fine. His technique was flawless, and his style so graceful and elegant as to make chess look easy. No player in all the world's history has equalled in artistry, logic, and crystalline clarity the masterpieces produced by Capablanca.

The four world champions who were contemporaries of Capablanca expressed their admiration for this master of masters, thus:

Euwe. In the endgame and in pure position play, Capablanca had no peer. As a tactician Capablanca was unsurpassable; his many meetings with combinative players provide the proof.

Botvinnik. Capablanca was the greatest talent, he made the best impression on me of all the champions I have met.

Alekhine. Capablanca was snatched from the chess world too soon. With his death we have lost the greatest genius of chess. There will never be anyone equal to him.

Lasker. I have known many chess players, but only one genius, Capablanca.

The ultimate compliment for the Kings of Chess from Morphy to Alekhine is to compare their play to that of Capablanca's. Here are some of the tributes:

Morphy. Of a Morphy game against Boden, König says, 'Morphy's endgame play recalls Capablanca's easy, elegant style.'

Alekhine. Winter praises Alekhine's outstanding positional play against Bogolyubov in the fifth game of their 1929 match, with: 'A very fine positional game by Alekhine. It might have been played by Capablanca, the highest praise that can be given to this sort of game.'

Botvinnik. Of the beautiful Botvinnik win against Alekhine at Avro in 1938, Reinfeld says, 'Botvinnik's masterly treatment bears comparison with Capablanca's finest efforts in this field.'

Smyslov. 'The clarity and logic of Smyslov's play,' says Stahlberg in his notes to the Botvinnik-Smyslov match in 1957, 'is highly reminiscent of Capablanca. The new World's Champion has a more modern opening repertoire than the famous Cuban, but he plays with the same amazing precision, is calm and collected in difficult positions, and is a big master of the endgame. Like Capablanca, he solves simply what at first sight are difficult problems arising in the course of the game.'

Petrosian. 'Capablanca could not have done better at the height of his powers,' says O'Kelly, commenting on the Petrosian-Smyslov 1961 masterpiece.

Karpov. Szabo says, 'Karpov's style reminds us of Capablanca's—once he has a small advantage in the middle-game, you can be sure his opponent will not be able to get out of his embrace.'

Fischer. Discussing Fischer's technique in the Larsen-Fischer game at Santa Monica in 1966, Robert Byrne says, 'Fischer's play here reminds one of none other than Capablanca in his heyday. His opening is a model of clarity in its logical and direct development which prevents White from obtaining any initiative. The method is carried through into the middle game until White's chances have been reduced to zero. Finally the exploitation of White's weaknesses is carried out with that simple and lucid efficiency for which his great Cuban predecessor was famous. And the same question arises out of Fischer's play as it often did out of Capablanca's—how does he get such an incisive conclusion out of such a modest beginning? Don't expect me to answer that as regards Fischer—no one ever answered it in regard to Capablanca.'

Capablanca's achievements in tournament and match play are astonishing. Here are a few record-breakers:

Capablanca played 567 tournament and match games, of which he won 296 games, drew 236, and lost 35, showing a 5½ per cent loss against total games played.

Alekhine (his closest rival) played 1097 tournament and match games, of which he won 623 games, drew 361, and lost 113, showing a 10 per cent loss against total games played.

Lasker (another formidable rival) played 519 tournament and match games, of which he won 298 games, drew 164, and lost 57, showing an 11 per cent loss against total games played.

All the games that Capablanca lost in tournament and match play in the course of a lifetime career in chess are contained in a book called *Capablanca's Samtliche Verlustpartien.* The book is only 1/64th of an inch thick, but then not much space is needed to print the scores of 35 games!

In 10 years of tournament and match chess (1914-24), including the match with Lasker for the World's Championship, Capablanca lost only one game!

Capablanca came first or second in 30 out of the 35 tournaments in which he played.

Attacking players (and many positional ones as well) could make little or no impression on Capablanca, some of the scores being as follows:

Opponent	Capa's Wins	Draws	Capa's losses
Janowsky	9	1	1
Marshall	20	29	2
Yates	8	3	0
Colle	4	0	0
Bogolyubov	5	2	0
Mieses	2	0	0
Tartakover	4	8	0
Kostić	5	5	0
Nimzowitsch	4	6	0
Vidmar	3	6	0
Lasker	6	16	2
Grand totals	*70*	*76*	*5 (Phenomenal!)*

Some of the tournaments deserve brief mention:

Capablanca won first prize in his début at an International Tournament, coming in ahead of Rubinstein, Vidmar, Marshall, Nimzowitsch, and Tarrasch, incidentally carrying off the first brilliancy prize as well.

At New York in 1913, Capablanca won all 11 games in a row.

At Hastings in 1919, his score was 10 wins and one draw.

At London in 1922, Capablanca came in first ahead of Alekhine, Vidmar, Rubinstein, and Bogolyubov, losing no games.

At New York in 1927, to pick a challenger to the title, Capablanca came in first, ahead of the runner-up Alekhine by 2½ points.

At Moscow in 1936, in a double-round tournament, Capablanca won first prize ahead of Botvinnik, Flohr, and Lasker.

At Nottingham in 1936, where the entry list included five past, present, and future world champions, Capablanca tied with Botvinnik for first and second, ahead of Alekhine, Lasker, Euwe, Fine, and Reshevsky.

Capablanca won five of the six matches in which he engaged, the victims being Corzo (when Capablanca was 12) by 4 wins to 2, Marshall by 8 wins to 1, Kostić by 5 wins to 0, Lasker by 4 wins to 0, and Euwe by 2 wins to 0.

The one match Capablanca lost was to Alekhine for the World's Championship in 1927. Capablanca won 3 games, lost 6, and 25 games were drawn. The match was hard-fought, the last game in fact (one of Alekhine's very best) lasting 82 moves! It is safe to say that at least 8 of the 9 wins were masterpieces of a high order of merit.

Capablanca's speed in ten-second chess is legendary, as well as his speed and accuracy in simultaneous play.

Two of his simultaneous records deserve to be noted here:

On a tour made in 1909, Capablanca played simultaneous chess, and games with individual opponents, with this remarkable result: out of 720 games, 686 wins, 20 drawn games, and only 14 losses! (At that time, Capablanca was not yet recognized as a master!.)

Capablanca played 103 games simultaneously in Cleveland in 1922. While the total number of games has been exceeded, the phenomenal number of wins achieved has never been approached. Capablanca won 102 games, lost none, and allowed one player to escape with a draw!

Capablanca's most important contributions to chess literature are *My chess career, Chess fundamentals,* and *A primer of chess.* The last two may have been intended as elementary texts, but they are gold mines of instruction for almost any grade of player. *My chess career* is absolutely fascinating, and I recommend it to you whether you have read it before or not. The games are top-drawer, and the story of Capablanca's early days in the chess arena is absorbing.

I consider Capablanca the greatest chess player of all time.

101

White **J.R. Capablanca**   Black **J. Corzo**
Queen's Pawn Opening
Havana, 1900

This game, played by Capablanca at the age of twelve, is nothing less than magnificent.

It shows an astonishing maturity in its various aspects

There is the characteristic quick sight of the board, reflected in his turning out a 60-move masterpiece 42 minutes!

There is deep feeling for strategy in the middle-game maneuvering.

There is tactical play to secure a positional advantage, the complications therein being handled with consummate ease.

There is a sacrifice of a queen, the brilliancy of which is enhanced by its being offered as a matter of course.

Finally, there is the transition to an ending, which is played with flawless accuracy.

In my opinion, it is the finest game ever played by any chess prodigy.

1 P-Q4   P-Q4

2 N-KB3   P-QB4

3 P-K3   N-QB3

4 P-QN3   P-K3

5 B-N2   N-B3

6 QN-Q2   PxP

7 PxP

The proper way to recapture. White gets a grip on the strong point K5 and also opens the king file for the use of his rook later on.

7 ...   B-Q3

8 B-Q3   0-0

9 0-0   N-KR4

Begins a maneuver which loses time, and one should avoid losing time when playing prodigies.

A better course was either 9 ... N-QN5   10 B-K2 N-K5 followed by 11 P-B4, or simple development of the queen bishop by 9 . . . P-QN3 and 10 . . . B-N2.

10 P-N3

This prevents an incursion by the knight at Black's B5.

10 ...   P-B4

Black's forces are arranged in a stonewall formation, a hard defence to break through.

A drawback, though, is the weakening of his K4 square—on which a knight promptly settles!

11 N-K5   N-B3

12 P-KB4   BxN

Centralization by 12 . . . Q-K2 (with the positional threat of 13 . . . B-R6)   13 P-QR3 N-K5 was more to the point.

13 BPxB   N-KN5

On 13 . . . N-K5 instead, there follows 14 BxN BPxB (if 14 . . . QPxB   15 N-B4)   15 Q-K2, and White keeps the initiative.

14 Q-K2   Q-N3

15 N-B3   B-Q2

The bishop must be brought out, if only to establish communication between the rooks. Its prospects look bleak, though, with so many pawns blocking its path.

Black could eliminate one of the bishops by 15 . . . N-N5   16 B-R3 R-Q1   17 BxN QxB, but after 18 P-B4 it's hard going.

16 P-QR3

Now even that opportunity is denied him.

16 ...   K-R1

17 P-R3   N-R3

18 Q-B2   N-B2

19 K-N2   P-N4

This attempt to attack leaves Black with a minute weakness on the long diagonal. But who would suspect danger from White's harmless-looking queen bishop?

20 P-KN4!

The first move in the grand plan to demolish the whole center.

20 . . .   N-K2

Black is careful not to make a hasty move with his bishop pawn. *Par exemple*, if 20 . . . PxP   21 PxP followed by 22 R-R1 triggers off a K-side attack, or if 20 . . . P-B5   21 R-R1 followed by 22 P-KR4 pries open the rook file against the king.

21 Q-K3   R-KN1

22 QR-K1   N-N3

23 PxP   N-B5ch

24 K-R2   NxB

25 QxN   PxP

Preparations are complete, and White is ready to break things wide open. This is the position:

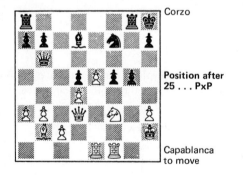

Corzo

Position after 25 . . . PxP

Capablanca to move

26 P-B4!

This is to eliminate Black's queen pawn. With its disappearance, White will be left with two passed pawns in the center, and the prospect of clearing the long diagonal for the bishop patiently waiting in the background.

26 . . .   Q-K3

27 PxP   QxQP

28 P-K6!

The combinations begin! Black is forced to attack the queen, as 28 . . . BxP loses a piece by 29 RxB (29 . . . QxR   30 P-Q5 dis.ch wins the queen).

28 . . .   B-N4

29 QxB!

Brilliant, forceful, and decisive—the way of a genius! There may have been 'a much simpler win,' as a commentator says, by 29 Q-Q2 BxR   30 PxN QxBP (if 30 . . . QxN   31 P-Q5ch! R-N2   32 R-K8ch and wins)   31 P-Q5ch R-N2   32 NxP Q-N3   33 R-K7 R-KN1   34 N-B7ch and White wins.

We may be grateful though that Capablanca, who saw this line of play, preferred the queen sacrifice, as that was the continuation he had in mind when he played 28 P-K6. *There was no reason to look for other ways to win.*

29 . . .   QxQ

30 P-Q5 dis.ch   R-N2

31 PxN   P-KR3

If Black tries to counter-attack by 31 . . . QxQP or 31 . . . QxNP   32 R-K8ch forces mate, while on 31 . . . R-KB1 Capablanca intended 32 N-Q4 (attacks the queen and threatens 33 N-K6) QxQP   33 R-K8 QxBP (or 33 . . . R(N2)xP   34 NxPch K-N1   35 N-R6 mate)   34 RxRch QxR   35 NxP and White wins.

32 N-Q4   QxR

Against 32 . . . Q-Q2, Capablanca had prepared a beautiful win. His analysis goes: 32 . . . Q-Q2   33 NxP QxBP   34 BxRch K-R2 (if 34 . . . K-N1   35 NxPch wins the queen)   35 R-K7 winning the queen, as 35 . . . QxP (clearly 35 . . . Q-R4   36 B-K5 dis.ch K-N1   37 R-N7ch K-B1   38 N-Q6 dis. ch leads to mate)   36 B-K5ch K-N3   37 R-N7ch K-R4   38 N-N3ch K-R5   39 R-B4ch PxR   40 R-N4 is mate!

33 RxQ   RxP

34 RxP   RxR

35 NxR dis.ch   K-R2

Corzo

Position after
35 ... K-R2

Capablanca
to move

36 N-K7
The master's touch! This cuts the king off from
approaching the precious queen pawn.

36 ...   R-KB1

37 K-N2
From this point on, Capablanca demonstrates that he
had the requisite technique, even as a boy, to win an
ending precisely and painlessly, as though it were a
composed study entitled *White to play and win*.

37 ...   P-KR4

38 P-Q6   P-N5

39 PxP   PxP

40 B-K5   K-R3

41 P-Q7
Threatens 42 B-B7 and P-Q8(Q), winning the rook.

41 ...   R-Q1

42 N-N8ch!
'Otra jugada de maestro!' says Corzo himself,
admiringly.

42 ...   RxN
Or 42 ... K-N3   43 N-B6 K-B2   44 B-B7, and
Black must part with his rook.

43 B-B6   K-N3

44 P-Q8(Q)   RxQ

45 BxR   P-N4

46 K-B2   K-B4

47 K-K3   K-K4

48 K-Q3   K-Q4

49 K-B3   P-N6

50 B-R4   P-N7

51 B-B2   P-R4

52 P-N4   K-K5

53 B-N6
But not 53 PxP, which allows a draw, since the bishop
does not control the rook pawn's queening square.

53 ...   K-Q4

54 K-Q3   K-B3

55 B-N1   K-Q4

56 B-R2   K-B3

57 K-Q4   P-R5

58 K-K5   K-N3

59 K-Q5   K-R3

60 K-B5!
Destroys Black's last hope! The natural move
60 K-B6 allows 60 ... P-N8(Q)   61 BxQ, and Black
escapes with a draw by stalemate.
    But Capablanca did not fall into traps, either as a
child prodigy, or in his entire chess career.

60 ...   Resigns
A typical Capablanca game—a masterpiece!

102

White **F.J. Marshall**   Black **J.R. Capablanca**
Queen's Gambit Declined
23rd Match Game, New York, 1909

In this delightful book *200 open games*, David Bronstein
writes,
    'Why is so little attention paid in our time to the end-
game?

Perhaps it is because that, whilst the great Capablanca was alive, few people could boast about their endgame!'

Capablanca himself stressed the importance of the endgame when he said, 'In order to improve your game, you must study the endgame before anything else, for whereas the endings can be studied and mastered by themselves, *the middle-game and the opening must be studied in relation to the endgame.'*

It may be paradoxical but Capablanca's endings often began from the opening, as in this game against Marshall.

As early as the 12th move, Capablanca has secured an endgame advantage in his three pawns to two on the Q-side. What more does a Capablanca need?

True, there are some interesting midgame maneuvers, but essentially the whole game is an endgame study, and in Capablanca's capable hands it is that, and more. It is an entertainment.

1 P-Q4   P-Q4

2 P-QB4   P-K3

3 N-QB3   P-QB4

Highly recommended by Tarrasch, this defence is, as he says, 'based on the undeniably correct idea that in the queen's gambit, . . . P-QB4 is the freeing move for Black, and must therefore be made as soon as possible. By this defence Black gets a fine, free game for his pieces, but an isolated queen's pawn.'

Neglected for many years (as the thought of being left with an isolated queen's pawn struck terror into the hearts of most masters) the Tarrasch Defence has had a successful revival recently, even to the extent of helping Spassky attain the world championship in 1966.

4 BPxP   KPxP

5 N-B3   N-QB3

6 P-KN3   B-K3

7 B-N2   B-K2

8 0-0   N-B3

9 B-N5

A better line is 9 PxP BxP 10 N-QR4 B-K2 11 B-K3 as in the game won by Réti against Tarrasch at Pistyan in 1922.

9 . . .   N-K5!

This excellent move, with which Mieses subdued Rubinstein in their match, impressed Capablanca and induced him to try it against Marshall.

10 BxB

It's too late to turn back now, as 10 B-K3 NxN 11 PxN P-B5 is in Black's favour.

10 . . .   QxB

11 N-K5

'One of those nervous attacking moves that one attempts when no safe, solid moves are at hand,' says Tarrasch.

Marshall apparently did not like the looks of 11 PxP NxN 12 PxN QxP, when his Q-side is ripped up.

11 . . .   NxQP!

This is superior to 11 . . . NxN(B6) 12 PxN NxN 13 PxN Q-Q2 14 P-KB4 0-0 15 Q-B2, when White has a decent position.

12 NxN   PxN

13 P-K3

But not 13 BxP B-R6, and at one stroke Black opens an attack on three pieces!

13 . . .   N-B6ch

14 NxN

Somewhat better (though still to Black's advantage) was 14 BxN PxB 15 Q-R4ch K-B1!

14 . . .   PxN

15 QxP   0-0

'I think the American Champion was overawed by the will and extraordinary calm of his young adversary,' says Goetz. 'Since Morphy, no one has ever seen such *sang-froid* in so young a player.'

16 KR-B1

Marshall was not attracted to 16 QxP, as the continu-

ation 16 . . . QxQ   17 BxQ QR-N1   18 B-K4 RxP
left Black with a passed pawn and a rook on the seventh
—clearly with much the better of it.

The move he selects is no great improvement,
since his rook bites on granite, in Nimzowitsch's
felicitous expression.

Marshall should have started the pawns rolling on
the K-side, where he has the majority, say by 16 P-K4,
followed by Q-K3, P-B4 and P-B5. He would then have
the makings of an attack.

Capablanca's comment on Marshall's move is illuminating from the psychological standpoint: 'White's
inactivity on his stronger wing took away all the
chances he had of drawing the game.' No mention is
made of the possibility of Marshall winning the
game!

16 . . .   QR-N1

17 Q-K4

Pins the bishop in preparation for 18 B-R3, which
would lead to an exchange of bishops, or force the
weakening 18 . . . P-B4.

17 . . .   Q-B2

18 R-B3

This move looks aggressive, but accomplishes little,
as the rook stays at this square for the next ten
moves.

This is the position, with Black to move:

Capablanca
to move

Position after
18 R-B3

Marshall

18 . . .   P-QN4!

Capablanca starts playing out his trumps—the Q-side
pawn majority. From now on the pawns will push on
every chance they get.

19 P-QR3   P-B5

A bit of a trap here. On 20 P-N3, the reply 20 . . .
Q-R4 (attacking the rook) either wins the knight pawn
or compels its advance, leaving Black with a powerful
passed pawn.

20 B-B3   KR-Q1

Capablanca never misses a trick! He seizes the only
open file.

As Tarrasch puts it, 'Capablanca points out all his
opponent's inexactitudes to him: first he gets the
Q-side majority into motion, and now he takes command of the queen file.'

21 R-Q1   RxRch

22 BxR   R-Q1

Lasker said at this point, 'Capablanca has full command of the board. His play is an example of how
slight advantages should be utilized.'

Capablanca (pleased) commented, 'No better
compliment is required.'

23 B-B3   P-N3!

This provides an outlet for the king, and frees the
rook from guarding the last rank, so that it may invade enemy territory.

Note that 24 R-B2 (to prevent the rook from
coming in) is penalized by 24 . . . B-B4, garnering a
whole rook for Black.

24 Q-B6   Q-K4!

This is better than 24 . . . QxQ   25 BxQ, when
Black must lose a tempo guarding the knight pawn.

25 Q-K4   QxQ

26 BxQ

A glance at the position indicates that
'Things are seldom what they seem
(Skim milk masquerades as cream).'
Theoretically, White's position is superior, as his

bishop occupies a square different in colour than those occupied by his pawns, while Black's light-squared bishop is restricted in its movements by the five black pawns standing on light-coloured squares.

Which proves once again that formulas, axioms, theorems, and conventions are generalities, and must be applied with discretion. Knowing when to violate the principles governing position play is the mark of the master.

26 . . .   R-Q8ch!

This prevents the king from coming to the center, and expedites the rook's chief function in the end-game—to get behind the pawns.

27 K-N2   P-QR4

The key to Black's strategy: he will advance the Q-side pawns, and also institute an attack on White's queen knight pawn—a weak point.

28 R-B2   P-N5

29 PxP   PxP

30 B-B3

If White tries to get the king into play by 30 K-B3, he might fall into this embarrassing loss: 30 . . . P-N6   31 R-K2 B-R6!, and suddenly White's rook is surrounded, and threatened with capture by 32 . . . B-B8.

30 . . .   R-QN8

31 B-K2   P-N6!

The proper caper. If instead 31 . . . P-B6   32 PxP P-N6   33 R-Q2 P-N7 (hoping for 34 . . . R-N8ch followed by queening the pawn)   34 B-Q3, and the precious pawn is lost.

32 R-Q2

If 32 R-B3 RxP   33 BxP R-B7, and Black wins a piece by this little finesse.

32 . . .   R-QB8

With a threat of 33 . . . R-B7, to which there is no defence.

33 B-Q1

The bishop prevents the rook move, but at the cost of its life.

33 . . .   P-B6

34 PxP   P-N7

35 RxP

Clearly, not 35 B-B2 (which seems to halt the pawn), as 35 . . . RxB wins instantly.

35 . . .   RxB

36 R-B2

The position, with Black to move:

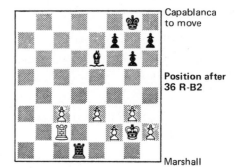

Capablanca to move

Position after 36 R-B2

Marshall

The rest could be a textbook lesson in the art of winning a won game. Capablanca, with a slight material advantage, brings the game to a conclusion with a few simple, energetic moves.

36 . . .   B-B4

This drives the rook away from its best post, behind the passed pawn.

37 R-N2   R-QB8

And, adding insult to injury, Capablanca moves *his* rook behind the dangerous pawn.

38 R-N3   B-K5ch

Forces the king to the edge of the board, as 38 P-B3 costs a pawn after 38 . . . R-B7ch.

39 K-R3   R-B7

40 P-KB4   P-R4

Threatens quick mate beginning with 41 . . . B-B4ch
42 K-R4 RxPch   43 K-N5 K-N2.

41 P-N4   PxPch

42 KxP   RxRP

43 R-N4   P-B4ch

44 K-N3

On 44 K-N5 K-N2 forces mate.

44 . . .   R-K7

45 R-B4   RxPch

46 K-R4   K-N2

47 R-B7ch   K-B3

48 R-Q7   B-N7

49 R-Q6ch   K-N2

Now if 50 R-Q7ch K-R3 followed by 51 . . . R-R6
mate. Or if 50 K-N5 R-N6ch   51 K-R4 R-N5 is mate.

Capablanca himself considered this game to be one of
the most accurate he had ever played.

103

White **J.R. Capablanca**   Black **R. Blanco**
French Defence
Havana, 1913

The story of this game can be told in a few words:

Capablanca creates a weakness in his opponent's
position at K3, in the form of a backward pawn. On this
weakness he concentrates his forces. So effective is this,
that when the pawn disappears, the weakness remains!

Capablanca's play is crisp, clear, harmonious—in a
word, artistic.

Dr. Lasker praised the game highly, saying, 'If White's
play were properly analyzed, it might be found that
there was no way to improve it.'

1 P-K4   P-K3

2 P-Q4   P-Q4

3 N-QB3   PxP

Though favoured by Rubinstein, this line is weak, as
it abandons the center. The simple 3 . . . N-KB3 is
preferable.

4 NxP   QN-Q2

5 N-KB3   KN-B3

6 NxNch   NxN

7 N-K5

What's this? Capablanca seems to be violating what
he himself emphasized as one of the general principles
in the opening, 'Do not move the same piece twice
before full development has taken place.'

Capablanca explains that he wanted to try this
move, shown him by M. Ayala, a talented amateur. The
idea is to prevent the development of the queen bishop
at N2 (after 7 . . . P-QN3), the usual procedure in this
variation of the French.

The reply now to 7 . . . P-QN3 would be 8 B-N5ch,
ruining Black's plans.

7 . . .   B-Q3

A better spot for the bishop is K2, anticipating a pin
of the knight.

Black's threat with the text move is to win a pawn
by 8 . . . BxN   9 PxB QxQch   10 KxQ N-N5.

8 Q-B3

Capablanca's own comment: '8 B-KN5 might be
better. The text move gives Black an opportunity of
which he does not avail himself.'

8 . . .   P-B3

(Capablanca again) '8 . . . P-B4 was the right move.
It might have led to complications in which Black
might have held his own; at least, White's play would
be very difficult. The text move accomplishes nothing,
and puts Black in an altogether defensive position.
The veiled threat . . . BxN followed by . . . Q-R4ch
is easily met.'

9 P-B3

The attempt to win a couple of pawns by 9 NxQBP
PxN   10 QxPch B-Q2   11 QxB(Q6) is a will-o'-the-

wisp, as Black simply answers 9 NxQBP with
9 . . . Q-B2, and regains the pawn.

9 . . . 0-0

10 B-KN5 B-K2

A tacit admission that the bishop should have been
posted at K2 in the first place.

11 B-Q3

More than routine development, this threatens to
weaken Black's K-side by forcing the advance of one
of the pawns guarding the king.

White intends 12 Q-R3 next move, with the threat
of 13 BxN, when Black is helpless to recapture. This
would compel him to weaken his position seriously
by 12 . . . P-KN3 (not 12 . . . P-KR3, which allows
the winning sacrifice 13 BxP).

11 . . . N-K1

12 Q-R3 P-KB4

For the time being, Black is safe from attack, but at
the cost of being saddled with an organic weakness
in his backward king pawn.

Every move from now on, as Capablanca says, is
directed to make the weak king pawn untenable, or
to profit by the inactivity of the Black pieces defending the pawn, in order to improve the position of
White at other points.

13 BxB

The exchange eliminates a chief defender of the
weakened black squares.

13 . . . QxB

14 0-0 R-B3

15 KR-K1!

Opens fire (even if only indirectly) on the weak point.

Black's game may be lost strategically but it still
needs precise technique to consummate the win.

15 . . . N-Q3

16 R-K2 B-Q2

17 QR-K1 R-K1

18 P-QB4 N-B2

A subtle move, tempting White to win a pawn. The
play would go like this: 19 NxB QxN 20 BxP
N-N4 21 Q-N4 RxB 22 P-KR4 P-KR4 (of course
not 22 . . . N-B2 23 QxR, and Black dare not take
the queen, the penalty being mate in two) 23 QxR
PxQ 24 RxRch K-R2 25 PxN QxP, and a win for
White is out of the question.

But Capablanca is not lured into premature action.

19 P-Q5!

Capturing twice at Q5 leads to ruin—total ruin. After
19 . . . BPxP 20 PxP PxP there follows 21 NxB,
and White wins everything in sight.

19 . . . NxN

20 RxN P-KN3

21 Q-R4 K-N2

22 Q-Q4!

Strategically, the queen centralizes her position.

Tactically, she pins the king rook.

Practically, she supports a threat to win the king
pawn or the queen rook pawn.

22 . . . P-B4

23 Q-B3 P-N3

Black probably feared 24 Q-R5 P-QR3 25 Q-N6
B-B1 26 P-Q6, and the queen bishop pawn falls.

Black's position is in any case untenable, his
pieces being tied down to defending the king pawn,
while White's pieces have complete freedom of
action.

24 PxP B-B1

Clearly Black may not recapture at once, but he hopes
to pick up the pawn soon.

Undeniably, Capablanca has the advantage, but
how does he bring it to fruition?

The position is shown on page 291.

25 B-K2!

A profound maneuver, this retreat must have come as
a surprise to Black. The bishop is to be brought around
to Q5, where it will help paralyze the opponent.

Blanco

Position after
24 . . . B-B1

Capablanca
to move

25 . . .   BxP

26 B-B3

The bishop continues on its little trip. Meanwhile
there is a threat of 27 RxB, winning a piece.

26 . . .   K-B2

Black's forces are huddled together like sheep in a
thunderstorm.

27 B-Q5   Q-Q3

28 Q-K3

White intends to bring his queen to R6, and then
advance his rook pawn to R5 to break up the king's
pawn-shelter.

28 . . .   R-K2

If 28 . . . K-N2, to prevent the queen's intrusion,
29 BxB wins a piece.

29 Q-R6!   K-N1

30 P-KR4!   P-R3

31 P-R5   P-B5

32 PxP

Begins a pretty concluding combination.

32 . . .   PxP

If 32 . . . RxP instead, 33 RxB, and Black can choose
one of these finishes:

(a) 33 . . . RxQ   34 R-N6 dbl.ch and mate next move.

(b) 33 . . . R(N3)xR   34 RxR and wins.

(c) 33 . . . R(K2)xR   34 QxRch PxR   35 RxR and

wins, as the queen cannot escape capture by discovered
attack.

(Capablanca does not mention any of these possibilities, probably considering them to be elementary).

33 RxB

Now if 33 . . .   R(K2)xR   34 RxR RxR   35 QxPch
followed by 36 QxR leaves White a piece ahead.

33 . . .   Resigns

104

White **O.S. Bernstein**   Black **J.R. Capablanca**
Queen's Gambit Declined
Exhibition Game, Moscow, 1914

Dr. Bernstein and Capablanca met three times over the
board, each time enriching us with a masterpiece.

At San Sebastian in 1911, Capablanca beat Bertstein
so impressively as to be awarded the First Brilliancy
Prize.

At St. Petersburg in 1914, Capablanca won gloriously,
and again received the First Prize for Brilliancy.

Now a preamble about this beauty:

Frank Marshall once asked Capablanca what game he
regarded as his (Capablanca's) best. The reply was, 'It is
difficult to say; so much depends on the point of view.
There are three possible types of best game—a fine attack,
a brilliant defence, or a purely artistic treatment.'

Marshall then asked which he considered his best game
from the artistic point of view, and Capablanca's answer
was, 'I think my most finished and artistic game was the
one I played against Dr. Bernstein on February 4, 1914.'

1 P-Q4   P-Q4

2 P-QB4   P-K3

3 N-QB3   N-KB3

4 N-B3   B-K2

5 B-N5   O-O

6 P-K3 QN-Q2

7 R-B1 P-QN3

8 PxP PxP

9 Q-R4 B-N2

10 B-QR6 BxB

11 QxB P-B4

12 BxN

There was no hurry about this move, which releases the pressure.

12 ... NxB

13 PxP PxP

Black is left with two 'hanging pawns.' Such pawns are notoriously weak, and require constant care.

Occasionally, though, they become obstreperous, by their threats to advance and spearhead a counter-attack.

14 0-0 Q-N3

15 Q-K2

The queen chooses to retreat in lieu of an exchange which would strengthen Black's pawn center.

15 ... P-B5!

Capablanca explains that the advance of the bishop pawn lets his bishop have some air and take an active role in the game, instead of being tied down to the defence of the pawn. It also gives Black a point of attack in the fixed and weakened queen knight pawn. 'The fact that the text move opens Q4 for one of White's knights is of small consequence,' says Capablanca, 'since by posting a knight there the attack on the queen pawn is blocked for the moment, and thus Black has time to assume the offensive.'

16 KR-Q1

More to the point was 16 P-K4, to break up the opposing pawns.

16 ... KR-Q1

17 N-Q4 B-N5!

The bishop, that stood meekly at K2, becomes aggressive!

In fact, this move threatens 18 ... BxN, after which the black knight can be deployed to Q6, by way of K5 (or Q2) and QB4.

18 P-QN3

The purpose of this move is to saddle Black with a weak, isolated pawn. Dr. Bernstein was completely unsuspicious of any danger in the position, or he would have played 18 Q-B2 followed by 19 N(Q4)-K2 and 20 N-B4.

18 ... QR-B1

19 PxP PxP

Bernstein has accomplished his object, but the 'weak isolated pawn' is also a passed pawn, and apt to be dangerous.

20 R-B2 BxN

21 RxB N-Q4!

To drive off the blockader, and then advance the pawn.

22 R-B2

Of course not 22 RxP N-B6, and Black wins the exchange.

22 ... P-B6

'As White is forced to retreat, the black pawn advances, and being well-supported and far advanced it becomes a source of great strength.'

Capablanca

23 R(Q1)-QB1 R-B4

Now comes some maneuvering by White's knight as Bernstein tries to win the weak-looking bishop pawn.

24 N-N3 R-B3

25 N-Q4 R-B2

26 N-N5

Looks good, since the knight's threat against the rook gains a tempo for the attack on the pawn.

26 ... R-B4

Apparently White can now win the pawn. It is attacked three times, and protected only twice. So

Bernstein, not suspecting the stunning surprise that awaits him, takes the pawn.

27 NxBP NxN

28 RxN RxR

29 RxR

This is the position:

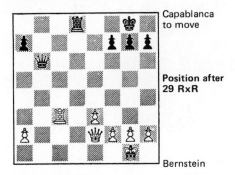

Capablanca to move

Position after 29 RxR

Bernstein

Capablanca now uncorks a million-dollar move.

29 . . . Q-N7!!

What a move!

White must lose his rook or be mated!
If 30 QxQ R-Q8 mate.
If 30 R-B2 Q-N8ch wins the rook.
If 30 R-Q3 Q-N8ch wins the rook.
If 30 R-B8 Q-N8ch 31 Q-B1 QxQch wins the rook.
If 30 Q-K1 QxR 31 QxQ R-Q8 mate.
If 30 Q-B2 QxQ 31 RxQ R-Q8ch forces mate.
If 30 Q-Q3 Q-R8ch! 31 Q-B1 QxR wins the rook.

Bernstein resigned gracefully. Playing even one more move would have been an anti-climax.

(Besides, there is no reply to a thunderbolt.)

105

White **J.R. Capablanca**   Black **B. Villegas**
Queen's Gambit Declined
Exhibition Game, Buenos Aires, 1914

In Anderssen's time, a sacrifice of the queen was usually the means of luring the hostile king to his doom.

Here, a spectacular offer of the queen has the objective of securing a positional advantage. This grand strategy leads to control of the queen file, and this in turn is converted to the advantage of a Q-side majority of three pawns to two.

Skilful play resolves this into a lone passed pawn, that is heavily blockaded by the enemy. Then another queen sacrifice by Capablanca opens wide the gate.

1 P-Q4 P-Q4

2 N-KB3 N-KB3

3 P-K3 P-B3

4 B-Q3 B-N5

5 P-B4!

Alert play! This opens the bishop file for the convenience of the heavy pieces, and holds out prospects of a raid by Q-N3 on Black's Q-side, weakened by the absence of his bishop.

5 . . . P-K3

6 QN-Q2 QN-Q2

7 0-0 B-K2

8 Q-B2 B-R4

Black prepares to swing the bishop over to N3, to exchange it for White's aggressive king bishop.

Had he castled instead, the continuation 9 N-K5 B-R4 (if 9 . . . NxN 10 PxN N-Q2 11 BxPch wins a pawn for White) 10 P-B4 gives White a powerfully centralized knight and excellent attacking prospects.

9 P-QN3 B-N3

10 B-N2 BxB

11 QxB

Capablanca has a strong initiative, though he has done nothing but build up his position quietly.

He can now choose one of these procedures:

(a) A breakup by P-K4, to open lines of attack for his pieces.

(b) The establishment of an outpost at K5 by the knight.

(c) A hemming-in process, beginning with P-B5.

11 . . .   0-0

12 QR-K1

Before committing himself, Capablanca brings another piece into play.

12 . . .   Q-B2

13 P-K4!

This opens up lines of attack, and allows less counter-play than 13 P-B5 P-K4   14 PxP NxBP, or 13 N-K5 NxN   14 PxN N-Q2   15 P-B4 P-B3.

13 . . .   PxKP

14 NxP   NxN

15 RxN!

This is much stronger than capturing with the queen, as the sequel will show.

15 . . .   B-B3

On 15 . . . N-B3 instead, White plays 16 R-R4, when the threat of 17 P-Q5 followed by 18 BxN forces 17 . . . P-KR3, weakening his pawn structure.

Black's actual move involves a pretty threat in 16 . . . N-B4   17 PxN BxB, simplifying to Black's advantage.

16 Q-K3!

Puts an end to that little scheme!

16 . . .   P-B4

This certainly looks attractive! Black plans 17 . . . PxP, a capture which White cannot avoid, his queen pawn being pinned. With the disappearance of White's center pawn, the squares K4 and QB4 become available to Black's knight, and the queen bishop file opens up for counterplay by his queen and rook.

17 N-K5

The knight establishes an outpost. It seems harmless enough; it threatens nothing, and does not interfere with whatever ideas Black has in mind.

17 . . .   PxP

Counting on the continuation 18 BxP BxN   19 BxB NxB   20 RxN KR-Q1, and his control of the open queen's file greatly increases Black's chances.

But the refutation is brilliant!

Villegas

Position after 17 . . . PxP

Capablanca to move

18 NxN!

What a shock for Black!

The concept is remarkable, not so much in the fact that White's combination involves a sacrifice of the queen, but in the circumstance that the offer of the queen is only a detail! It is subordinate to the over-all strategy of the game.

The game is conducted on positional lines, and that's the way it will be won. Any combinations that arise will be incidental to the general plan, which is to create a passed pawn, move it up at every opportunity, and promote it to a queen.

18 . . .   QxN

If he accepts the offer and plays 18 . . . PxQ, White reveals this combination: 19 NxBch K-R1 (or 19 . . . PxN   20 R-N4ch K-R1   21 BxP mate) 20 R-R4 (threatening 21 RxP mate) P-KR3   21 RxPch! PxR   22 N-Q5 dis.ch K-N1   23 NxQ, and White with two pieces for a rook wins easily.

19 BxP

Regains the pawn, and aims at checkmate by 20 BxB PxB   21 R-N4ch K-R1   22 Q-R6 R-KN1   23 QxBPch and mate next move.

19 ...   BxB

20 RxB   Q-B2

21 KR-Q1   KR-Q1

Black must oppose rooks before White establishes a rook on the seventh rank, or triples pieces on the file.

22 P-QN4!

This starts the Q-side pawns rolling!

Capablanca does not even cast a glance at such a transparent trap as 22 RxRch RxR   23 RxRch QxR   24 QxRP Q-Q8 mate.

22 ...   RxR

23 QxR   P-QN3

24 P-N3   R-QB1

25 R-QB1

Necessary, to save the pawn. But now the rook is in back of the bishop pawn (the candidate for the coronation) and is in position to keep it under protection no matter how far the pawn moves up the file.

25 ...   R-Q1

Now he has the open file; but this is of slight consequence, as there is no useful point of invasion available.

26 Q-K3

A shrewd move: the queen keeps in touch with the rook, prevents Black's rook from coming in at Q2, and keeps a weather eye on the strategic square QB5, the bishop pawn's next stop.

26 ...   K-B1

The king approaches the field of action. In the event of a general exchange of pieces, he is prepared to head off the bishop pawn.

27 P-B5   PxP

Expecting White to recapture by 28 PxP, whereupon he blockades the pawn effectively by 28 . . .Q-B3.

28 Q-K4!

Very clever! White need not recapture immediately, as Black's pawn is pinned and cannot escape.

Meanwhile the queen's move stops the intended blockade by 28 . . . Q-B3, and prepares for 29 PxP

followed by 30 P-B6.

28 ...   R-Q4

There is a temptation for White to go pawn-hunting now by 29 QxRP followed by 30 Q-R8ch and 31 QxP, picking up a couple of pawns and creating for himself a passed rook pawn. But this sort of random play would not be consistent with White's orderly, economical conduct of the game, and entirely out of character for a Capablanca!

29 PxP

A passed pawn at last!

29 ...   P-N3

Of course not 29 . . . RxP, as 30 Q-QN4 pins and wins the rook.

30 P-B6

Passed pawns must be pushed! With each step forward of the pawn, the field of action of White's rook increases, while the freedom of Black's pieces becomes more limited.

30 ...   K-N2

Bringing the king to the center could lead to regicide, thus: 30 . . . K-K2   31 Q-R4ch K-Q3   32 Q-QN4ch K-K4   33 Q-KB4 mate!

31 P-QR4!

In order to play 32 Q→QN4→N7. Then, after Black plays . . . QxQ and White replies PxQ, Black must play . . . R-Q1 (. . . R-QN4 is impossible) whereupon R-B8 wins.

Note the enormous power of White's passed pawn!

31 ...   R-Q3

The pawn is now under heavy guard. But White lifts the blockade with one shot!

32 Q-K5ch!   P-B3

33 QxR!   QxQ

34 P-B7   Resigns

The pawn becomes a queen next move, leaving White a whole rook ahead.

An elegant composition, from 1 P-Q4 to 34 P-B7.

106

White **J.R. Capablanca**   Black **C. Molina** and **E. Ruiz**
King's Gambit Declined
Buenos Aires, 1914

The great Capablanca generally preferred simple positions in which he could display his wonderfully polished technique with moves of an unsurpassed crystal clarity.

But there were times when he lashed out with thrilling attacks.

It is masterpieces of this sort, such as feature in this game, which must have inspired Vuković's appreciative comment, 'If we delve into the whole of chess literature looking for games which serve to illuminate the logical integration of the attack on the castled king and the game in its entirety, then those of Alekhine and Capablanca remain the unsurpassed models; side by side with them may be placed a few of the games of Rubinstein, Keres, and Bronstein, though we shall find scarcely any new discoveries in them; the whole period from Alekhine's death to the present day has not been particularly fruitful in the sphere of the attack on the king. So one is justified in going back to Alekhine and Capablanca to discover knowledge which to this day has been neither refuted nor superseded.'

1 P-K4   P-K4
2 P-KB4   B-B4
3 N-KB3   P-Q3
4 N-B3   N-QB3
5 N-QR4!

Better than the book move 5 B-N5, this eliminates Black's strong bishop, makes early castling feasible, and secures the two bishops for White.

5 . . .   B-N3
6 B-N5   B-Q2
7 NxB   RPxN
8 P-Q3   KN-K2

9 0-0   0-0

An attempt to simplify by means of 9 . . . N-Q5 would cost a pawn by 10 BxBch QxB   11 PxP.

10 P-B5

The pawn's advance cramps Black's game, and presages a strong K-side attack. The immediate threat is 11 P-B6, a worthwhile pawn sacrifice.

10 . . . P-B3
11 B-B4ch

Just to restrain Black from freeing his game by 11 . . . P-Q4.

11 . . . K-R1
12 P-QR3

And this provides a shelter for the bishop against 12 . . . N-R4.

12 . . . B-K1
13 B-K6   B-R4
14 Q-K1   Q-K1

Now was the time for Black to effect an exchange of bishops. Later, the opportunity is denied him.

15 Q-R4   N-Q1
16 B-R2   B-B2
17 P-B4!

Rather than exchange, he prefers to bury his bishop alive! Only a player supremely sure of himself could dare play such a move.

17 . . . P-B4

Better than this effort to nail down White's bishop pawn is 17 . . . P-QN4.

18 P-KN4

Indicating that he intends to break up the king's pawn-barricade by pushing the pawn on to N5 and N6.

18 . . . N-N1
19 B-Q2   P-QN4
20 P-N5   PxNP

A compulsory capture, in view of the threat of 21 P-N6, winning a piece.

21 NxNP

White's advance of the king knight pawn has briskly stepped up the tempo of his attack: his knight has become very menacing, and the king knight file has been opened.

21 ...   N-KB3

22 R-B3   PxP

23 NxP!

Capablanca begins a combination which is remarkable for its imaginative sustained brilliance.

'This is better,' says Capablanca, 'than 23 R-R3, when there would follow 23 ... P-KR3   24 NxBch NxN   25 BxBP P-Q4!

I daresay very few masters would have made this sacrifice. It requires not only very great powers of combination, but what is still more, accurate judgment. A very careful analysis will demonstrate that the sacrifice is absolutely sound.'

23 ...   NxN

24 R-R3   B-N1

25 BxP

The buried bishop is resurrected; White threatens to win at once with 26 BxB.

25 ...   R-B2

Black would happily surrender the exchange to slow down the attack.

Against the plausible 25 ... N-B2, Capablanca shows this fine continuation: 26 P-B6! P-KN4 (if 26 ... PxP   27 QxP mate!)   27 Q-R5 N-Q1 (else 28 Q-N6 forces mate at N7)   28 Q-R6 R-B2   29 BxP Q-B1   30 K-R1! QxQ   31 BxQ RxBP   32 R-KN1, and Black is helpless.

26 K-R1!

Clearance for the queen rook to take part in the attack.

26 ...   P-QN4

Black's response is to clear the second rank, for his queen rook to come to the defence.

27 B-Q5   QR-R2

28 R-KN1   R-B3

29 B-N5

Obviously threatening sudden death by 30 BxR PxB   31 QxPch and mate next.

29 ...   R(R2)-B2

This is the position:

Molina & Ruiz

Position after 29 ... R(R2)-B2

Capablanca to move

Black is tied up in knots on the K-side, and powerless to stir. But how does Capablanca break down resistance and force capitulation, when his pieces are as well posted as they can be? How can he add power to the attack?

Answer: With a quiet little move on the Q-side! A quiet little move whose effect will be irresistible! Watch carefully!

30 P-N3!!

Far from the madding crowd, a pawn will begin a journey to the eighth square!

30 ...   Q-B1

Black must move something! If 30 ... R-R2 (to stop the rook pawn) 31 BxR, and Black may not recapture, or if 30 ... R-B1   31 BxB wins at once.

Throughout, of course, Black's bishop is tied to N1 in order to guard the knight at KR2.

31 P-R4!

White gets a passed pawn, whose every step forward will add to Black's difficulties on the K-side.

(Note that Capablanca is still a piece behind, but serenely unconcerned with such matters as material possessions.)

31 ...   PxP

32 PxP   Q-K1

It is futile to take steps against the passed pawn: if 32 ... R-R2   33 BxB QxB   34 BxR and wins! Or 32 ... N-N2   33 B(N5)xR PxB   34 BxR QxB. 35 R(R3)-N3, and White wins.

33 P-R5   N-B3

34 P-R6   N-N5

35 B(N5)xR   N(N5)xB

A pretty finish, showing the power of the passed pawn, follows other defences by Black:

If 35 ... PxB   36 RxBch! QxR   37 BxR QxB 38 QxNch! QxQ   39 RxQch KxR   40 P-R7, and the terrible pawn queens!

Or if 35 ... RxB   36 QxR! PxQ   37 RxBch QxR 38 BxQ KxB   39 P-R7, with the same result.

36 BxPch   RxB

37 RxR   KxR

38 Q-R6ch   K-R1

Capablanca says: 38 ... K-B2 would be no better. White would have three or four ways to win, of which 39 R-N3 looks strongest, as then we would have 39 ... K-K2   40 R-N7ch B-B2   41 Q-K6ch K-B1 42 RxBch QxR   43 QxQch KxQ   44 PxN winning. The position is most remarkable, as with two pieces ahead Black is helpless, although all that White has left is a queen and rook.

39 QxP!   Resigns

Black cannot meet all the threats: If 39 ... N(Q4) moves, the reply 40 Q-B6 is instant mate. If 39 ... Q-K2 (to save the knight)   40 QxQ NxQ   41 P-R7 wins. Finally, if 39 ... Q-B2   40 QxPch N-B3 41 Q-R1!! (the prettiest way to apply the *coup de*

grâce) Q-R2   42 QxNch wins, or if 41 ... K-N2 42 P-R7 does the trick.

A marvellously sustained combination by Capablanca, and for us superb entertainment.

107

White **J.R. Capablanca**   Black **R.T. Black**
Ruy López
New York, 1916

Capablanca's unknown games are as fascinating as his familiar masterpieces.

This one, for example, is one of my happy discoveries. Despite its length, it holds your interest every step of the way. I can picture its highlights being pointed out by an announcer some day in the future, when chess brilliancies are featured on television.

'See Capablanca handling the Ruy López opening in his own inimitable style!'

'Watch him force a bishop back to the sidelines, cutting it off from the theater of action!'

'See him surround the black queen, and capture her alive!'

'Watch him set a trap to catch the king with a long-distance mate!'

'See him corner the king and compel him to surrender!'

1	P-K4	P-K4
2	N-KB3	N-QB3
3	B-N5	P-QR3
4	B-R4	N-B3
5	0-0	B-K2
6	R-K1	P-Q3
7	P-B3	0-0
8	P-Q4	P-QN4
9	B-B2	B-N5
10	P-Q5	N-N1

11 P-KR3   B-R4

The alternative 11 . . . B-B1 would leave Black terribly cramped after 12 P-QR4.

12 QN-Q2   QN-Q2

13 N-B1   R-K1

14 P-KN4

Dispatches the bishop to N3, where it is shut out of play for a long time.

14 . . .   B-N3

15 N-N3

Ostensibly the knight is headed for B5, a splendid outpost.

Capablanca reserves this option, though, as there is no reason to let Black exchange his useless bishop for a potentially powerful knight.

15 . . .   P-KR3

16 P-QR4

White starts operations on the Q-side, to maintain the initiative on the whole front.

16 . . .   N-R2

17 Q-K2   R-N1

18 PxP   PxP

19 P-N4

This curbs any ambitions Black may have entertained of Q-side expansion by means of 19 . . . P-N5 and 20 . . . N-B4.

19 . . .   Q-B1

20 B-Q3

Evidently Black is to be kept busy defending Q-side, K-side, and the center of the board simultaneously.

20 . . .   P-QB3

21 PxP   QxP

22 R-R5

'This move is quite safe,' says Capablanca, 'and apparently has no other object than to win the queen knight pawn in exchange for the queen bishop pawn. In reality it is the beginning of a very long combin-

ation, which will ultimately force Black to give up his queen for rook and bishop.'

22 . . .   QxBP

23 BxNP

This is better than the natural move 23 B-Q2, as the queen must return to B2 in any event. In addition, the bishop will be more useful at K3.

The text move gains time to pursue the attack.

23 . . .   Q-B2

The queen hurries back; capturing the pawn would not do, as after 23 . . . QxP comes 24 B-Q2, and White wins the unguarded knight.

24 B-K3   KR-Q1

25 R-QB1

Seizing control of the open file, the rook attacks the queen, forcing her to flee to N2, the one safe square left.

25 . . .   Q-N2

26 B-B6

Capablanca says: I hesitated a long time before I made this move, as I suddenly realized that while I could win the queen, Black would obtain rook, bishop, and pawn for it, besides a very solid position. What finally decided me was the fact that Black's extra pawn would be the pawn at Q3, a backward pawn not much to be feared. Otherwise I would have played differently. I remember that I seriously considered the following variation: 26 BxN QxB   27 P-QN5 with an excellent game.

26 . . .   QxP

27 R-R4   Q-N6

Once more, the only square open, as 27 . . . Q-N7 loses by 28 QxQ RxQ   29 R-R7 N(R2)-B3   30 BxN RxB   31 RxR NxR   32 R-B7, winning one of the unprotected pieces—triumph of the seventh rank!

28 R-R7

The star move in the combination!

28 . . .   N(R2)-B1

29 N-Q2   Q-N7

The queen may flee to the K-side, but the villains still pursue her, thus: 29 ... Q-K3 30 B-Q5 Q-B3 31 N-B3 (threatens 32 P-N5 PxP 33 BxP, winning the queen) 31 ... B-R2 (on 31 ... N-R2 32 R(B1)-B7 wins a piece) 32 P-N5 Q-N3 33 N-R4, and White wins the queen.

30 Q-Q1   B-N4!

This offers the most resistance. Against 30 ... QR-B1 instead, White had this neat combination *in petto:* 31 R-B2 Q-N5 (on 31 ... Q-N1 32 R-N7 Q-R1 33 RxN wins a piece) 32 R-B4 Q-N7 33 BxN!, and White remains a piece ahead, despite Black's choice of three ways to recapture.

31 R-B2   BxB

If 31 ... Q-N5 32 R-R4 catches the queen *en plein jour.*

32 RxQ   BxR

33 RxR   NxR

The best way to recapture, as 33 ... RxR loses a piece after 34 Q-R4, while 33 ... BxR removes the bishop from its command of the long diagonal.

34 B-Q5   N-K3

35 N-K2

The threat is stronger than the execution: the knight never does reach KB5.

Meanwhile, it is important to prevent Black's knight from occupying the counterpart KB5 square.

35 ...   N-Q2

36 Q-R4   B-N1

Black avoids 36 ... B-B4, fearful of having the bishop exchanged for one of the knights.

37 Q-R2   N(Q2)-B4

38 P-B3   K-B1

39 N-QB4   K-K2

This turns out to be fatal; here is one of those rare cases where the king should stay at home in the endgame.

40 N-R5   K-B3

41 N-B6   R-QB1

42 P-KR4   B-B2

Black

Position after 42 ... B-B2

Capablanca to move

43 P-B4!

Threatens to win a piece in either of two ways: by 44 P-B5 attacking two pieces, or by 44 P-N5ch PxP 45 RPxPch, and Black must give up his knight for two pawns.

43 ...   BxP

Black avoids being the victim of a brilliancy! Had he played 43 ... NxBP, the finish would have been 4 NxN PxN 45 Q-R1 mate—a beautiful long-distance mate!

44 P-N5ch   PxP

45 RPxPch   NxP

Forced, as 45 ... K-B4 (or N3) loses a rook by the knight fork at K7.

46 PxNch   KxP

47 BxB   NxB

48 QxP   B-N3ch

49 K-N2   RxN

Just a temporary loan, as Capablanca regains the knight instantly.

50 QxPch   K-R4

Loses the knight by a double attack, but the alternative 50 ... K-B4 loses a rook by 51 Q-Q7ch.

51 Q-R7ch   K-N4

52 QxN   R-B2

53 N-N3

Intends this continuation: 54 Q-B5ch K-R3
55 Q-B6ch K-R2   56 N-B5, and the threat is
57 N-K7 followed by 58 Q-N6ch K-R1   59 Q-R6
mate.

53 ...   K-B3

54 Q-Q5   B-B4

55 N-K4ch   K-K2

56 K-B3   K-Q2

57 K-N4   R-B3

58 Q-B7ch   K-B1

Quick loss follows 58 ... K-Q1 by 59 N-B6, when
the threat of mate forces 59 ... K-B1, and
60 Q-Q7ch wins a rook.

59 N-B6   R-B2

60 Q-K8ch   K-N2

61 N-Q5   R-B1

62 Q-N5ch   K-R2

63 N-K7   Resigns

Any rook move is followed by 64 N-B6ch, forcing
Black to give up the exchange or be mated.

108

White **J.R. Capablanca**   Black **A. Schroeder**
Queen's Gambit Declined
New York, 1916

This is not merely a favourite game. It is a game I love.

I have played it over a thousand times (well, a hundred
anyway). It is elegant all the way through, and notable for
the award of a brilliancy prize for superb combination
that Capablanca had in mind, but which never appeared
on the board!

The ending, with a bishop trapped in the corner by a
pawn, is exquisite, and as neat a finishing touch as I have
ever seen.

It is a game such as this that must have moved Gilbert
Highet to say, 'Some of Capablanca's finest games remind
me of the compositions of De Falla in their blend of intri-
cacy, elusiveness, dignity, and basic simplicity.'

1 P-Q4   P-Q4

2 N-KB3   P-K3

3 P-B4   N-KB3

4 N-B3   QN-Q2

5 B-N5   B-K2

6 P-K3   0-0

7 R-B1   P-QR3

Ready to start the pawns rolling with 8 ... PxP
9 BxP P-N4   10 B-Q3 B-N2 followed by 11 ... P-B4,
with vigorous, but perhaps premature, counterplay.

The safer move is the conventional 7 ... P-B3,
strengthening the pawn center.

8 Q-B2   R-K1

9 B-Q3   PxP

10 BxP   P-N4

11 B-Q3   B-N2

12 P-QR4!

Capablanca does not allow Black to continue with
12 ... P-B4, but forces the knight pawn to advance.

12 ...   P-N5

13 BxN!

An unexpected exchange, but the recapture will divert
the knight from its surveillance of the key square
QB4, as well as from the possibility of swinging over
to KB1 to defend the K-side.

13 ...   NxB

14 N-K4!

Suddenly White has queen, rook, knight, and pawn
bearing down on one point—QB5!

The immediate threat is either to win a pawn by

15 NxNch BxN   16 BxPch, or to anchor the knight at QB5, with a death grip on the position.

14 ...   NxN

15 BxN   BxB

Capablanca suggests 15 ... P-N6 as the alternative, 'the move that Black should play, even if it leads to ultimate defeat. White could answer 16 Q-Q3, or 16 BxPch followed by 17 Q-Q3.'

16 QxB   P-QB4!

Win or lose, Black must advance the bishop pawn, or be left with a strategically lost position. Any delay will allow White to play 17 Q-B6 with intolerable pressure.

17 PxP   Q-R4

18 P-QN3

Simple and strong! Black will have to lose time capturing the bishop pawn, and in consequence his pieces will be somewhat awkwardly placed.

18 ...   BxP

19 N-N5   P-R3

Black has only a choice of evils. He feared 19 ... P-N3, which weakens his black squares, and could lead to trouble after 20 Q-B3 R-KB1 (protecting the bishop pawn by 20 ... R-R2 loses a piece by 21 Q-B6) 21 Q-KB6, and White threatens 22 NxRP followed by 23 R-B4.

20 Q-R7ch

Begins an extraordinary combination. Capablanca sacrifices a knight and compels the king to make a long journey to QN3, and into a state of virtual *zugzwang*.

20 ...   K-B1   See diagram.

21 Q-R8ch

Capablanca continues the attack, though it involves giving up a piece, in preference to this safe procedure: 21 N-K4 B-N3   22 R-B6 Q-KB4   23 QxQ PxQ 24 N-Q6 KR-N1   25 NxP(B5) R-B1   26 RxR RxR 27 K-Q2, and White, a pawn ahead, would win eventually, though it would take time and trouble.

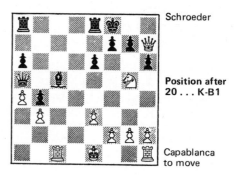

Schroeder

Position after 20 ... K-B1

Capablanca to move

21 ...   K-K2

22 QxNP   PxN

23 QxNPch   K-Q3

The king must protect the bishop, and is thus open to attack by all of White's pieces.

24 K-K2!

Beautiful, and the key to the attack! The king is perfectly safe here, while the rooks are enabled to get in touch with each other.

24 ...   QR-B1

Black cannot free his pieces by 24 ... B-N3, as 25 KR-Q1ch wins on the spot.

25 R-B4   K-B3

26 KR-QB1   K-N3

Black can hardly stir after this move: his queen cannot move at all; a move by his king loses the bishop; the rook at QB1 must stay put to protect the bishop, and the bishop may not move lest a rook be lost.

Black's pieces being thus tied up, Capablanca plays a trump.

27 P-R4!

Capablanca makes no attempt to exploit the helpless position of his opponent. He pays no further attention to it, but with delightful (and enviable) insouciance starts a pawn off on its way to the queening square!

This is the way the board looks:

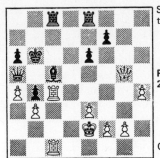

Schroeder
to move

Position after
27 P-R4!

Capablanca

27 ...   P-B4

This is what Black played, and it lost quickly, as follows:

28 Q-N7   R-K2

On 28 ... R-B2, White can finish brusquely with 29 QxRch KxQ   30 RxBch, and it's all over.

29 Q-K5

This exerts the maximum of pressure, and commands the queening square of the pawn.

29 ...   R-B3

30 RxB!   Resigns

If 30 ... RxR   31 Q-Q6ch R-B3   32 RxRch K-N2 33 R-B5, and White wins the other rook.

Now back to the diagram above:

Immediately after the game, Capablanca demonstrated the following combination, which he had prepared against the best defence. It was impressive enough to influence the committee to award him a brilliancy prize:

27 ...   R-B2

In order to double rooks, and free the bishop and the queen.

28 P-R5   KR-QB1

29 P-R6   B-Q3

Any other bishop move loses a rook.

30 QxQch   KxQ

31 RxR   RxR

Most amusing would be 31 ... BxR, when 32 R-B6 paralyzes all of Black's pieces!

32 RxR   BxR

33 P-B4

To keep the bishop from occupying the long diagonal.

33 ...   B-Q1

34 P-N4   B-B3

Otherwise 35 P-N5 follows, and the bishop is completely shut out.

35 P-N5   B-R1

White's aim is to advance his knight pawn to N7.

In order to advance the knight pawn, he must advance the bishop pawn.

In order to advance the bishop pawn, he must advance the king pawn.

And that explains the following moves.

36 P-K4   K-N3

The king is unfortunately too far away to come to the rescue in time.

37 P-B5   PxP

38 PxP   K-B4

39 P-N6   PxP

40 PxP   K-Q3

41 P-N7 and wins

A witty finish, and worthy of a picture:

109

White **D. Janowsky**   Black **J.R. Capablanca**
Queen's Gambit Declined
New York, 1916

How do you describe a game that is outstanding (even in a selection of Capablanca's greatest games) in tactical brilliance and depth of strategy?

Combinations are there, but not as pretty displays of fireworks. The combinations are means to an end, that of obtaining an advantage in position. It is Capablanca's exploitation of this advantage that represents strategy of a high order.

It is games such as this that elicited Alekhine's admiring comment, 'Capablanca's planning of the game is so full of the freshness of his genius for position play that every hypermodern player can only envy him.'

It is truly a masterpiece in the grand manner, whose every move merits recording in letters of gold.

1 P-Q4   N-KB3

2 N-KB3   P-Q4

3 P-B4   P-B3

4 N-B3   B-B4

5 Q-N3

> The better line is 5 PxP PxP   6 Q-N3 Q-N3   7 NxP NxN   8 QxN P-K3   9 Q-N3 QxQ   10 PxQ B-B7 11 B-Q2 BxP   12 P-K4!, and Torre eventually trapped Gotthilf's wandering bishop (temporarily) and later won the game (permanently) in their encounter at Moscow in 1925.

5 . . .   Q-N3

6 QxQ   PxQ

7 PxP   NxP

8 NxN   PxN

> It is true that Black's Q-side pawns have been split up, but in return he has two open files for his rooks to gallivant in.

9 P-K3   N-B3

10 B-Q2

> One would now expect 10 . . . P-K3, to get the king bishop into play. But development for its own sake is aimless.
>
> Capablanca knew then, what masters later rediscovered, that random development was not good enough. The pieces must be brought to their best squares, *as quickly as possible.*

10 . . .   B-Q2!!

> Two exclamation marks for one of the most profound moves ever played. It surpasses easily the highly-praised 19 QR-Q1 in the celebrated Anderssen-Dufresne game, and equals in subtlety the 36 R-Q5 move in the Alekhine-Tartakover masterpiece, played at Vienna in 1922.
>
> Not only does Capablanca *undevelop* the bishop, but he locks it in next move by 11 . . . P-K3.
>
> The idea is to continue with . . . N-R4, . . . P-QN4 (the pawn now being under the protection of the bishop), and . . . N-B5, with the knight occupying a strong outpost, stoutly supported by pawns.
>
> Should White take the knight off, the recapture straightens out Black's pawns, and leaves him with the two bishops.

11 B-K2

> Janowsky, completely in the dark about Black's plans, does nothing to hinder them. Instead of playing 11 B-N5 he proceeds in the old-fashioned way (development for the sake of development) to bring the bishop into play, and then follows by safeguarding the king by early castling.

11 . . .   P-K3

12 0-0   B-Q3

13 KR-B1   K-K2!

> Once queens are off the board (lessening danger to the king) and the endgame is in sight, the king belongs in the center, rather than on the wing.

14 B-B3   KR-QB1

15 P-QR3

Preferable to this, which creates a hole at his QN3, was the energetic 15 N-K5.

15 . . .   N-R4!

Black goes on with his plan of posting the knight at B5, incidentally threatening to win the exchange by 16 . . . N-N6.

White could remove the knight, but that would forfeit one of his much-prized bishops, and also un-double Black's pawns.

16 N-Q2   P-B4!

Squashes any White thoughts of freeing himself by 17 P-K4.

17 P-KN3   P-QN4!

18 P-B3   N-B5

'Black's first plan is completed,' says Capablanca. 'White will now have to take the knight, and Black's only weakness, the doubled queen knight pawn, will become a great source of strength at QB5. Now for two or three moves Black will devote his time to improving the general strategic position of his pieces before evolving a new plan, this time a plan of attack against White's position.'

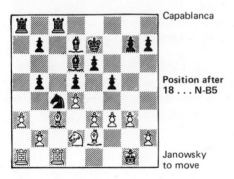

Capablanca

Position after
18 . . . N-B5

Janowsky
to move

19 BxN

Janowsky would love to keep his bishop, but he needs the knight to support an advance by the king pawn, a move he wants to play as quickly as possible.

19 . . .   NPxB

20 P-K4   K-B2

Vacates a good square for the bishop in the event of its being attacked by 21 P-K5.

21 P-K5

This move, and White's next, are anti-positional, if only for the fact that placing pawns on black squares reduces the mobility of his bishop—that can travel on black squares only!

Far better was 21 PxQP PxP   22 P-B4 followed by 23 N-B3 and 24 N-K5.

The knight would then be strongly placed, while its removal would cost Black one of the bishops, and leave White with a protected passed pawn.

21 . . .   B-K2

22 P-B4   P-QN4

Black threatens, after suitable preparation, to play . . . P-N5, fixing White's pieces on the Q-side.

Then he plans to switch suddenly to the K-side, break up that wing by . . . P-KN4, and attack on the open file with his rooks.

Speaking in general of the force of the threatened attack, Capablanca says, 'One of the best and most successful maneuvers in this type of game is to make a demonstration on one side, so as to draw the forces of your opponent to that side, then through the greater mobility of your pieces to shift your forces quickly to the other side and break through, before your opponent has had the necessary time to bring his forces for the defence.'

23 K-B2

Against 23 B-N4 instead (to prevent the impending . . . P-N5) the continuation 23 . . . BxB   24 PxB R-R5   25 RxR PxR followed by 26 . . . R-QN1 wins a pawn for Black.

23 . . .   R-R5

24 K-K3   KR-QR1

Threatens to trap the bishop by 25 . . . P-N5.

25 R(R1)-N1   P-R3

26 N-B3   P-N4

27 N-K1   R-KN1

28 K-B3

More resistance was offered by 28 N-N2, in order to reply to 28 . . . PxPch with 29 NxP, thereby bringing the knight to a good square.

28 . . .   PxP

29 PxP   R(R5)-R1

30 N-N2   R-N5

Auguring difficulties for White along the open knight file.

31 R-N1   QR-KN1

'Black is now ready to reap the reward for his well developed plan,' says Capablanca. 'All that is now needed is to bring the bishop at Q2 to bear pressure against White's position.'

32 B-K1

Janowsky fights hard to escape from the pin. He plans to rescue the knight from the attack threatened on it by Black's rook pawn, with this line of play: 32 . . . P-R4 33 B-B2 P-R5 34 P-R3 R(N5)-N2 35 N-K3, and he's out of the woods.

But Capablanca crosses him up by switching the action to the Q-side!

This is the situation:

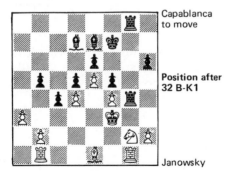

Capablanca to move

Position after 32 B-K1

Janowsky

32 . . .   P-N5!

A brilliant sacrifice to give his white-square bishop more mobility. This bishop has been waiting patiently at Q2 since the memorable 10th move.

The planned itinerary is . . . B-QR5, . . . B-B7, and . . . B-K5ch, throwing terror into the ranks of the enemy.

33 PxP

If 33 BxP BxB 34 PxB, Black can either regain the pawn by 35 . . . R-N1, or advance 35 . . . P-R4 with threats against the pinned knight.

33 . . .   B-QR5!

Threatens (as mentioned before) 34 . . . B-B7 and 35 . . . B-K5ch. If White stops this by 34 R-QB1, then 34 . . . RxPch! 35 KxR B-N4ch 36 K-B3 BxR wins for Black.

Capablanca's games are studded with these little tactical finesses.

34 R-QR1   B-B7

35 B-N3

Interferes with the attack on the knight, but Capablanca finds a way to renew the pin.

35 . . .   B-K5ch

36 K-B2   P-R4

Threatens to win a piece by the simple but brutal 37 . . . P-R5 38 NxP BxN 39 BxB RxB.

37 R-R7

There being no relief in 37 N-K3 P-R5 38 NxR PxBch followed by 39 . . . RxN, winning two pieces for a rook, White plays for some vague hope of a counter-attack.

37 . . .   BxN

38 RxB   P-R5

39 BxP   RxRch

40 K-B3   RxRP

41 BxB

On 41 RxBch instead, Black wins by 41 . . . K-B1 42 B-B6 R(N1)-R1! (the threat of mate on the move

cleverly forces a reduction of pieces) 43 BxR KxR,
and the rest is child's play.

41 ...   R-R6ch

42 K-B2   R-QN6
With every piece and pawn standing on a white square,
Black is immune to any discovered check!

43 B-N5 dis.ch
Shuts out one of the deadly rooks . . .

43 ...   K-N3

44 R-K7   RxPch

45 K-B3   R-QR1
. . . but not forever!

46 RxPch   K-R2
Does he really hope to swindle Capablanca by 46 . . .
K-R4   47 R-R6 mate?

47 Resigns
If 47 K-N3 (to escape mate in one) 47 . . . R-R6ch
48 K-R4 R-R7 effects the mate in two.

110

White **J.R. Capablanca**   Black **S. Tartakover**
Dutch Defence
New York, 1924

If it is indeed true that Capablanca studied more than a
thousand rook-and-pawn endings to refine his incomparable technique, then in the ending of this game he offers
us the quintessence of his acquired and inborn mastery.

  This ending, which may very well be the best of its
kind, is one to delight the connoisseur, and one to grant
the student a priceless lesson in the art of finishing a game
with elegance and accuracy.

1 P-Q4   P-KB4

2 N-KB3   P-K3

3 P-B4   N-KB3

4 B-N5   B-K2

Instead of this passive defence, Alekhine suggests
4 . . . B-N5ch   5 QN-Q2 N-B3   6 P-K3 0-0, followed
eventually by . . . P-Q3 and . . . P-K4. This would
develop the queen knight without further weakening
Black's basically unsound pawn structure.

5 N-B3   0-0

6 P-K3   P-QN3

7 B-Q3   B-N2

8 0-0   Q-K1
Tartakover improves on 8 . . . N-K5, which had cost
him a pawn in an earlier round against Marshall, when
this ensued: 9 BxB QxB   10 BxN PxB   11 N-Q2 Q-R5
12 N(B3)xP, and Tartakover realized too late that
12 . . . BxN would be met by 13 P-KN3 R-B3
(threatens mate if the queen be taken)   14 P-B4,
and White remains a pawn ahead.

  With the text move, Black threatens the customary
attack in the Dutch—9 . . . Q-R4, 10 . . . N-N5, and
11 . . . BxN.

9 Q-K2!
Causes an immediate change of plans, as 9 . . . Q-R4
allows 10 P-K4 to White's advantage.

9 ...   N-K5

10 BxB   NxN

11 PxN   QxB
To make up for his pawns being doubled on the bishop
file, White has the open knight file for his rooks.

12 P-QR4!
More than just preventing an unwelcome entry by the
queen at R6, this fine move prepares to counter 12 . . .
N-B3 by 13 KR-QN1 (threatening 14 P-R5) 13 . . .
N-R4   14 P-B5, undoubling the pawns by force, as
14 . . . PxP favours White after the response 15 R-N5.

12 ...   BxN
Tartakover exchanges pieces to avoid the above variation, and in the belief that his remaining minor piece,
the knight, will prove to be stronger than Capablanca's
bishop.

13 QxB   N-B3

14 KR-N1   QR-K1

15 Q-R3

Another preventive move. Black may not free himself by 15 . . . P-K4 as 16 BxP wins more than a
mere pawn.

The queen's move also makes it possible for
White to play 16 P-B4, securing a grip on the square
K5.

15 . . .   R-B3

16 P-B4!   N-R4

17 Q-B3

The queen returns to a stronger post, commanding
the long diagonal.

17 . . .   P-Q3

18 R-K1

Its work being finished on the knight file, the rook
moves to the center, to support a break by P-K4.

18 . . .   Q-Q2

Black temporizes, as 18 . . . P-K4   19 P-K4 opens
the lines to White's benefit.

19 P-K4!   PxP

20 QxP   P-N3

21 P-N3

With this move and the next White stabilizes his
position before starting hostilities on the K-side by
P-R4 and P-R5.

21 . . .   K-B1

22 K-N2   R-B2

Cautious measures such as this may have won
battles for the Roman general Quintus Fabius, but
against Capablanca this amounts to waiting for the
blow to descend.

Better chances were offered by 22 . . . Q-B3
23 QxQ NxQ   24 P-B5 R-K2   and the knight returns
from the sidelines.

23 P-R4   P-Q4

This leads to an exchange of queens, and a rook-
ending favouring White.

Black can avoid this by adopting Alekhine's half-
hearted suggestion, 23 . . . NxP   24 BxN P-Q4, but
after 25 BxP QxB   26 P-QR5, the prospects are likewise uninviting.

24 PxP   PxP

25 QxRch! QxQ

26 RxQch   KxR

27 P-R5!   R-B3

On 27 . . . PxP   28 R-R1 K-B1   29 RxP, and White
wins a pawn next move.

28 PxP   PxP

29 R-R1

Good players always seem to hold the high cards!

Capablanca's rook controls an open file, and will
seize the seventh rank next move. Should Tartakover's
rook become ambitious and try to counter-attack by
29 . . . R-B3, the reply 30 B-N5 would come like a
flash and pin the unfortunate piece.

29 . . .   K-B1

30 R-R7

Rook to the seventh—the magic move in rook-and-
pawn endings. What are the secrets in the strength of
this move?

(a) The rook is in perfect position to attack any pawns
that have not yet moved—those still standing on the
second rank.

(b) The rook is prepared to attack any pawn that has
moved, by getting behind it *without loss of time*. The
pawn would be under constant threat of capture, no
matter how many squares it advanced on the file.

(c) The rook's domination of the seventh rank con-
fines the opposing king to the last rank, preventing
his participation in the fighting.

30 . . .   R-B3

31 P-N4!

In keeping with the spirit of rook endings, Capablanca plays aggressively, instead of moving his king towards the Q-side.

31 ... N-B5

The knight hastens to get back into active play. Black naturally avoids 31 ... RxP, as the reply 32 32 BxP lets his opponent have two connected passed pawns.

32 P-N5

Fixes the knight pawn, and threatens to win it by 33 R-R6 K-N2 34 P-B5 N-K6ch 35 K-N1! (the only move).

32 ... N-K6ch

To no avail is blocking the diagonal by 32 ... N-Q7 33 R-R6 N-K5, as 34 P-B4 will pry it open.

33 K-B3

This is the position:

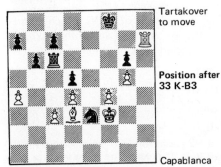

Tartakover to move

Position after 33 K-B3

Capablanca

Tartakover intended to play 33 ... N-Q8, but he changed his mind when he saw that Capablanca could steer the position into a pawn ending, which he would turn into a win, though he had only three pawns against four (or if Tartakover did not resign in time, Capablanca would win it with one pawn against two!).

The idea being so pretty, let's see what fate Tartakover escaped:

33 ... N-Q8 34 R-R6 K-N2 35 P-B5 NxP 36 K-B4! N-K5 37 BxN PxB 38 P-B6ch! RxP

39 PxRch KxR 40 KxP K-R2 41 K-Q5! K-N1 42 K-B6 P-KN4 43 KxP P-N5 44 P-Q5 P-N6 45 P-Q6 P-N7 46 P-Q7 P-N8(Q) 47 P-Q8(Q)ch K-R2 48 Q-K7ch K-R3 49 Q-N7ch QxQ 50 PxQ KxP 51 K-N7 K-B2 52 KxP K-K2 53 KxP K-Q2 54 K-N7 and wins!

33 ... N-B4

34 BxN PxB

Now comes a brilliant continuation, which Capablanca must have planned many moves before. In a simplified ending, where pawns are worth their weight in gold, he gives away two pawns! Moreover he lets Black capture them with check!

35 K-N3!

Le roi s'amuse! The king is headed for B6, a square from which he can assist the rook in threats of mate, and also help the passed pawn take these last three steps.

35 ... RxPch

36 K-R4 R-B6

Should Black try to exchange rooks instead, this follows: 36 ... R-B8 37 K-R5 R-R8ch 38 K-N6 RxR 39 KxR P-B4 40 P-N6, and the pawn crashes through.

37 P-N6

Once more Capablanca allows a pawn to be captured with check!

As compensation though, Capa's king will gain an important tempo or two.

37 ... RxPch

38 K-N5

Gains time by attacking the rook.

38 ... R-K5

Capturing one more pawn would be fatal: 38 ... RxP 39 K-B6 K-N1 (on 39 ... K-K1 40 R-R8ch K-Q2 41 P-N7, and Black must give up his rook for the pawn) 40 R-Q7, and mate follows.

39 K-B6!

Far superior to the petty 39 KxP. The disdained pawn will in fact be useful to White in acting as a buffer against annoying checks.

Capablanca's king is now in a dominating position, and faces Black with the threat of instant mate, as well as 40 P-N7ch followed by queening the pawn.

39 ...   K-N1

40 R-N7ch   K-R1

41 RxP

Removes one pawn, and the renewed threat of mate will enable White to gather in another.

41 ...   R-K1

42 KxP   R-K5

43 K-B6

There is no rest for the weary! White's threats on the K-side (mate, or queening the knight pawn) will give him time to simplify the position on the Q-side and create another passed pawn.

43 ...   R-B5ch

44 K-K5

Contrasting the activity of the two kings, White is practically a king ahead!

44 ...   R-N5

45 P-N7ch   K-N1

Black does not dare take the pawn. If 45 . . . RxP 46 RxR KxR 47 KxP K-B2 48 K-Q6 K-K1 49 K-B7 K-K2 50 P-Q5, and the pawn has clear sailing ahead.

46 RxP   R-N8

47 KxP   R-QB8

48 K-Q6   R-B7

49 P-Q5   R-B8

Hope (for a miracle) springs eternal.

50 R-QB7   R-QR8

51 K-B6   RxP

52 P-Q6   Resigns

Réti says, 'No one has ever played these endgames with such elegant ease as Capablanca; no one else has looked upon these technical difficulties so casually as a matter of course.'

111

White **A. Nimzowitsch**   Black **J.R. Capablanca**
Caro-Kann Defence
New York, 1927

'One might suppose from this game that Capablanca had carefully read *My system,* and then used the theories contained therein against their inventor,' says Keene in *Aron Nimzowitsch: a reappraisal.*

Even Nimzowitsch himself must have been fascinated by the way Capablanca's rooks glided into his position to settle down on the weakened white squares.

And the final arrangement of pieces, which found Nimzowitsch at the wrong end of an *Immortal Zugzwang,* must have stirred his admiration as an artist.

1 P-K4   P-QB3

2 P-Q4   P-Q4

3 P-K5   B-B4

4 B-Q3   BxB

A retreat to N3 could run into trouble by 5 P-K6! PxP 6 BxB PxB 7 Q-N4 K-B2 8 N-KB3, and the knight leaps in next move with a deadly check.

5 QxB   P-K3

6 N-QB3   Q-N3

7 KN-K2

The knight moves here rather than to B3, making it possible to protect the king pawn by P-B4.

7 ...   P-QB4

Capablanca avoids an exchange of queens, which he could bring about by 7 . . . Q-R3, as that would facilitate the draw.

Instead he plays to undermine the base of the hostile pawn-chain—strategy recommended by Nimzowitsch (but no secret to the higher echelon).

8   PxP   BxP

9   0-0

Attacking the K-side by 9 Q-N3 looks inviting, but after 9 . . . N-K2   10 QxP R-N1   11 QxRP RxP, the attack suddenly changes hands.

9 . . .   KN-K2

10   N-R4

Exclamation point or question mark?

White considers this a good move, as it eliminates a potentially troublesome bishop, and enables his own bishop to come into the game with a gain of tempo.

Black considers this a doubtful move, as the exchange of pieces will leave him with an able knight against an inferior bishop.

10 . . .   Q-B3

11   NxB   QxN

12   B-K3   Q-B2

13   P-KB4

Unavoidable, as the king pawn needed support, but it emphasizes the weakness of his white squares, notably K4, KB5, and QB4.

13 . . .   N-B4

An ideal spot for the knight! It can be dislodged from this square, but only at the cost of creating further weaknesses.

14   P-B3

Nimzowitsch overprotects the central square Q4 with queen, knight, bishop, and pawn, in accordance with his theories.

Alekhine, whose style is restless and energetic, suggests a dynamic approach, such as this line of play: 14 QR-B1! N-B3   15 B-B2 P-KR4   16 P-B4 PxP 17 QxP 0-0   18 KR-Q1, and after shifting the knight to K4 (by way of B3) White should hardly lose.

14 . . .   N-B3

15   QR-Q1   P-KN3

Capablanca could fortify his knight's position by 15 . . . P-KR4, but instead deliberately invites an attack on the knight, which dislodges it from its present fine position.

Réti's comment is illuminating: Capablanca's style exhibits several peculiarities, the explanation of which must be sought in the fact that they are a consequence of his sovereign insight into all the elements of a position. For instance, he is sometimes content with surprisingly small advantages, although the position may be such that many a master would feel justified in trying to obtain more than that. The thing is that very early he clearly perceives small nuances as real advantages, and turning them to account is for him a matter of definite and perhaps not too laborious technique.

Another characteristic of Capablanca's style is that he does not cling stubbornly to an advantage he has gained, but is always ready to exchange one advantage for another. Thus we believe that in the present game, most masters would have held fast to the advantage in position with 15 . . . P-KR4; and there does not seem to be any objection to this method. But Capablanca readily admits 16 P-KN4, as he realizes that then, even after the exchange of White's ineffective bishop, the too far advanced pawn position will offer him other permanent advantages.

16   P-KN4

Alekhine calls this 'an unbelievable maneuver for a player of Nimzowitsch's class,' as it forfeits his prospects on the K-side, and frees the opponent of worry about the black squares (since the bishop will come off).

Alekhine regards White's game as strategically lost, but admits that it would take proper technique to demonstrate a win. He suggests instead this continuation: 16 B-B2 P-KR4   17 R-Q2 followed by 18 R-QB1 with a view to P-B4.

Capablanca explains his thought processes (about

16 P-KN4): White has accepted the invitation to drive away the knight. He probably considered that if he did not drive away the strongly posted knight, Black would play . . . P-KR4 and then the knight would be a source of trouble for the rest of the game. Black had considered other factors before allowing this move. He felt that after the exchange of the knight for the bishop, he would play . . . P-KR4, forcing White to play P-N5. As a result White's king bishop pawn would be very weak. The whole king's side would be open to any Black piece able to enter that territory. It is true that it does not seem possible to penetrate White's defence, but Black felt that there would be a way to do it. His judgment was vindicated, since he was able to prove that White's stronghold could be conquered and that the weak king bishop pawn, combined with the exposed position of the White's K-side, would be the cause of White's downfall.

16 . . .   NxB

17 QxN   P-KR4

18 P-N5

Forced, as after 18 P-KR3 PxP   19 PxP 0-0-0 Black's threats of . . . P-KN4 and . . . R-R5 are hard to meet.

18 . . .   0-0

19 N-Q4   Q-N3

20 R-B2   KR-B1

21 P-QR3   R-B2

22 R-Q3   N-R4

23 R-K2   R-K1

A precaution against 24 P-B5 KPxP   25 P-K6.

24 K-N2   N-B3!

One would expect the knight to go to B5, but that square is reserved as a point of entry for the rooks in their projected attack along the fifth rank.

25 R(K2)-Q2

Alekhine suggests as offering the best practical chances: 25 NxN QxN   26 R-Q4 (certainly not 26 QxP P-N3

27 Q-R6 R-R1, and the queen has no exit), though Black should still win with best play.

25 . . .   R(K1)-QB1

26 R-K2   N-K2

This begins the final phase, which Capablanca conducts with his customary accuracy.

27 R(K2)-Q2   R-B5

The magic square!

28 Q-R3   K-N2!

The purpose of this will be clear shortly.

29 R-KB2   P-R4

30 R-K2

The position with Black to move:

Capablanca to move

Position after 30 R-K2

Nimzowitsch

30 . . .   N-B4!

The point is to eliminate Black's most useful defensive piece (the knight) after which Black can concentrate his fire on the king bishop pawn.

31 NxNch

The alternative 31 R(K2)-Q2 allows 31 . . . NxN (the exchange at a different square, but just as effective) 32 RxN RxR   33 PxR Q-N4, and after 34 . . . R-B8 Black wins much as in the actual game.

31 . . .   NPxN!

Nimzowitsch may have thought that his 28 Q-R3 move prevented this capture, only to discover that 32 QxRP (the move he relied on) fails after 32 . . .

R-KR1 (now we see the point of 28 . . . K-N2!)
33 Q-B3 R-R5, and Black wins in all variations, thus:
34 R-Q4 R-N5ch, and

(a) 35 K-R1 QxR! 36 PxQ R-B8ch with mate to
follow.

(b) 35 K-B2 RxR 36 PxR QxPch 37 Q-K3 (best)
RxPch and wins.

(c) 35 K-B2 RxR 36 PxR QxQP 37 R-KB2 Q-B5ch
38 Q-K2 Q-B8ch 39 Q-K1 R-N8ch, and Black wins
the queen.

32 Q-B3   K-N3

33 R(K2)–Q2   R-K5

34 R-Q4   R(B1)-B5

Whether White chooses to exchange or not is im-
material, as his king bishop pawn remains weak in any
event, and Black's queen will insinuate herself into the
enemy camp.

35 Q-B2   Q-N4!

36 K-N3   R(B5)xR

37 PxR

But not 37 RxR, when 37 . . . R-K7 wins.

37 . . .   Q-B5

The queen takes command of the only open file.

38 K-N2   P-N4

This and the next couple of pawn moves are intended
to rid the board of any superfluous elements.

39 K-N1   P-N5

40 PxP   PxP

41 K-N2

White is reduced to moves by his king, the only
piece that dares move. His queen and rook, tied to the
defence of the bishop pawn and queen pawn, may not
stir.

41 . . .   Q-QB8

Begins a series of beautifully forceful moves that
render Nimzowitsch utterly helpless.

42 K-N3

What else is there? A queen move loses the rook, a
rook move loses the valuable bishop pawn (and the
game, of course) and if 42 P-R3 P-N6 43 K-R2
R-K8 44 K-N2 Q-QN8 45 R-K2 R-QB8 followed
by 46 . . . R-B7 wins for Black.

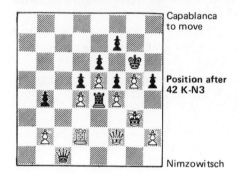

Capablanca
to move

Position after
42 K-N3

Nimzowitsch

42 . . .   Q-KR8

Threatens a decisive invasion by 43 . . . R-K8 and
44 . . . R-KB8.

43 R-Q3

If White tries to exchange queens or rooks, this is
what happens:

(a) 43 R-K2 RxR 44 QxR Q-N8ch, and Black wins
the queen pawn.

(b) 43 Q-N2 QxQch 44 KxQ (or 44 RxQ RxQP)
RxBP and wins.

(c) 43 Q-B3 P-R5ch 44 K-B2 Q-K8ch and Black
wins a rook.

43 . . .   R-K8

Now the threat is 44 . . . R-KB8 45 Q-K3 R-N8ch,
and White must give up his queen or be mated in two.

44 R-KB3   R-Q8

White is in *semi-zugzwang*. If 45 K-R3 Q-Q7
46 Q-N3, and 46 . . . P-R5 is the knockout blow. Or if
45 R-N3 Q-K5 46 RxP R-Q6ch 47 K-R4 R-KB6
does the trick. Finally, if 45 P-R3 R-N8ch 46 K-R4
R-N5 is mate.

45 P-N3   R-QB8!

This is *zugzwang!* The proof: If

(a) 46 K-R4 R-B7   47 QxR QxR   48 P-R3 QxBP mate.

(b) 46 P-R3 R-N8ch   47 K-R4 R-N5 mate (pretty!).

(c) 46 Q-K2 R-B7!   47 QxR P-R5ch   48 KxP QxR 49 P-R3 QxBP mate.

(d) 46 Q-Q2 P-R5ch   47 KxP (or 47 K-B2 R-B8ch and mate next) 47 . . . QxR and Black wins.

46 R-K3   R-B8
Now on 47 Q-K2 there follows 47 . . . Q-N8ch 48 K-R3 R-K8   49 QxR Q-N5 mate.

47 Resigns
A magnificent game.

112

White **E. Bogolyubov**   Black **J.R. Capablanca**
Queen's Indian Defence
Bad Kissingen, 1928

No one ever drew a game with Capablanca by exchanging pieces. Somehow an exchange or two left Capablanca with slightly the better game—but that little was enough for his purpose.

In the fine art of exchanging pieces, Capablanca had no equal.

In this game, for example, he takes a position that seems barren of resources and molds it into a picture of beauty.

With consummate artistry he fashions a web to ensnare the king, and hold him tight. Then, while his rooks and a knight surround the king, a pawn, quietly waiting in the background, steps forward to administer the *coup de grâce*, a checkmate in problem-like style.

1 P-Q4   N-KB3

2 P-QB4   P-K3

3 N-KB3   P-QN3

4 N-B3   B-N2

5 B-N5   B-K2

6 P-K3
Rather mild for a Bogolyubov. One would expect 5 Q-B2, if only to prevent the freeing 5 . . . N-K5.

6 . . .   N-K5

7 BxB   QxB

8 NxN   BxN

9 N-Q2
The better move is 9 B-K2, but Bogolyubov wants to exchange as many pieces as he can.

9 . . .   B-N2

10 B-K2   Q-N4
Clearly, nothing is to be gained by 10 . . . BxP, when 11 R-KN1 B-N2   12 RxP gets the pawn back with advantage to White.

11 B-B3   BxB

12 QxB   N-B3

13 Q-N3   QxQ

14 RPxQ   K-K2
'Almost any other master would reconcile himself to a draw in such a position,' says Beheim, 'but Capablanca, along with Rubinstein, won a reputation for peerless endgame skill which enables such minimal advantages as Black has here to be gradually increased.'
(Capablanca does win it, and beautifully!)

15 P-KN4   P-KR3

16 P-R3   P-R3
There is a great difference in the two moves by the queen's rook pawn: White's is a fearful precaution against 16 . . . N-N5; Black's rook pawn will act as support for a breakthrough by . . . P-QN4, and an opening of lines for his rooks.

17 K-K2   KR-QN1!
Reminiscent of the Winter-Capablanca game, played at Hastings in 1919, this move seems almost con-

temtuous of any excitement that White could stir up
on the K-side.

So far as the Q-side is concerned, Black is prepared
to meet 18 P-N4 with 18 . . . P-QN4, and if then
19 P-B5, P-QR4 assures him the better game.

18 N-K4   P-QN4

19 P-B5

As good as forced, since 19 PxP RxP   20 P-N4
P-QR4 wins a pawn for Black.

19 . . .   P-Q4!

20 PxP en passant, ch

Retreating the knight to Q2 allows a breakthrough by
20 . . . P-K4, while 20 N-B3 permits it by 20 . . . P-N5.

20 . . .   PxP

21 P-B4   R-QB1

22 P-B5

Instead of this optimistic attempt to attack, White
should have played 22 KR-QB1, to counter Black's
Q-side pressure.

22 . . .   N-R4

23 K-Q3   N-B5

24 QR-QN1   P-Q4!

Capablanca's play here and to the end of the game
is perfect in its economic and beautiful exploitation
of a won position—Golombek.

25 N-B3

On 25 N-B5, Black's reply is the energetic 25 . . .
P-K4 (threatens 26 . . . P-K5ch)   26 P-K4 PxPch
27 NxP (if 27 KxP, N-Q7ch wins the exchange)
R-Q1, and Black wins a valuable pawn.

25 . . .   R-B3

26 PxP   PxP

27 P-N5

White gives up a pawn, hoping to derive some benefit
from the open rook file. Besides he must do something about preventing 27 . . . K-B3 and 28 . . . K-N4.

27 . . .   PxP

28 R-R5   K-B3

29 R-R3   QR-QB1

Beginning of the end. Capablanca has all the elements
of victory in his unremitting pressure on the bishop
file, his strongly-placed knight, and an extra pawn as
a trump.

Incidentally, he threatens to win two pawns by
playing 30 . . . NxPch.

Strategically, the game is won, but the best is yet
to come, with Capablanca weaving a beautiful mating
net around the king.

30 N-R2

This is the situation:

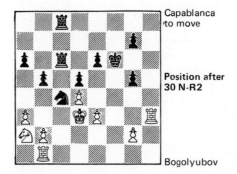

Capablanca
to move

Position after
30 N-R2

Bogolyubov

30 . . .   P-R4!

This keeps the knight from emerging, and begins the
process of encirclement.

31 R-B3ch   K-N3

'Secure from worldly chances and mishaps.'

32 P-KN4   N-Q3

Already indicating his intentions: 33 . . . N-K5,
34 . . . R-B7, and 35 . . . R-Q7 mate.

33 N-B3   P-N5

34 PxP   PxP

35 N-Q1

There is no escape from destiny by this alternative
line: 35 N-R2 N-K5!   36 NxP R-B5   37 N-R2 R-B7
38 R-Q1 RxP   39 N-B1, and now instead of 39 . . .

RxN! (recommended with exclamation marks included by Spielmann, Panov, Reinfeld, and Beheim) R-B6 is checkmate.

35 ...   R-B7

Once again the ominous rook to the seventh!
    Threat: 36 . . . N-K5 and 37 . . . R-Q7 mate.

36 R-B2   P-N6!

A pretty pawn push of paralyzing power.
    White may not exchange rooks, as that costs a rook; nor may he separate his opponent's rooks by 37 N-B3, for that costs a rook too.

37 R-R1   N-K5

Draws the net tighter.

38 R-K2   R(B1)-B3

Tighter and tighter! What moves are left to White? If 39 R-K1 R-Q7 is mate, or if 39 RxR, RxR followed by 40 . . . R-Q7 is mate. Finally, if 39 N-B3, RxNch 40 PxR RxP is mate.

39 R-N1   P-K4!

A delightful touch! Mate will come by a pawn, and from another direction!

40 R-R1

If 40 PxP, R(B3)-B5 wins.

40 ...   R(B3)-B5

41 R-R5   N-B4ch!

42 Resigns

Mate will come next move by 42 . . . P-K5.

113

White **J.R. Capablanca**   Black **H. Steiner**
Queen's Gambit Declined
Budapest, 1928

This game against Steiner is beyond praise.
    It is *the* classic Capablanca game (but then every Capablanca game I look at is *the* classic game).
    So elegant and crystal clear is it, that I was impelled

to place an exclamation mark after every move I admired—only to find that I had to adorn every move with this symbol of excellence! Later I was persuaded (against my better judgement) to single out only the moves that really shine.

1 P-Q4   N-KB3

2 P-QB4   P-K3

3 N-QB3   P-Q4

4 B-N5   QN-Q2

5 P-K3   B-K2

6 N-B3   O-O

7 R-B1   P-B3

8 B-Q3   PxP

9 BxP   N-Q4

Capablanca's freeing maneuver, but as Steiner discovers, it works for Capablanca, not for Steiner.

10 BxB   QxB

Taking the knight first loses in a hurry, so: 10 . . . NxN 11 BxQ NxQ 12 B-K7 R-K1 13 B-R3, and the knight is captured alive.

11 O-O

Capablanca has no taste for the complexities of 11 N-K4, favoured by Alekhine. He prefers clarity above all.

11 ...   NxN

12 RxN   P-QN3

Black should play 12 . . . P-K4 immediately to free his game. If then 13 PxP NxP, and his bishop can see daylight.
    Steiner's idea is to continue with 13 . . . B-N2 and 14 . . . P-QB4, but this turns out to be slow.
    Capablanca exploits Black's minute positional weakness in admirable style.

13 Q-B2!

This embodies a threat of 14 B-Q3, winning a pawn.
    Against the natural development by 13 . . . B-N2,

White proceeds 14 B-Q3 P-KN3 15 B-K4, and wins
the bishop pawn.

13 . . . P-QB4

14 PxP!

'This apparently simple continuation contains, as is
customary with Capablanca, a wealth of hidden,
positional meaning,' says Golombek.

Capablanca does not plunge into combinations
that have a surface glitter, but abound with treacherous reefs beneath, such as: 14 B-N5 PxP 15 R-B7
Q-Q1 16 PxP N-B3 17 Q-B6 N-Q4 18 RxBP RxR
19 QxR N-B2 20 Q-B6 B-Q2, and Black wins a piece.

14 . . . NxP

On 14 . . . PxP 15 B-N5 wins a pawn, by removing
the defending knight.

15 P-QN4!

Brilliant, as it forces the knight to the side of the
board.

15 . . . N-R3

Black could ill afford 15 . . . N-Q2, the sequel to which
could be: 16 B-Q3! QxP 17 BxPch K-R1 18 R-B4!
Q-K2 19 R-R4, and the two-fold threat of 20 B-N8
dis.ch, and 20 B-K4 dis.ch, is decisive.

Or if 16 . . . P-N3 (instead of 16 . . . QxP) 17 R-B7,
and the various threats of 18 Q-B6, or 18 B-N5, or
18 B-K4, or 18 N-K5 would be too much for mere
mortal to contend with.

16 P-QR3 B-N2

17 B-Q3!

By attacking the rook pawn, Capablanca cleverly gains
time to triple his heavy pieces on the bishop file.

17 . . . P-N3

18 R-B1!

With such domination of the bishop file, White can
say with *The Count of Monte Cristo*, 'The world is
mine!'

18 . . . QR-Q1

Black cannot dispute control of the bishop file with

18 . . . QR-B1, as after 19 RxR RxR 20 QxRch!
BxQ 21 RxBch K-N2 22 BxN, White's material
superiority is enough to win.

Black hopes to get the knight back into play by
19 . . . N-N1, and if then 20 R-B7 R-Q2.

19 N-K5

Seizes a fine outpost, once more with a gain of time,
as there is a threat of winning the exchange by
20 BxN BxB 21 N-B6.

19 . . . Q-Q3

The attractive 19 . . . Q-N4 is easily repulsed by
20 P-B4.

20 P-B4

Now the threat of winning a pawn by 21 Q-R4 is
one that Black is helpless to meet.

20 . . . N-N1

Attacking the knight instead by 20 . . . P-B3 would
let Capablanca unfold a beautiful combination involving play against pieces on both sides of the board—
one of those brilliant concepts that appear in the
notes, and which 'slumber beneath a thin coverlet.'

The combination (after 20 . . . P-B3) would go
like this: 21 NxP! PxN 22 BxN (makes room on
the diagonal for the queen—line-vacating, as the
problemists call it) 22 . . . BxB 23 QxPch K-R1,
and now, not 24 P-K4 (clearance for 25 R-R3 mate)
as that loses by 24 . . . Q-Q5ch, and Black does the
mating, but 24 P-N5! B-N2 (on 24 . . . BxP
25 Q-R5ch wins the bishop) 25 P-K4! Q-Q5ch
26 K-B1, and 27 R-R3ch next move wraps the game
up.

21 R-B7!

*If there is one magic move that wins every game, it
is R-B7!*

21 . . . B-R1

Capablanca's superb strategy seems to take every
form of counterplay into account. Here, the plausible
21 . . . R-B1 is refuted by 22 NxBP! QxR 23 QxQ
RxQ 24 N-R6ch K-N2 25 RxRch KxN 26 RxB

and White has won a pawn.

22 RxRP N-B3

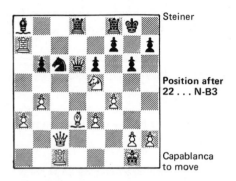

Steiner

**Position after
22 . . . N-B3**

Capablanca
to move

White could now win a second pawn by 23 NxN BxN
24 QxB QxB 25 QxNP. But then Black retaliates
with 25 . . . Q-K7! (threatening 26 . . . R-Q7 27 Q-N7
QxKPch 28 K-R1 R-K7! 29 R-KN1 R-K8 forcing
mate) 26 P-R3 R-Q7 27 Q-N7 QxKPch 28 K-R1
R-Q2! 29 QxR QxRch 30 K-R2 QxPch, and Black
draws by perpetual check.

Capablanca is content to simplify—remaining one
pawn ahead. And nobody, but nobody, could simplify
so well as Capablanca!

23 RxB! NxN

Naturally, Black avoids 23 . . . RxR, as 24 QxN
leaves White with two pieces for a rook.

24 RxR RxR

25 B-K2!

The bishop retreats quietly, and leaves the knight
stranded.

The knight, ideally situated in the center of the
board, must move and can move, but only into a
fatal pin, thus:

If 25 . . . N-Q6 26 R-Q1 wins the unfortunate
creature, or if 25 . . . N-Q2 26 R-Q1 Q-K2 27 Q-B7
K-B1 28 B-N5 K-K1 29 RxN wins by exchanging
all the pieces, and leaving a pawn ending that is easily
won for White.

25 . . . Q-Q7

26 QxQ!

'Position comes first, material next,' Capablanca himself advised in his admirable *A primer of chess.*

Capablanca follows his own advice, and rejects the
win of a piece by 26 PxN, when the continuation
26 . . . QxPch 27 K-R1 R-Q7 28 Q-B8ch K-N2
29 B-B3 QxRP might still offer some difficulties.

26 . . . RxQ

27 R-B8ch K-N2

28 K-B1

Once again the knight will be mercilessly pinned
wherever it goes.

28 . . . N-Q2

On 28 . . . N-Q6 instead, 28 R-Q8 follows, and the
knight is doomed.

29 R-Q8

The immediate threat is of course 30 B-N5, with a
double attack on the knight.

29 . . . K-B3

30 B-N5 R-Q4

31 P-QR4!

Accurate to the last detail! On the hasty 31 BxN, the
play goes: 31 . . . K-K2 32 R-QN8 RxB 33 RxP
R-R2 followed by 34 . . . RxP, and Black can still put
up a struggle.

31 . . . RxB

Desperation, but anything else loses by 32 RxN!

32 PxR K-K2

33 R-QB8! P-K4

34 R-B6! P-K5

35 K-K2 P-B4

36 K-Q2 K-B2

37 K-B3 Resigns

Steiner is convinced, seeing no defence. If 37 . . .
K-K2 38 K-Q4 K-B2 39 K-Q5 K-K2 (if 39 . . .

N-B3ch   40 RxNch wins) 40 R-B7 K-Q1   41 K-Q6,
and Black runs out of moves.

114

White **J.R. Capablanca**   Black **H. Mattison**
Nimzo-Indian Defence
Carlsbad, 1929

Capablanca is at his best in this miniature.

In the economical style for which he is famous,
Capablanca simply develops his pieces. So beautifully
are his moves timed, though, and so skilful are his
thrusts at the enemy pieces, as to cause Mattison's game
to fall apart.

Underneath the placid surface there lurk all sorts of
clever little combinations, but they all end in favour of
Capablanca!

The last combination is merely a threat, but it is
menacing enough to make Mattison resign! The thought
of losing by smothered mate is too much to bear!

A Capablanca jewel!

1 P-Q4   N-KB3

2 P-QB4   P-K3

3 N-QB3   B-N5

4 Q-B2   P-B4

The preference nowadays is 4 . . . P-Q4, or 4 . . .
N-B3 (the Zurich variation) with a view to building
up a pawn center by 5 . . . P-Q3 and 6 . . . P-K4.

5 PxP   N-B3

6 N-B3   BxP

7 B-B4

At first glance this appears less energetic than 7 B-N5
B-K2 8 P-K4, but there is a lot of poison in Capa-
balanca's quiet little bishop move.

Could he have foreseen, at this early stage, the
great influence the bishop would exert on the square
Q6?

7 . . .   P-Q4

8 P-K3   Q-R4

Black spies a chance to saddle his opponent with an
isolated bishop pawn—a slight positional weakness.
So he begins an action against the knight: but, as
Tartakover says, 'Such artificial maneuvers can hardly
succeed against a Capablanca.'

Instead of this, Black should try to get his queen
bishop into play, somewhat as follows: 8 . . . P-QR3
9 B-K2 PxP 10 BxP P-QN4 11 B-K2 Q-N3 (not at
once 11 . . . B-N2 on account of 12 NxP) 12 0-0
B-N2.

9 B-K2   B-N5

In contrast to White's classically simple method of
development, Black moves the bishop a third time
in the opening, in order to inflict his opponent with
an isolated pawn. Such an attempt is premature in
view of Black's incomplete development.

Some interesting play would follow 9 . . . 0-0
one possibility being:
10 0-0 PxP   11 BxP B-Q2 (unites the rooks)
12 P-QR3 B-K2   13 P-QN4 Q-R4   14 P-N5 N-R4
15 B-K2, and now 15 . . . Q-QB4, but not 15 . . .
Q-N3, when 16 Q-R4 P-N3   17 N-K5 Q-B4   18 P-N4!
wins a piece or two.

10 0-0   BxN

11 PxB

The bishop has moved four times to make this exchange for a knight which has moved only once! So
much shifting around of one piece indicates that the
strategy impelling it must be faulty.

Despite the doubled bishop pawn, White enjoys
these advantages:

(a) He has two active bishops against Black's knight
and bishop.

(b) All his minor pieces are in play, while Black's
bishop is still on the first rank.

(c) His rooks are in touch with each other, and ready
to seize the open knight file, and the half-open queen file.

(d) His king is safely tucked away in a corner, while Black's is out in the open.

(e) His queen is ideally posted, and has more influence on the center than does Black's, standing at the side of the board.

(f) An exchange of pawns in the center (which looks inevitable) will open lines of attack—a circumstance favouring the player whose development is superior—in this case, White.

(g) He maintains the initiative.

11 . . .   0-0

It's now or never. It was risky to develop the bishop, as after 11 . . . B-Q2   12 QR-N1 (attacks the knight pawn) P-QN3   13 B-Q6 (stops K-side castling and threatens 14 R-N5 Q-R3   15 PxP PxP   16 RxQP, and the discovered attack on the queen enables White to win a pawn).

12 QR-N1!

Seemingly an unobtrusive move, but the kind that Capablanca employed with great effect.

In compensation for White's broken-up pawn position, the rook has an open file, along which it manages to exert uncomfortable pressure on Black's Q-side, makes normal development difficult for Black, and creates permanent weaknesses which lend themselves to exploitation.

12 . . .   Q-R6

It would be dangerous to play 12 . . . P-QN3 instead, in order to develop the bishop. There would follow 13 B-Q6 R-Q1   14 R-N5 Q-R3   15 PxP, and White wins at least a pawn, as 15 . . . PxP is met by 16 RxQP discovering an attack on the queen, while 15 . . . RxB   16 PxN RxP is even worse, as 17 R-Q5 attacks the queen and threatens mate.

13 KR-Q1!

With the posting of this rook on the partly open queen file, development has been completed in an ideal way, *every piece taking its best post in no more than one move.*

White has not so much as hinted at an attacking combination until every piece has been put to work.

13 . . .   P-QN3

This is to enable the bishop to come out, without losing the knight pawn. The advance of the pawn takes away the knight's support, and weakens its position.

The weakness is so slight as to be almost imperceptible, but it does not escape Capablanca's eagle eye.

Note, incidentally, that Black could not simplify by 13 . . . PxP, as 14 B-Q6 in reply wins the exchange.

14 PxP

The attack begins! Capablanca now demolishes the enemy position with half a dozen energetic shots.

14 . . .   NxP

Recapturing with the pawn would be fatal: if 14 . . . PxP   15 P-B4! is the key to the win. Black could not then play 15 . . . PxP, since 16 B-Q6 attacks queen and rook, while protecting the pawn by 15 . . . B-K3 yields to 16 PxP BxP   17 RxB NxR   18 QxN, and White has won two pieces for a rook.

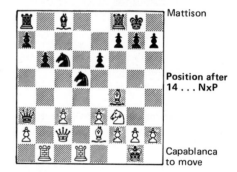

Mattison

Position after 14 . . . NxP

Capablanca to move

15 N-N5!

A master stroke! The obvious threat of 16 QxP mate disguises the two real purposes of the move: the strategical concept of forcing Black to weaken his defensive structure by moving one of the K-side pawns, and the clearance of the square KB3 for the benefit of the king bishop, who will bear down heavily on the long diagonal.

15 ...   P-B4

This weakens the king pawn, tying the bishop down to its defence, but what else was there?

If 15 ... P-N3, Black's position is riddled with black-square weaknesses.

Or if 15 ... N-B3, to avoid moving one of the pawns, 16 B-Q6 wins the exchange.

16 B-B3!

This arrangement of bishops gives them tremendous raking powers along the two parallel diagonals.

White's major threat is 17 RxN PxR   18 BxPch K-R1   19 BxN followed by 20 BxR, sweeping away a good part of Black's army.

16 ...   Q-B4

The queen rushes to the aid of the vulnerable knights. Other defences are no better:

(a) 16 ... N(Q4)-K2   17 B-Q6 Q-R4   18 BxN(K7) NxB   19 BxR, and White wins a whole rook.

(b) 16 ... N(B3)-K2   17 P-B4 N-N5   18 RxN QxR 19 BxR, and White wins a piece.

(c) 16 ... NxB   17 BxN R-N1   18 PxN, and White has won a piece.

(d) 16 ... QxBP   17 QxQ NxQ   18 BxN NxR(Q8) 19 RxN B-R3   20 BxR RxB, and White is a piece ahead.

After his actual move, Black seems to have escaped the worst, but White has an ingenious way to get at the knights.

17 P-B4!

One little combination follows another!

This stab at the knight seems harmless, as the pawn is pinned and unable to capture. But the pawn threatens to support an attack by 18 R-N5, which will drive the queen off, and make the capture 19 PxN possible.

17 ...   N(Q4)-N5

Mattison attacks the queen, in lieu of other defences which he finds wanting. For example, if

(a) 17 ... N-B3   18 B-Q6 Q-R4   19 BxN, and both Black's rooks are *en prise*.

(b) 17 ... NxB   18 R-N5 (a pretty *zwischenzug*) Q-K2 (or 18 ... N-N5   19 Q-Q2 QxBP   20 RxN, and White wins)   19 BxN QxN   20 PxN, and Black has no time to save his rook, as his queen is under attack.

(c) 17 ... N(Q4)-K2   18 B-Q6 Q-R4, and White can take either knight and win the exchange after Black recaptures.

18 Q-N3   P-K4

Black hopes to curb the terrible bishops by putting obstacles in their paths, there being no other specific against 19 B-Q6.

19 P-QR3!

Starts a beautiful combination at one end of the board, which involves a smothered mate away over at the other!

19 ...   N-R3

If 19 ... PxB instead, White forces the win by 20 PxN Q-K2   21 BxN R-N1   22 PxP, and the extra piece wins easily.

The position at this point:

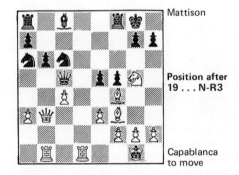

Mattison

Position after 19 ... N-R3

Capablanca to move

20 BxN

After the recapture by 20 ... QxB, there comes this dénouement: 21 P-B5 dis.ch K-R1   22 N-B7ch K-N1 (if 22 ... RxN   23 R-Q8ch, and White forces mate)   23 N-R6 dbl.ch K-R1   24 Q-N8ch! RxQ 25 N-B7 mate!

Black did not wait to be convinced by a demon-

stration over the board, but turned down his king
in surrender.

20 . . .   Resigns

An exquisite game, played with elegance and precision.
Capablanca's own comment on it was, 'I made a few
little combinations in this game.'

115

White **J.R. Capablanca**   Black **K. Treybal**
Queen's Gambit Declined
Carlsbad, 1929

With the versatility of genius, Capablanca creates a
masterpiece that borders on the fantastic.

The opening theme of encirclement is introduced by
Capablanca's pawns, which spread out in a V-shaped
chain to embrace Black's pieces in a grip of steel. These
unfortunate pieces are driven further and further back
onto the last rank. There they can take a single step
forward to the second rank—but no further than that!

Capablanca's pieces meanwhile array themselves
along an open file in a manner that is unique in chess
literature. No less than five pieces in a row occupy the
queen's rook file!

The king, away from his army, watches the scene
from a distance (not caring to be involved in any violence).

The position on the board, just before the decisive
blow is struck, is picturesque. All White's pieces except
one stand on the queen rook file, while all Black's pieces
except one stand on the last rank. The final *coup,* a
knight fork attacking the queen and both rooks, is a nice
artistic touch, in keeping with the rest of this remarkable
game.

The whole production constitutes an impressive
achievement by the greatest chess player that ever lived—
José R. Capablanca.

1 P-Q4   P-Q4

2 P-QB4   P-QB3

3 N-KB3   P-K3

4 B-N5   B-K2

There is nothing wrong with the natural move 4 . . .
N-B3, but Treybal wants originality.

He gets it—in a hurry!

5 BxB!   QxB

For now he is left with a bishop hemmed in by pawns
while Capablanca's bishop will enjoy a fine, free
development at Q3.

6 QN-Q2   P-KB4

Sets up a hard-to-crack Stonewall, a defence though
that has a drawback in that it leaves black-square
weaknesses in its wake.

7 P-K3   N-Q2

8 B-Q3   N-R3

The knight's destination is B2, from which square it
can bear down on K4 and KN4.

9 0-0   0-0

10 Q-B2   P-KN3

Supports the bishop pawn before switching the knight
over. If at once 10 . . . N-B2, then 11 PxP BPxP
(forced, as 11 . . . KPxP loses a pawn) 12 QR-B1,
and White owns the bishop file.

11 QR-N1   N-B3

12 N-K2   N-B2

13 P-B4   B-Q2

Misses his chance! Black should exchange by 13 . . .
NxN (to replace White's strongly-posted piece by a
pawn) 14 QPxN N-N5 (but not 14 . . . N-K5   15 BxN,
and White's agile knight will prove far superior to
his opponent's almost lifeless bishop)   15 R-B3
P-KN4, and he can still put up a struggle.

14 N(Q2)-B3   KR-Q1

15 P-QN4

Starts an enveloping movement on the Q-side, with
similar action to follow later on the K-side.

15 ...   B-K1

16 KR-B1   P-QR3

This emphasizes the plight of Black's 'bad' bishop. Its career is badly hampered by the fact that all eight of Black's pawns stand on white squares.

17 Q-B2   NxN

18 NxN   N-Q2

19 N-B3!

No, thank you! An exchange would only ease Black's defence.

19 ...   KR-B1

20 P-B5!

Fixes the position on one wing, in preparation for a breakthrough at QN5.

20 ...   N-B3

21 P-QR4   N-N5

22 Q-K1   N-R3

23 P-R3   N-B2

Indicating that he will try to get in 24 ... P-KN4, but White gets there first by doubly attacking the king bishop pawn.

24 P-N4

Now of course 24 ... P-KN4 loses a pawn by 25 PxBP.

24 ...   B-Q2

25 R-B2   K-R1

26 R-N2   R-KN1

27 P-KN5!

Fixes the position on this wing as well, stifling any attempt at counter-attack.

The critical points now are Black's KN3 and QB3, to which Capablanca will devote his careful attention.

27 ...   Q-Q1

28 P-R4   K-N2

29 P-KR5   R-R1

30 R-KR2   Q-B2

31 Q-B3   Q-Q1

32 K-B2   Q-B2

Black can do little but await the turn of events.

33 QR-KR1   QR-KN1

34 Q-R1   R-N1

35 Q-R3

One would expect Capablanca to lock up the Q-side, then triple his heavy pieces on the king rook file, and follow up by breaking through with PxP PxP and R-R7ch.

Instead, Capablanca does the opposite. The breakthrough comes on the Q-side, the locking up on the K-side!

35 ...   QR-KN1

36 P-N5!   RPxP

Naturally, if 36 ... BPxP   37 P-R6ch K-B1   38 P-B6 dis.ch, and White wins a piece.

37 P-R6ch   K-B1

38 PxP   K-K2

39 P-N6

Forces the queen to retreat. Notice that none of Black's pieces can venture beyond the second rank.

39 ...   Q-N1

The harmonious arrangement of White's pawns makes a pleasing picture, and deserves a diagram.

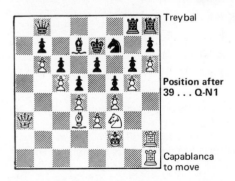

Treybal

Position after
39 ... Q-N1

Capablanca
to move

40 R-R1

White controls the queen rook file. His object now is to establish an outpost at QR7, and then exert irresistible pressure on Black's queen knight pawn.

40 ... R-QB1

To contest the open file is of no avail, as after 40 ... Q-R1 41 Q-N2 Q-N1 42 R-R7 is the consequence, with immediate pressure on the critical knight pawn.

41 Q-N4   KR-Q1

42 R-R7

For the rook this is Seventh Heaven!

42 ...   K-B1

43 R-KR1   B-K1

44 R(R1)-R1   K-N1

45 R(R1)-R4   K-B1

46 Q-R3   K-N1

Black must guard his first and second ranks simultaneously. If he tries to protect the vital queen knight pawn by 46 ... R-Q2, the reply 47 R-R8 wins his queen for a rook.

47 K-N3   B-Q2

48 K-N2

Care is needed even in a position like this, where Black seems unable to stir. If for example, 48 N-Q2 (to bring the knight to N3 and R5) NxNP would come like a shot.

48 ...   K-R1

49 Q-R1   K-N1

50 K-N3   K-B1

51 K-N2   B-K1

52 N-Q2!

Everything being proof against surprise attack, the knight starts out on its tour.

There is no danger in 52 ... NxNP, as after 53 PxN Black's queen still has no point of entry.

52 ...   B-Q2

This is the unhappy bishop's fourth (and last) little walk to Q2.

53 N-N3   R-K1

The alternative (or properly speaking, another way of losing) is 53 ... B-K1 54 N-R5 R-Q2 55 NxNP! RxN 56 R-R8, and Black loses his queen.

54 N-R5   N-Q1

55 B-R6!

Brilliant, and must have been foreseen many moves back by Capablanca.

The picture on the board is extraordinary! White's pawns are arranged in a V for Victory design, and all his pieces (except the king) are lined up on one file, while nearly all his opponent's pieces stand fearfully on the back rank!

The bishop, completely surrounded by pawns and rooks occupying white squares, is a truly 'bad' bishop.

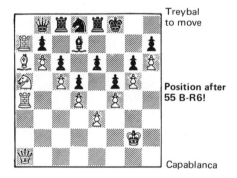

Treybal to move

Position after 55 B-R6!

Capablanca

55 ...   PxB

After this forced capture, Capablanca just rips the position apart.

56 RxB   R-K2

If 56 ... K-N1, White can win by this lovely continuation: 57 R-N7ch K-R1 58 R-N4!, and since *none of Black's pieces can stir beyond the first rank,*

he is helpless to stop the following: 59 P-N7 R-B2
60 RxR QxR   61 P-N8(Q) and wins.

57 RxNch!
Elegant, as usual.

57 ...   Resigns

Black does not care to see the pretty knight fork after 57 ... RxR   58 NxP, when the knight attacks the queen and the two rooks.

A magnificent performance by Capablanca, King of Chess.

Eugene Alexandrovich Znosko-Borovsky (a resonant name if ever there was one) once published a monograph called *Capablanca's Mistakes.*

Capablanca's response to this was to tell the author that he had tried to write a work called *Znosko-Borovsky's Good Moves*, but had to give it up, as he could not find enough material.

Milan Vidmar was scheduled to be Capablanca's opponent in the tenth round of the Nottingham Tournament of 1936. The game was postponed on Vidmar's request, as he pleaded illness, and play was set for the next free day, the fourteenth round. The other competitors, however, insisted that the game be played before the start of the eleventh round.

Capablanca refused to co-operate, saying, 'I did a favour for a colleague when he was ill. Surely Vidmar can understand that it is out of the question for me to cancel a date with a lady'?

Capablanca kept the date with the lady, and eventually married her. As for the game with Vidmar, that was played the day before the semi-final round, and resulted in an easy victory for Capablanca.

Bibliography

GENERAL WORKS

Alekhine, Alexander — *My Best Games of Chess, 1908-23*
— *My Best Games of Chess, 1924-1937*
— *Deux Cents Parties D'Échecs*
Alekhine, Alexander, and Euwe, Max — *The World's Chess Championship 1937*
Alexander, C.H.O'D. — *Alekhine's Best Games of Chess, 1938-1945*
— *A Book of Chess*

Barden, Leonard — *How Good is Your Chess?*
Beheim, Martin — *Chess With the Masters*
Bisguier, Arthur, and Soltis, Andrew — *American Chess Masters from Morphy to Fischer*
Bjelica, Dimitrije — *Grandmasters in Profile*
Bogolyubov, Ewfim — *Klassische Schachpartien aus Modernen Zeiten*
Botvinnik, Mikhail — *100 Selected Games*
— *Botvinnik's Best Games, 1947-1970*
Bronstein, David — *200 Open Games*
Burger, Robert E. — *The Chess of Bobby Fischer*

Cafferty, Bernard — *Spassky's 100 Best Games*
— *Tal's 100 Best Games*
Capablanca, José R. — *My Chess Career*
— *Chess Fundamentals*
— *A Primer of Chess*
— *Last Lectures*
Chernev, Irving — *Logical Chess Move by Move*
— *The Bright Side of Chess*
— *The Chess Companion*
— *The Most Instructive Games of Chess Ever Played*
— *Combinations: The Heart of Chess*
— *Wonders and Curiosities of Chess*
— *The 1000 Best Short Games of Chess*
— *The Russians Play Chess*

Chernev, Irving, and Reinfeld, Fred — *The Fireside Book of Chess*
Clarke, Peter H. — *Tal's Best Games of Chess*
— *Petrosian's Best Games of Chess, 1946-1963*
Coles, R.N. — *Dynamic Chess*
— *Battles Royal of the Chessboard*
Cozens, W.H. — *Boris Spassky's Road to the Summit*
— *Tal since 1960*

Euwe, Max — *Meet the Masters*
— *Judgment and Planning in Chess*
— *The Development of Chess Style*
— *Chess Archives, 1952-1959*
Euwe, Max, and Prins, Lodewijk — *Das Schachphänomen Capablanca*
Evans, Larry — *Modern Chess Brilliancies*
— *Chess Catechism*

Fine, Reuben — *The Middle Game in Chess*
— *The World's a Chessboard*
— *Chess Marches On*
— *Basic Chess Endings*
— *The World's Great Chess Games*
— *Psychoanalytic Observations*
Fischer, Robert J. — *My 60 Memorable Games*

Gelabert, José A. — *Glorias del Tablero 'Capablanca.'*
Gligorić, Svetozar — *Selected Chess Masterpieces*
— *Fischer vs. Spassky, the Chess Match of the Century*
Golembek, Harry — *Capablanca's 100 Best Games of Chess*
— *The World Chess Championship 1954*
— *The World Chess Championship 1957*
— *Fischer vs. Spassky—The World Chess Championship 1972*

Hannak, J. — *Emanuel Lasker—The Life of a Chess Master*
Hooper, David — *Practical Chess Endgames*
Hooper, David, and Brandreth, Dale — *The Unknown Capablanca*

Keene, Raymond D. — *Flank Openings*
— *Aron Nimzowitsch: A Reappraisal*
Keene, Raymond D., and Levy, David N.L. — *How to Play the Opening in Chess*
Kmoch, Hans — *Rubinstein Gewinnt!*
König, Imre — *Chess from Morphy to Botvinnik*
Kotov, Alexander — *Think Like a Grandmaster*
— *Das Schacherbe Aljechin's*
Kotov, Alexander, and Yudovich, Mikhail — *The Soviet School of Chess*
Kramer, Hans, and Postma, S.H. — *Das Schachphänomen Robert Fischer*
Krogius, N.V. — *Chess Psychology*

Lasker, Edward — *Chess Strategy*
— *The Adventure of Chess*
Lasker, Emanuel — *Manual of Chess*
— *Common Sense in Chess*
Levy, David N.L. — *How Fischer Plays Chess*
Lionnais, François Le — *Les Prix de Beauté aux Échecs*
Lionnais, François Le, and Maget, Ernst — *Dictionnaire des Échecs*

Müller, Hans — *Botvinnik Lehrt Schach*
— *Das Zentrum in der Schachpartie*
Müller, Hans, and Pawelczak, A. — *Schachgenie Aljechin*
Murray, H.J.R. — *A History of Chess*
— *A Short History of Chess*

Nimzowitsch, Aron — *My System*
— *Die Praxis Meines Systems*

O'Kelly de Galway, Albéric — *Tigran Petrosian, World Champion*

Pachman, Ludek — *Modern Chess Strategy*
— *Attack and Defence in Modern Chess Tactics*
— *Entscheidungspartien*

Reinfeld, Fred — *Nimzowitsch the Hypermodern*
— *The Immortal Games of Capablanca*
— *Botvinnik the Invincible*
— *The Human Side of Chess*
— *Great Games by Chess Prodigies*
Reinfeld, Fred, and Chernev, Irving — *Chess Strategy and Tactics*
Réti, Richard — *Modern Ideas in Chess*
— *Masters of the Chessboard*

Saidy, Anthony — *The Battle of Chess Ideas*
Sergeant, Philip W. — *Championship Chess*
Smyslov, Vassily — *My Best Games of Chess, 1935-1957*
Sokolsky, A.P. — *The Modern Openings in Theory and Practice*
Soltis, Andrew — *The Best Chess Games of Boris Spassky*
Stahlberg, Gideon — *Chess and Chess Masters*
Sunnucks, Anne — *Encyclopaedia of Chess*

Tarrasch, Siegbert — *Die Moderne Schachpartie*
— *Der Schachwettkampf Lasker-Marshall 1907*
Tartakover, Savielly — *Die Hypermoderne Schachpartie*
— *Die Zükunfteroffnung*
— *Führende Meister*
Tartakover, Savielly, and du Mont, Julius — *500 Master Games of Chess*
— *100 Master Games of Modern Chess*
Toran, Roman — *David Bronstein*

Vasiliev, Vik L. — *Tigran Petrosian, His life and Games*
Vuković, Vladimir — *The Art of Attack in Chess*

Wade, Robert G. — *Soviet Chess*
Wade, Robert G., and O'Connell, Kevin J. — *The Games of Robert J. Fischer*
Winter, William — *Kings of Chess*
— *Chess for Match Players*

Yates, F.D., and Winter, William — *Modern Master Play*

Znosko-Borovsky, Eugène — *How to Play the Chess Endings*
— *The Art of Chess Combination*
— *The Middle Game in Chess*

MAGAZINES

American Chess Bulletin, 1904-63
Chess, 1936-75
Chess Life, 1961-9
Chess Life and Review, 1970-5
Chess Review, 1933-69
Chess World, 1946-67
Wiener Schachzeitung, 1898-1933

TOURNAMENT BOOKS

Alekhine, Alexander — *The New York International Tournament 1924*
— *Das New Yorker Schachturnier, 1927*
— *The Book of the Hastings International Masters' Chess Tournament 1922*
— *Internationales Schachturnier, Zurich 1934*
— *The Book of the Nottingham International Chess Tournament 1936*
Bogolyubov, Ewfim — *Das Internationale Schachturnier Moskau 1925*
Botvinnik, Mikhail — *Championship Chess: Match-Tournament for the Absolute Championship of the U.S.S.R. 1941*
Cafferty, Bernard (editor) — *Candidates' Matches 1971*
Capablanca, José R. — *Torneo Internacional de Ajedrez 1913*
Cheshire, Horace E. (editor) — *The Hastings Chess Tournament 1895*

Fischer, Robert J., and Bjelica, Dimitrije — *Chess Meets of the Century*
Gligorić, Svetozar, and Matanović Milan — *Interzonen-Turnier, Portoroz 1958*
Gligorić, Svetozar, and Ragosin, V. — *Kandidatenturnier für Schachweltmeisterschaft Bled, Zagreb, Belgrad 1959*
Grünfeld, Ernst, and Becker, Albert — *Die Partien des Internationalen Meisterturniers Teplitz-Schönau 1922*
Kashdan, Isaac (editor) — *First Piatigorsky Cup 1970*
Keene, Raymond D., and Levy, David N.L. — *Siegen Chess Olympiad 1970*
— *Chess Olympiad Skopje 1972*
Kmoch, Hans (editor) — *IV Internationales Schachmeisterturnier Karlsbad 1929*
Lasker, Emanuel — *International Chess Congress St. Petersburg 1909*
Marco, Georg, and Schlechter, Karl — *Das Internationale Schachmeisterturnier in Karlsbad 1907*
Maroczy, Geza (editor) — *The Book of the London International Chess Congress 1922*
Najdorf, Miguel — *Aspirantes al Campeonato Mundial Suiza 1953*
Rabinovich, I.L. (editor) — *Vtoroi Mezhdunarodny Schachmatny Turnir Moskva 1935*
Tarrasch, Siegbert — *Das Grossmeisterturnier zu St. Petersburg 1914*
Tartakover, Savielly — *Internationales Schachturnier Bad Kissingen 1928*
Wood, Baruch H. (editor) — *The World Championship Candidates' Tournament Switzerland 1953*

Index of openings

Index of players

The references are to game numbers

Alekhine   91, 92, 93, 94, 95, 96, 97, 98, 99, 100
Aronin   60
Averbach   52

Barendregt   58
Bauer   82
Behting   2
Benko   62
Bernstein   1, 104
Black   107
Blanco   103
Bogdanovich   54
Bogolyubov   16, 96, 112
Bolbochan   77
Boleslavsky   68
Bondarevsky   67
Botvinnik   19, 64, 65, 66, 67, 68, 69, 70, 71, 72
Bronstein   19, 20, 21, 22, 23, 24, 25, 26, 27, 31
Byrne   73

Capablanca   66, 88, 101, 102, 103, 104, 105, 106, 107, 108, 109, 110, 111, 112, 113, 114, 115
Chekover   65
Cohn   14
Corzo   101

Denker   41
Dubinin   21
Duras   11

Evans   32

Fischer   51, 57, 73, 74, 75, 76, 77, 78, 79, 80, 81
Furman   22
Fuster   49

Geller   45

Gligorić   50
Grünfeld   97
Guimard   74

Hage   7
Hromadka   17

Janowsky   109
Johner   5
Jopen   55

Keres   25, 35
Kevitz   100
Klovan   33
Kotov   23
Kottnauer   40

Larsen   36, 79, 80
Lasker   13, 82, 83, 84, 85, 86, 87, 88, 89, 90
Letelier   53, 75
Lipnitzky   43
Lissitzin   46

Makogonov   37, 69
Mannheimer   9
Marshall   85, 86, 90, 102
Mattison   8, 18, 114
Molina   106

Najdorf   24
Nimzowitsch   1, 2, 3, 4, 5, 6, 7, 8, 9, 91, 111

Palmiotto   27
Petrosian   55, 56, 57, 58, 59, 60, 61, 62, 63, 81
Pillsbury   83
Pilnik   30, 56
Pinkus   100